MANITOBA STUDIES IN NATIVE HISTORY

Manitoba Studies in Native History publishes new scholarly interpretations of the historical experience of Native peoples in the western interior of North America. The series is under the editorial direction of a board representative of the scholarly and Native communities in Manitoba.

I *The New I*   *ca,* edited by
Jacqueline Pe

II *Indian-Eu*   *iver Region to*
1840, by Pau

III *"The Ord*   *rthern Ojibwa*
Religion and   *man*

IV *The Plain*   ohn S. Milloy

V *The Dakot*   Peter Douglas
Elias

VI *Aborigino*   *cts,* edited by
Kerry Abel ar

VII *Severing*   *ous Religious*
Ceremonies o

Severing the Ties that Bind: Government Repression of Indigenous Religious Ceremonies on the Prairies

KATHERINE PETTIPAS

THE UNIVERSITY OF MANITOBA PRESS

© The University of Manitoba Press 1994
Winnipeg, Manitoba R3T 2N2
Printed in Canada
Printed on recycled, acid-free paper ∞

Design: Norman Schmidt

Cover/jacket illustration: Cree celebrants at a ceremony in File Hills, Saskatchewan, with a local Royal Canadian Mounted Police officer, 1926 (the National Museum of the American Indian / Smithsonian Institution, NA-1463-36).

Canadian Cataloguing in Publication Data

Pettipas, Katherine

  Severing the ties that bind

  (Manitoba studies in native history, ISSN 0826-9416 ; 7)
  Originally presented as the author's thesis (Ph.D.),
University of Manitoba, 1989.
  Includes bibliographical references and indexes.
  ISBN 0-88755-151-3 (bound) – 0-88755-638-8 (pbk.)

1. Cree Indians - Rites and ceremonies. 2. Cree
Indians - Government relations. 3. Indians of North
America - Prairie Provinces - Rites and ceremonies.
4. Indians of North America - Canada - Government
relations - 1860-1951.* 5. Indians of North
America - Prairie Provinces. I. Title. II. Series.

E99.C88P47 1994   971.2'00497   C94-920188-X

This series is published with the financial support of the people of Manitoba, the Honourable Harold Gilleshammer, Minister of Culture, Heritage and Citizenship. The publication of this volume was also assisted by a grant from the Canada Council.

Manitoba Studies in Native History Board of Directors: J. Burelle, J. Fontaine, G. Friesen, E. Harper, E. LaRocque, R. McKay, W. Moodie, G. Schultz, D. Young.

For my parents,
Peter and Rose

Contents

Foreword by A. Blair Stonechild   *ix*

Preface   *xi*

Acknowledgements   *xiii*

Introduction   *3*

Piapot's Story   *9*

1 Imperial Policy and Local "Customs"   *17*

2 The Ties that Bind: The Plains Cree   *43*

3 From Independence to Wardship: 1870 to 1895   *63*

4 The Indian Act and Indigenous Ceremonies: 1884 to 1895   *87*

5 Regulating Sun Dances and Giveaways: 1896 to 1914   *107*

6 Responses to Religious Suppression: 1896 to 1914   *127*

7 Other Forms of "Objectionable Customs": 1914 to 1940   *145*

8 Persistence, Reason, and Compromise: 1914 to 1940   *167*

Contents continued

9 A Matter of Religious Freedom: 1940 to 1951   *193*

Summary and Conclusions   *211*

Appendix   *233*

Notes   *237*

Bibliography   *279*

Index   *297*

Foreword

In their writing on First Nations history, traditional historians tend to miss the forest for the trees. They read endless reams of official documents in the archives, but few have been able and willing to try to examine the overriding cultural and spiritual issues. Often, they disregard any information that is not written. This creates a nagging dilemma – how to account for the fact that First Nations history on the Canadian prairies, as expressed by Aboriginals ourselves, was essentially an oral phenomenon. But the problem goes even further, and it involves questions of whether there is a basic understanding and respect for First Nations cultures on the part of traditional historians. Have today's historians fully overcome the attitudes of cultural superiority that were so deeply entrenched during the imperialist, colonialist era?

In this book, Katherine Pettipas takes serious steps to rectify these problems. Her goal is to examine the suppression of First Nations religions during the period of Indian Department administration. Her emphasis is on hearing the First Nations voice as it emerges in the written records. She uncovers the complex public and government attitudes surrounding oppression and reveals how the pattern of oppression that prevailed on the Canadian prairies was a feature of colonialism on an international level. But she has gone further than just considering the written records. She has gone directly to the elders with an attitude of respect and a willingness to understand their point of view. As an observer who is not Aboriginal, she is to be credited for that. In doing so, she is on the right path to respecting First Nations traditions.

Katherine Pettipas deals sensitively with the subject of First Nations beliefs. She does not seek to expose beliefs for the sake of sensationalism, nor does she want to convert the reader, but instead she reflects on the significance of spiritual belief in the lives of the people of First Nations societies. She shows that an attack on First Nations spirituality is an attack on the core of First Nations identity, since spirituality pervades all aspects of the First Nations lifestyle. European colonizers tended to treat First Nations spirituality as an isolated segment of the culture, which could be methodically eradicated by deploying missionaries. But it was not eradicated; First Nations people adapted their beliefs, sent their spirituality "underground," and it survives today. Katherine Pettipas notes how the healing aspects of ceremonies such as the Thirst Dance will be needed in the future for the struggle by First Nations people to re-assert control over their lives.

First Nations elders would never consider a history whole or relevant without a full accounting of how a spiritual understanding was central to the way First Nations people understood the unfolding of their world. Katherine Pettipas understands this idea. I believe that the publication of this book has great potential to create a wider and more sensitive understanding of the history of First Nations people.

A. Blair Stonechild
Dean of Academics
Saskatchewan Indian Federated College
Regina Campus

Preface

This is a study of the conceptualization and implementation of an aspect of Canadian Indian policy that can best be described as the repression of indigenous religious systems among Aboriginal[1] peoples residing in the prairie region. Subsequent to the Potlatch Law of 1885, a number of amendments were made to the Canadian Indian Act to discourage the persistence of specific ceremonial activities. Both missionaries and administrators contended that such practices were immoral. Moreover, they argued that certain forms of Aboriginal religious expression and associated customs undermined the objectives of federal Indian policy, that is, the assimilation of Aboriginals into European-Canadian society. The attitudes of missionaries and civil servants were the typical product of the Christians' intolerance of other religions. But they also rested on an accurate analysis of the interconnections between religious life and ceremonies, and with the social, economic and political aspects of Aboriginal cultures. The European-Canadian overseers of the transformation of Aboriginal societies believed that such values must be destroyed if they were ever to join fully in Canadian life as citizens.

While this study is a history of the administrative aspect of the repression of indigenous religious practices, it is equally an analysis of Aboriginal responses to the attempts by the Department of Indian Affairs to undermine this important aspect of their culture. Aboriginal resistance took many forms, some of which have left clear traces in the historical records of this era. In addition to challenging the legitimacy of the terms of the Indian Act and the manner in which anti-ceremony regulations were implemented, prairie Indians altered their ceremonial life – the time and place and rituals of the ceremonies – but they did continue to worship in their traditional ways. I examine the experience of one major group, the Plains Cree, in some detail to illustrate the degree of Aboriginal religious persistence and change under the law. I address a number of questions: In what manner did Aboriginal reaction and resistance influence the development of Canadian Indian policy regarding ceremonial repression between 1895 and the 1930s? Was ceremonial life left largely intact as a result of this resistance to inadequate regulations and their coercive implementation?

Paradoxically, the very system that was supposed to destroy prairie Aboriginal societies actually ensured the survival of many important aspects of their cultures. However, the regulations against certain forms of religious expression were not totally ineffective and, in combination with other assimilative programs, they did have a profoundly important effect, which is felt to this day.

Acknowledgements

The impetus for my interest in the subject of Aboriginal religions and their changes throughout history can be traced to my work experience as the Curator of Native Ethnology at the Manitoba Museum of Man and Nature. Some of the most culturally sensitive collections in museum institutions are the sacred materials that were collected from numerous First Nations. At the Manitoba Museum of Man and Nature there are significant collections of sacred items that were collected from a small number of Saskatchewan reserves. It was during my work with both Saskatchewan and Manitoba Aboriginal elders in discussing the appropriate care for such items and their possible repatriation that the subject of religious repression by the local missionaries and Indian agents often arose. I have also had the privilege of speaking with members of the younger generation who, along with their elders, are committed to rebuilding the strength of their people through principles inherent in "traditional" forms of spirituality. As a result of my professional and personal relationship with the Aboriginal community I have also been privileged to attend local ceremonies including the Midewiwin, the Sun Dance and the Sweat Lodge to further my understanding of the meanings of Aboriginal spirituality. I would like to express my appreciation to all those in the First Nations communities who, with profound generosity and patience, have welcomed me into their ceremonial lodges and helped me go beyond the printed page to gain knowledge of their spiritual beliefs and cultural values.

The manuscript for this book was initially written for a dissertation, and I would like to acknowledge Dr. Jean Friesen, who introduced me to the wealth of historical material available for research in the RG10 files of the Department of Indian Affairs. The editorial comments and guidance offered by Dr. Jean Friesen on the various drafts of the dissertation and the many hours of editing of the various stages of the manuscript by Dr. Gerald Friesen are greatly appreciated. In addition, a number of other individuals made significant contributions to the anthropological and historical approaches used in this study. The guidance and advice of Dr. Joan Townsend, Dr. John Kendle, Dr. Noel Dyck, Dr. David Mandelbaum and Bennett McCardle were invaluable. Blair Stonechild and David Miller read the final draft of the text, and their comments are also appreciated. Particular thanks are due to Patricia Dowdall, Carol Dahlstrom, and Allison Campbell at the University of Manitoba Press for their editorial work and constructive comments.

During the initial research stage of this study, I had the unexpected honour of meeting Dr. David Mandelbaum at a conference sponsored by the Canadian Plains Research Center in Regina in 1975. Dr. Mandelbaum responded to my many questions concerning his fieldwork among the Plains Cree in the mid-1930s, even in moments of illness. His effort to repatriate copies of his valuable fieldnotes and photographs back to Saskatchewan through the auspices of the Canadian Plains Research Center was a significant contribution for both the First Nations and western scholars. As I worked through the boxes of notes, I was particularly moved by the story of Dr. Mandelbaum's return of a personal gift that he had received from Fineday, an elder who had provided him with a wealth of traditional information. This gift was a small hide pouch containing a lithic biface.

Much of the time I spent researching and writing the manuscript would not have been possible without the support of the administrative staff and my colleagues at the Manitoba Museum of Man and Nature. I would also like to thank Marlene Gentile, who helped with the typing of the final manuscript; Carolyn Trottier, who produced the map; and David Pentland, who assisted with the translation work.

Finally, I would like to acknowledge the support of my husband, Leo, who not only assisted with proofreading various drafts of the text, but also was an important source of encouragement in this undertaking.

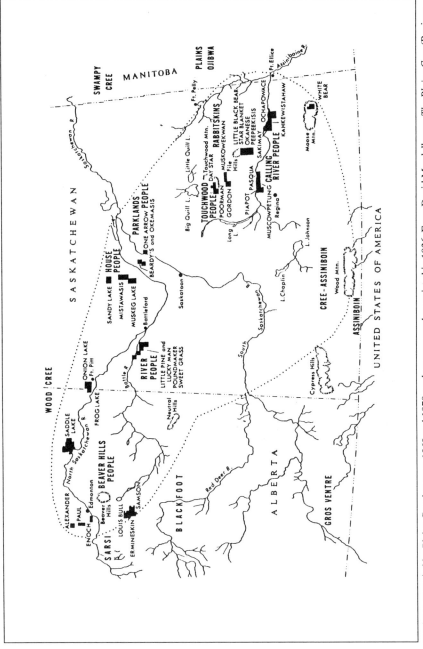

Territory occupied by Plains Cree between 1860 and 1870, and reserves as they existed in 1936. From David Mandelbaum, *The Plains Cree* (Regina: University of Regina, 1979), p. 13 (map drawn by Carolyn Trottier).

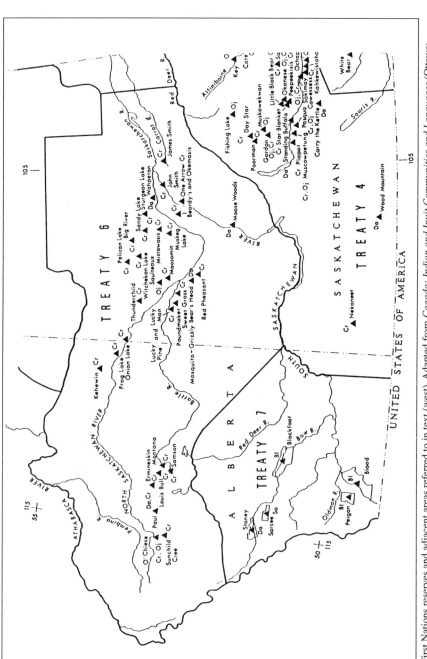

First Nations reserves and adjacent areas referred to in text (west). Adapted from *Canada: Indian and Inuit Communities and Languages* (Ottawa: Survey and Mapping Branch, Department of Energy, Mines and Resources Canada, 1980) (map drawn by Carolyn Trottier).

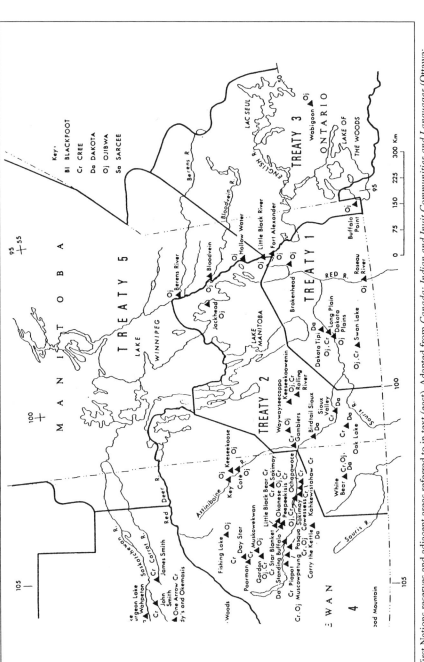

First Nations reserves and adjacent areas referred to in text (east). Adapted from *Canada: Indian and Inuit Communities and Languages* (Ottawa: Survey and Mapping Branch, Department of Energy, Mines and Resources Canada, 1980) (map drawn by Carolyn Trottier).

Chief Piapot (front centre, holding war club) and followers, with Edgar Dewdney (Indian Commissioner for the North-West Territories) and members of the Montreal Garrison Artillery, 1885 (Piapot's Story). Photo courtesy of National Archives of Canada, PA118775.

The physical transformation of Thomas Moore, who was admitted to the Regina Industrial School in 1896, was visually recorded and published in the *Annual Report of the Department of Indian Affairs for 1897* (Chapter 3). Saskatchewan Archives Board, R-A8223(1) and R-A8223(2).

Seasonal work such as fall threshing and harvesting was an important source of economic support for many prairie Aboriginal families, ca. 1908 (Chapter 3). Photo courtesy of Provincial Archives of Manitoba, Agriculture-Harvesting 60, N12137.

Father Joseph Hugonnard, Principal of the Industrial School at Qu'Appelle, Saskatchewan, with school children, teachers, and some adult members of the community, ca. 1885 (Chapter 6). Photo courtesy of the National Archives of Canada, PA118765.

European-Canadian immigrants were accustomed to seeing indigenous dancing in their towns and at local fairs and stampedes, such as this celebration by local Cree at South Edmonton in 1898. By 1914, prohibitions had been enacted against the performance of off-reserve dancing (Chapter 7). Photo courtesy of Glenbow Archives, Calgary, Alberta, NA-614-1.

Elders such as Wanduta (a Dakota from the Oak Lake area in Manitoba), who persisted in performing their ceremonies despite government regulations, were considered to be serious obstacles to the assimilation of school graduates; ca. 1913 (Chapter 5). Photo courtesy of National Archives of Canada, PA-030027.

A delegation from the Treaty Four area met with Department of Indian Affairs officials in 1911 to petition for numerous changes to the Indian Act, including the repeal of legislation against their ceremonies. Extreme left, Louis O'Soup; extreme right, Alex Gaddie, both from the Cowessess Reserve (Chapter 6). Photo courtesy of Saskatchewan Archives Board, R-B584.

Participants at the Brandon Fair, Manitoba, with dignitary Lieutenant Sousa, ca. 1919 (Chapter 7). Photo courtesy of National Archives of Canada, PA-30375.

Three generations from File Hills, in traditional and civilian and military dress, with Indian Commissioner William Graham, prior to the departure of the young World War One recruits for England as part of the 68th Regina Regiment (Chapter 8). Photo courtesy of National Archives of Canada, PA-66815.

American anthropologist David Mandelbaum (centre) was allowed to document certain aspects of the Sun Dance and other ceremonies in the 1930s. Solomon Blue Horn (back row, second from left) and Elder Maskwa (first row, third from left), provided Mandelbaum with information for his studies; Sweetgrass Reserve, 1934 (Chapter 8). Photo courtesy of Saskatchewan Archives Board, R-A25774.

Missionary, teachers, and school girls celebrating a Christian service at the Crooked Lakes Sun Dance in 1934 (Chapter 8). Photo courtesy of Saskatchewan Archives Board, R-A25770-4.

Reverend Edward Ahenakew (seated front centre) at a chiefs' conference on the Thunderchild Reserve, Saskatchewan, in 1922 (Chapter 9). Photo courtesy of Saskatchewan Archives Board, R-A10196.

Metis Dance troupe organized by Joseph Dion (back row, extreme right), a Cree-Metis. Dion, a teacher and political activist for the Alberta Aboriginal people, also defended traditional forms of religious worship; ca. 1931 (Chapter 9). Photo courtesy of Glenbow Archives, Calgary, Alberta, NA-927-2.

Today, elders continue to play a vital role in the persistence of indigenous spirituality and ceremonies. Here, an unidentified elder addresses Sun Dance celebrants inside the sacred lodge; photographed by David Mandelbaum, 1965. Photo courtesy of Saskatchewan Archives Board, R-A25814.

Severing the Ties that Bind

Introduction

In 1885, the Canadian government outlawed the ceremonial distribution of property through potlatches and other forms of religious expression practised by many Northwest Coast Aboriginal cultures in British Columbia by amending the Indian Act of Canada. Subsequent modifications to this legislation (in 1895) allowed the federal government, under the auspices of the Department of Indian Affairs, to undermine certain religious practices among other Aboriginal cultures. In particular, certain rituals associated with the Sun (or Thirst) Dances were prohibited, as were giveaway ceremonies involving the massive distribution of goods. Over the years, other legislated regulations were introduced in support of a more general level of religious repression as well as locally imposed government restrictions on cultural behaviour that went "beyond the law."

Government officials and missionaries contended that certain indigenous religious practices were immoral and seriously undermined the assimilative objectives of Canadian Indian policy. However, the rationale for adopting coercive measures against indigenous religions had much deeper roots, which were grounded in Christian Victorian ethnocentric notions of cultural inferiority and inherent contradictions between Western capitalism and pre-industrial societies. The repressive measures adopted by the Department of Indian Affairs against various ceremonial practices were not simply indicators of European-Canadian intolerance for non-Christian religions or customs foreign to their own. Rather, they were based on a belief on the part of Department officials – and it was correct – that there existed a direct connection between indigenous worldview, ceremonial life, and the social, economic, and political structures of the community. Furthermore, the official vision of Canada was that of a culturally and politically homogeneous nation. No politician of the day could imagine the continued existence of numerous Aboriginal nations that differed significantly from their own. The ultimate goal of Canadian Indian policy was the political, economic, and cultural absorption of all Aboriginal peoples into the general citizenry and economy of the Canadian nation-state. The Canadian government adopted special legislation that imposed a wardship political status on all Aboriginal people and officially supported the destruction of indigenous cultural systems.

In addition to examining the history of the development and implementation of federal policies to suppress ceremonies, this study also explores the various forms of Aboriginal response to these measures. The initiatives undertaken by Aboriginal communities to resist or to mitigate the circumstances of their repression had a direct effect not only upon their cultural expression but also upon government policy and its implementation. For those who wished to retain their traditional forms of religious worship, the repressive measures provided a very real challenge to their cultural integrity. Officially powerless within the nation-state and governed by the Indian Act, which provided the federal government with sweeping powers over almost every aspect of their lives, prairie Aboriginal peoples initiated a number of culturally accommodative responses to the suppression of ceremonial life.[1]

My research has involved an investigation into both the historical and the anthropological literature. My approach is based on the premise that the inter-relationships between indigenous societies and Western colonial powers can be best documented and evaluated through a "holistic and diachronic" method whereby both the "local level social history and the larger scale social history and cultural environments that affected that history" are taken into consideration.[2] The principles guiding Canada's policy makers on Indian matters in the prairie region during the late nineteenth century were well established and were essentially identical to those that determined Britain's imperial relations with other non-Western societies in other areas of the world. Victorian attitudes towards non-Western cultures, political and economic interest, local environments, and the various forms of indigenous societies encountered by British colonials all affected the development of Canada's Indian policy and its implementation. The effectiveness of these policies can be evaluated only if there is an understanding of indigenous cultures and their particular historical experiences. While the Aboriginal nations of the northern prairie and parkland regions shared much, both culturally and historically, they nevertheless differed from group to group. In order to prevent over-generalization regarding the implementation of and effect on the various Native communities of policies against ceremonies, I've chosen the relationship between ceremonial practices and the social, economic, and political system of one particular nation, the Plains Cree, as the major illustration of the Aboriginal experience.[3]

With the exception of two historical studies written by Jacqueline Gresko on Canadian Indian policy and Indian education in western Canada between 1870 and 1910, and a study of the administration of Deputy Superintendent General Duncan Scott by Brian Titley, there are no detailed studies of the Canadian federal policy of cultural suppression in the prairie region.[4] Two major works on the history of the potlatch law on the Northwest Coast are used for comparative purposes.[5] In general, the authors who have examined the legislation in question to date have generally tended to minimize the impact of this aspect of Canadian Indian policy. I suggest that, despite the adeptness of Aboriginal peoples at evading and resisting prohibitions, there was a significant effect, especially when other forms of assimilative measures are taken into consideration.[6] The large volume of petitions and extensive ceremonial modifications attest to the fact that people took the legislation seriously.

Researchers in the disciplines of anthropology, sociology, and religious studies who have examined changes in indigenous religions as a result of contacts with Christian missionaries and colonial regimes have yet to consider the role of specific policy implementation as a factor in cultural transformation. The focus of this scholarship has been on changes in religious ideology and ceremonial life and the emergence of nativistic movements as one form of response to repressive colonial administrations. Such movements as the Gaiwiio religion (the Good Word, or Message of Handsome Lake), the Peyote religion (Native American Church), the Ghost Dance religion, the "Sun Dance" religion, Prophet movements, and more contemporary versions of the Pow-wow have been subjects of this scholarship.[7] Similarly, in other former British settlement colonies, such as Australia and New Zealand, regulations against "local customs" have yet to be investigated.

The richest source of materials pertaining to Canada's Indian policy is the RG10 Indian Affairs Records, Black Series (Western Canada) located in the National Archives of Canada. This collection of documents consists of policy statements, official correspondence, and directives from senior officials with the Department of Indian Affairs; field reports submitted to Ottawa by Indian commissioners, inspectors of agencies, Indian agents, farm instructors, principals of Indian schools, missionaries, and medical officers; and the police reports related to their assistance to the Department. While fewer in number, there are also petitions and letters from the Aboriginal community. This series of documents also contains agency reports, numerous working papers relating to amendments to the Indian Act, special reports of Aboriginal participation in indigenous ceremonies and White-sponsored agricultural exhibitions, fairs, and stampedes, as well as policy statements regarding traditional healing practices, the ritual use of peyote, and the protection of sacred sites and "monuments."

Other relevant documents in the Public Records Division of the National Archives of Canada are: the Privy Council Records (RG2, Series 18); Records of the Secretary of State including the Ministry of Indian Affairs (RG6, Series A1, C1); North-West Mounted Police / Royal Canadian Mounted Police Record Group (RG18); External Affairs Records (RG25, Series A1, A5); and the Records of the Department of Citizenship and Immigration (RG26). I have also reviewed, with permission, contemporary unindexed files held by the Department of Indian Affairs.

Published annual reports of the administration of the Department of Indian Affairs are available in the *Sessional Papers of Canada*; however, the reports dated after World War One are only abbreviated summaries of field activities and policy. Another published source, the *Federal Statutes of Canada*, contains committee reports and discussions relevant to the passage of amendments to the Indian Act of 1876. Of particular importance to my research were the hearings of the Special Joint Committee of the Senate and the House of Commons Appointed to Examine and Consider the Indian Act from 1946 to 1948.

Official agency reports and the private papers of some agents, missionaries, teachers, and Aboriginal politicians are located in the National Archives of Canada, the Provincial Archives of Manitoba, the Saskatchewan Archives, and the Glenbow Archives. Another valuable archival resource is the archives of the Ethnology Division of the Canadian Museum of Civilization in Ottawa, which houses correspondence and fieldnotes on anthropological activities conducted under the sponsorship of the National Museum of Canada. Of note are the correspondence files of E. Pliny Goddard, Diamond Jenness, Alanson Skinner, Wilson Wallis, and Clark Wissler.[8] Only one document from this collection addressed the issue of religious suppression, and this is Marius Barbeau's commissioned report based largely on Department of Indian Affairs files, which he submitted to the Department of Indian Affairs.[9]

Other primary documentation relevant to Plains religious ideology and forms of expression are available in unpublished and published ethnographies and cultural histories produced by anthropologists and Aboriginal historians.[10] The most important collection of fieldnotes on the subject of the Plains Cree Sun (or Thirst) Dance and other forms of ceremonialism was documented by David Mandelbaum, who was permitted to record the ceremonial life of the Plains Cree during the summers of 1934 and 1935. At this time, Mandelbaum was allowed to witness these ceremonies despite the existence of government policy against their practice. A copy of Mandelbaum's fieldnotes and photographs is housed with the Saskatchewan Archives Board in Regina.[11]

Finally, important descriptions of prairie Aboriginal cultures and histories have been written by a number of Aboriginal historians such as Reverend Edward

Ahenakew, Reverend Stan Cuthand, Joseph Dion, Mike Mountain Horse, John Tootoosis, Abel Watetch, and Alexander Wolfe.[12] Other oral histories collected by the Saskatoon Indian Cultural College have also been published.[13]

In addition to the abovementioned sources, I have had the privilege of attending a Midewiwin initiation ceremony on a Manitoba reserve. This ceremony had not been held in this particular community in over fifty years. I also had the honour of attending two Sun Dance ceremonies on the same reserve. On these occasions and in my capacity as the Curator of Native Ethnology at the Manitoba Museum of Man and Nature, I have spoken with Aboriginal people about the repression of their ceremonies. The history of repression and their rights to religious freedom remains an important issue to this day. Even after the regulations were deleted from the 1951 Indian Act, many elders and ritualists remained fearful of performing their ceremonies openly, and some continued to believe that the laws against their ceremonies were still in effect.

Across North America, many issues relating to Aboriginal religious freedom remain unresolved and occupy an important place in the political agenda. Of particular note are concerns over the access to and use of religious objects held in museum repositories; the protection and use of sacred lands and sites in the face of development; the right to practise indigenous forms of religious expression within the prison system; and the transport of sacred materials across state, provincial, and international boundaries.[14] In the United States, the American Religious Freedom Act (albeit inadequate) was passed in 1978 to protect Aboriginal religious freedoms, and, in Canada, the protection of Aboriginal cultures is a major issue in the ongoing discussions on self-government occurring between the federal government, the provinces, and the First Nations.

The general term *Aboriginal*, while used inconsistently, has gained recognition in Canada as a broad designation for the nation's indigenous peoples. While the people of the First Nations prefer their own names for themselves, the term is also increasingly used among them. I use the term *Indian* because it was the operative term of the historical period under consideration. This nomenclature was used within federal administrative circles and among indigenous peoples who undertook to defend their interests vis-à-vis the administrative regime engendered by the Indian Act. According to the Indian Act, there was a further classification of Indians into "status" and "non-status" categories. My research deals with the status Indian populations, or those individuals and their families who were officially registered to receive the benefits derived from treaties. Non-status Indians included those who were not registered, were enfranchised as Canadian citizens, or, until 1985, Indian women who had married non-Indians, and their children. The federal government did not recognize any obligations to non-status Indians.

Piapot's Story

According to oral tradition, the year was 1816 and the day was filled with the rumbling of thunder, turbulent winds, and flashes of lightning as the sacred and powerful Thunderbeings ripped open the prairie sky for miles around. In the camp of humans below, a newborn's cry broke through the voices of the Thunderbirds themselves, announcing the arrival of a new life.[1] The newborn's Assiniboin father and Cree mother soon after invited an elder with powerful spiritual guardians to name their child. The Naming Ceremony was a special occasion marked by a community feast. As was the custom, a male elder chose the name for newborn male children. After careful contemplation, the elder named this infant kîsikâw-awâsis, or Flash-in-the-Sky Boy, in recognition of the spiritual circumstances surrounding his birth.

Young children spent a great deal of their time in the care of their grandparents as their parents went about sustaining the household. It was the elders who possessed knowledge and wisdom through their life experiences and assumed a major responsibility in the instruction of their grandchildren. Some children were immediately recognized as possessing spiritually powerful gifts. In the case of kîsikâw-awâsis, his grandmother took a special liking to him, and he spent much time in her care, learning the traditions of his people.

Kîsikâw-awâsis's early years proved to be as turbulent as the conditions accompanying his birth. One day, tragedy struck when warriors returned to the camp unsuspectingly carrying smallpox with them. The disease took its toll on the village, but kîsikâw-awâsis and his grandmother were among the survivors. Shortly after, they were captured by a raiding party of Dakota warriors and were taken to Montana, where they lived with the Dakota. When the boy was about fourteen, these Dakota were in turn raided by the Plains Cree, who took the pair

back to their homeland in the Qu'Appelle area. Because of the mixture of Cree and
Dakota characteristics reflected in the young man's behaviour, kîsikâw-awâsis was
renamed nêhiyawi-pwât, or Sioux Cree. He was given the nickname of Payepot,
or Hole in the Sioux, since he was knowledgeable in the ways, or "secrets," of the
Dakota enemy.[2]

During his early adolescent years, the young kîsikâw-awâsis would have spent
a great deal of his time with boys of his own age and his older male relatives, learning
to hunt, fish, ride and care for horses, and defend himself. He would have undergone
a "vision quest," during which time he would have fasted and been visited by
protective guardian spirits. All the basic skills for survival would have been acquired
by this time. He would have witnessed the communal seasonal bison hunts and even
assisted in certain aspects of the hunt itself – perhaps by helping to drive the herds
down the v-shaped, stone-piled channels that led to a pound enclosure. By his late
teens, the young man would have travelled with his male relatives on raiding parties
for horses, and to other Indian villages and European fur posts to trade. His identity
was grounded deep within his cultural upbringing and was reflected not only in his
language and behaviour, but also in the way he wore his hair, the colours and designs
painted and quillworked onto his hide clothing, and individual and communal
expressions of spirituality.

As he grew older, Piapot's skills as a hunter, trader, and warrior were recognized,
and he sat in the council of the Rattler's Society Warriors' lodge. In this position of
status, he was expected to be a "free-giver" by offering his life in the defence of the
community and freely distributing material goods, including horses, that he captured on raids. He would also demonstrate his leadership qualities by playing a major
role in the bison communal hunts, by conducting favourable trade with other groups,
and by assisting in the performance of religious ceremonies.

A noted warrior, Piapot led his men, along with other Cree headmen and
Assiniboin allies, into battles against the Dakota and the Blackfoot. His association
with a mixed band of Assiniboin, Cree, and Ojibway known as the *nêhiyawi-pwât*
(Young Dogs), however, undermined his position as a trader and provisioner with
the Hudson's Bay Company. Some of the warriors belonging to the Young Dogs
were notorious for their raiding and terrorizing behaviour, and for this reason they
were not given favourable treatment by European traders. As a result, Piapot was
unable to receive a *masinahikan,* "little writing," or letter of acknowledgement,
from the Company confirming his status as a leader in their eyes and a "good Indian"
who was worthy of special gifts and consideration on the part of fur post factors.
His frustration with the Company led him to compel a "Half-Breed" traveller to
write a note declaring, "I am PIAPOT, LORD of the HEAVEN and EARTH."[3] Whether

Piapot was mocking the pretentiousness of the European traders or hoping for more favourable trade relations through this action is not clear.

Eventually, Piapot left the Young Dogs and continued to gain status and prestige among the Plains Cree as a major leader in raids conducted against the enemies of the Cree. One of his last major battles occurred in 1870 near the present site of Lethbridge, Alberta. Here, the Cree and the Assiniboin suffered heavy losses at the hands of the combined forces of the Blackfoot, Blood, and Peigan, who out-numbered the Cree and possessed superior weapons.

Reputedly a speaker of five languages – Plains Cree, Dakota, Ojibway, Assini-boin and Peigan – Piapot's reputation as a trader and negotiator of peace between groups was probably surpassed by few. His influence ultimately extended over nearly a thousand people, including a number of families belonging to the Cree-Assiniboin *nêhiyawi-pwât* (Young Dogs), the Qu'Appelle Cree, the southerly Upstream People, and some Assiniboin groups.[4] That he was a successful provider, commercial hunter, and trader is evident in his ability to support six wives and their families in the early 1880s.[5]

By the 1860s, life for Piapot and his followers had taken a dramatic turn for the worse. Food resources were being over-exploited, European-introduced diseases had decimated the population, and violent outbreaks resulted in a further loss of lives, as Indians, Metis, and White commercial traders and hunters competed for access to the diminishing bison herds. For example, in 1873, the North-West Mounted Police had been sent into the Cypress Hills area to restore law and order following the massacre of some twenty Assiniboin by American wolf hunters and traders, and to curtail the liquor trade.

During this period, a number of Cree leaders, including mistahi maskwa (Big Bear), Piapot, and his brother-in-law, Little Pine, had attempted to restrict hunting in their homelands by American and Metis commercial traders. These efforts were unsuccessful, and fears of impending starvation and rumours of the increasing interest of the European Canadians in their lands for settlement prompted some headmen to consider negotiating access to resources on their lands. Cree leaders were well aware of the precedents set by the treaty negotiations that had taken place in Manitoba in the early 1870s with representatives of the British and Canadian governments, and this measure was seriously considered as a means to ensure their livelihood. By the summer of 1874, land cessions were negotiated by the Assiniboin, Cree, and Ojibway who occupied lands between Fort Ellice and Cypress Hills. Treaty Four was concluded with Lieutenant Governor Alexander Morris in the Qu'Appelle area. Piapot was not present at the signing of this treaty. That he was not impressed with the terms of this agreement was indicated by his request for additional items when he finally agreed to negotiate land cessions in an adhesion to Treaty Four in 1875.[6]

Between the years 1875 and 1885, Piapot's leadership skills were severely tested as he attempted to protect the interests of his followers in the face of a changing physical environment and a new order of political relations with the Canadian nation-state. Dissatisfied with the lack of assistance forthcoming through the terms of Treaty Four, Piapot initially refused to select a permanent location for a reserve. He eventually decided to locate his followers in the relatively game-rich area of Cypress Hills. However, living off the land proved to be difficult, and people suffered from starvation, tuberculosis, and the effects of the unchecked whisky trade. Piapot's followers were forced to live off small game and the meat from their own horses, and they finally petitioned the Canadian government for rations of flour and salt pork.

As it became clearer to Piapot that the "buffalo hunting days" were over, he and other Cree leaders increasingly sought instruction in agriculture. The government had established a "home farm" in the Maple Creek area near the Cypress Hills in 1879, and in 1881 Piapot selected lands for a reserve approximately ten miles north. Despite shortages of government supplies, Piapot's band began to plant gardens and to raise wheat. In the following spring, Piapot's band, along with other Cree and Assiniboin families, were informed that all rationing would be cut off unless they relocated to their former hunting territory. This government directive was issued as a measure to prevent large numbers of Cree and Assiniboin from concentrating in the Cypress Hills area, a situation that might have future military consequences.

In June 1882, with seventeen days of rations and promises of more food at Old Wives Lake, Piapot left for the Qu'Appelle area with approximately 470 people. It proved to be a difficult journey for the band, and many became sick and died. At Qu'Appelle, Piapot met with other Cree headmen, Major J.M. Walsh, and White settlers to discuss a reserve location.[7] Piapot explained that he had been promised his choice of land for a reserve. He had considered settling in the Touchwood Hills area but now he was favouring the Qu'Appelle "flats." That the Canadian government was not prepared to honour its word regarding the freedom of choice in selecting reserve lands became clear to Piapot when he discovered that Indian Agent Allan MacDonald had already chosen a site for the band at Indian Head. Once again Piapot voiced his concerns for his people, who were not only facing starvation, but also succumbing to illness resulting from a shift in their diet from fresh meat to salt pork.

Piapot refused to settle on the land chosen by the Indian agent, and once again he led his people on a trek to the Cypress Hills area. In retaliation, the Department of Indian Affairs refused to supply rations, and finally Piapot and his followers were forced to reconsider the Indian Head location. Along with their property and horses, they were removed from Maple Creek in boxcars, one of which ran off the tracks and slid down an embankment during the journey.[8] By this time, Piapot's band had been even further reduced in numbers as they made their way back to an area immediately south of Sintaluta. During the devastating winter of 1884, it was reported that one out of three died, many suffering from a form of scurvy brought on by inadequate diet. The son of one homesteading family observed: "Many a time, while herding my father's flocks on the old reservation, I passed aspen groves where there were dozens of platforms lashed to the poplar trees with rawhide thongs, sepulchres that bore mute evidence of that tragic winter."[9] By mid-May of 1884, Piapot had moved off the reserve at Indian Head, insisting upon a reserve site of his choice where his people could survive on a staple of fish. In the meantime he camped on an Assiniboin reserve and at Pasquah's reserve.

Throughout 1883–84, Piapot persisted in voicing his dissatisfaction with the terms of Treaty Four, and the unfulfilled treaty promises, to police, Indian agents, and government officials. In the early summer of 1883, Piapot, along with Big Bear, Lucky Man, and Little Pine, officially met in the Cypress Hills with Commissioner Edgar Dewdney to request rations for their communal ceremony known as the Thirst, or Sun, Dance. Dewdney's objective, however, was to make sure that these Cree moved out of the area as soon as possible and located on reserves. The request was turned down. Piapot's dismay at the commissioner's position once again prompted him to criticize the government for not following through with their promises and for refusing to allow his people to settle in the Cypress Hills area.[10] Venting his frustration, Piapot "angrily tore down his treaty flag, took the medal from around his neck, passed them both to the interpreter and stalked out of the council."[11] These defiant stances were not easily forgotten by officials of the Indian Affairs Department.

The police and the survey workers with the Canadian Pacific Railway (CPR) were particularly concerned over the opposition of the Cree to the building of the railway line through their lands. According to a firsthand account by Piapot's son John, headmen Poundmaker, Big Bear, and Little Blanket favoured more forceful action, but Piapot preferred to negotiate.[12] Surveying stakes were pulled up in 1883, and Piapot camped his people at the right-of-way of construction near Maple Creek. The police stepped in before the construction crew arrived on the scene, and, after a verbal exchange, Piapot restrained his people from taking up their arms and agreed to move camp on the condition that his people could have half-fare passage on the trains.[13]

In the end, Piapot was allowed to settle his people in the Qu'Appelle area near the Pasquah and Muscowpetung reserves. Despite his many battles with the Canadian government over his right to select a reserve location and his dissatisfaction with inadequate government aid, Piapot remained loyal to the Crown during the turbulent years of the Saskatchewan Uprising of 1885. His important role in persuading his allies in southern Saskatchewan to refrain from taking up arms against the Canadian government was officially recognized by Prime Minister Sir John A. Macdonald and the Manitoba government, and was mentioned at public events that he attended later in life.

By comparison, Piapot's treatment by the Department of Indian Affairs officials was callous. And yet he was not averse to compromise. Once settled on his reserve, he finally agreed, at the behest of Father Joseph Hugonnard (Principal of the Qu'Appelle Mission Industrial School), to have two of his sons sent to an Indian school to be educated in the "ways of the Whites." A young employee of the Indian Office in Regina had several meetings with Piapot and considered him to be "an exceedingly able man" who was regarded as a "sort of prophet, priest, and king among the Southern tribes."[14] The small, slight man, however, had a "strong sense of sardonic humor," which he used most frequently in his verbal exchanges with Department officials. One of his most cited remarks, regarding the failure of the government to supply the promised assistance for his people, was made when he criticized their Indian agent as being "so mean he carries a linen rag in his pocket into which to blow his nose for fear he might blow away something of value."[15] When William Graham was appointed their Indian agent, Piapot used the fact that Graham had lost one of his legs to emphasize his frustration with unfulfilled treaty promises and the starvation of his people by stating: "Now I know the Government is going to break the Treaty because when it was signed it was understood that it would last as long as the grass grew, the winds blew, the rivers ran, and men walked on two legs, and now they have sent us an Agent who has only one leg."[16]

Given the strong convictions and personalities of Piapot and Indian Agent William Graham, it is perhaps not surprising that the two men did not have a good relationship. Convinced that assimilation was in the best interests of Indians, Graham had little patience with Piapot's criticisms of government policy. In his memoirs, he described Piapot as a "very obstinate man" who was "always complaining about the Government's treatment of him."[17] By the end of the nineteenth century, Piapot, who had personally come to terms with the new order and had even agreed to send two of his sons to school, was stripped of his position as chief and sent to prison.

An appreciation of the strength of Piapot's spiritual power can be gleaned from a historical record of a Thirst (or Sun) Dance that was held in Montana around 1890. At this time, Montana was suffering from drought. Piapot, who periodically travelled south to celebrate the Thirst Dance with the Assiniboin and Gros Ventre, was asked to conduct the ceremony. The aftermath of the singing of the fourth sacred song by celebrants under his leadership has been described in oral tradition:

Thunder was heard in the distance, the voice of the Thunder Bird. A sudden quickening of the wind took place, bringing the clouds closer to the camp. Lightning in the sky reminded them that Chief Piapot's name to them was kîsikâw-awâsis Flash-in-the-Sky Boy.

He kept them going, dancing, singing, without let up, as a plea to the Great Spirit, to favor them with the rain they desperately needed. They did not stop, and the rains came. . . . The entire encampment gazed with wonder out upon the muddy sight, drenched from the plentiful rains, filled with awe and a sense of religious fulfillment. The equivalent of a miracle had happened; they felt it.

They tell the story to this day in Montana of how Chief Piapot demonstrated his prowess as a Medicine Man.[18]

As a spiritual leader and healer, however, Piapot refused to take personal credit for the blessing of healing rains. Rather, he informed the gathering that the power came from the strength of the people themselves and advised that "only the whole community joining together can call upon the Great Spirit to act in pity for us."[19] Piapot's message was one of community empowerment – love for one another and cooperation were the ties that bound the people together and ensured their survival in trying times.

While fulfilling his sacred vows to perform the Thirst Dance for his people on his reserve in the late 1890s, the Holy Man who once brought the rains to the sun-parched grasslands of Montana was arrested and prosecuted by the Department of Indian Affairs for encouraging and participating in ceremonial acts of self-mortification. According to regulations contained in amendments made to the Indian Act in 1895, rituals involving flesh-offerings were prohibited.[20] According to a young school graduate, Harry Ball, who was taken to visit the elderly Piapot during his incarceration, the official charge was "drunkenness."[21] However, Piapot informed his young visitor that the real reason for his incarceration was due to his having conducted the piercing ritual for some twenty young men at a Thirst Dance. At the time of his prosecution, Piapot was removed from his official position as chief. His followers protested this action by refusing to recognize this official decision and refrained from electing another leader until Piapot's death. In 1901, Piapot was again sentenced for encouraging six people to resist arrest at a giveaway.[22] He was to spend two months in a Regina prison for interfering with an officer in the discharge of his duties.

Piapot's second arrest was perhaps not unexpected given the stormy relationship between the leader and William Graham, who was now the Indian Commissioner. Graham claimed that Piapot obstructed progress by not encouraging his people to farm or to send their children to school. Graham considered Piapot to be one of the worst troublemakers, "who appeared to have a grudge against the White people, claiming that if they had not come into the country the buffalo would still be there in abundance and the Indians would be happy."[23]

A popular personality with the local press and visiting dignitaries, the aging Piapot was described as having a dignified appearance, especially as his two long hair-braids became white. Although he was a friend of Father Hugonnard, he resisted the priest's efforts to convert him. Apparently, in his old age Piapot decided to learn more about Christianity, and when the obviously pleased Hugonnard suggested baptism, Piapot, in his typical style of compromise, protested: "Oh! No. . . . I am only going to accept half of your religion. I will belong half to the Christian Religion and half to the Indian, because you may turn out to be wrong after all, and the Indian Religion might happen to be right and then I would have nothing to fall back upon.[24] Although he was described as the leader of the "pagan element" on his reserve, Piapot did attempt to accommodate the Christians in his own extended family and community by offering his lodge for Christian services. He persisted in performing his traditional ceremonies, and as late as 1894 he refused to be pressured to give up the Thirst Dance, informing Indian Commissioner A.E. Forget: "I will agree that my people will not pray to their God in their way if the Commissioner will agree not to pray to his God in his way."[25]

In 1908, Piapot succumbed to old age, and, unlike his forefathers who would have been buried on a scaffold, he was laid to rest in a White man's coffin. However, according to the traditional manner of burial, his knees were drawn up to his chest.[26] Thus, he returned to "Mother Earth" as he left his own mother's womb at birth.

In retrospect, it seemed only fitting that the maker of Piapot's coffin was a young nephew, Abel Watetch, who later recorded Piapot's story for future generations. Watetch, or Herald of the Sky, had attended the Lebret School, where he learned to be a carpenter, wheelwright, tinsmith, and cobbler, but he did so at the cost of losing much of his traditional language and knowledge about his culture. After returning to his home reserve, the young man spent many long hours with the aging Piapot, re-learning his language and listening to a way of life that could now be experienced only through the stories.

After World War One, returning war veterans from the Piapot Reserve formally appealed to the Indian Commissioner, William Graham, for permission to perform their Thirst Dances. Some also became active in the various newly formed Indian political organizations to seek redress from the Canadian government for broken treaty promises, among which was the freedom of religious expression. These men and their children would be the new warriors in the new social order, and would continue to carry Piapot's message of protest to the Canadian government.

The story of Piapot's determination to practise his religion and traditions in the face of government regulations contained in the Canadian Indian Act puts a human face on the "other side" – the Aboriginal side – of Canadian Indian policy. It is a story that many others across the prairie region were to tell as they recounted their experiences to younger generations. Many Aboriginal people carry the memories and hurts of these episodes deep within their hearts to this day. It is time the story was told.

Imperial Policy
and Local "Customs"

1

The period from the 1870s to the turn of the century was a watershed for indigenous societies residing in the prairie and parkland regions. The lives of men, women, and children were radically altered as they were forced to come to terms with a series of major ecological, demographic, social, economic, and political changes. The depletion of natural resources, family dislocation, the reductions in population brought on by illness and starvation, as well as the instability of the commercial provisions market, all contributed to the crisis. By the mid-1870s, indigenous peoples who had survived on the land as hunters, gatherers, fishermen, and provisioners for the commercial trade were faced with the necessity of negotiating the use of their lands with European Canadians. While arrangements for land cessions and economic assistance were made through a treaty-making process, federal regulations regarding the administration of Indian concerns were unilaterally imposed. The authority and sweeping powers of this Indian administration were defined in regulations contained in the Indian Act of 1876 and its amendments. These regulations were developed to transform "Indians" into "Canadians" through a colonial relationship characterized by wardship and tutelage.

The vision of the Canadian nation-state in the 1870s was not based on a concept of political, economic, or cultural pluralism. Rather, it was assumed that, as in eastern Canada (and in other White settlement colonies throughout the British Empire), indigenous populations would disappear as they conformed to the Christian capitalist state. Federal administrators felt that, while this transformation was taking place, Indian societies, whose social, economic, and political structures and behaviour differed radically from their own, should be controlled at the very least. It was argued that such controls would not only facilitate the tutelage of

Indians, but would also ensure the economic and political incorporation of the prairie region into the nation within a climate of law and order.

The repression of indigenous religious practices was perceived as being an important aspect of the cultural transformation of prairie Indians into European Canadians. Regulations against specific types of religious expression and related behaviour were not adopted merely because Victorian Canadians abhorred non-Christian forms of worship and were driven by a humanitarian impulse to "better" their fellow beings. The federal government supported various means of religious control because administrators and missionaries understood the connections between religious ideology and practices and the persistence of indigenous social, economic, and political systems.

The form of colonial rule imposed upon prairie Indians had its roots in British Native Imperial policy as it was developed for the administration of temperate-climate settlement colonies such as Australia, New Zealand, and British North America. This policy was described by Herman Merivale, the Undersecretary of State for the British Colonial Office (1848 to 1874), as one of "perpetual compromises between principle and immediate exigency."[1] Although the sovereign rights of "first inhabitants" were officially recognized, in practice this principle was continually undermined by the imperial government's commitment to fostering economic self-sufficiency and self-government in the settlement colonies in order to establish its own economic and political hegemony in the non-Western world. For the Australian Aborigines, the New Zealand Maori, and Canadian Indians, these "perpetual compromises" led to similar colonial experiences. The incorporation of indigenous populations into the newly emerging nation-states dominated by the newcomers was achieved through unilaterally imposed special legislation, the destruction of local economies, and attempts to dismantle traditional beliefs, customs, and social organization.[2] The result was the reduction of politically independent societies to powerless minorities within the industrialized Western nation-state system.

Several factors influenced the development of imperial Native policy. Local environmental conditions, the historical period of colonization, the prevalent ideology of the day, the varying types of cultural systems encountered by colonials, and indigenous responses to colonization all affected the implementation of a Native policy. Most important, inherent contradictions between Victorian principles of humanitarianism and the political and economic exigencies of managing imperial interests often prevented the adoption of a uniform policy. This administrative dilemma has been summarized by Beverley Gattrell in her examination of colonial expressions of liberal democratic ideologies. She concludes that, while the imperial government was expected to "clear the land of indigenes," it was also committed by its humanitarian principles to refrain from destroying those considered to be "human beings," albeit existing at the stage of "savagery."[3]

The implementation of a Native policy was also impeded by financial constraints on the imperial and colonial governments. Ultimately, the extent to which indigenous labour remained relevant to the economic growth and development of settlement colonies and the willingness on the part of indigenous populations to participate in this new order determined the success of imperial Native policy. In order to promote the peaceful and orderly incorporation of indigenous peoples into the social, economic, and political realities of the colonies, administrative systems of protective trusteeships were established. Indigenous peoples were expected to contribute to the prosperity of the colonies through their labour; and for its part, the Colonial Office assumed the responsibility of protecting Native workers from harsh treatment and exploitation.[4] More direct involvement in "civilizing" Native populations was left to the missionaries.

The development of imperial Native policy can be traced to the humanitarian lobby that followed in the tradition of the anti-slavery reform movement of the late eighteenth and early nineteenth centuries. During this period, influential Low Church evangelicals known as the Clapham Sect, or Exeter Hall, pressured the British Parliament to enforce the principles behind the Abolition of Slavery Act of 1833 throughout the Empire. This meant that the "natives of the British Empire" were to receive "due observance of justice and the protection of their civil rights."[5] It was within the context of the anti-slavery act that Lord Glenelg issued a dispatch to Governor Bourke in 1837 with instructions to deal with Australian Aborigines as "Subjects of the Queen."[6] The official recognition of the inherent rights of indigenous populations and the extension of the British system of justice to protect these rights was premised, in part, on the evangelical belief in the "unity of the human family." Observable cultural differences and what were perceived to be degrading forms of behaviour were attributed to environmental conditions, lack of knowledge of the Christian message, and the unscrupulous exploitation of Native peoples and their resources by colonists.[7] It was believed that non-Western societies could be transformed through programs of directed change and by exposure to the British system of values. Thus, the imposition of British political rights and justice was based on the ethnocentric assumption that Victorian values and lifestyle had "universal application" and, indeed, would be desired by Native colonials once they became aware of the benefits of "civilization."[8]

These attitudes towards colonized indigenous peoples were espoused by members of the various Christian reform movements who were convinced of the "theoretical universality of the Christian religion," and by secular humanitarians who promoted the "idea of progress" for the betterment of the human condition.[9]

The term *progress* was understood as a process by which all would enjoy the opportunity to attain the highest stage of civilization as exemplified by Victorian Protestant industrialized England. Considering themselves to be "leaders of civilization" and successful "pioneers of industry and progress," Victorians evaluated the cultural systems of other societies against their own image. It was a hierarchical world, with Britain at the apex of material and moral progress. The capacity for "freedom" and "enterprise" was the measure by which others were judged. The ladder of Victorian progress took on the following configuration:

The British [were] at the top, followed a few rungs below by the Americans, the other "striving, go-ahead" Anglo-Saxons. The Latin peoples were thought to come next, though far behind. Much lower still stood the vast Oriental communities of Asia and North Africa where progress appeared unfortunately to have been crushed for centuries by military despotisms or smothered under passive religions. Lowest of all stood the "Aborigines" whom it was thought had never learned enough social discipline to pass from family and tribe to the making of a state.[10]

According to the evolutionary thought of the times, humanity was perceived as evolving through a number of regular and predictable stages of development ranging from savagery and barbarism to civilization. This social theory had moral and political implications, and mid-Victorian humanitarians "with a vivid sense of superiority and self-righteousness, if with every good intention," considered it their Christian duty to hasten this process among the "uncivilized."[11] This duty would be fulfilled through the proselytization of Christianity and the establishment of the principle of free enterprise as a precondition for material progress. And, in fact, many believed that "Divine Providence" had especially endowed the English with such a mission by providing access to non-Western peoples through their imperial commercial contacts.[12]

In addition to the impetus for the development of an imperial policy provided by "armchair" humanitarians, the firsthand observations made by missionaries and travellers to the colonies confirmed the need for regulations governing the relations between colonists and the colonized populations. These reports contained descriptions of the devastating effect of uncontrolled frontier colonialism upon the well-being of indigenous peoples. Mission reports received by home offices in London detailed the high incidence of mortality brought on by European-introduced diseases, accelerated levels of warfare, and starvation, which resulted from the over-exploitation of food resources or territorial dispossession. If not physically exterminated (as were the Beothuks, Tasmanians, and certain Australian Aboriginal groups), once viable societies were reduced to a disintegrated, demoralized, and impoverished state. Reacting to these reports, the government struck a fifteen-member parliamentary committee in 1835 to investigate the treatment of indigenous peoples in South Africa, British North America, Australia, New Zealand, the South Seas, and British Guiana. In the committee's report, entitled *Official Report and Minutes of Evidence of the British House of Commons Select Committee on Aborigines,* published in 1836–37, numerous cases of mistreatment were recorded, and state intervention in the colonies was recommended. Other organizations, such as the Aborigines Protection Society, also felt that the Colonial Office should take steps to exert a firm control over the relations between indigenous and colonial societies.

In general, humanitarians distrusted local colonial legislatures to treat fairly with Natives, and were opposed to unjust land seizures and to the use of slave labour. Although the various humanitarian elements were not politically organized and differed in their particular schools of thought, they nevertheless espoused a number of common principles that served to define the nature of British colonial trusteeship. These humanitarians appealed to the moral conscience of British society, and thereby challenged the commonly held belief in a natural law that implied that the destruction of the weak by the strong was a normal aspect of human development.[13] The influence of the humanitarians on administrators such as Lord Glenelg was clear when he identified "civilization" and "protection" as the underlying principles of imperial Native policy.[14]

By the mid-nineteenth century, the initial public expressions of humanitarianism were being modified by a current of social theory that espoused a more explicit doctrine of racial supremacy. Historians such as Douglas Lorimer and George Stocking have traced this development to the "armchair investigations of the new science of anthropology," which occurred at the same time that historians were expounding on the "national character" through glorified folk myths.[15] From these early anthropological investigations, a theory of race was postulated to suggest that, in addition to physical traits, moral and intellectual qualities were biologically determined. The social application of this racial theory not only resulted in a re-evaluation of the work of social reformers among the English poor at home, but also allowed Victorians to define non-Europeans in racial terms that rationalized cultural differences in terms of "inferior inherited characteristics."[16] Accordingly, the new anthropological science encouraged a philosophical shift in the definition of trusteeship in that "paternalism was no longer a trusteeship until maturity was reached, but a perpetual guardianship over ageless children."[17]

The destruction and displacement of non-Western societies was implicit in the notion of the "survival of the fittest" as it was defined in the theory of social Darwinism. Charles Darwin's *The Origin of Species*, published in 1859, provided social theorists with the first formal scientific statement of the theory of biological evolution as a process of natural selection. When applied to human societies within the context of imperial contacts, this theory provided the rationale for arguing that the "means justified the ends." In her study of Victorian attitudes articulated in popular literature of the day, Christine Bolt discovered that most writers believed in the inevitable destruction of indigenous forms of pre-industrial societies:

> The principle of the survival of the fittest seen to be working itself out in these regions was proving conclusively that civilized and uncivilized races could not mix, and in a conflict situation the latter must perish. Everywhere the inferior organization makes room for the superior. As the Indian is killed by the approach of civilization, to which he resists in vain, so the black man perishes by that culture to which he serves as a humble instrument.[18]

The application of socio-cultural evolutionism to non-Europeans contributed to the view that societies could be ranked on the basis of types of subsistence strategies, technology and resource use, forms of social and political organization, and "customs." Pre-industrial societies were considered to be at a level comparable to that which Britain had known during earlier phases of its history. Lack of material advancement, measured according to British standards, and the apparent unwillingness of indigenous peoples to strive for "progress," were seen as indicators of self-imposed conservatism, backwardness, and cultural stagnation. It was held that only direct intervention could reverse this situation. This ethnocentric bias was dominant in the ideology of imperial Native policy well into the twentieth century and was a determining force behind the imposition of colonial systems of wardship. As Bolt has pointed out, the challenge to these theories did not emerge until the first decade of the twentieth century when the association between technological development and morality was seriously questioned and "armchair" anthropological studies were replaced by a method that encouraged the study of other cultures through direct field observations rather than from indirect sources.[19]

These "armchair" concepts not only influenced the ways in which Victorians perceived themselves in relation to others, but also contributed to the adoption of racial stereotypes that permeated Native policy development and implementation. These theories served to explain and justify the destruction of Native societies in the name of progress. Indeed, the expansion of Western capitalism seemed to take its toll despite the intervention and good intentions of the Colonial Office.

In comparison with England, non-industrialized societies were perceived as technologically inferior and inefficient in terms of producing surpluses for the international market. The terminology used to describe indigenous forms of multi-household levels of production and distribution – "backward," "wasteful," "crude," "tradition-bound," and "unproductive" – attests to the conviction that such systems were irrelevant to a self-sufficient and prosperous settlement colony.[20] For Victorians, these societies seemingly lacked the "striving go-ahead" or enterprising nature of Anglo-Saxons, that is, "the desire to keep moving" and "to be trying and accomplishing new things" for themselves and humanity.[21] Often the lack of visible surpluses comparable to those of European societies was attributed to "indolence," believed to be a "common characteristic" of uncivilized people.

Many of the adaptive strategies developed by non-industrialized societies in order to maximize resource use, to ensure orderly biological reproduction, and to enhance the chances for cultural survival were viewed as "irrational." Commonly referred to as "local customs," the ideologies and associated religious expressions of these groups were denounced as "gross superstitions" and even "ferocious forms of worship."[22] Since these cultural practices were thought to be responsible for the lack of material and moral progress, they were targeted for suppression. The various forms of non-Christian religious expression were analyzed within the framework of socio-cultural evolutionary theory, and few Europeans believed that pre-industrial societies had beliefs that could be properly associated with a religion.

Anthropologists of the day, such as American scholar Lewis Henry Morgan, believed that non-Christian religious experience was derived from the imagination and the emotions. Behaviour associated with these beliefs was interpreted as irrational. Some of his British counterparts did attempt to define stages of religious evolution; in *The Origin of Civilization,* published in 1870, Sir John Lubbock traced the development of religious thought by identifying various types of behaviour associated with atheism, fetishism, nature-worship, shamanism, and idolatry.[23] Lubbock and his contemporaries, like anthropologist Edward Tylor, explained religious expression in terms of stages in human social evolution. Religious beliefs and organization changed with the development of a greater "scientific" understanding of the occurrence of natural events. Scholars such as Lubbock represented the more "optimistic, Christian" side of this viewpoint and felt that, "while savages show us a melancholy spectacle of gross superstitions, . . . the religious mind cannot but feel a peculiar satisfaction in tracing up the gradual evolution of more correct ideas and nobler deeds."[24]

Implicit in this evolutionary scheme of morality was the European assumption that spiritual and material progress were inter-related. Lubbock, for example, believed that "advanced ideas" were "entirely beyond the mental range of the lower savages."[25] While he made only a brief reference to the relationship between his defined levels of religious expression and social organization, Lubbock did note that the power of chiefs and priests increased from the lower to the higher levels, and he associated the stage of "idolatry" with sacrifices, temples, and priests.[26]

During the same period, Edward Tylor produced a similar evolutionary scheme to explain cultural differences in religious expression. He traced humanity's progression from polytheism to monotheism in *Primitive Culture* (1871).[27] Tylor's analysis suggested that there was evidence for a functional correlation between religious systems and social, economic, and political institutions. He specifically cited the association between religious beliefs and customs such as the "prohibition of special meats, observance of special days, regulation of marriage or kinship, division of society into castes, ordinance of social law and civil government."[28] Tylor also observed that vestiges of Britain's pre-Christian past were still evident in the folk beliefs and customs prevalent among the illiterate of British and European peasant societies. For Tylor and other nineteenth- and twentieth-century scholars, religious beliefs, organization, and practices were related to levels of "mental and cultural evolution." Accordingly, the practice of "magic" indicated an "infantile" stage of human understanding of the world; organized "religion" reflected a more "mature stage" of human evolution; and "science," the "true" world view, was the "culmination of mental development."[29]

Another influential scholar in the field of anthropology, Sir James Frazer, published *Totemism* in 1887, and his most renowned work, *The Golden Bough,* in 1890. Central to Frazer's interpretation of the evolution of religion was his differentiation between magic as "an early expression of science based on a false notion of the regularity of cause and effect processes" and nineteenth-century Christian religion as representing a "higher achievement, substituting uncertainty and prayerful conciliation for misguided notions of causality."[30]

Using a comparative approach to develop his theory of religion, Frazer derived his descriptive material from the observations of explorers, traders, missionaries, gentlemen travellers, and colonial administrators.[31] The "apparent universality" of the state of savagery was undeniable because it was evident in Britain's own past. In a section of *The Golden Bough* entitled "Our Debt to the Savage," Frazer acknowledged the contribution made by previous levels of human society to the "perfection of theories of thought," and suggested that "contempt and ridicule or abhorrence are too often the only recognition vouchsafed to the savage and his ways."[32] While Frazer praised the cultural legacy of his ancestors, he was less tolerant in his portrayal of the religious behaviour of others. For instance, he referred to practitioners of homeopathic imitative magic as "cunning and malignant savages."[33] According to Frazer's explanatory model, political evolution progressed with religious change as seen in the historical transition from "medicine man" (magician) to monarchy (religion). In ritualistic terms, this transition involved the replacement of "magic" with the "priestly functions of prayer and sacrifice."[34]

In his comparison of colonial indigenous cultures, Frazer concluded that the Australian Aborigines were representative of the "most backward state of humanity" in the world, and lacked any religion.[35] He observed that among these "rudest savages" sympathetic magic was the major means of controlling one's fellow beings or natural occurrences. Nevertheless, Frazer did appear to be impressed with the social and economic role of the clan systems in the performance of specialized rituals associated with food procurement. While not considered to be as backward as the Aborigines, the Maori of New Zealand were described in similar terms. In the Americas, Frazer argued that the greatest advance had been made by the monarchical and theocratic governments of Mexico and Peru. In other societies, including those of the Plains Indian nations, the "sorcerer or medicine man" was the most important source of influence. Drawing upon the writings of traveller-artist George Catlin, Frazer concluded that the source of political power in a "state of savagery" on the plains was a "council of elders" who consulted closely with their shamans.[36] He claimed that this form of oligarchy was responsible for the lack of progress among the Plains Indians. As Frazer explains, "no human being is so hidebound by custom and tradition as your democratic savage; in no state of society consequently is progress so slow and difficult."[37] In his comparison of political systems, he argued that there was more "liberty to think our own thoughts and to fashion our own destinies" under despotism and "grinding tyranny" than "under the apparent freedom of savage life, where the individual's lot is cast from the cradle to the grave in the iron mould of hereditary custom."[38]

The relationship between religious systems and social organization was the subject of other studies, including W. Robertson Smith's *Religion of the Semites* (1889), in which the function of religion in promoting social solidarity was explored, and Herbert Spencer's *The Principles of Sociology* (1891), which discusses the role of religion in terms of social cohesion and political organization and continuity.[39] The majority of treatises on social evolution were grounded in the "cultural idealist heritage of the Enlightenment," for, while material progress was an important physical indicator of evolution, the "pre-eminence of mind" in determining material progress was never questioned.[40]

This theoretical orientation would be seriously challenged only by Marxian models of society as exemplified in Karl Marx's *Preface to the Critique of Political Economy* (1859), in which all aspects of human culture were said to derive from a material base.[41] According to Marx, cultural differences were inherent in the "social production" that humans carry on as "they enter into different relations that are indispensable and independent of their will; these relations of production correspond to a definite stage of development of their material powers of production."[42] Marxians favoured the evolutionary scheme propounded by the materialist-oriented American anthropologist Lewis Henry Morgan. Morgan correlated the stages of human development with various types of technologies and subsistence patterns – hunting and gathering (savagery); to the raising of livestock and cultivation (barbarism); to the conversion of natural products through mechanical and industrial means (civilization).[43]

These Victorian concepts of social evolution were popularized in the literature of the period and reached an influential audience through public lectures. The oral and written accounts of traders, explorers, missionaries, administrators, and colonial settlers were also made available to the public through the lecture circuit. Personal testimonies lent further credence to the theory of social evolutionism and seemingly justified imperial policies designed to protect indigenous peoples. This combination of social theory and humanitarian idealism influenced policy makers such as the Permanent Undersecretary of the Colonial Office, Herman Merivale. A former professor of political economy at Oxford University, Merivale was consulted on issues related to British Native policy by his successors well after his own incumbency had ended.

Merivale was committed to developing a Native policy that would counteract the destructive effect of colonialism, and was very active in promoting his ideas. The issue of metropolitan intervention in the affairs of colonists and indigenous peoples was addressed by Merivale in two major lectures, known as *Lectures on Colonization and Colonies,* first published in 1841 and revised in 1861. In these two sets of lectures, there appears to be a noticeable shift in Merivale's approach to the inevitable "contact-conflict" situations existing throughout the Empire.[44]

In the 1841 edition of the *Lectures,* the undersecretary supported the regulation of colonial-Native relations by the Colonial Office. This policy would temporarily insulate indigenous peoples from White colonists on reserves or in other locations until the two populations could be amalgamated.[45] The conviction that colonial legislatures would not act in the interests of Native peoples was evident in Merivale's insistence that the colonial governors, as representatives of the British government, be responsible for the implementation of the policy. For, while imperial Native policy was premised on the belief that "inferior" indigenous systems would disappear once the British colonies became self-governing, this process was to be achieved within the guidelines inherent in humanitarian principles.[46]

In light of the failure of his Native policy in British North America and South Africa, Merivale's second lecture series reveals a disillusionment with the ability of the Colonial Office to fill its mandate of protection. The best of intentions had been undermined by the principles of free trade, the struggle for colonial economic self-sufficiency and demands for self-government, a retrenchment in parliamentary funding needed to support metropolitan-controlled administrations, the problems associated with enforcing an equitable and uniform policy from London, and indigenous resistance to assimilative measures.[47]

Merivale's support for the cultural transformation of indigenous societies was explained in the 1861 lecture series. In these addresses, he outlined broad areas of objectionable behaviour that would not even be tolerated by the Colonial Office. These included: "violations of the eternal and universal laws of morality"; "less horrible" but nevertheless "pernicious" customs; and what he termed as "absurd" and "impolitic" customs that were not "directly injurious."[48] Merivale was convinced that the acceptance of British customs, values, laws, and the Christian religion by indigenous populations was necessary if indigenous peoples wished to have a meaningful place in self-governing White colonies. Until the colonized were "elevated," colonial self-sufficiency and prosperity were dependent upon the ability of the more "progressive" colonists to control "land, capital, and labour" even at the expense of "less progressive societies."[49] Towards this end, Merivale recommended that colonial authorities have the right by virtue of their "relative position of civilized and Christian men to savages, to enforce abstinence from immoral and degrading practices," and to "compel outward conformity to the law of what we regard as better instructed reason."[50]

Christian conversion was supported as a major means for the physical and moral "uplifting" of indigenous colonials. In Africa, missions were established in coastal settlements, and energies were directed towards undermining the slave trade. The creation of a bishopric in Zanzibar, the heart of the Arab slave trade market, is one example of the force behind this commitment.[51] African religious practices were denigrated as ancestor worship, fetishism, and witchcraft. While some missionaries credited Africans in the south and west for having "spiritual pretensions," even the most liberal-thinking missionaries believed that millions of Africans were held in "cruel control" by "charlatanism," "ventriloquism," and "scarcely disguised fraud and legerdemain."[52] Spiritual leaders and healers, commonly referred to as "witch doctors," were perceived as major obstacles to progress. Legislation was sometimes used to undermine the status and influence of this class of people; for example, the colonial government of Rhodesia passed witchcraft regulations in 1895 and a Witchcraft Suppression Act in 1899 to suppress witchcraft and various forms of divination.[53] The latter legislation was still in effect in the 1960s and was directed against believers as well as practitioners.

In contrast, the religions of India were more highly regarded. The existence of temples, priesthoods, and religious documents provided Victorians with visible signs of more organized and evolved religious systems than those found in Africa, Australia, or North America. Nevertheless, evangelicals lobbied the Colonial Office for support for the establishment of missions. Hinduism, in particular, was considered idolatrous, corrupt, and immoral. It was felt that believers indulged in their ceremonies for sensual gratification rather than spiritual reasons. Associated customs such as the caste system, "widow burning" or "Thuggee," infanticide, "hook-swinging" rituals, self-mutilation, human sacrifice, polygamy, and prohibitions on widow remarriage and female education all provided missionaries with justification for attempting to draw Hindu believers away from their religion.[54]

Although the commercial charter of the British East India Company encouraged Christian missions, the Company had actually restricted missionary activity until 1833. In the interest of promoting a favourable commercial climate, the Company had adopted a neutral position with regard to religion and local customs. Missionaries claimed that the Company's neutrality in these matters was self-serving at the expense of the well-being of the indigenous population. The Company's opposition to providing locals with a Christian education was, according to the missionaries, motivated by the fear that enlightened Indians might demand a more equitable share in commercial transactions.[55] The Indian Mutiny of 1857 brought the argument to a head. While missionaries blamed the mutiny on the absence of a Christian presence, their opponents argued that a "departure from strict neutralism" had contributed to the uprising by defending Indian traditionalists.[56] By this time, the colonial government itself had shifted from a policy of non-interference by passing legislation to discourage polygamy, the Thuggee, and infanticide. Soon after the shock of the Indian Mutiny had reached Britain, Queen Victoria issued a proclamation in 1858 in an attempt to prevent a recurrence of this type of revolt. The proclamation implied that missionary activity would be supported but that the conversion of Moslems, Hindus, and Buddhists would not be forced. The Act declared that it was the royal will that "none be in anywise favoured, none molested or disquieted by reason of their religious faith or observance, but that all alike shall enjoy the equal and impartial protection of the law."[57]

In the colonies of Africa and India that were not White-dominated in terms of population, customary practices and religious systems were suppressed to some degree. These efforts, however, were largely ineffective. Administrators, missionaries, and settlers often disagreed over the extent of intervention into local affairs. Furthermore, the general nature of directives issued by the Colonial Office allowed for a significant latitude of local interpretation and implementation by the colonial governments. This inconsistency in imperial Native policy resulted in some level of tolerance as exemplified among colonial Indian tribal peoples who were allowed to practise their customs provided that they were compatible with British notions of "justice," "humanity," and "good government," and were not "wasteful" or "cruel."[58]

Unlike non-settlement colonies, interference in the lives of indigenous peoples was much more pervasive in the White settlement colonies. A brief examination of the development of policies that directly or indirectly affected ceremonial life in Australia, New Zealand, and British North America will illustrate the pattern of religious suppression that occurred among the Aboriginal peoples of the western-Canadian prairies.

From the time of the establishment of the first penal colony in New South Wales in 1788, relations between White colonists and Aborigines were typified by the annihilation, exploitation, and dispossession of the latter. As historian C.D. Rowley explained, the relationship between Britain and the Aborigines was to a large extent determined by the demand for fine wool and cheap suitable land. New South Wales proved to be ideal for the commercial raising of sheep, and it was expected that the use of lands for this purpose would meet with little effective resistance on the part of the Aborigines.[59] Unlike other colonial relationships, no formal trade or military alliances were made, and no arrangements for land cessions were undertaken. Existing clan ownership of tracts of land went unrecognized, and a legal decision passed in 1899 declared that the new nation, Australia, was a *territorium nullius* at the time of contact and was therefore "unoccupied." It was the desire for the land itself and not indigenous-produced goods that determined the historical relations between the colonists and the Aborigines.

By the mid-nineteenth century, the Aborigines had been reduced in number to the point where colonists believed that these original inhabitants would soon vanish. Lacking the technology and forms of military organization required to resist the colonists effectively, these semi-nomadic hunters and gatherers had been unable to limit colonial expansion into their clan tracts. In an effort to at least "smooth [the Aborigines'] dying pillow" as expeditiously as possible, the Colonial Office instructed its governors to support the activities of missionaries and the establishment of schools for Aboriginal children.[60]

The Colonial Office had envisioned the incorporation of indigenes into colonial society as a process whereby people "would learn by precept and example to live in equality with the lower orders of the colonial society with all the protection of the law."[61] Directives from the Secretary of State for the colonies encouraged governors to foster a cooperative and peaceful relationship and even recommended the punishment of those Whites who attempted to destroy the Aborigines or unnecessarily interrupted their lives.[62] At the same time, governors were instructed to help develop the Aboriginal sense of religion and to support their education. In 1837, the Select Committee on Aborigines, organized to investigate charges of colonial maltreatment, advocated these same policies in addition to proposing the creation of a reservation for hunting land and "special codes of law to protect the Aboriginal until he learned to live within the framework of British law."[63]

Initially, the Colonial Office had advised against interference in local internal affairs, and thus the Aborigines were to be left free to exercise "their own customs upon themselves" as long as they were not practised "too immediately in the presence of Europeans."[64] Before his appointment as Governor of South Australia, however, Captain George Grey informed the Colonial Office in 1840 that certain "barbarous" customs should not receive official recognition. Grey believed that the Aborigines were inferior to Europeans, but was convinced that cultural mores, rather than biological or environmental factors, were responsible. In his opinion, Aboriginal religion, or what was referred to as superstitions, or "traditional laws," was responsible for the lack of material and moral progress. Grey, along with his contemporaries such as British Whig leader Lord John Russell, had little patience with those philosophers who "idealized the freedom and equality of natural man" and firmly believed that these qualities were absent in the Aboriginal clan system that "bound the Aborigines to 'barbarism' by allowing the monopolization of advantages by strong male elders."[65] For Grey, the erosion of the power base of traditional male elders was a necessary step towards the integration of Aborigines since it was the elders who, through the supernatural sanctions of traditional laws, would attempt to retain their positions of influence by discouraging those who indicated an inclination to assimilate.

While conversion to Christianity was a major mechanism through which morality and liberality would be achieved, the incorporation of Aborigines as labourers into the capitalist economy was also an important objective. Towards this end, Grey and his predecessor, Governor Gipps, supported the introduction of training facilities and apprenticeships whereby new technical skills and European work habits could be learned.[66] This transformation of Aboriginal hunters and gatherers into members of the British working class was also the prerequisite for the attainment of citizenship status. The continued use of Aborigines as casual labour was considered to be inadvisable since the low wages (attributed to the lack of skills rather than racism) only served to draw labourers back into the "bush" once they were no longer needed.[67] The location of people on reserves during the transition phase was to serve both protectionist and assimilative objectives.

With the exception of Western Australia, responsible government had been granted to the Australian colonies by 1856. The colonial frontier had advanced over Aboriginal lands, and competition for resources led to violence. Aboriginal families increasingly found that their access to water holes was restricted, that fences and grazing cattle and sheep had driven off the game, and that they were forbidden to hunt or congregate near settled areas. Some family groups settled near pastoral stations where they were employed as casual labour; others sought refuge at mission stations; some relocated on the outskirts of townships; while still others, particularly in the desert areas, retreated as far as possible from the European.[68]

A system of trusteeship in the form of two administrative offices called the Protectors had been established since 1840 to prevent the total annihilation of the

Aborigines. Food rations, blankets, and medical aid were distributed through the offices of the resident magistrates. In 1886, the Aborigines Protection Act was passed by a five-member Aborigines Protection Board of Western Australia; however, no bureaucracy was created to implement its provisions. Rather, the provisions of the Act were simply added to the myriad of other duties performed by resident magistrates, police, and government medical officers. This situation was rectified in subsequent legislation, which established an administrative arm to supervise policy implementation in the form of a Chief Protector and a Department of Native Affairs. To facilitate the administration of protectionist policies, the Aboriginal population was to be relocated on a series of small reserves. These reserves would serve as areas of refuge rather than as bases for viable economic development and incorporation into the new order. Through the plan to settle Aborigines on lands not coveted for development, the races were effectively separated, and, at the same time, the political and economic interests of the colonists were served. For the most part, the future welfare of the Aborigines was left to the missionaries.

Assimilative programs received support through legislated measures such as the Queensland Act of 1897 and similar acts passed in 1911 by state governments. The comprehensive nature of these acts has been described in these terms:

> Aborigines were denied the right to vote, the right to testify under oath and the right to participate in certain religious and cultural ceremonies. Moreover, liquor and firearms were prohibited, admission and expulsion from reserves were stipulated, interracial marriages were discouraged, children could be made wards of the state, work permits were granted to those eligible for employment. . . . Institutional regulations on missions and stations were formulated whereby work was assigned, punishment of insubordination enforced, monies and wages controlled.[69]

The failure of the Colonial Office to successfully put in place mechanisms for the protection of Aboriginal rights while at the same time facilitating their incorporation into the political economy was rationalized in racist terms. According to C.D. Rowley, to this day "their failure or refusal to conform to middle-class *mores* has been monotonously explained as due to the stubborn resistance of Aboriginal 'mentality' or custom, or culture, to 'civilising influences.'"[70]

In contrast to the Aboriginal semi-nomadic hunters and gatherers, the Maori of New Zealand practised a subsistence economy based on horticulture supplemented by hunting, fishing, and collecting. Fundamental to their economic, political, and social institutions was a hierarchical system of kin-related families headed by chiefs who were responsible for pooling household products and supervising their distribution. The Maori lived in fortified villages in order to maintain protection from rival feuding groups. For Europeans, the existence of chiefdoms, villages, a horticultural subsistence, military organization, the presence of "slaves," and highly decorative art forms placed the Maori on a higher level of social evolution than was accorded to the Australian Aborigines.

Following the initial period of contact with commercial whalers in the eighteenth century, the Maori soon became important suppliers to the trading centres established on the North Island. During this phase of contact, the Maori traded their communally produced surpluses of timber, flax, and later potatoes and pigs, with colonists on the islands and in New South Wales. Even the smoked tattooed heads of Maori slaves and enemies became coveted trade items on the commercial market. While the participation of the Maori in the mercantilist system was originally beneficial, some tribes experienced extensive cultural disintegration as they became more entrenched in the European market economy. Competition for access to markets, trade goods such as woollen blankets, and new forms of technology such as metal knives, axes, and firearms resulted in an intensification of inter-tribal wars. The loss of life through warfare, European-introduced diseases, and the abuse of alcohol resulted in the deaths, dislocation, and impoverishment of thousands of Maori.

With the influx of British settlers at the height of the industrial revolution in Europe, the Maori increasingly found themselves competing for access to their own lands. Lord Glenelg and James Stephen, the Permanent Undersecretary of the Colonial Office, both supported British intervention to protect Maori interests while ensuring peaceful colonization. In 1839, a decision was made to annex the South Island as a "right of discovery," to formally negotiate land cessions, to appoint a "protector" to prevent land frauds, and to generally oversee the welfare of the Maori. In 1840, New Zealand became a British colony. The principle of Maori sovereignty was recognized when the Treaty of Waitangi was signed with a provision that further land alienation would be negotiable only through the Crown. Five years later, war broke out between the colonists and those chiefs who refused to consider land sales; this was the first of many armed conflicts that took their toll on the Maori.

As is evident in its directives concerning New Zealand, the Colonial Office had every intention of implementing the humanitarian lessons learned from its failure to regulate colonial relations with the Australian Aborigines, the Tasmanians, the North American Indians, and the Africans. The instructions signalled a "new and noble beginning" for British Native policy in which imperialism and evangelical humanitarianism would "march together."[71]

The years immediately following the wars of the 1840s were peaceful ones, and the Maori were able to expand their horticultural activity on the North Island and even exported food surpluses to Australia. Under the governorship of George Grey, agricultural production was encouraged, and communally organized Maori work crews were hired for public-works programs. At this time no serious consideration was given to the removal of the Maori due to their numerical majority, their nearness to White settlements, and their reputation as adept warriors. The colonial government, however, did initiate a policy of "Europeanization" to foster the assimilation of the Maori through subsidized mission schools, industrial boarding schools, and the provision of medical aid in hospitals. A system of resident magistrates who were responsible for educating the Maori chiefs in British legal procedures and law was also introduced. While some attempt was made to accommodate customary law (through a provision of the Resident Magistrate Court's Ordinance of 1847 and the Native Circuit Courts Act of 1858) by consulting local leaders and adapting to needs, the British system of law predominated. These same magistrates were also expected to provide the Maori with support in the Land Court created to facilitate the exchange of communal land title for individual property ownership, with the surplus land being made available to settlers.

In addition to transforming the Maori economy through the introduction of the concept of private property, assimilation was also encouraged by allowing Maori participation in the colonial political system. This political concession is considered to have been a "diplomatic" move rather than a serious effort to provide some level of political representation. The creation of seven Maori seats in the colonial legislature did, however, give the Maori some access to political power in the new order.

By 1860, racial hostilities had increased as settlers made further encroachments on Maori lands. The conflict was not only over land, but also over the ways in which the land resources were being used by the two cultures. For their horticulture, the Maori required large sections of land that were left to return to a forest stage to lie fallow, whereas European commercial agriculture required both smaller areas of permanently cultivated lands and large areas of grasslands for grazing sheep.[72] The stripping of forests for grasslands seriously affected the Maoris' ability to live off wild resources. As in the case of the Australian Aborigines, the Maoris' spiritual relationship to their land was reflected in their political economy. A leader's ability to productively manage resources earned him the respect of followers, and, in turn, enhanced his power, or "mana," in a material (property), social (status and prestige), and spiritual sense.[73]

In response to these pressures, an inter-tribal political movement emerged in the form of the King Movement under the leadership of the chief, Wiremu Kingi. United under Wiremu Kingi, several central North Island chiefs became involved in an unsuccessful twelve-year effort to preserve Maori control over their lands. Two subsequent militant messianic religious movements, the Hau Hau (or Pai Marire) religion (led by Te Ua Hamene) and the Ringatu religion (led by Te Kooti Rikirangi), also failed in their objective to drive out White colonists. The Hau Hau followers were defeated in 1872 and disbanded, and, while the Ringatu religion was immobilized in the 1880s, a form of it persists to this day.[74]

The initial policy of non-interference in local customs and religion did not imply acceptance or tolerance of Maori cultural behaviour. The terms *depraved* and *obscene,* as well as *unprogressive,* were used to describe much of Maori life. A passage from the *Wellington Independent* describes typical White attitudes towards the Maori:

Scrape a Maori, the most civilised, and the savage shows distinctly underneath. The 'Haka' [war dance] is an *exposé* of the evil which really lies at the root of their present prostrate condition, an exhibition of the substratum of utter immorality, depravity, and obscenity, which forms the ground work of their race; and in spite of the veneering with which we clumsily cover the rough wood, we shall do nothing until we alter their entire character, by taking in hand the education, *per force* of the young growing saplings.[75]

In addition to the "war dance," another major communal ceremony, the Tangi, was discouraged. The Tangi was a funeral ceremony lasting for a week or more, which involved the congregation of numerous kinfolk who came to mourn and pay their respects to the dead.[76] During this ceremony, large quantities of food were prepared by the deceased's relatives and consumed by the visitors. Attempts were made by the colonial authorities to reduce the size and duration of these gatherings. Such ceremonies were considered a "drain on foodstuffs," a "burden on public transport," and a "danger to public health."[77] For the Maori, the funerary ceremony was a "social rite *par excellence*" that not only signified the ritual passage from life to death but also served to reinforce solidarity and moral obligations among kin-related households. As with other communal ceremonies, these practices perpetuated traditional forms of production and distribution. On these occasions, food surpluses and labour were directed away from the commercial market since the obligation to pool one's resources undermined the accumulation of property by individual producers.[78] Consequently, such ceremonial practices were viewed as hindrances to Maori participation in wage labour, successful family farming, and, ultimately, assimilation.

Throughout the Oceanic region, other British colonial governments treated indigenous customs in a similar manner. If the customs shocked Victorian morality, had no utility in terms of colonial objectives, or, as in the case of the anti-colonial religion-driven movements of the Maori, threatened the lives of colonists and law and order, steps were taken to regulate indigenous behaviour. Ordinances passed against customary practices and their implementation varied from area to area.

The Colonial Office was confronted with a more complex situation in British North America, where it attempted to develop a Native policy over a comparatively vast area occupied by many culturally diverse societies. While some peoples had economies based upon semi-sedentary patterns of hunting, fishing, and gathering, others were sedentary villagers who combined horticulture with hunting and gathering. Their socio-economic and political organization varied in types from bands, to tribes, to ranked societies, and to chiefdoms, but all were characterized by "subsistence level" economies based on a domestic mode of production. Material goods were produced and distributed through kin-related groups and inter-group trading partnerships. Such networking facilitated the flow of new technologies, ideas, and people (primarily through marriage). Territorial boundaries between groups and societies were recognized but there was no exclusive individual ownership of land in the European sense of the concept.

Before the unification of eastern British colonies as the Confederation of Canada in 1867, imperial Native policy in British North America followed precedents established by the British government in the English (or Thirteen) Colonies of the present-day United States; that is, there was a political recognition of the legitimacy of indigenous ownership of occupied lands. Accordingly, any extinguishment of land ownership ideally involved the processes of negotiation and purchase rather than seizure.[79] Control over land transfers was to be within the purview of the British Crown rather than of individuals. Although the British government recognized the principle of aboriginal rights to land ownership, in practice there was no uniformly implemented Native policy until the 1750s. Following the cession of Acadia (Nova Scotia) by the French to the British in 1713, the government attempted to introduce the process of negotiated land surrenders to the Micmacs; however, it was not until 1752, when conflict over the region ended, that Governor Peregrine Hopson was able to ratify a treaty with the Micmacs. In this treaty, Micmac "hunting and fishing rights" in British territory were recognized, and the government agreed to supply provisions.[80] Apparently the terms of this treaty were not enforced.

In a subsequent proclamation issued some ten years later by Lieutenant Governor Jonathan Belcher, the British Crown guaranteed the Micmacs their "just rights and possessions," and further stipulated that all European squatters on Indian lands would be duly prosecuted.[81] This proclamation contained the essence of the pattern of imperial Native policy to be followed in later negotiations with other indigenous groups. By the mid-eighteenth century, Britain had adopted a "protectionist" policy not only to prevent the economic exploitation of Indians by colonists, but also to stabilize its commercial and military relations with the various Indian nations. Such alliances, including arrangements for neutrality, were considered necessary in the successful establishment of British political and economic hegemony in North America.

With the surrender of New France to Britain in 1763, Indian land rights were re-affirmed in principle. Not only were Indian allies of New France granted the right to occupy their lands in Article 40 of the Capitulation of Montreal in 1760, but, as well, the subsequent Proclamation of 1763 established an Indian Territory "west of the Appalachians and the Thirteen Colonies and east of the Mississippi and south of the height of land dividing the waters flowing into the Arctic from those flowing into the Atlantic Ocean."[82] The Proclamation provided for due consultation before the establishment of military fortifications in Indian territory and assurances that the British government would secure to them previously held "Rights and Privileges."[83]

In recognition of these rights, the British offered Indians protection against colonial encroachment in their hunting territory and stipulated that future transfers of land involve formal negotiations and "fair" purchase through the agency of the Crown. This system of extinguishing Indian claims to territory was later applied to cessions in Ontario and the prairie provinces. Lands were to be set aside for exclusive occupation by Indians (called reserves), and monies accruing from sales of their lands were to be applied to projects benefiting them. In practice, however, such funds were frequently misappropriated, and until the twentieth century there were few mechanisms in the Indian administration to prevent fraudulent dealings.[84]

The protective role of the imperial government was also reflected in the nature of the administrative structures that were created to establish and maintain formal relations with the Indian nations. In 1670, colonial governors were instructed to offer Indians British protection when it was requested. By 1755, an Indian superintendency had been based in the Mohawk Valley (New York State), and Sir William Johnson was appointed to administer political and economic relations on behalf of the imperial government between the colonists and Indian nations. After the American Revolution, the Indian superintendency was relocated in Canada.

The Indian superintendents and their agents were expected to function as both protectors and diplomats. Much of their work involved the negotiation of trade and military alliances through formal meetings and the annual distribution of gifts. According to historian John Milloy, the political relationship between the British government and indigenous societies was conducted on a "nation-to-nation" basis whereby the Indian Department, in effect, operated as a "foreign office."[85] This type of relationship implied that Aboriginals were allowed to retain their autonomy despite the government's support for "civilizing" programs. Milloy contends that there was a major shift in imperial Indian policy after the unification of Upper and Lower Canada in 1841, particularly when (as in 1860), the British government transferred its responsibilities for Indian affairs to the United Canadas.[86] This shift was reflected in a change in the Indian administrative structure. At the time of unification, the management of Indian affairs was assumed by the Crown Lands Department, with the commissioner also being the Chief Superintendent of Indian Affairs. Under the provisions of the British North America Act in 1867, the responsibility for Indian affairs was handed over to the Secretary of State, and in

1873 it became a branch of the Department of the Interior. With the passing of the Canadian Indian Act of 1876, the social, economic, and political position of Indian nations was dramatically transformed into one of "dependence." This formalized relationship between Indian nations and the new Canadian state had not been negotiated, but, rather, it was unilaterally imposed. By 1880, the Department of Indian Affairs had been created to implement the terms of this act.

While this transformation in the political relations between Indian nations and the imperial government might be attributed to efforts on the part of politicians to "consolidate" a new nation, Milloy argues that the process started much earlier and received its impetus from "a continuing quest for a more perfect [colonial] developmental strategy in an atmosphere of escalating political conflict involving Native leaders and local civilizers, such as Indian agents and missionaries."[87] Before the War of 1812, the British government had favoured a Native policy characterized by protectionism and "conciliation," whereby the Christianization and civilization of Indians was not discouraged if the missionaries received indigenous support; otherwise, forced cultural change was not supported.[88] An increased demand for Indian lands, and the state of economic dependency in which many Indian groups located near the colonies found themselves, provided the motivation for imperial intervention. For many communities, the situation had reached a crisis level for several reasons: the over-exploitation of food resources as settlement and the commercial fur trade moved into the hinterland; the loss of hunting and fishing territories; and the decimation of populations through starvation, disease, and increased warfare.

John Webster Grant has traced the first official movement for support of "civilization" programs in eastern Canada to Sir Peregrine Maitland, who was the Lieutenant Governor of Upper Canada and a former vice-president of the Church of England evangelical Church Missionary Society.[89] During 1820–21, Maitland proposed a program of primary education, training in agricultural and industrial skills, and Christianization for the Indian inhabitants of the communities of Grand and Credit rivers. His successor, Sir John Colborne, extended this idea into the Coldwater area of Georgian Bay and Lake Simcoe in 1829. According to historian Leslie Upton, the official commitment to these social experiments in cultural transformation by the Indian Department "came into official policy through the back door of self-interest" and was an attempt on the part of Major General Darling, the Superintendent of the Indian Department, to deflect imperial plans for the dissolution of the Department by creating a new official function in the form of "civilizing" the Indian.[90] For its part, the Colonial Office verbally supported the establishment of Christian Aboriginal agriculturally based farms as a means to rescue indigenous peoples from "a state of barbarism," but no funds were allocated. As part of a more general move towards economic retrenchment, and in recognition of the changed role of Indians as military allies, the Indian Department was transferred from military to civil control in 1830, the governors of Upper and Lower Canada assuming responsibility for Indian Affairs.[91]

The only serious internal challenge to the "civilization" program came in 1836 through the office of the newly arrived lieutenant governor of Upper Canada, Sir Francis Bond Head. Convinced that Indians were "a doomed race" and were "melting like the snow before the sun," he recommended the physical isolation of Indians from all White contact.[92] Towards this end, Bond Head undertook negotiations for the removal (without compensation) of Chippewa, Ottawa, and Sauking to Manitoulin Island. Protests from the London-based Aborigines Protection Society and mission agencies such as the Wesleyan Methodist Conference undermined this scheme. By 1838, Lord Glenelg of the Colonial Office had issued an official statement of support for the cultural transformation program as outlined by Darling some ten years earlier, claiming that it was the only effective means to "protect and cherish this helpless Race" and to "raise them in the Scale of Humanity":

Wandering Indians had to be settled down; those who were more or less settled had to be made farmers. They had to be given a sense of permanency on their lands, "attached to the soil." . . . Still, their lands would be protected from creditors and would be inalienable without the threefold consent of governor, principal chief, and resident missionary. Education was basic to assimilation. The government gave its blessing to the missionaries by instructing the Indian agents to co-operate cheerfully with them.[93]

The education of indigenous children was a major focus of this assimilation program. Protestant missionaries had already established schools for Indian children patterned after those available to the English poor, but in certain areas Indians were allowed to attend White schools.[94] In 1879, the residential "manual labour" school system as it had been developed in the United States by American educators such as Richard Pratt, the Director of Carlisle Indian School at Carlisle, Pennsylvania, was adopted. The introduction of these off-reserve industrial residential schools, according to Grant, signified a "new era" for Indian missions. It was hoped that, by removing young children from the influence of their parents and relatives, they would become "effective emissaries of Christian civilization among their own people."[95] The ramifications of this education system for Indians was that assimilation would not be a matter of choice, but would be imposed on them by the dominant society.

Efforts were also made to integrate Indian adults into the mainstream of the dominant society. By the 1850s it had become evident that protective measures alone – such as the legislative acts passed to protect against encroachment on Indian lands (1839), to regulate the sale of alcohol to Indians (1839), and to attempt to insulate reserve populations from unscrupulous Whites by introducing punishment to trespassers (1850) – were not effective in promoting "civilization." Rather than adopt further insulating measures, the governor of Upper Canada felt that the offer of full citizenship might be an inducement for integration.[96] In 1857, the Act for the Gradual Civilization of the Indian Tribes in the Canadas made it possible for male adults to attain citizenship upon meeting certain criteria. Citizenship could be achieved through the surrender of all rights to Indian lands and privileges. In return, Indian citizens would receive compensation in the form of fifty acres of reserve land to be held in fee simple and a payment from band funds.

When the responsibility for Indian affairs was transferred from the imperial government to the Province of Canada in 1860, these same principles and strategies were upheld. They were incorporated into the British North America Act of 1867, which empowered the newly formed government of Canada to pass legislation with respect to Indians. It was at this time that formal mechanisms through which Indians were to become politically incorporated into the Canadian nation-state were defined. Towards this end, the Indian Act was passed in 1869, and under Section 10 provisions were made to undermine traditional forms of political leadership through the imposition of the European version of the "democratic, elective" process. As in Australia and New Zealand, traditional forms of hereditary leadership were considered to be major impediments to progress because they prevented the political ascendancy of young "educated" men. Furthermore, it was hoped that the power concentrated in the office of the traditional leaders would be delegated to elected councillors in the new system. The hereditary leaders who were allowed to continue in office and the newly elected chiefs, as they were termed, were subject to removal on the grounds of "dishonesty, intemperance, or immorality."[97] In the new Indian Act of 1876, incompetency was added as a reason for dismissal.

In their analysis of this legislation, historians Wayne Daugherty and Dennis Madill maintain that, whereas colonial legislation had emphasized the process of "gradual civilization," the new act promoted "gradual enfranchisement."[98] It was specifically created for those groups (for example, the Six Nations) who had a long history of contact, and was designed to provide a means for educating adults in European-Canadian political and social values.[99] Concomitant with this legislation was the promotion of the idea of individual ownership of property through the granting of "location tickets" to holders of individually held land on reserves. The demonstration of ownership and proper use of private property was a prerequisite for the transformation of "Indians" into "Canadian citizens."

In summary, the development of imperial Native policy in British North America was regionally inconsistent, reflecting the historical nature of changing political and economic relations between the various Indian nations and the British government. Formal statements of policy were generally communicated in a language consistent with Victorian evangelical humanitarianism; in other words, it was the sacred duty of a more advanced nation to enlighten those inferior peoples whom they had contacted through the expansion of commerce. The intervention of the Colonial Office in the internal affairs of indigenous societies was motivated by the need to ensure that Britain's political and commercial interests would be pursued within a climate of law and order. The level and type of controls exerted by the Colonial Office varied on a regional basis. Historian David McNab has concluded that by the mid-nineteenth century the Colonial Office, in consultation with its resident governors in the colonies, had developed an "expedient" approach to the management of relations with Indian populations, following a policy of non-interference unless local circumstances forced a re-evaluation of its position.[100] In the Maritime region, Indian peoples were to be insulated on reserves until they could be assimilated. In the Canadas, the objective was the reduction of the necessity for reserve lands through amalgamation with the White population and education. In the western territories, amalgamation was also adopted as a strategy because the commercial fur trade persisted, and because, in Rupert's Land, the welfare of Native people was administered by the Hudson's Bay Company. On Vancouver Island and the Northwest Coast, the Colonial Office under Merivale was guided by Governor James Douglas's firsthand experiences. Douglas promoted insulation for Indian populations living in the vicinity of White settlements, and eventual amalgamation for more remote populations.

This approach was similar to that used in other areas of the British Empire. In situations where the productive labour of indigenous populations was considered irrelevant (Australian Aborigines) or became redundant over time as a result of European immigration (the Maori and Canadian Indians), official policies were less tolerant of traditional cultural systems.[101] The greater part of the legislation introduced by the Colonial Office and subsequently adopted by colonial governments was directed towards standardizing property relationships, creating greater access to land resources, and defining the process of cultural transformation. With the exception of Australia, legislation pertaining to the protection of traditional lands was not intended to safeguard the lands *per se,* but rather to protect indigenous populations in the "land conveyance process" and to ensure the orderly transfer of indigenous lands for settlement.[102] Once White colonials predominated, the need for political and economic interdependency disappeared, and the indigenous peoples became irrelevant to the European colony's self-sufficiency and prosperity.

During the 1870s, the newly formed Canadian government continued to develop and codify its Indian policy. These same principles formed the basis for the

Dominion's official dealings with the Indian nations residing in present-day western Canada. Accordingly, entitlement to occupied lands was formally acknowledged and land transfers to colonists were possible only through the process of formally negotiated land sales by a representative of the Crown. In exchange for surrendered lands, reserves were set aside for the exclusive occupancy of those who had signed the treaties. The "civilization" and "assimilation" of Indians into the dominant society through paternalistic social programs and legislation were long-term objectives supported by the Canadian government.

The Ties that Bind:
The Plains Cree

2

The many bands of Algonquian-speaking Cree who make up the Plains Cree nation of present-day Saskatchewan can be traced to a number of subarctic woodland Cree groups who gradually moved into the parkland and prairie regions in the late eighteenth century. From 1670 to the early nineteenth century, these Cree, along with their Assiniboin allies, were the middlemen for the northwestern commercial fur trade extending from Hudson Bay to the prairies. In addition to trapping and trading in furs and food products, the Cree also bartered European trade goods with other Aboriginal nations. Trading alliances were established with the Blackfoot in the early eighteenth century, and along with their Assiniboin allies, the Plains Cree formed a strong trade and military partnership with the Mandan and Hidatsa in the Missouri River region.

From 1763 to 1821, major shifts in the distribution of the Cree and Assiniboin occurred.[1] Their movement northwest was halted when several Cree bands succumbed to the smallpox epidemic of 1784. Their subsequent loss of military strength forced them to withdraw from the northern regions occupied by the Dene (Chipewyan) and to look to the parklands and prairie regions to the south of the North Saskatchewan River. These shifts to the southwest were also a response to a move into the hinterland by the Hudson's Bay Company and its Montreal-based competitors. By the 1790s, many of the Cree bands followed this expansion of the commercial trade along the Saskatchewan River system. Here they became more oriented to bison hunting and enhanced their trade in furs and food provisions with bison meat, pemmican, and hides. Their use of the rich food environments of the parklands and prairie regions, successful participation in the fur trade, and their adoption of new forms of technology (the horse and the gun) resulted in unprecedented affluence for the Plains Cree.[2]

The movement of the Cree into the prairie/parkland region continued throughout the first quarter of the nineteenth century. By the 1850s, the seasonal movements of the *nêhiyawak,* or the "exact-speaking," people extended along several
major river systems. In the summer months, many camped along the Qu'Appelle
River and Missouri Coteau where they came into contact with the Dakota and
Assiniboin. For the remainder of the year, these Cree exploited the resources of
the Saskatchewan valley extending from "the Neutral Hills south of the Battle
River to the Beaver Hills and Fort Edmonton." Here they shared territorial
boundaries with the Blackfoot.[3]

One of the most powerful and largest nations residing in the prairie region, the
Plains Cree had an estimated population of 11,500 in the early 1860s. In comparison
to other groups that had been drastically reduced in numbers by smallpox epidemics
in the periods between 1780 and 1782, and between 1810 and 1820, the Cree
population continued to rise as more of their woodland relatives joined them. By
the late 1850s, however, the Plains Cree were also on the decline due to smallpox
and starvation, which was brought on by both their incapacity to hunt in their
weakened state, and the decline of the bison herds.[4]

The foundations of Plains Cree society were the networks of related extended
families who generally resided together. These encampments of families are often
referred to in the literature as "bands." Each group of families had a stable nucleus
of close relatives associated with a headman.[5] While each band tended to frequent
its own hunting and gathering territory, it did not possess exclusive ownership of
resources or land and did not accept strictly defined boundaries.

Mandelbaum and others have identified at least eight major Plains Cree bands
and several smaller family groupings. These bands varied in number from 200 to
800 people.[6] The larger bands and their homelands have been identified as follows:
the Calling River People, *kâ-têpwêwi-sîpîwiyiniwak* (valley of the Qu'Appelle);
the Rabbit Skin People, *wâposwayânak* (wooded country between the Assiniboine
and Qu'Appelle rivers); the "Cree-Assiniboin," *nêhiyawi-pwât* (southwest of the
Qu'Appelle River into the Wood Mountain region); the Touchwood Hills People,
posâkanacîwiyiniwak (between Long Lake and Touchwood Hills); the House
People, *wâskâhikaniwiyiniwak* (congregated near Hudson's Bay Company posts,
particularly Fort Carlton); the House, Willow, or Parklands People, *pask-
wâwiyiniwak* (descendants of the Scottish trader George Sutherland and his Cree
wife, located immediately to the southwest of the confluence of the South and
North Saskatchewan rivers); the River People, *sîpîwiyiniwak* (located between the
North Saskatchewan and Battle rivers, ranging as far west as the Edmonton area
and south to the forks of the South Saskatchewan); and the most numerous and
westernmost of the bands, the Upstream or Beaver Hills People, *natimîwiyiniwak*

or *amiskwacîwiyiniwak* (ranging along the North Saskatchewan to the Edmonton area and southward to the Battle River).

There was another way of identifying these bands. The Calling River People, Rabbit Skins, and Touchwood Hills People were referred to as the Downstream People, or *mâmihk iyiniwak,* while the more westerly groups, including at times the "Cree-Assiniboin," were known collectively as the Upstream People, or *natimîwiyiniwak.*[7] On the western fringes of the Plains Cree homelands resided their enemies, the nations of the Blackfoot Confederacy; and to the south and southwest resided the Dakota. By the 1860s, the Cree knew the Blackfoot and Dakota nations as *ayahciyiniwak,* or enemy. In the early years of the nineteenth century, the Cree, along with their Assiniboin allies, were conducting raids against the Crow, Gros Ventre, and some of the Missouri village groups, particularly the major suppliers of horses, the Mandan-Hidatsa, whom they knew as the *k'ôtasiskîwikamikôwak,* or Mud House People.

The membership of any one band was flexible, and its size varied. An individual became a member of a band through birth, marriage, adoption, or simply by living with a group of families for a period of time. Most members, however, were related through consanguinal ("blood," or genetic) or affinal (marriage) ties. While band size varied with the seasonal fluctuation of food resources and the re-alliance of individuals (such as young men who were reported to have travelled to distant groups to marry and take up residence), the core of families associated with any one headman remained relatively constant. Members from other cultural groups either camped in close proximity to the Plains Cree bands or became members through marriage. Still others were forced to live with the Cree as captives.

A number of culturally mixed groups developed over time. The bilingual Cree-Assiniboin bands resulted from the practice of exogamous marriage (marriage outside of one's group).[8] In 1868 the trader Isaac Cowie reported that a mixed encampment located some twenty miles northeast of the Cypress Hills consisted of about 3,000 allied Assiniboin, Cree, Cree-Assiniboin, Ojibway, and Metis. These groups had gathered to celebrate the Sun Dance, to secure mutual defence while hunting bison in enemy territory, and to organize a communal hunt.[9] These groups were socially, politically, and economically independent, and any formal political organization uniting the efforts of these groups was "non-existent" or "transitory."[10]

Individuals traced their descent through their fathers' family lines. Residency also tended to be patrilocal, or oriented towards the husband's male line. Marriage tended to be endogamous; that is, marriage partners were chosen from among the Plains Cree themselves. A couple generally resided with the husband's family after spending some initial time following marriage with the wife's relatives. Despite his place of residence, a new husband was expected to contribute to his father-in-law's household and also to fulfill gift-giving obligations to his wife's brother. Upon the death of a young husband's parents, he might take up residence and become part of his wife's paternal household. Men of status were able to enlarge their households by acquiring more than one wife. In this case, the preferred form of marriage was sororal polygyny, in which a man married women who were sisters.

In addition to marriage alliances, friendships were important means of widening supportive networks among families. For example, friendships struck by young boys from different groups were often formally recognized through residence-sharing and gift-giving. Their relationship was known as *nîcêwâkan,* "the one with whom I go about."

While the availability of food resources played a key role in determining band followings, the quality of leadership was also important. In some cases, a larger band might have more than one leader, each with his own following. As in other egalitarian societies, leadership was not defined in terms of authority, for a headman did not have the power to coerce followers into complying with his decisions. Cree leadership was male and often hereditary, although an unworthy son could be superseded by another individual who had earned a greater degree of support. Personal and spiritual charisma, bravery, oratory, hunting skills, diplomacy, and an outstanding raiding record were valued leadership qualities. Ultimately, the ability of a leader to provide for the physical and spiritual well-being of followers determined the strength of his political power. The ability to amass relatively larger quantities of provisions and a willingness to share these goods with others was vital to good leadership. One elder, Fineday, described the relationship between political and economic life through an explanation of the quality of generosity.

> It happened many times that a man would be brave and bring back many horses. But he would trade the horses for clothes and would be too lazy to get hides for a tipi cover and so he could never be a chief. . . . It is not an easy thing to be chief. . . . He has to have pity on the poor. When he sees a man in difficulty he must try to help him in whatever way he can. If a person asks for something in his tipi, he must give it to him willingly and without any bad feeling.[11]

Finally, headmen were responsible for maintaining peaceful relations among their followers. Conflicts between individuals and families were resolved through established customary laws. The process of conflict resolution generally involved an obligatory mutual exchange of propitiatory gifts. The only recorded instance of forceful coercion occurred during communal bison hunts when individual transgressions of hunting codes were punished by members of the Warrior Society.[12]

The tasks and working relationships associated with subsistence activities and the production of goods were organized through the kinship networks. Many tasks were performed according to age and sex. In practice, these divisions of labour were generally reflected in the different stages of gathering and processing raw materials. For example, the capture and processing of bison would ultimately involve a cross-section of family members. As families became more involved in the commercial hide and provisions market, however, the dichotomy between men as procurers and women as processors of meat and tanned hides became more fixed.[13] As the Cree economy shifted from an emphasis on subsistence to production for exchange in the commercial market, the need for processors of raw materials in meat and hides increased the need for women labourers. Researchers examining the changing roles of women during this time have documented an increase in multiple wives, or polygynous marriages, and associated this occurrence with the demand for bison products in the commercial trade.[14]

Larger households with more workers were able to produce more goods and to distribute relatively greater amounts of goods. Their increased capacity to distribute or share goods, in turn, enhanced the status of these families and their headmen. Such a respected leader was often able to attract other people into his camp besides those closely tied to him through kinship. These included orphans and the offspring of poorer relations. Known as *otôskinîkîma,* they often helped the households of men of higher rank in exchange for food, clothing, access to horses, and training in hunting and warfare.[15]

The network for support in difficult times was also achieved through the extension of kin-like relationships with people from other areas. Amelia Paget, a White captive in Big Bear's camp during the Saskatchewan Uprising of 1885, remarked on this networking.[16] Strangers were addressed with "friendly expressions" such as *"nîs-tâw,"* or "brother-in-law," or *"niciwâmis,"* meaning "parallel cousin." Through this form of friendship, strangers were put at ease and soon became part of the household kinship network. Even Plains Cree strangers who visited one another's camps would soon find a "real or imaginary" relationship with their hosts, leading Paget to comment that "they trace their kindred to wonderfully distant sources, and one might almost believe that the whole Cree nation was related or connected in some way."[17] In addition to creating supportive networks through their contacts, including those established at the fur-trade posts, the Plains Cree increased their success at exploiting their resources by adjusting their habitation and hunting and gathering patterns to the seasonal movements of game. Of particular importance were the bison. Local family groups congregated along the southern Saskatchewan rivers to take advantage of the southward-moving bison herds during June and July. After these major communal hunts, encampments were relocated on the plains between the Grand Coteau of the Missouri and the Saskatchewan rivers. With the northward shift of certain herds in the fall, communal hunts were once again held. At the onset of cold weather in January and February, the Cree either dispersed into smaller encampments to hunt in sheltered wooded areas or stayed out on the prairies if the herds remained plentiful and the winter was not too harsh. Many factors affected the success of the hunts, and the bison were periodically unpredictable in their movements. Should dispersal and movement have been necessary, however, the flexibility in the social, economic, and political organization of the Cree ensured that such survival strategies could be called upon in an expeditious manner.

In addition to bison, a number of other animals were hunted, including moose, deer, elk, smaller game, and birds and fish. Vegetable foods, such as prairie turnips and other wild roots, berries, and even maple sugar were harvested. Until the early 1800s, some of the Cree bands, along with their Assiniboin allies, supplemented their larders with food products obtained through trade with Mandan horticulturalists in the Missouri River region. Commercial European trade goods were exchanged for Mandan-produced beans, corn, and tobacco.[18] Medicines and wild rice were obtained from the Anishinabe (Ojibway) residing to the east.

Of all the trade goods obtained through the exchange networks, the horse was perhaps the most important. Horses were first acquired through trade with the Mandan and the Blackfoot, who bartered these animals along with wolf pelts, tanned bison robes and hide garments for guns, hatchets, metal knives, kettles, and iron projectile points.[19] First acquired by the Plains Cree in the latter half of the eighteenth century, the horse had a profound effect on their culture for the next fifty years.[20] While it did not immediately replace the dog as a beast of burden, the horse did have an effect for those fortunate enough to possess it. The horse had the potential of increasing a group's mobility, and it enabled hunters to locate bison more easily and to kill them more effectively by using the chase technique. The riding, training, and care of horse herds required new knowledge and skills. The availability of suitable pastures became a factor in the location of encampments. Those who possessed horses could acquire and transport more goods and live in larger lodges. New forms of technology associated with the horse, such as bridles and pad saddles, were acquired. Special herbal medicines were used to treat sick or injured horses. The highly prized horse became a standard of trade and an important medium of exchange.[21] As visible symbols of wealth, horses brought their owners prestige and status, particularly through their distribution as gifts. Furthermore, horse herds were often augmented by raiding enemy camps; and, because great stealth and courage were needed for this undertaking, the capture of enemy horses was highly honoured.[22]

Apart from its involvement with the communal bison hunts, every household had the necessary means for its survival. Bison were often hunted by individuals; deer, moose, elk, and smaller game were hunted by both individuals and groups of related men. Various households operated fish weirs and distributed the catch to the community. The technology and labour needed for communal hunts, however, involved the application of specialized knowledge, the use of trained horses known as buffalo runners, and a relatively high degree of organization. Certain individuals were recognized as having special skills related to various methods of bison hunting, including the chute, or pound, method, a technique that was commonly used to capture bison in the autumn and early winter. Specialists known as poundmakers supervised the construction of a pound and possessed spiritual powers that enabled them to "call a herd" in for the kill. These leaders also conducted ceremonies associated with the bison hunts.

In the late winter and early spring, bison were stalked on foot by smaller groups of hunters, but in the summer they were taken by the "chase," which involved the use of trained buffalo runners. Not every household possessed these horses.[23] The headman Fineday informed Mandelbaum that only one household in ten owned a good buffalo horse. Therefore, a number of families would ally themselves to the owner of such a horse in order to increase their chances of obtaining bison. The responsibilities and status of the owners of such horses were increased by their ability to kill more bison, and in turn distribute relatively more meat and robes. Successful poundmakers attracted similar followings.

The fact that certain individuals possessed specialized knowledge or buffalo runners did not mean that the products of the hunt were individually owned. Ideally, they were distributed throughout the community. No particular household had exclusive rights to resources or territory. In addition, one's use of goods produced by another household was not necessarily restricted. While a horse, gun, dog, and other items were considered to be "individually owned," close relatives made "free use" of each other's goods.[24]

Any tendency to take unfair advantage of the labour of others was checked in a number of ways. An individual was rarely physically coerced into contributing his or her share of labour or goods. Ostracism, ridicule, and kinship pressure (particularly by a man's brothers-in-law) were methods used to discourage laziness and stinginess. A sense of duty for the support of one's kin, instilled from childhood and reinforced with spiritual sanctions, ensured that individuals fulfilled their obligations.

The ability to produce goods and to share them was one of the major factors in determining power relationships. In political terms, "the economic relation of giver-receiver is the political relation of leader-follower; . . . it is the operative ideology."[25] Those who could not reciprocate in kind for goods and services offered their loyalty and labour; this was particularly the case for older and impoverished people. While Plains Cree society was not rigidly stratified, there was some degree of ranking among individuals and households. To what extent the commercial fur trade influenced this development, and the characteristics of leadership, warrants further study. Mandelbaum indicates that European-Canadian companies favoured "peaceful, industrious trappers" over "aggressive warriors" and, in fact, may have encouraged a new type of leadership by according prestige, status, and preferential treatment to the former in trade negotiations.[26] Such favourable treatment for headmen would have enhanced their access to coveted trade goods and ultimately their status among their own people. Other historians have argued that good "war" leaders often excelled at trading; this resulted in "a concentration of horses and valued goods in the hands of the wealthy and successful, producing a differentiation between richer and poorer, between chiefs and their dependents."[27]

The system of ranked leadership was not formalized to the point of precluding an individual's rise in the power structure, and the fact that some enjoyed more privileges associated with their status than others was at least tacitly acknowledged. This acknowledgement was demonstrated in the respect and honours given to individuals of status and their families by other members of the community. In instances where status was questioned, doubt was usually clarified "by a word or hint from a respected old man."[28] There were other, more formal, methods used to confirm status, as in the assigned seating arrangements at council meetings and the weight attached to one's opinions in decision-making. The more impoverished members of the council were seated near the doorway of the lodge (a place of lesser status) and might not be given a buffalo robe on which to sit.[29]

The system of ranking in Plains Cree society was evident in other positions. With the exception of the role of headman, a title that was generally passed from father to son, other positions of status were earned rather than inherited. The headman had the prerogative to initiate council meetings and to announce final decisions on issues. However, decisions were generally reached through consensus in discussion with other leading men and elders. Elderly men with good war records were honoured with the role of camp crier, or *osâkitostamâkêw*. The headmen and other men of rank were responsible for the *osâkitostamâkêw*'s material well-being. In addition to announcing the decisions of council meetings to the camp, the crier possessed a number of powers in the absence of the headman, including the preservation of public order, the distribution of the headman's material possessions upon request, and the announcement of public occasions of gift-giving. A third position, also occupied by an elder, was known as the *otêpwêstamâkêw,* or caller. Again, the holder of this position was materially supported by a man of rank. It was the duty of the *otêpwêstamâkêw* to summon people to meetings and the headman's lodge. A fourth official responsibility was that of camp leader. This position was generally filled only during the larger summer village gatherings. The camp leader was chosen for his ability to designate a safe and productive camp site. Because of the importance of this undertaking, it was thought that such a man had "powerful spirit helpers to guide him."[30]

This type of differentiation in status and associated responsibilities was also evident in the informally organized men's associations. The *kihtoskinîkiwak* (Worthy Young Men) was a title conferred on younger men who had demonstrated their bravery. Their primary responsibilities were to defend the camp and to host visitors. In addition, each band had at least one of the more formally organized men's associations known as the *okihtsitawak* (Warriors).[31]

Membership in a Warrior's lodge or society was by invitation, and members were recognizable by their insignia and performances of specific ceremonial dances and songs. While the qualities of bravery and liberality were held in esteem, a good hunter who possessed horses was welcome to join a society. The achievement of these positions of honour was marked by the public distribution of gifts such as horses and hides. On occasion, an unproven adolescent might obtain the right to dance with the Warrior Society if his parents were able to contribute sufficient gifts. Each Warrior society had a formal leader, or Warrior chief, who ensured that the society's obligations were carried out. Along with Warrior chiefs from other bands, he also assisted with the coordination of joint forays into enemy camps and the supervision of communal bison hunts. The Warrior chief was endowed with the authority to punish those hunters who had transgressed the rules of the communal hunts. Above all, Warriors and Worthy Young Men were expected to demonstrate exemplary behaviour in all aspects of life. They were expected "to part with their material possessions freely and willingly; they were expected to be above jealousy; they took it upon themselves to prepare corpses for burial, an unpleasant and dread task."[32] These voluntary societies cut across kinship lines and were important in promoting an even greater cohesion among the various Plains Cree bands. The elders of these Warrior societies were accorded political power and special status, which accrued from the knowledge and wisdom they had gained from their experiences. Younger Warriors generally deferred to the elders and, when appropriate, provided them with material assistance.

While the religious experiences of the Plains Cree cannot be adequately communicated on the written page, a basic appreciation of the inter-relatedness of what Western society defines as the "sacred" and "secular" is necessary for an understanding of the impact of Canadian government regulations pertaining to indigenous forms of religious expression. The "pervasiveness" of spirituality throughout the individual and collective lives of people has been described by scholars such as Alvin Josephy:

Legends, ceremonies, songs and dances and arts were integrated parts of the spiritual systems, instructing the people not only in sacred matters but about many of the ends and purposes of the systems themselves – what the group expected of an individual, right and wrong behavior, and the position and obligations of each person within the group. The systems were further strengthened by sacred symbols – fetishes, pipes, painted designs, medicine bundles, shrines, the first runs of fish, and the first fruits of harvest – that with the help of rituals made real and living the spiritual attachments between man and the sun and the unseen world and assured food, well-being, and the satisfaction of the needs and wants of the society and its members.[33]

As in other religions the world over, the spiritual beliefs of the Plains Cree and other indigenous peoples define and sanction the cultural values and behaviour that are necessary for personal well-being and the survival of the society.[34]

Although both men and women could acquire the right to perform certain rituals, shamans were the predominant source of power and leadership in religious matters. Their shamanistic abilities were conferred upon them by spiritual beings, and their influence flowed from their relatively greater access to spiritual knowledge and supernatural power. Therefore, their advice in both material and spiritual matters was highly valued. The shamans not only provided ceremonial leadership but also served as counsellors, healers, and transmitters of sacred knowledge and teachings associated with ritual life.

Plains Cree rituals enabled participants to obtain guidance in their lives through communication with the spiritual world. Many preparations were necessary before an individual could undertake this search. The vision quests involving long periods of fasting and prayer, along with purification rituals, were particularly important as a means of receiving spiritual guidance. This was especially true for male adolescents. The content and power of certain visions varied, and the recipients of the more potent visions were expected to assume greater responsibilities within the community. In a sense, the most valued positions of power were reflected in a "hierarchy" of visionary experiences. These included poundmaking, conducting the Sun Dance, healing, divining (valued by war leaders to locate enemies), communicating with the spiritual world through "conjuring," and the right to make or own certain types of religious objects (especially the powerful protective war bundles and sacred pipestem bundles).[35]

Receiving a vision, however, was not sufficient in itself, for the recipient was obliged to have its meaning validated by the spiritual elders and to demonstrate this acquired power to the community. Another limitation on the access to spiritual power accruing from visionary experiences was the right of a father to transfer visionary prerogatives to his son. The right to lead a "vowed" ceremony (the most powerful and demanding type of ceremony) is an example of one type of transferable power.[36]

In their study of the vision quests of the Plains Indians, Patricia Albers and Seymour Parker correlate the vision experience with access to positions of status and suggest that as a belief system it "'explained' to members of the society why certain individuals were more capable or had greater right to assume positions of prestige and privilege than others."[37] According to this observation, the visionary experiences of the Plains Cree served to perpetuate and to legitimize the right of certain individuals to hold the few status positions. The teachings and interpretations associated with the content of vision quests not only provided individuals with a sense of identity and social purpose but also enabled the teachers and elders to channel and reinforce behaviour in "socially approved directions."[38] The legitimacy of powers acquired through visions became apparent to the community as the appropriate teachers undertook to train recipients of visions.

There were also material manifestations of spiritual powers and prerogatives in the form of religious objects and symbols. These items were believed to possess a life and power of their own. While every member of Plains Cree society possessed such items, some were more powerful than others, particularly those that could be used for the well-being of the community. The use of these communal objects was restricted to exemplary individuals who had earned the public trust, and their ownership remained with the community. Other sacred materials, such as the coveted war bundle, were held by individuals. While knowledge concerning this bundle was received through a vision, younger men undertook to negotiate its transfer from the maker once its supernatural power had been demonstrated through successful forays into enemy camps.[39] In contrast was the sacred pipestem bundle, which was held in the collective trust and was cared for by a worthy keeper on behalf of the community. This bundle was important for the protection of the community, and was used to resolve conflicts through the good offices of its keeper. The status granted to the bearer of this bundle could be conferred only by the council.

Other religious materials were obtained through visions, gift exchange, or, in some cases, inheritance. The possession of these objects afforded their owners and families increased opportunities to demonstrate their generosity and to enhance their prestige.[40] In addition to serving as tangible symbols of status, religious para-phernalia, along with their associated teachings, prayers, songs, and dances, were important "repositories" of sacred knowledge.

Much of Plains Cree ceremonial life centred around the celebration of individual "rites of passage" that socially demarcated the movement of an individual from one status to another. All households participated in rituals pertaining to transitory phases of the human life cycle – that is, birth, puberty, adulthood, and death. Similar rituals were performed for healing, conflict resolution, and the creation of "economic or political bonds" between families and bands.[41] Many of the rites-of-passage rituals had a communal aspect to them in order that newly acquired statuses became public knowledge. On these occasions, relatives pooled their resources to make spiritual offerings, to provide gifts to ritualists and celebrants, and to host a feast.

There were also important communal rites, or "rites of solidarity." Among the Plains Cree, the Thirst (Sun) Dance, Smoking Tipi ceremony, the Masked (or *wîhtikôw*) Dance, the Give Away Dance, the Prairie-Chicken Dance, the Pipestem

Bundle Dance, the Round Dance, the *mitêwiwin* (Medicine Society Dance, associated with healing), and the Horse, Elk, and Bear dances were the major communal ceremonies. A communal ceremony was generally sponsored by a pledger who had made a sacred vow to hold the ceremony. For the pledgers and their kin, the sponsorship of the larger ceremonies was a major material and spiritual undertaking, which took many months of preparation.

The requirements associated with the production of goods for the communal ceremonies served to draw the various households together and to reinforce kinship responsibilities. The status of sponsoring households was a function of their ability to provide the pledger with the necessary goods for ceremonial distribution. This was particularly the case for headmen, who "were expected to contribute a larger share of the feast than the other tribesmen," and to host visitors.[42]

Offerings of prayers, tobacco, food, prepared hides, horses, consecrated dogs, and one's person through self-mortification were all means of sacred communication. The sacrifice and distribution of labour-intensive products, such as tanned hides or the highly valued and costly red woollen cloth (stroud) obtained from the fur-trade posts, occurred during these ceremonies. In his reference to the stroud wrappings used for the Thunderbird bundle in the Sun Dance, Abel Watetch explains that "the Crees never hesitate to give what is best to the Great Spirit."[43] Offerings of highly valued commodities and personal physical sacrifice were considered to be most potent in establishing favourable and harmonious relationships with the spiritual world. These demonstrations of liberality and sacrifice for the general well-being of the community were intended to induce these same patterns of reciprocity in the spiritual world. This relationship of religious ideology to the "material" (or "secular") world was described by Mandelbaum:

When the spirit powers partook of food offering, they could hardly turn a deaf ear to the petitions addressed to them by the host. . . . Every gift received imposed a reciprocal obligation on the recipient. A man who was given a new robe during some public demonstration of wealth, often gave clothing away at the same ceremony or at one soon after. An old man who received a gift paid off his obligation by publicly praising and praying for the giver. In the same way cloth offerings were considered to be gifts to spirit powers, in return for which they were duty bound . . . to return favors in proportion and kind.[44]

While material offerings and the distribution and exchange of gifts were part of every ceremony, the *mâhtâhitowin* epitomized all levels of the economic, political, and social relationships of Plains Cree society. *Mâhtâhitowin* translates as "passing off something to each other" or "gifts exchanged are a blessing," and is commonly known as the "Give Away Dance."[45] This ceremony involved the most conspicuous public demonstration of the distribution of goods. Held in the fall or early winter, the Give Away Dance was pledged by one who had received the spiritual prerogative from the spirit Pâkahkos (or Bony Spectre). Descriptions of this spirit are fairly consistent, indicating that it is a "small and mischievous" being residing in the bush country who enjoys frightening humans. Having sacrificed itself so that others may live, it was associated with starvation. Rarely seen, Pâkahkos made its presence known by whistling.

The giveaway involved communal feasting, the ritual consumption of hardened bone grease (the favourite food of Pâkahkos), and the giving of gifts. Successful hunts and long life were believed to be within the power of Pâkahkos, and offerings to this spirit reflected Cree concerns regarding their well-being during the ensuing winter months.[46] The importance of fostering the ideology of sharing one's good fortune during the winter months when game was more scarce was instilled through the ritualized obligatory exchange of goods.

According to Mandelbaum's version of the giveaway ceremony, there are three levels of exchanges: (1) between the ceremonial sponsor and male celebrants; (2) among all members of the community; and (3) by the children through cloth offerings made to Pâkahkos.[47] Joseph Dion mentions additional exchanges between the wife of the headman and other women as well as a generalized distribution throughout other camps.[48] Dion noted that major giveaway ceremonies were known to have lasted for days, with leaders travelling from camp to camp carrying the wooden image of the spirit Pâkahkos. The period of their stay in any one camp was "governed by the size of the camp or until the gifts began to go back to their original owners."[49]

In this system of obligatory sharing, the types and amounts of goods exchanged were significant. The accumulation of goods for its own sake was considered to be immoral. As Chief Thunderchild explained, "It is because Pah.kahkus can be so lavish in his favors, that those who take part in the dance which honours him give away their horses, harness, clothing, bedding – anything that is theirs."[50] Although some people did accumulate more than others, any deliberate contrivance to amass goods was discouraged. It was believed that the giving of poor gifts or the accumulation of goods at the expense of others would result in ill health and poor hunting. Sincere generosity was rewarded with "prestige and supernatural blessings."[51]

The obligatory acceptance and return in kind of gifts were at the heart of the several types of giveaways that were celebrated. If an item of equal exchange value was not reciprocated, the imbalance was at the recipient's expense. The Plains Cree headman Fineday explained to Mandelbaum that, "if someone gives only poor little things for good gifts, he will generally not enjoy them," and went on to describe how a man grew blind after he had "cheated" him out of a good hunting horse.[52] According to written accounts, there was considerable competition involved in matching or surpassing the value of gifts. Such rivalry was generally amiable. The psychology of "unrequited good measure" was evident from these attempts to over-reciprocate, and by this means to create a relationship of indebtedness between the giver and the receiver.

Giveaway ceremonies functioned to re-affirm pre-existing kinship ties and to establish new networks among households and between diverse communities. This practice optimized the availability of natural resources, goods, and labour over considerable distances. In addition, the giveaways promoted the cooperative pooling of labour and goods on the part of related households. This cooperation not only increased the headman's ability to distribute goods and better care for his followers, but also brought prestige to his household. Sacred sanctions ensured that this system was perpetuated. Despite the seeming one-sidedness of some of the transactions, it is important to keep in mind that, "inasmuch as what one gave, another got" and "the aggregate of possessions remained the same" within the community.[53] However, this did not mean that everyone in the community possessed equal amounts of goods, but rather that resources necessary for survival were available to all at the expense of those able to accumulate.

The major communal ceremony was the *nipâhkwêsimowin* or Thirst Dance (Sun Dance). The vow to sponsor the Thirst Dance was (and remains) one of the most demanding spiritual commitments an individual could undertake. It was celebrated as a public communal ceremony by many Indian societies residing in the prairie and plains regions. Although its original form is not known, it is generally agreed that the Sun Dance evolved into its classic "high plains" form during the period between 1800 and 1883.[54] Its rapid spread throughout the plains is attributed to the acquisition of the horse, which placed more people in contact with one another over greater distances, and to the availability of bison herds, which enabled large numbers of people to congregate during the summer months. The popularized term for the ceremony, *Sun Dance,* is derived from a sun-gazing ritual performed by the Oglala during the ceremony.[55] While the expression of this ceremony varied from group to group, community well-being, world regeneration, and thanksgiving through communal worship were commonly shared motivations for its celebration.

Knowledge of the Sun Dance was probably transmitted to the Plains Cree from their Assiniboin allies. It was held in the early summer when the bison were forming large herds as they migrated to the northern prairies and the earth was lush with the new growth of grass – a time of year known as "the moon of the young birds" or *pâskâwêwi-pîsim* (Hatching Moon). At this time the relatively smaller camps of families who had made their winter home in sheltered river valleys gathered together nearer the open prairies in preparation for the early summer communal bison hunts.[56]

Both Sun Dance ritualists and informed scholars emphasize the fact that regeneration and thanksgiving were the major purposes of the ceremony; it "is a ceremony of new creation, the lodge is the world, and its centre post the world-tree, the communications channel between man and the powers above."[57] During the ceremony, celebrants entered a sacred time and space where the Plains Cree traditions and beliefs were ritually dramatized, renewed, and re-affirmed. Society was renewed as the values and appropriate ethical behaviour were transmitted through song, sacred teachings, public testimonials by exemplary persons, and disciplined behaviour and sacrifice associated with rituals. It was through ceremonies such as the Sun Dance that the children were most dramatically introduced to their cosmos and heard teachings explaining their role as humans in a world where all elements were inter-related. It was here that the children "saw either actually functioning or ritually imitated the major social institutions, the approved conduct of [their] culture, and the reward granted to those who follow the ideals of . . . life."[58]

Despite the proliferation of scholarly analyses of the Sun Dance, the ideological components of the ceremony are not fully understood.[59] The prerogative to perform a Sun Dance as a ritual leader was obtained through spiritual revelation and required formal instruction. One ritualist, Fineday, informed Mandelbaum that this privilege could be passed from father to son.[60] A woman might also pledge a Sun Dance, but it was common practice to have a male member of the family, such as a husband or a son, sponsor it on her behalf. Visions regarding the right to hold a Sun Dance were often received in crisis situations. This was Fineday's experience:

Years ago my first born son was sick. I tried many medicines and gave away many horses but he was no better. Then one night I dreamed that I was to make a Sun Dance. When I woke I promised manito (the Creator) that I would make one the next summer. That morning it seemed as though the boy improved and by next morning he is definitely better.[61]

The sponsorship of a Sun Dance was a major undertaking and required the productive and organized cooperation of households far in advance of the actual ceremony. A number of preliminary rituals known as *inikimah nipâhkwêsimowin* ("the singing rehearsals for the Sun Dance") were held throughout the year preceding it.[62] The "Sings" brought sponsor, ritualists, and other worshipers together to prepare for the summer celebration. Throughout the year, those who had vowed to perform the Sun Dance prepared themselves by prayer, purification through fasting and the Sweat Lodge, the pledging of vows, and formal instruction.

The ceremonial encampments lasted from a few days to several weeks. The ceremony was sponsored or pledged by a person who had received spiritual direction to perform the dance. If the pledger was not a Sun Dance ritualist, he or she was obliged to provide the material offerings necessary to engage a ritualist to conduct the ceremony. This meant that the pledger required extensive support from relatives and friends. Other individuals who had received spiritual direction to dance in the ceremony did so to fulfill a sacred vow for spiritual assistance.

According to the precepts of sacred teachings and instructions from a ritualist, a sacred lodge and altar were constructed. A number of poles, which served as rafters, were ritually felled, while a specially selected centre pole served as a "tree of life." A Thunderbird's nest and a number of offerings were attached to the top of the central pole; other offerings were affixed to the lower part and base of the pole. The whole lodge was then covered with hides and leafy boughs. The dancers were separated from the central part of the lodge and from each other with bough partitions. It was inside the sacred lodge that the ritual leaders, their assistants, drummers, singers, and dancers, along with supportive relatives and friends, would spend their next few days. Along with the dancers, many would abstain from food and water. Continual prayers were offered by the celebrants for spiritual intercession in their lives as well as on behalf of the whole community.

Dancing as an expression of worship consisted of bending at the knees and taking small steps in one place in time with the drumming; the dancers often blew sacred eagle-bone whistles. Dancers were instructed to concentrate their vision on the centre pole. During the periods of dancing, numerous prayers were made by the ritualists and elders. The final phase of the earlier-period Plains Cree ceremony involved various forms of personal sacrifice through flesh offerings. It was at this time that male worshipers engaged in a number of forms of "piercing." Some were connected to the centre pole with rawhide ropes, the ends of which had been skewered through incisions made on either side of the upper chest, the back, or the arms. Other worshipers attached numbers of guns, bison skulls, or even horses to the ropes. As the dancers pulled back on the ropes, their flesh tore away. Other offerings of this nature included the severing of a finger joint or the cutting away of small portions of flesh on the arms or legs. Female celebrants are reported to have engaged in the latter practice.[63] Following the completion of these rites, a number of closing songs, prayers, dances, and orations, along with giveaways and a communal feast, were held. The sacred lodge was not re-used and was left to the elements. Many of the sacred offerings were taken and placed in spiritually "clean" locations in the bush where they would not be mishandled.

While fasting from food and water for the duration of the Sun Dance was a common means of personal offering, it was the "piercing" ritual that captured the attention and disapproval of White observers. This form of self-mortification was generally misinterpreted as a means of testing the courage of young warriors. While courage and inner strength were indeed required for such an undertaking, the underlying principle was that the sacrifice or offering of oneself was the ultimate gift that mortals could offer to their Creator. Through personal sacrifice, celebrants placed themselves in a receptive state to experience visions, acquire spiritual power, and obtain the fulfillment of personal requests.[64] These forms of religious expression also dramatically demonstrated the ideals of inner strength, conviction, heartfelt sincerity, and generosity.

The Sun Dance gathering also afforded people an opportunity to demonstrate their worthiness through the distribution of goods and the public recounting of honourable deeds. Participants brought dressed hides, blankets, clothing, trade goods, horses, and other valued articles, as offerings and for distribution. There were many occasions for the sharing of these goods. For example, at one point in the ceremony, the "foremost fighters" danced and publicly recited their acts of courage. Those who had "counted coups" gave clothing and horses according to need, kin relations, and rank.[65] These goods were distributed from the south side of the centre pole by an official known as the Shouter, who dispersed them to the people of his choice. The elderly or infirm received the first distribution, then visitors received their share, and men who had a reputation for their liberality also were given gifts. The generosity of the donors was publicly acknowledged as each recipient offered a prayer or word of praise for the donor.[66]

On each day of the ceremony, blessed food was served in the dance lodge for all those not fasting. Donors of the food, and the women who had prepared the meals, were publicly acknowledged by the Shouter. On the final day of the ceremony, a more general giveaway occurred:

The gifts given by a man were placed near the center pole; the giver and his family came forth and danced beside their gifts. Then the Shouter distributed the presents to visitors or to tribesmen. The gifts undoubtedly added prestige to the donor's name, but officially they were regarded as offerings to the supernaturals. The people who received the presents prayed for the welfare of the donors and by means of such prayers divine favor might be procured.[67]

The prayers and blessings received in exchange for these material offerings not only benefited the giver, but also the entire community.

As a renewal ceremony, the Sun Dance provided a sacred time and space in which the regeneration of the universe, the community, and the self were celebrated and intensified through ritual. In the sacred lodge stood the "tree of life," the *axis mundi,* or "center of the world," where all forces became concentrated. It was a place where "the spiritual, the temporal, the gross, the profane, the common all come together at one time," and where "the individual transcends all that we know of this life and finally arrives at the real world, the real place."[68] It was the place where the drama of creation and rebirth and the unity of all things were ritually dramatized and personally experienced. And it was here that physical and spiritual transformation were possible by obtaining transcendental power that might offer redemption and healing.

The corporate nature of the ceremony was crucial to its effectiveness; the Sun Dance ritual leader was simply an intermediary through whom ordinary humans could communicate with the powerful spirit beings. The cooperative efforts of the whole community were needed to make contact with this power. As Fineday explained to Mandelbaum, "Making rain is something that is not in my power. . . . Not one or two can do this. Only the whole community joining together can call upon the Great Spirit to act in pity for us."[69] Cooperation, sharing, and a proper sense of one's place relative to the whole of creation were at the heart of Plains Cree spirituality.

The ceremonial communal Sun Dance gatherings were also used for other sacred and secular activities important to the survival of Plains Cree society. The Sun Dance was also a time for the re-alignment of group memberships through marriages and the initiation of alliances. In addition, there were numerous opportunities for socialization: "Bands reunited; military associations convened; tribal chiefs met in formal council; people who had not seen each other all year renewed old friendships. . . . Feasting and dancing, storytelling and courting, gambling and horse racing, and visiting of all kinds abounded."[70] Of equal importance was the education of the children in the belief systems and wisdom of their elders through observation, listening, and participation.

Religious expression through ceremonies reflected and re-affirmed the world view and cultural practices of the Plains Cree. The values of cooperation, generosity, fortitude, and universal harmony or balance – all prerequisites for the spiritual, emotional, and physical well-being of the members of society – were not only ritually dramatized but also operative in the ceremonial cycle itself. The production of goods for distribution and exchange at ceremonies required a constant pooling of labour, and in turn it enhanced the existence of the cohesiveness of kin networks. The prerogative to perform sacred rituals and to use associated religious parapher-nalia enabled their users to demonstrate publicly their worthiness and power. This process not only reflected and validated one's privileged access to spiritual power not shared by others, but also obliged men of rank and their households to use this power for the corporate good – the material expression of which was the distribution of goods. Among the Plains Cree and other Indian societies, the concentration of religious knowledge resided with the elders, who throughout their lifetimes ac-quired both practical and spiritual expertise to guide their people. They were the ultimate repositories and teachers of cultural knowledge, which was transmitted through a strong oral tradition from one generation to the next. In a very real way, the survival of Plains Cree society depended upon the ability of the elders to function as protectors, "keepers," and promulgators of this knowledge. Ceremonies offered occasions through which elders transmitted it.

Finally, ceremonies such as the Sun Dance served to integrate otherwise politically autonomous bands of families and their allies. Participation in collective religious rites also provided the bands with a means to expand their kinship ties and gain access to a wider variety of resources than might be available in their own hunting-and-gathering territories. In this way, social, economic, and political cooperation was made possible in order to ensure the survival of the Plains Cree.

From Independence to Wardship: 1870 to 1895

3

In the late 1860s, the Plains Cree faced several major changes in their lives. Food resources were being increasingly over-exploited; European-introduced diseases had seriously reduced the population; and violence erupted as Indian, Metis, and White traders competed for access to the ever-diminishing bison herds. Cree leaders were increasingly concerned that European-Canadian settlement would encroach on their homelands without prior approval. It was in this context that the Plains Cree and their allies, the Assiniboin and Ojibway, negotiated Treaty Four (1874) and Treaty Six (1876) with representatives of the British Crown.

By the mid-1800s, the commercial fur trade was becoming highly competitive for Indian traders as the French Metis exerted their control over the provisions market for southern Manitoba posts as well as for the establishments located along the Assiniboine River and the North and South Saskatchewan rivers and their tributaries.[1] The Plains Cree were among those who were able to maintain their trade with the more westerly posts. The commercial demand for more bison robes and food provisions to sustain the fur-trade labour force not only accelerated competition among the Indians and Metis but also pitted these same groups against American traders from Fort Union who had come to hunt in the Saskatchewan and Assiniboine river areas. Furthermore, the comparative economic advantages of the shorter distances involved in transporting provisions to American markets, combined with a more efficient transportation system, drew traders southward and undermined Cree trading networks.[2] Other factors also contributed to the collapse of the market in bison products for the Cree. New methods of procuring and commercially processing bison robes radically altered the need for indigenous suppliers. A technological evolution in the commercial tanning industry enabled buyers to by-pass Indian and Metis women as the labour for hide processing.

In order to protect their interests in the bison trade, the Plains Cree and their allies, along with the Dakota, attempted to restrict Metis and White hunting-and-trading activities in their territories. During a Cree council held at Qu'Appelle in 1857, headmen demanded that these commercial hunters procure dried meat, pemmican, hides, and robes by trading with them rather than obtaining them firsthand in Cree territory.[3] Another major concern for the Cree was the dwindling bison herds whose numbers diminished with the increase in market demands for bison products. The introduction of the breach-loading and repeater rifles reduced the margin of chance in the hunt, enabling hunters to kill more animals. Historical observers reported that the herds had been seriously reduced north of the Qu'Appelle and South Saskatchewan rivers by the 1860s and in southwestern Saskatchewan and southern Alberta by the early 1870s.[4] During the same period, other forms of alternate subsistence resources such as larger mammals, small game, and fisheries were also diminishing with the increase in their exploitation by Indians, Metis, and European-Canadian traders and settlers.

The strain on the local natural resources for livelihood and trade intensified competition and hostilities between groups. By the 1860s the Plains Cree and their allies were moving into the westernmost part of a "neutral zone" in the Cypress Hills area. This natural zone traditionally served as a buffer between the Plains Cree and their Blackfoot enemies. Until 1865, relations between the Cree and the Blackfoot had consisted of intermittent periods of horse raiding, trading, and truce; however, the intrusion of the Cree into the Cypress Hills led to frequent violent conflicts.[5] Despite initial efforts to negotiate peace, a virtual state of "war" had broken out by 1870 along the frontier line from the Missouri River to Fort Edmonton.[6] A final battle at the Oldman River resulted in the death of 200 to 300 Cree and forty Blackfoot. A further loss of twenty Assiniboin allies occurred in 1873 in the Cypress Hills Massacre, which was instigated by American whisky traders and wolf hunters. In addition to the loss of life sustained in these outbreaks, several thousand Cree and their allies died as a result of two smallpox epidemics and associated bouts of starvation.

While in this weakened state, and confronted with economic uncertainty, the prairie Indians were also faced with new forms of political incursions into their homelands. By 1870, the land holdings and administrative responsibilities under the control of the Hudson's Bay Company in Rupert's Land and the North-West Territories had been officially transferred to the Dominion of Canada. In the same year, following the suppression of the provisional government under the leadership of Louis Riel, the District of Assiniboia (Red River area) entered the Canadian confederation as the province of Manitoba. The remaining prairie region was administered by an appointed governor and council established in 1872, and later, under the provisions of the North-West Territories Act, by a council of appointed and elected representatives. Initially situated at Battleford, the territorial council was relocated to Regina in 1882 and continued to be Ottawa's formal link to the territories until the creation of the provinces of Saskatchewan and Alberta in 1905. During its existence, the council received little in the way of monies or official support for its ordinances from Ottawa. Rather, Ottawa preferred to depend upon its own Department of the Interior, especially the Dominion Lands Branch, for the administration of the region and the conduct of surveys and resource management.[7] Indian-related matters were dealt with through a branch of the Department of the Interior.

The transfer of Rupert's Land and the North-West Territories was negotiated with the Dominion of Canada without the political representation of any of the indigenous populations. There was, however, a stipulation in Article Fourteen of the Order-in-Council of June 23, 1870, that acknowledged the principle of Aboriginal rights in future land transfers; that is, "any claims of Indians to compensation for lands required for purposes of settlement shall be disposed of by the Canadian government in communication with the Imperial government."[8] Implicit in this provision was an understanding that the Dominion of Canada would acquire access to Indian lands according to precedents established in the eastern provinces, including the negotiation of formal treaties. In return for land cessions, indigenous peoples were to receive monetary compensation and a choice of lands to be set aside for their exclusive use.[9] The subsequent imposition of federal policies supporting "wardship, civilization, and assimilation" clearly indicated that social control in the interest of settlement, rather than the preservation of indigenous societies as political and cultural entities, was the underlying objective of treaty negotiations. While traditional forms of government were used to officially facilitate the transfer of eastern lands, there was no intent to recognize Indian traditional political systems beyond this point as evident in the passage of the 1869 Act for the Gradual Enfranchisement of Indians and the Better Management of Indian Affairs. This act authorized the governor to order the elections of chiefs and council on a three-year term and to dismiss leaders for "dishonesty, intemperance or immorality."[10]

Similar plans for the eventual absorption of prairie Indian nations into the Dominion of Canada had been voiced by administrators such as Commissioner J.A.N. Provencher. In 1873, the commissioner had advocated assimilation as a solution to dealing with Indian populations:

There are two modes wherein the Government may treat the Indian nations who inhabit this territory. Treaties may be made with them simply with a view to the extinction of their rights, by agreeing to pay them a sum, and afterwards abandon them to themselves. On the other side, they may be instructed, civilized, and led to a mode of life more in conformity with the new position of this country, and accordingly make them good, industrious and useful citizens.

> Under the first system the Indians will remain in their condition of ignorance and inferiority, and as soon as the facilities for hunting and fishing disappear, they will become mendicants, or be obliged to seek refuge in localities inaccessible to immigration or cultivation.
> Under the second system, on the contrary, they will learn sufficient for themselves, to enable them to pass from a state of tutelage, and do without assistance from the Government.[11]

This approach to establishing political relationships with indigenous nations was typical of the racial attitudes that pervaded British imperial Native policy. The Plains Cree were considered inferior to Europeans and incapable of determining their own best interests in the new order. Since it was assumed that indigenous cultures had little to offer to the Canadian state, the morality of transforming Indians into European Canadians was never questioned, and, indeed, assimilation was considered mandatory if they were to survive at all and share in the "benefits of civilization."[12]

In its dealings with the western Indian nations, the federal government chose to follow the example of the land transfer process as established in the Robinson Treaties of 1851. These treaties resulted in land cessions in the Lakes Huron and Superior region for annuities, parcels of land to be used only by Indian bands (reserves), and assurances of traditional hunting-and-fishing rights on unoccupied portions of ceded lands.

Treaties One, Two, and Three were concluded according to similar arrangements. The terms of Treaty One, negotiated with the Ojibway and Cree in the Red River area, and Treaty Two, negotiated with the Ojibway residing immediately to the northwest of the Treaty One region in 1871, involved massive land cessions and provided the basis for negotiations with the Plains Cree. In these two treaties,

the Indians agreed to surrender title to all their territory, to keep the peace, and not to molest the property or persons of Her Majesty's other subjects. In return, they were to receive an immediate gratuity of three dollars each, an annuity of fifteen dollars in cash or goods per family of five, reserves in the amount of 160 acres per family of five, a school on each reserve, and protection from intoxicating liquor. A number of additional items – clothing for the headmen, farm animals, and implements – were not contained in the written text but rather were assented to informally.[13]

Although the Canadian government was prepared to refrain from negotiating further land cessions until settlement progressed further westward, Cree concerns regarding the anticipated arrival of settlers on their lands, the increasing unilateral use of resources and travel into their homelands by commercial traders and government personnel, and diminishing food supplies, provided the impetus for the initiation of talks. In 1871, a delegation of chiefs had met with William Christie of the Hudson's Bay Company at Fort Edmonton to register their apprehension over rumours that their lands would be settled and sold without their permission.[14]

Aware of the plight of the Indians to the east and the fate of Indian nations of the American plains, the Cree, Assiniboin, and Ojibway attempted to secure their political and economic independence by insisting that their homelands could not be used for resource exploitation or settlement until their rights had been recognized.[15] Appeals for the regulation of bison hunting and support for those who chose to practise agriculture indicated that Indian leaders were motivated to conduct negotiations at this early date out of fear for the physical survival of their people. Another point of contention was the future landholdings of the Hudson's Bay Company and the payment that it had received for the lands turned over to the Dominion of Canada. Despite the efforts of Ojibway headmen Gambler and Pasqua, the government would not permit these terms of the land releases to be altered in negotiations.

In 1874, Treaty Four was concluded at Fort Qu'Appelle. Its terms were essentially identical to those of Treaties One and Two. In return for the surrender of lands, each chief was to receive $25, each headman $15, and every man, woman, and child $5. Provisions of powder, shot, ball, and twine ($750 worth) were to be distributed annually among the bands. The amount of land allotment anticipated the transition of Indian peoples to an agricultural economy, and each family was allotted up to one square mile of reserve land for its use. The actual ownership of the land base was held by the Crown while the administration of Indians, and lands reserved for Indians, was the responsibility of the Canadian government (Section 91, British North America Act 1867). In addition to reserves, clothing for headmen, seed, farm implements, and livestock were also promised. The government also agreed to control the trafficking of intoxicants and to provide schools for all reserves. Hunting, fishing, and trapping activities were allowed to continue on unoccupied ceded lands subject to government regulations, excluding lands required for settlement and economic development such as mining. In return for these guarantees, Indian negotiators agreed to maintain peace and order among themselves and between their band members and other British subjects.[16]

Meanwhile, other Plains Cree groups located further west had been waiting for government representatives to initiate terms for access to their lands. Once it had become evident that these Cree would not tolerate further incursions into their homelands without negotiations, the government was forced to mediate. That the issue of political sovereignty would be a point of contention was clearly demonstrated when the Cree became alarmed over the activities of surveyors who had been sent out to record land around the Hudson's Bay Company posts in 1872. In 1873, the geological surveying party headed by Robert Bell was interrupted by local Indians who confronted the surveyors and threatened their property and lives. The surveyors were also ordered to discontinue their work. An international boundary survey that cut across Cree homelands was also perceived as a challenge to Cree authority.[17] Three years later, the Cree once again interfered with the work of government surveyors and the construction of a telegraph line running from Edmonton to Winnipeg.

By the summer of 1876, the government began negotiations with the Plains Cree at Fort Carlton and Fort Pitt. Headmen such as Sweetgrass were initially adamantly opposed to any alienation of their lands. Poundmaker, an influential man of rank, reacted to the government's offer of 640 acres per family by warning the commissioner, "This is our land. It isn't a piece of pemmican to be cut off and given in little pieces back to us. It is ours and we will take what we want."[18] The apprehension expressed by some headmen over uncontrolled access to their resources prompted Commissioner Morris to promise that they would be able to pursue hunting and fishing "through the country, as you have heretofore done."[19]

Those Plains Cree who signed Treaty Six in 1876 were able to negotiate more favourable terms for economic support including promises of farm equipment, seed, livestock, wagons, and handmills; and upon the settlement of two or more reserves, a sum of $1,000 of provisions (up to three years' duration) was allocated for the promotion of agriculture. In addition, the government promised to supply medical aid by equipping each Indian agent with a medicine chest. Assurances were also given to the effect that in the event of pestilence or famine, the Queen, acting upon the advice of the Indian agent and the chief superintendent of Indian Affairs, would supply the amount of assistance deemed to be "necessary and sufficient."[20]

It was also understood that the Cree could select their lands freely and that they could settle onto their reserves with minimal interference in their lives. Undoubtedly, of equal importance to the Cree were government promises that their cultural autonomy was not a point of negotiation. For them, the treaties were guarantees that they could continue to live in their territories according to their customary ways and that they would receive assistance in establishing an alternate economic base. Judging from Morris's words, there was no reason to believe that there would be interference in their daily lives.

Numerous problems arose at these negotiations, including the lack of representation on the part of the Plains Cree. Only twenty-five of 107 lodges belonged to the Plains Cree, and the majority of the Fort Pitt Cree (the largest of the bands) were still hunting on the plains. The rejection of the terms of Treaty Six by some leaders resulted from their concerns over unhindered access to food supplies and their fear of losing political independence. Poundmaker, Piapot, and Red Pheasant (represented by a Saulteaux, Joseph Thoma), felt that the economic provisions offered by the government were insufficient to either support their present needs or adequately facilitate their transition to agriculture. Big Bear arrived at Fort Pitt only after the treaty was signed. He had been previously consulting with other bands of Cree and Assiniboin on the prospect of negotiations with the government, and continued to resist making any commitments in the absence of the other representative chiefs. One of his primary concerns was the protection of bison herds, and at this point he was unwilling to "be led by the neck," that is, to have terms dictated to him.[21] Little Pine also refused to negotiate. Chief Piapot agreed to sign an adhesion to Treaty Four in 1875 only after receiving promises that he would be able to obtain assistance in the form of "mills, blacksmith and carpentry shops and tools, and instructors in farming and the trades."[22] For other leaders, the devastating effects of smallpox and starvation left them little room for choice and delay. The two Carlton-area chiefs, Atahkakohp (Star Blanket) and Mistawâsis (Big Child), may have been more amenable to taking treaty for these reasons. Leaders such as Sweetgrass followed the lead of Atahkakohp and Mistawâsis.

Headmen who did not sign Treaty Six found it increasingly difficult to retain their independence and to provide for their followers. Piapot (headman of the Cree-Assiniboin in the Qu'Appelle area) and Little Pine (who headed the largest following in the Saskatchewan River area) nevertheless attempted to live off the land according to their traditional seasonal rounds. While Big Bear had received a promise from Morris that bison hunting would be regulated, an ordinance passed by the North-West Council in 1877 was not only unenforceable, but it also restricted Indian methods of hunting.[23] Initiatives taken by the Plains Cree to negotiate hunting restrictions with the Blackfoot and Sitting Bull's Teton Dakota also failed.[24] Pressured by economic necessity, Little Pine finally accepted the terms of Treaty Six, as did half of Big Bear's followers who had left the dissident leader's side to join with the bands headed by Lucky Man and Thunderchild.

In order to administer the terms of Treaties One and Two, an Indian commissioner was appointed in 1871. Initially established in Winnipeg, the commissioner's head office was relocated in Regina in 1887 and transferred back to Winnipeg in 1897. The Indian commissioner was directly accountable to the Indian Affairs Branch of the Department of the Interior in Ottawa. The commissioner was responsible for implementing Indian farm policy, overseeing the survey of reserve lands, and establishing twelve farm instructorships to aid in the transition to agriculture. During the preliminary phases of this transition, rations were to be distributed to those who agreed to farm. Arrangements had already been made to supply the sick, aged, and orphaned with supplies; these particular rations were clearly to be used as incentives for would-be farmers.[25]

Despite the fact that most headmen had now accepted the terms of Treaties Four and Six, the Plains Cree leadership remained politically committed to negotiating more favourable provisions. By 1881, official protests had been sent to Governor

General Lorne, and several council meetings had been held to discuss treaty revisions and the idea of an "Indian territory."[26] A number of Cree leaders hoped that they would be able to retain their political autonomy and control over strategic resources by selecting reserve lands in close proximity to one another. The Cypress Hills area was chosen for this "homeland." This movement was politically signifi-cant, since this location for reserves would have resulted in a "concentration of the Cree nation and the creation of an Indian territory that would comprise most of what is now southwestern Saskatchewan."[27]

In the 1880s, as the Cree began to congregate in the Cypress Hills area, the government responded with coercive measures. Subsistence rations were with-drawn from Fort Walsh and provisioning was curtailed in the Cypress Hills region. Indian Commissioner Edgar Dewdney attempted to block the Cree political unification movement by opposing the concentration of reserve sites in any one location, restricting off-reserve travel, and limiting access to arms, ammunition, and horses. In order to implement this "policy of compulsion," Dewdney recom-mended the enlargement of the police force and suggested incarceration of recalcitrant leaders. The wisdom of coercion was re-assessed particularly follow-ing confrontations between the police and the Cree at Piapot's and Big Bear's Sun Dances in 1884. An alternate policy of "rewards and punishment" was introduced. It entailed not only subtle inducements to settle, but also intimidation and surveillance.[28] Towards this end, Dewdney approved the issuing of more rations, farming equipment, oxen, ammunition, and twine, and invited a number of Cree chiefs to visit Regina and Winnipeg to view for themselves the power of the "civilized world." In order to enforce the Indian Department's mandate more expeditiously and to keep a close watch for opposition, he increased the number of employees assigned to the reserves.

A number of Plains Cree leaders continued to hold council meetings in an effort to unite their people and to discuss treaty revisions despite government efforts to deter this movement. The details of Cree petitions to the government are perhaps best represented by the stand taken at the Duck Lake Council of 1884. The council was headed by Chief Beardy and was attended by twelve bands among whom were representatives from the followers of Big Bear, Lucky Man, and Poundmaker. There was a general mood of frustration and hostility towards the government's failure to provide assistance as promised during the treaty negotiations. According to histo-rian John Tobias, the Cree claimed that the government failed to deliver cattle and oxen, sent inferior wagons and farm equipment, and provided insufficient rations and clothes.[29] In addition, the government failed to supply medicine chests to Indian agents for the benefit of Indians under their charge. If their grievances were not adequately addressed by the summer of 1885, the headmen warned that, while they would not declare a state of war with the government, measures would be taken to correct the situation.

Their commitment to resolving outstanding issues with the Dominion of Canada through non-violent means, and their wish to honour their promises given with the signing of the treaties, resulted in the refusal on the part of major Cree leaders to support the Metis in the Saskatchewan uprising of 1885. Contemporary re-examinations of Indian involvement in the events of 1885 have revealed that most hostilities can be attributed to a number of dissident younger warriors belonging to the bands of central Saskatchewan, particularly those led by Big Bear's warrior "chief," Little Poplar.[30] Dewdney himself admitted that the violent outbreaks that did take place at Frog Lake, Duck Lake, Battleford, and Fort Pitt were precipitated in part by fears of impending starvation.[31]

The events leading up to Poundmaker's decision to join Louis Riel's forces after the Battle of Cutknife Hill require further investigation. At least one historical source suggests that millennial expectations may have played a part in this decision. According to Department Farm Instructor Robert Jefferson, Poundmaker claimed that his military response was spiritually ordained for purposes of reviving pre-European conditions. According to Poundmaker, the Cree would find spiritual redemption and be delivered out of their suffering to a life of plenty once Whites were prevented from intruding into their lands. Jefferson, in his conversations with Poundmaker, reported that the chief believed that their suffering was partly caused by "the hand of God, whom the Indians had temporarily deserted"; it was only by returning to "God" that "the buffalo would emerge from the hiding places to which God had diverted them; that Indian stomachs would again know plenty, and they would be happy once more."[32] There was little confidence expressed in the ways of the "white man," and Poundmaker was convinced that others would rise to join with the Metis under Riel's leadership to oust the European Canadians.

The participation of the Plains Cree in the uprising was limited, but the potential military threat was a lesson not easily forgotten by the Dominion of Canada, and the Indian commissioner used every opportunity to terminate the "treaty revision movement."[33] Troops sent out to put down the uprising arrested dissidents, and eighty-one Indian men were sent to trial. Forty-four were convicted, and the leaders Big Bear and Poundmaker were sent to Stony Mountain Penitentiary in Manitoba to serve out their sentences.

By the end of 1885, the political "subjugation" of the Plains Cree was complete. Dissident leaders had been deposed; their followers were ordered to settle on reserves; horses and arms were seized; and treaty payments were suspended for a number of years.[34] Both Big Bear's and Lucky Man's bands were subdivided. Rather than being considered "homelands," where the Plains Cree could determine their future and adjust to the changing order on their own terms, the reserves now became places of confinement, where government programs of transformation and legislative regulations would be unilaterally enforced. Politically, the Plains Cree were now wards of the Canadian government until it was determined by the superintendent general of Indian Affairs that they were sufficiently "civilized" to be enfranchised as Canadian citizens.[35] Because the Indian leaders were excluded from the political process either by direct representation as a "nation" or by individual vote, they had no formal access to power within the new order. Their relations with the Dominion of Canada were formally defined in the Indian Act of Canada, which provided the legal authority to the superintendent of Indian Affairs to manage Indian lands, property, and ultimately many other aspects of Indian life.[36]

During his term as Indian Commissioner and later as Deputy Superintendent of Indian Affairs (1890 to 1898), Hayter Reed undertook to impose further political restrictions on the Plains Cree.[37] Determined to dismantle the "tribal," or "communistic," system underlying the indigenous social, political, and economic institutions and to undermine the influence of "unprogressive" leaders, Reed refused to support the immediate implementation of the chief and councillor elective system as it was outlined in the Indian Advancement Act of 1884 (S.C. 1884, c. 28, 47 Vict.). He argued that even the progressive leaders were often reduced to becoming mere mouthpieces "for the ventilation of imaginary grievances and the presentation of utterly unreasonable demands."[38] The Department, however, refused to support Reed's move to abolish the elective system in western Canada.

The implementation of the elective process did not provide for any meaningful level of political independence. The elected chief and council were considered, in effect, to be employees of the Department and were expected to work closely with the Indian administration. The governor-in-council had the right to dismiss leaders and councillors on the grounds of "dishonesty, intemperance, immorality, or incompetence" (sections 96 and 75 of the Indian Act).[39] The definition of competent leadership provided the Department with considerable latitude to undermine leaders who were not supportive of their policies. In spite of the provision for an elective system, the selection of band officers continued to be made according to traditional customary practices on most reserves. However, the powers inherent in these positions were severely curtailed over the years.[40]

The traditional forms of "chiefly" authority were considerably altered. Wrongdoing and appropriate punishment were no longer defined only according to customary laws. Headmen were obliged to report breaches of the Canadian law to the Indian agent or police and were expected to defer to the Canadian justice system. Furthermore, in cases where disputes would have been settled internally between families, the headmen were now instructed to intervene, and they were made personally responsible for the maintenance of law and order. In this sense, chiefly authority was expanded "mostly at the expense of individual autonomy and at the same time the placing of final authority in the hands of the whites."[41] The physical isolation of most reserves from police detachments, however, allowed for the persistence of many customary laws in internal community relations.

Some of the traditional roles of members of the Warrior societies were assumed by the Canadian police force and the military. The continuity of their functions was perhaps most evident at the larger inter-reserve gatherings. The methods of attaining access to positions in Warrior societies were undoubtedly altered because raids against other villages, and the taking of lives, property, and horses during these forays, were now criminal acts according to the Canadian justice system. Some historians have suggested that the voluntary involvement in Canadian war efforts on the part of young men was linked to the opportunity to demonstrate one's worthiness and to achieve a status similar to that enjoyed by Warriors. Participation in rodeos and the development of competitive pow-wows have similarly provided opportunities to earn public recognition through the demonstration of traditionally valued skills.[42]

Another major element in Plains Cree society was also undermined. Once valued for their knowledge and guidance, the elders were viewed by the Department and, eventually, by many of their own people, as "unprogressive." Their power and authority were constantly challenged and at times ridiculed by the Department's employees, mission teachers, and even the more acculturated graduates from the Indian schools who were taught to reject their own cultural values and ways. The relevancy of the learning and wisdom that the generation of bison-hunting elders had to offer to their communities in the face of changes that were required for survival in the new order largely went unacknowledged. It was the Indian agent, the missionary, the farm instructor, and the teacher who now possessed the necessary knowledge for survival. In many reserve communities it was the next generation of school children, educated in the ways of the European-Canadian system, who assumed more control over leadership positions and decision-making.

Although the Plains Cree had been informed during treaty negotiations that they would be treated as British subjects, the signatories did not comprehend the sweeping implications of this shift in their political status. Nor were they fully informed about the implications of the extension of the Indian Act and other related legislation into their lives. Thus reduced to a status of wardship and forced to abide by the regulations of an Indian Act that was simultaneously paternalistic and coercive, the Plains Cree essentially found themselves in a colonial form of relationship similar to that of Indians residing in eastern Canada or of other indigenous peoples occupying lands in British agriculturally based settlement colonies. The regulations imposed under the Indian Act, in combination with the demise of natural game resources and insufficient government aid to promote agriculture on a viable basis, plunged the Plains Cree and others into the lowest stratum of Canadian society.

Initially, the Canadian government supported the scheme of encouraging western Indians to become profit-making cereal agriculturalists and cattle-breeders.[43] Several officials were of the opinion that the practice of farming would instill capitalistic values in Indian people by encouraging them to participate in the market system and by supplanting the "communal" system of property holdings. Indian Commissioner Hayter Reed was unwavering in his determination to eradicate the "tribal" or "communal" system. In an annual report for 1888, Reed wrote, "[The] policy of destroying the tribal or communistic system is assailed in every possible way, and every effort made to implant a spirit of individual responsibility instead."[44] The qualities of self-reliance, independence, and individuality were closely associated with the practice of agriculture in the minds of European Canadians. Farming was promoted among homesteaders as a "noble and sacred occupation" that was the "foundation" of the nation's wealth, and one could be transformed and elevated by working one's quarter section in an independent and diligent manner.[45] This "country life ideology," pervasive throughout Canadian thinking at the time, seemingly "endowed the land with an almost mystical power to transform and elevate, even the lowest or weakest of men."[46]

In order to "elevate" Indian peoples, to provide them with an alternate subsistence base, and to encourage the taking of individualized land holdings with the future release of "unfarmed" lands in mind, the government officially promoted the homestead pattern of agriculture on prairie reserves. Subject to the consent of the Indian Department and the band councils, an individual was able to apply for a "location ticket" that functioned as a certificate of entitlement to a share of reserve land. Because such lands could be alienated from the bands only through the Crown, the Indian farmer had control over only the *use* of his holding rather than outright legal title.

Several strategies were adopted by the government to encourage Indian farming. During 1878–79, a model, or "home farm," system had been introduced in a number of Indian agencies. Based upon the British landlord-tenant farm system, the objectives of the scheme were to instruct adults in knowledge needed for farming and to raise surpluses for rations during the training period. Many of the instructors and their assistants lacked the necessary skills to subsist on their own farms and so proved to be ineffective teachers. Farm Instructor Robert Jefferson reported that the first instructors among the Plains Cree were lumbermen from the Ottawa district who "at least knew all there was to know about driving men, in addition to being experienced wire pullers."[47]

The home-farm strategy was in operation from 1879 to 1884 and grew from an initial seventeen to twenty-four farms. It was rejected as a viable system for promoting Indian farming for a number of reasons, including the refusal of the Department to tolerate the high costs of supporting the instructors, their families, and the staff; poor returns from the farms; and the difficulties experienced in providing instruction to the would-be farmers.[48] In practice, the staff of home farms were obliged to expend a greater part of their time in making their own farms productive and hardly served as suitable models for their Indian charges. Many of these agency farms were located outside the reserve boundaries, a situation that further handicapped the instructors.[49]

Environmental adversity and the lack of proper instruction, provisions, machinery, capital for investment, and even adequate food and clothing undermined the efforts of those Plains Cree who tried to farm. The challenge to the traditional authority and decision-making powers of the chiefs and their councils also served only to increase tensions in an already stressful transitory period. It was now the Department officials and employees who possessed political power and the knowledge necessary for a transition to the new order, and who controlled access to the means of production (draft animals, seed, cattle, and wagons, for example) and played a determining role in the distribution of the products of Indian labour. The resentment of this situation was evident in the reactions of such chiefs as Poundmaker. Forced to move his followers onto a reserve under economic duress, the headman was described by the farm instructor as "resenting all, even advisory interference, . . . showing pretty plainly that it was only the dire pressure of circumstances that had brought them to accept the restraint of Reserve life."[50] When Poundmaker insisted upon having more say in the affairs of his reserve, it was denied on the grounds that he was not considered to be "sufficiently advanced to be entrusted with the care of government property or with the supervision of farm work."[51]

In spite of these drawbacks, some headmen, such as Poundmaker, did make an effort to farm. However, they were constantly thwarted in their efforts owing to departmental parsimony and other adversities experienced by European-Canadian farmers. As historians have pointed out, "The development of suitable crops, farming techniques and agricultural equipment for the northern climate still lay ahead."[52] From the Department's perspective, the lack of agricultural productivity was attributed to preconceived notions of cultural "backwardness." This opinion was typical of that of Department officials, including the deputy superintendent of Indian Affairs, who believed that those Indians who refused to change with the times were indifferent and lazy, and that "if such Indians would not help themselves, there was nothing the department could do for them."[53]

By the 1890s, a new strategy for promoting Indian agriculture was adopted by Indian Commissioner Hayter Reed. In 1895, the commissioner lent his support to the "peasant" model of farming, which would consist of the development of small family-operated, subsistence-level mixed farms with minimal technology. All forms of "tribalism" or "communalism," including cooperative labour, the pooling of resources to purchase and share machinery and livestock, and traditional multi-family settlement patterns, were to be discouraged. The denial of access to techno-logically advanced farm machinery to Indian farmers was grounded in the belief that the more labour-intensive methods of "peasant" farming would promote more rigorous work habits.[54] The dismantling of the communally oriented village pattern typical of reserves and its replacement with individual landholdings was encour-aged. One official report noted that proximity of dwellings to one another afforded too much opportunity for excessive visiting, gossiping, and gambling among men during the winter evenings, and strengthened "the clannish feeling which renders it so difficult to deal with individual members."[55] Another, more practical, problem with traditional settlement patterns was the tendency of people to live in sheltered river valleys rather than on the uplands where their allotted farms were located.[56]

In order to encourage the individualization of productivity, Reed undertook to "restrict the area cultivated by each Indian to within such limits as will enable him to carry on his operations by the application of his own personal labour."[57] Accordingly, reserves were subdivided into forty-acre allotments and parcelled out to individual families, and farms were spaced throughout the reserve to discourage a communal pattern of production and settlement. As early as 1899, families on the Piapot, Muscowpetung and Pasquah reserves had resettled on their family plots. Heads of families were advised that permission from the local Indian agent was required for travel away from their reserves during the agricultural season, and in some areas this involved obtaining an official document.[58]

Other regulations were adopted to control the distribution of Indian-raised farm products and their sale in the market. A permit system prohibited off-reserve sales without the approval of the Indian agent. Whites attempting to purchase goods from Indian farmers who had not obtained a permit were liable to fines. No Trespassing signs were posted on reserve lands, and White storekeepers refused to extend credit because the Indian Act prevented them from collecting debts on reserve lands. The cumulative effect of these repressive measures was to curtail the free flow of outside capital into the Indian reserve economy, a situation that led to under-development.[59]

These regulations, or forms of "kindly supervision" as they were termed by officials, served only to further discourage would-be farmers, and they intensified hostile feelings towards the Department. One Cree historian, the Reverend Edward

Ahenakew, has documented the magnitude of the psychological and economic impact of the implementation of the system of government wardship:

> It is most wretchedly humbling to many a worthy fellow to have to go, with assumed indifference, to ask or beg for a permit to sell one load of hay that he has cut himself, on his own reserve, with his horses and implements. . . . What kind of policy is it that aims at bringing a people to a point of self-respect, and then by the nature of its regulations destroys the very thing for which it works? . . . I think that I would rather starve than go to beg for such a trifling thing . . . while I am trying to make every hour of good weather count. . . . From the standpoint of the government it may seem good, a kind of drill or discipline. . . . I have seen with my own eyes, Indians wasting a day, even two days, trying to get a permit to sell, when they are short of food. The Agent cannot always be at home, the clerk may be away, or busy, and the Indian must wait, though he may have to drive to the Agency from another reserve.[60]

Frustration with these conditions resulted in apathy towards government programs on the part of the Indians. Eventually, as a registration of protest against the lack of support and as an assertion of their right to self-determination, they refused to cooperate altogether. Joseph Dion, another Cree historian, describes an example: "[People] wanted to buy cattle when they had money after a successful hunt, but would not because the ID [Indian Department] brand would be put on the cattle."[61] Some families from the Frog Lake and Kehiwin bands even relocated to more distant reserve lands in the Onion Lake agency in order to have greater autonomy and a more secure economy by combining commercial trapping with marginal farming.[62] Other Plains Cree combined marginal farming efforts with seasonal employment as contracted labourers, clearing land and doing the fall harvest for White farmers. As one Cree observer noted, "We had become cheap labourers in the eyes of the white man, just as an economic commodity."[63]

By the turn of the twentieth century, the prairie agricultural region was being economically and demographically transformed as the Dominion of Canada supported programs to settle immigrant labour in the west to raise wheat and cattle for its export markets. Once the lands around the reserves were settled by immigrant farmers, and towns such as Moose Jaw, Maple Creek, Medicine Hat, and Swift Current were established, "unused" Indian lands were coveted. Over the next decade, a number of bands were pressured into releasing or exchanging their lands.

A number of government regulations were introduced to facilitate the alienation of Indian peoples from their land base. In 1911 an amendment to the Indian Act allowed for expropriation of reserve lands for public works, while a second amendment permitted the cession of reserve lands adjacent to towns with populations over 8,000 without a band's consent.[64] A bill introduced in 1914 by the Minister of the Interior, Arthur Meighen, to "lease [uncultivated] land to a third party without Indian consent" was approved in 1918.[65] In the following year, some 62,128 acres of Indian land, the majority of which were in Saskatchewan, were expropriated under the terms of the Soldier Settlement Act. Under the provisions of this act, a board was created to allocate Dominion and purchased reserve lands for soldiers returning from World War One. Indian soldiers were to be settled on their respective home reserves, and Indian Commissioner William Graham was authorized to provide loans of up to $1,000 to each veteran who wished to farm.

The Greater Production Program, introduced in 1918 as a war-time measure, also resulted in the procurement of uncultivated reserve lands for farming. Supervised by the Indian commissioner, the program was intended to raise food productivity. Through an order-in-council, Graham was directed to encourage Indian farming, to establish Greater Production farms using reserve labour, and to arrange for the leasing of reserve lands to White farmers.[66] All profits accruing from this program were to be diverted to the bands after expenditures for improvements were deducted.

The unilateral nature of leasing Indian lands was raised by the Liberals in 1924. Both the Conservative and Liberal parties, as well as Indian Department administrators, rationalized the government's land policy as an economic necessity associated with the costs of maintaining the wardship system. It was also felt that White lessees would not only increase food production for the nation, but would also serve as good examples to future Indian farmers.[67]

By the time the state-run Greater Production farms were phased out in the early 1920s, some 20,448 acres of reserve land were co-opted for farms located at the Crooked Lakes, Assiniboin, Muscowpetung, Blackfoot, and Blood reserves, and approximately 255,000 acres had been leased to White farmers. Of note is the fact that these state-run farms used cooperative labour forces and modern machinery to enhance production. The measure of Indian Commissioner Graham's success in alienating Indians from their lands during this period is indicated by the local reputation he earned as an aggressive and inflexible land dealer. According to one Plains Cree elder, John Tootoosis, the members of the Poundmaker Reserve had very strong feelings about Graham's dealings:

The Commissioner Graham was really hard on people. Those in the eastern part of Saskatchewan were really afraid of him, he really controlled them. . . . It was through him that the Indians were made to sell parts of their land, . . . persuading them to sell even if they didn't want to. He used to stack money on the table in order to entice them to sell their land and paid them right there . . . he kept bothering us.[68]

Other forms of development resulted in land expropriation, such as the 1,408 acres of Cree land in the Touchwood Hills and Qu'Appelle areas that were released for cottage development. In a 1919 amendment to the Indian Act, the superintendent general of Indian Affairs was empowered to lease "surface rights" on reserves for mining.[69]

The promotion of economic self-sufficiency among western indigenous populations was one of the major objectives of the Indian education system. Provisions for government-supported education once bands had settled on their reserves had been part of the treaty negotiations. It had been assumed by administrators that the objectives of Indian education would be to provide technical training for children as well as to bring them into "civilization" through Christian teachings and training in the values and behaviour of European-Canadian society.

The types of schools established for prairie Indian children had precedents in the mission-operated school systems in existence for indigenous peoples throughout the British Empire. Until the mid-1870s, various Christian denominations had taken on the responsibility of operating day schools, "boarding" schools, and orphanages for Indian children. European-Canadian Christian training was instilled in their young charges through a combination of book learning, Christian religious teaching, and vocational training. The latter was a major aspect in the day-to-day operations of the schools, for the children functioned as the primary source of labour for their operation.

By the late 1870s, the Canadian government began to examine the question of Indian education in the light of its own assimilative objectives and wardship responsibilities. Towards this end, lawyer-journalist Nicholas Davin was sent by the Conservative Macdonald government to meet with the American Secretary of the Interior, Carl Schurz, for purposes of evaluating the American Indian school system. Davin was particularly impressed with the strategy of isolating children from their home environments by locating them in schools off their reserves. As a result, he recommended that the government proceed with establishing a residential school system along with an emphasis on vocational training in order to promote a greater level of self-sufficiency among the graduates.[70] Davin also advocated the use of missionaries as appropriate teachers since they had already effectively demonstrated their commitment to educating indigenous children. Accordingly, he proposed that the government support three church-operated industrial schools. Among his other recommendations were "rewards to pupils and parents for attendance," "compulsory education," the employment of teachers of "high moral and intellectual character," and the inspection of the teachers' work.[71]

The Canadian government acted upon Davin's report in 1883, and the Commissioner of Indian Affairs, Edgar Dewdney, arranged for the creation of three joint state- and church-administered industrial residential schools to be located in each treaty area in the western region. A Catholic school was established at Qu'Appelle (Treaty Four) and at High River (Treaty Seven); the third, an Anglican institution, was to be built at Battleford (Treaty Six). The intent of the curriculum was to provide a limited education with practical training in crop planting, dairying, livestock care, carpentry, blacksmithing, laundering, cooking, and sewing. Competitive individualism was encouraged through sports activities and the submission of handiwork, as well as student-raised produce and livestock, for prizes at local fairs. Some pupils were hired out as labour to work for local settlers as farm hands or domestic help. Termed "outing," this practice not only brought much-needed funds into the school, but served as a form of apprenticeship into the real world.[72]

The development of "new, moral, self-supporting Christian citizens," who would either be integrated into the White community or return home to elevate "the pagan and dependent reserve community," was achieved through the implementation of a Victorian regime of discipline and school regulations. The transformation of Cree children began the moment of their arrival in the schools. Their identities were immediately physically altered as each child underwent a disrobing and received a thorough scrubbing and a haircut. Each child was then dressed in near-identical, European-Canadian-style, uniform-looking clothing that served to further strip any outward appearances of indigenous forms of individuality and cultural identity. Newly registered children were given Christian names, and the use of their traditional languages was forbidden. Behaviour was controlled by the application of numerous regulations, the regimentation of daily routines, and the administration of forms of punishment that were often unduly harsh, even for the standards of the time. Parents were discouraged from visiting their children to prevent their children from lapsing into traditional behaviour and to discourage homesickness. The preparation of Cree children for their future role in Canadian society also involved instruction in Christian religious ideology. Such instruction was intended to replace traditional religious beliefs and religious expression. Once children were selected for school attendance, parents were obliged to designate a Christian denominational affiliation at the time of enrolment. As one historian has astutely indicated, Indian religious rites were now replaced with the rites of Christianity.[73] Indigenous patterns of socialization and ceremonial rites of passage were now marked by the Christian holy sacraments of baptism, first communion, and confirmation. The more secular dimension of the children's transition was the passage of the child from student to graduate to farmer, mechanic, and homemaker through "territorial passages from junior classroom to half days in shops to drama groups or visits to fairs."[74]

At least twenty industrial schools had been opened in Manitoba, the Northwest Territories, and British Columbia by 1896. However, the government began to question the cost of the program. Of major concern was the "reversion" of graduates to their cultural ways once they returned home, and the resistance displayed by parents to having their children reside in distant schools for long periods of time.

The impetus for a revision in the federal Indian school system, however, came from the desire to reduce government spending and a widely shared scepticism regarding the "physical, mental or moral get-up" of Indian graduates to compete with their White counterparts.[75] Consequently, in 1910, the government adopted a more limited objective of fitting "the Indian for civilized life in his own environment" through the provision of a very basic program of education and practical training that persisted well into the mid-twentieth century.[76] There were now three school systems that served the Indian communities: day schools, which were on or near reserves; boarding schools, which were located on or near reserves; and industrial boarding schools, which were more distantly located.

The opposition of leaders and parents to the boarding and industrial schools continued throughout this period. One headman, Star Blanket, insisted that the off-reserve boarding or residential school system was a violation of treaty rights and that, in fact, the government had promised to establish a school on every reserve. In an appeal to the governor general, who was touring western Canada in 1912, Star Blanket protested the inhumanity of forcing parents to send their children to schools located hundreds of miles from home, where many of them died without ever seeing their parents again.[77]

During the 1920s and 1930s, Indian education continued to be supported by the churches and government monies received through attendance-rated grants. However, in 1923, the government agreed to assume responsibility for expenses incurred in the operation of residential schools, allowing church finances to be diverted to improving living conditions and hiring more qualified staff. While grants were available to promising graduates to enable them to attend high school, university, trade school, or business college, most students fell short of the high requirements for this aid. For example, a requirement that students pass grade eight by the time they were fourteen could not be fulfilled by children who often did not start school until they were between eight and ten.[78]

For the students who did manage to complete their school terms, there was little to look forward to either in White society or on their home reserves. Because of the poor quality of education and the racial prejudice of White employers, there were few employment opportunities for graduates beyond the seasonal casual jobs already open to their parents. Paid jobs on reserves were equally scarce. In addition to unemployment, the "acculturated" graduates were forced to confront a number of other problems associated with their alienation from their culture. According to Elder John Tootoosis, Indian graduates were literally suspended between two cultures:

On one side are all the things [the Indian] learned from his people and their way of life that was being wiped out, and on the other side are the white man's ways which he could never fully understand since he never had the right amount of education and could not be part of it. There he is hanging in the middle of two cultures and he is not a white man and he is not an Indian.[79]

In some schools, graduates were married to one another without due consideration for customary prohibitions inherent in traditional kinship or clan affiliations. These married couples were encouraged to establish their own family farms. In the early 1900s, William Graham, then Indian Agent in the Qu'Appelle Valley area, initiated a social experiment that involved graduates at File Hills. With the co-operation of the principals of various boarding schools such as the File Hills Boarding School and the Lebret Industrial School, ex-pupils were married to each other and settled on lands physically removed from the reserve proper. By 1907, there were some twenty families residing in this model colony designed to produce self-sufficient farmers living according to European-Canadian lifeways.[80]

By the 1930s, the third generation of Plains Cree since the signing of the treaties had little reason to expect more equitable treatment from the Canadian government and society than had been received by their grandparents. In an interview with Coming Day from the Sweet Grass Reserve, conducted in 1934, anthropologist David Mandelbaum was provided with a description of the level of Plains Cree integration into Canadian society.[81] While some families practised marginal farming and gardening, others chose to sell their labour by chopping wood, clearing land, or working as domestics. Many combined their options on a seasonal basis by contracting out as manual labourers on farms, and by trapping. Food resources such as fish, waterfowl, and small game remained important. The multi-family kinship network continued to be crucial for obtaining and sharing resources for survival.

The lack of integration of Indian workers into the Canadian economy as permanently employed wage labourers was attributed by administrators to racial prejudice rather than to ineffectual government programs.[82] Surprisingly, Indian agriculture was reported to be "remarkably prosperous" in comparison to White farms during the Depression years of the 1930s, undoubtedly owing to relatively greater degrees of aid provided to Indian farmers, including exemptions from taxes, mortgages, and overhead charges.[83] At the close of the thirties, however, the severe drought turned the tide for Indian farmers, as it did for all farmers, and they were forced to depend on their cattle for food and revenue. Other sources of income included proceeds from the harvest of seneca root and the manufacture of beaded handicrafts.[84]

In an attempt to revive Indian farming following the Depression, the Department introduced mechanized machinery such as tractors in addition to manual implements and horses. On some reserves, individualized labour was replaced through the creation of community-run gardens and farms. Ironically, the director of the Indian Affairs Branch announced that the success of these farms resulted from "showing the Indians the value of co-operative effort," a system of production that had been systematically discouraged through detribalization policies.[85]

Because of the shortage of White labour during World War Two, there was an increase in the employment of Indian labourers. Some Plains Cree men worked on White farms in spring and autumn and in lumber camps during the winter. Individuals were paid $8 to $10 per day for harvesting, and families received an average of $25. Women were able to find work in restaurants and as domestics, while their husbands found work in abattoirs, oil refineries, trucking or draying firms, railway companies, and in all types of processing plants. Once White workers were again available following the war, these sources of employment were considerably reduced for Indians.

In addition to unemployment and the lack of effective economic programs for the development of reserve economies, another problem confronting the Plains Cree during the inter-war years was the further disintegration of indigenous forms of social and political organization. This was evident from the factionalism that was developing between the older generation and those school graduates who chose to adopt a White-oriented lifestyle. This development was partially the consequence of the wardship system, which encouraged young people to look to White society for leadership and role models rather than to their own relations. Cree historian Stan Cuthand summarized his recollections of Plains Cree societal breakdown during the inter-war years:

Family-arranged marriages were opposed by the youths, and they often ran away to be married elsewhere. The younger generation refused to accept the traditional role of submitting to the wishes of their fathers and tended to question such traditional customs as giving away horses to visitors. The more educated Indians scoffed at Indian rituals and refused to participate. They danced square dances and quadrilles. They would speak English rather than the native tongue. The more traditional families ignored this and continued to show their Indianness.[86]

Generational differences were also apparent in the emergence of new types of political and economic leadership. While working on the Sweet Grass Reserve in 1934, Mandelbaum observed a growing tendency for an individual's status to be determined by one's ability to accumulate wealth rather than through the traditional method of the distribution of goods. Older leaders who were not able to successfully participate in the new agriculture-based economy were now losing their following and influence. For example, Fineday stood for re-election as chief on the "strength of his ancient prestige" as a warrior and his ability to care for his followers, while his rival, Sam Swimmer, who owned eighty cattle and farmed some two hundred acres of land, campaigned for "progress and cooperation with the whites."[87] Swimmer won the election by a small margin.

Like Swimmer, other Indian leaders were beginning to favour an assimilative approach as a solution to their problems, while still others lobbied "for the retention of Indian identity and the continuation of the Indian practice of adaptation.[88] The retention of cultural identity and the attainment of self-determination were key issues for most Plains Cree political figures in the inter-war years. In his analysis of this movement, historian John Tobias observed that the pre-1885 treaty revision movement continued, taking the form of a treaty-rights lobby.[89]

The first formalized treaty-rights lobby was organized by the "old men from southern Saskatchewan" in the Treaty Four area who sent a delegation to Ottawa in 1911.[90] The delegation confronted the Department of Indian Affairs on a number of issues, including a ban against their ceremonies, the unilateral deposition of their chiefs and councillors, and the lack of a voice in determining their own affairs. Their claim that the Department's regulations violated treaty rights was largely ignored by officials. Throughout the first half of the twentieth century, the Plains Cree found it difficult to mobilize a united front against the Canadian government. This problem partially arose out of government policies that were enacted to keep the Plains Cree and other Indian political movements in a state of powerlessness. For instance, John Tobias has indicated that, in the Treaty Four area and in the southern part of Treaty Six, traditional leaders were not replaced once they were deposed or had died, and, as a result, the Cree were in effect kept "leaderless" and had to depend upon the federal Indian administration for direction.[91]

A further obstacle to the treaty-rights movement was the difficulty that communities faced in formally organizing their efforts. In 1927, an amendment to the Indian Act prohibited anyone from raising or providing funds for the prosecution of claims against the Canadian government.[92] Originally directed against the land-claims activities of the British Columbia Indians, this amendment (Section 141, Chapter 98 of the Revised Statutes of 1927) was now being broadly interpreted to prosecute those who collected or solicited funds "to support an organized grievance or an organization for representing Indian grievances."[93] Although only one arrest was recorded under this section of the Act, the Department did use the clause to conduct investigations into the political activities of Indian organizations.

Despite these limitations, the political example established by the signatories of the treaties was followed by the next generation of school graduates that included John Tootoosis, Joseph Dion, Reverend Edward Ahenakew, and others, through their involvement with the Allied Bands (in the 1920s), the League of Indians of Western Canada (in the 1930s), and the Saskatchewan Indian Association and the Union of Saskatchewan Indians (in the 1940s). Their ability to overcome government restraints on their activities was evident in their formal written and personal representations before the Special Joint Committee of the

Senate and the House of Commons, which met in 1948–49 to reconsider the provisions of the Indian Act.

From the time of their initial formal dealings with prairie Indians in the 1870s, and throughout the 1880s and 1890s, the Canadian authorities attributed the lack of Indian material progress and expressions of resistance against federally imposed assimilation policies to "cultural lag," that is, the persistence of traditional customs and leadership. Ottawa's lack of commitment to creating an effective Indian policy and the methods that it adopted to implement its paternalistic programs were rarely considered to be factors contributing to the state of Indian under-development. One of the ways in which the Indian Department attempted to counteract the persistence of "unprogressive" indigenous beliefs and practices was to undertake and support the repression of one of the more potent and visible forms of cultural expression – religious ceremonies.

The Indian Act and Indigenous Ceremonies: 1884 to 1895

4

By the late 1860s, the acquisition of the land and resources of the prairie region had become a major objective of Sir John A. Macdonald's Conservative Party. They believed that access to a new "investment frontier" in the west would simultaneously open the region and materially benefit the east.[1] Their entrepreneurial vision involved the development of agriculture and primary resource industries, which were connected with eastern markets by means of a national railway. The labour force would be largely supplied by immigrant farmers and traders. In order for this vision to become a reality, the question of Indian title to the region had to be dealt with. To this end, the numbered treaties were negotiated, and in 1873 the North-West Mounted Police force was created to assert Canada's hegemony in the western interior and to ensure that settlement proceeded within a climate of law and order.

Once Canadian sovereignty had been established in the western prairie region, the various indigenous nations came under the same federal regulations as their eastern counterparts. They would be incorporated into the Canadian state through unilaterally imposed federal legislation and assimilative programs. Politically, "Indians" had been placed in a "distinct legal category" as wards of the Canadian government, subject to all "British rights and privileges" with the exception of those accruing from citizenship.[2] The Acts of 1868 and 1869 had served to consolidate the 1850s legislation regarding federal relations with eastern-Canadian Indians.[3] These acts increased government control over Indian lands and introduced measures to discourage European-Canadian encroachments onto reserves. An Indian act was drafted in 1874 (c. 21, 37 Vict.) that contained amendments for the extension of pre-existing legislation to the western interior and for more restrictive measures against the sale of intoxicants, but this act was not passed. However, the 1874 amendments and previous legislation regarding Indian affairs were applied to other parts of Canada including British Columbia, Manitoba, and the Northwest Territories. In 1876, An Act to Amend and Consolidate the Laws Respecting Indians to be Known and Cited as "The Indian Act, 1876" was passed.

Both protective and coercive, the terms of the Indian Act did not reflect a federal recognition of the cultural, political, and economic integrity of Indian societies. Rather, the Act demonstrated "little respect" for indigenous peoples or faith in their abilities to make a contribution to the building of the new Canadian nation as "Indians."[4] Before 1884, the Indian Act primarily dealt with matters concerning property acquisition and disposal, Indian government, and education. In that year, the first in a series of amendments to the Act was passed to facilitate the direct interference of the state in the ceremonies of the Northwest Coast and Plains Indian cultures. The development of a policy of religious interference was motivated by the political and economic tenets of Macdonald's National Policy and Victorian attitudes towards Indian religious systems.

The precedent for imposing controls over indigenous religious expression on the prairies had been set during the period between 1884 and 1895 when legislation was passed to outlaw ceremonial activities associated with potlatches among the Northwest Coast Indians.[5] Until 1858, when its charter was subject to re-negotiation, the Hudson's Bay Company had enjoyed a commercial monopoly in Rupert's Land, New Caledonia, and Vancouver Island. As part of its political mandate, the Company was responsible for maintaining law and order and ensuring that indigenous populations received fair treatment. In 1849, the imperial government had authorized the Company to promote the colonization and settlement of Vancouver Island. According to Herman Merivale, Permanent Secretary of the Colonial Office, it was in the Company's best interest to foster the social, economic, and spiritual well-being of indigenous populations; otherwise, "there was always a distinct possibility that the Company's supply of furs would either be disrupted or curtailed."[6] The Colonial Office had considered the Company's monopoly preferable to a free-trade environment, which it felt would have led to the destruction of Indians through unscrupulous competition. Despite local petitions to the Colonial Office that challenged the Company's monopoly on the grounds that it was not in fact fulfilling its mandate to protect the Indian population, the imperial government opted for expediency by continuing its support.

During the Company's period of control over these colonies, a number of Christian mission projects were initiated, but Christianity was not well received among most Northwest Coast cultures. As historian Robin Fisher suggests, "Their disposition towards western religion was the same as it was towards other aspects of European culture: they were free to select and reject as they pleased."[7] This is evident in the emergence of a number of syncretistic cults, known as Prophet movements, which blended indigenous and Christian beliefs. One of the more successful attempts at cultural transformation had occurred among the Tsimshian under the direction of Reverend William Duncan of the Anglican Church Missionary Society. In 1862, Duncan had established the village of Metlakatla in order to promote the well-being of Indian converts in a controlled social environment. He believed that this form of resettlement scheme would prevent the regression of converts to their traditional ways and, at the same time, protect them from exploitation by Europeans. His opinion of Tsimshian ceremonies and Northwest Coast Indian religions was typical of the times. Winter ceremonies were denounced as a "horrid fabrication of lies," shamans were "sinister" at best, dancing was "frivolous," and the potlatches were condemned as "wasteful."[8]

Following the establishment of the colony of Vancouver Island in 1849, a number of changes occurred in Britain's relations with indigenous populations as the creation of a viable settlement colony demanded more formal terms of co-existence. Under Richard Blanshard, the first governor of the colony, Indian-European relations were marked by territorial encroachment and coercion; recalcitrant Indians were punished, and there were instances of Indian villages being shelled and destroyed by naval vessels.[9] By contrast, Blanshard's successor, James Douglas, attempted to arrange for the purchase of Indian lands, and successfully negotiated eleven treaties. However, according to the instructions sent to him by the Hudson's Bay Company, the British notion of land tenure was the basis for negotiating access to Indian territory, with the result that only "village sites" and "enclosed fields" were reserved for the sole use of Indians.[10] All other lands were considered to be unoccupied and open for immigrant settlement.

As the numbers of settlers, land developers, and gold miners grew, the British House of Commons Select Committee on the Hudson's Bay Company recommended in 1857 that the mainland be granted the status of a Crown colony as British Columbia. The colonial Governor, James Douglas, was responsible for promoting agricultural settlement, supervising the commercial development of resources (timber, minerals, and fish), while at the same time protecting the rights of Indian populations. Douglas's initial attempts to address Indian concerns regarding White encroachment on their lands and traditional fishing grounds were undermined by his two successors, Frederick Seymour and Arthur Kennedy, and then by Joseph Trutch, the Commissioner of Lands and Works (1864 to 1871), who refused to recognize the legitimacy of Indian land claims to "unoccupied" lands. Before his retirement, Douglas had failed to entrench his Indian land policies by enacting legislation and thus left his successors with considerable latitude in their own dealings with the Indian nations. According to his successors, Douglas had been too lenient in his willingness to accord territorial rights to Indians, and they objected to the fact that Indians, as British subjects, had the right to pre-empt land by establishing habitations on their claims and cultivating the soil. Douglas even permitted Indians to purchase town lots.[11]

In 1871, British Columbia entered into the confederation of Canada and the indigenous populations residing within its boundaries came under federal jurisdiction. At this time there was no re-evaluation of the status of Indians or their lands. The single reference to indigenous groups, attributed to Trutch, was contained in Clause 13 of the terms of the Union and was essentially a defence of the status quo. The provincial legislation passed in 1872 and 1875 excluded Indians from the vote. As early as 1873, Dr. Israel Powell, the newly appointed Indian superintendent of Victoria, denounced potlatching because it hindered the "civilization" process and was generally considered to be a waste of productive time.[12] By 1879, there was some indication that missionaries were gaining more influence over certain groups. In that year a number of southern-interior tribes met in Lytton and reached a consensus to educate their children in the western system, to replace communal land use with individualized property holdings, and to abolish the potlatch.[13] These "regulations" were generated under the supervision of the Indian Reserve Commissioner Gilbert Sproat and were among the first official statements addressing the suppression of potlatches.

While many of the potlatches were performed at winter village sites distant from White settlements, these ceremonies were highly public affairs and could be readily monitored by local authorities. Because they involved the redistribution and the destruction of material goods, potlatches were denounced as wasteful and impoverishing by European settlers. In particular, the highly competitive potlatches sponsored by rival ranked households of the Nootka and southern Kwakiutl shocked the most tolerant of the Victorian colonists. While highly complex in nature, the essential features of the potlatch are summarized in the following observation made by anthropologist Philip Drucker:

The overt purpose of both feast and potlach was the announcement of an event of social significance: marriage of an important person, birth of a potential heir to one of the group's titles, crests, and high statuses, inheritance and formal assumption of one of these titles or crests and its corresponding position, and rescue or ransom and restoration to free status of a war captive. . . . Much of the legendary history of the group was recited to prove the right to use the name or privilege. Then the gifts were distributed in the name of the recipient of the title or crest. The first and largest gift went to the highest-ranking guest.[14]

In order for the new statuses to be validated, it was important that the guests bear witness through the recitation of family histories and transfers of rights. In addition, the distribution of household wealth served to substantiate these new privileges in a tangible manner. Not only did potlatches allow their sponsors to publicly demonstrate their status, but they were also fundamental to the political economies of these societies. Through this means, surpluses and locally produced items were distributed to other communities; political, economic, and social alliances were re-affirmed or initiated; and the cohesion of the hereditary family lineages of the households was strengthened.[15] It was a social system whereby guests could elevate their rank only by sponsoring a potlatch in which they would give more than they received from their host household.

From the point of view of European-Canadian observers, this system was no more than an economic relationship between creditor and debtor, and for this reason potlatchers were perceived to be victims of self-inflicted wounds caught up in a cycle of material impoverishment. Historically, the most blatant occurrences of conspicuous consumption occurred during rival potlatches that flourished in the late nineteenth and early twentieth centuries. The increase in the performance of potlatches and the goods distributed or destroyed at these ceremonies resulted from the relatively greater amount of wealth that households were able to accumulate through their participation in the commercial fur trade. The disruption of hereditary positions of rank due to the loss of life from warfare and disease also contributed to the rise in potlatching. Rival potlatches were held "to establish or alter the precedence of groups," and "to claim a vacant title or status."[16] There were even feigned rivalry potlatches for the re-enactment of traditional conflicts between lineage households. Other forms of ceremonial gift-giving or transfer of material goods also served to reinforce a system of reciprocal obligation of mutual support during crises, and to provide a means for the redistribution of pooled household resources. Gift-giving in these ranked societies created mutual bonds of obligations among all members, and symbolized, defined, and publicly validated an individual's status.[17]

For the Nootka and Kwakiutl, the potlatches demonstrated – indeed, underlay – the social, political, and economic integrity of their societies. On the other hand, for White observers, these communal ceremonies came to represent all that was inherently wrong with Northwest Coast Indians, and the rival potlatches undoubtedly served to escalate these feelings. Citing Superintendent Israel Powell's report, the deputy superintendent general of Indian Affairs urged the adoption of a policy of vigorous and systematic civilization for the purposes of "elevating their condition," and "rendering their future intercourse with an inflowing white population."[18] The potlatch was attacked for its role in perpetuating the powerful influence of traditional leaders. Department officials realized that these positions of power were closely associated with one's capacity to redistribute material goods, particularly through the potlatches.[19] The potlatches also were criticized on moral grounds. The observations recorded by William Lomas, Cowichan Indian Agent, were repeated over the years as the official rationale for the repression of potlatches. In a statement forwarded to Ottawa, Lomas wrote: "A few years ago I thought that these dances were only foolish imitations of their old savage customs"; however, he later believed that they were the primary causes of the reduction in population, destitution among the aged, sickness and death among the children, indifference to education, and the neglect of farms and livestock during the winters.[20] Missionaries, who had to this point won few converts among the Northwest Coast Indians, welcomed the government's support on the issue of potlatching. Rather than depending solely on their own energies to eradicate traditional beliefs and customs, missionaries of the late nineteenth century were "becoming accustomed to look to governments for the enforcement of elements of their moral code. . . . They readily extended this logic to the outlawing of traditional religious practices."[21]

By the early 1880s, the lobby for federal intervention in prohibiting certain types of indigenous religious behaviour had gained momentum. In their reports, agents consistently claimed that the lack of Indian material progress was due to their participation in lengthy winter ceremonies and to the "giving away" of property. The impoverishing aspect of potlatching was often cited as the reason for the need to continue the rationing system, an expense that the Department hoped to eradicate. These observations were reinforced by missionaries who believed that potlatches not only obstructed material progress and spiritual enlightenment, but also were responsible for the impoverishment of Christian converts who were pressured to provide labour and goods to their kin in support of the potlatches and feasts.

Thus, in April 1883, a lobby consisting of missionaries and Indian converts, including several headmen from Fort Simpson, Kincolith, and Greenville, petitioned Superintendent Powell for legislation against potlatching. While Powell was of the opinion that resident Indian agents and local forms of law enforcement would eventually undermine the potlatches, he nevertheless felt that the enactment of federal legislation against the potlatch and other "reprehensible customs" would be supported by both non-Christian and Christian Indians.[22] Until the appropriate legislation could be initiated, the Deputy Superintendent General of Indian Affairs, Lawrence Vankoughnet, recommended that the Conservative government pass an order-in-council against potlatches. The first official federal proclamation issued to ban potlatching appeared in a Report of a Committee of the Honourable Privy Council on July 7, 1883.[23] Concern for the safety of the colonists played a major role in the implementation of the proclamation. Leader of the national Conservative government Sir John A. Macdonald pointed out that the most expedient policy with regard to the potlatch was one of prevention rather than confrontation, since the settlers were easily outnumbered by the indigenous population and the police force was inadequate.[24] Officials including the leader of the Liberal opposition, Edward Blake, hoped that practitioners in the potlatches would voluntarily obey the proclamation as a demonstration of their loyalty to the British Crown. However, the lobby for legislative intervention continued, and by April 19, 1884, an amendment to the Indian Act was passed stating that participation in potlatches and Tamanawas (medicine, or healing, ceremonies) was a misdemeanour:

> Every Indian or other person who engages in or assists in celebrating the Indian festival known as the "Potlach" or in the Indian dance known as the "Tamanawas" is guilty of a misdemeanour, and shall be liable to imprisonment for the term of not more than six nor less than two months in any gaol or other place of confinement; and any Indian or other person who encourages, either directly or indirectly an Indian or Indians to get up such a festival or dance, or to celebrate the same, or who shall assist in the celebration of same is guilty of a like offense, and shall be liable to the same punishment.[25]

The federal government's decision to interfere in potlatching was rationalized in economic terms. It was argued that potlatches were not conducive to fostering notions of "thrift" and "personal acquisitions" among Indians because they involved the giving away and destruction of property, including European goods, which had been acquired through the fur trade.[26] While the intent of previous legislation contained in the Indian Act was the protection of persons and property, this regulation was the first of several official enactments designed to eradicate traditional customs, in other words, to "protect the Indians from themselves."[27] The Potlatch Law, as it was termed, set a precedent in the use of legislation to forcibly transform the cultures of Indian societies. In the wider context of imperial Native policy, the regulation was in keeping with the western-European liberal humanitarian tradition that gave rise to similar forms of suppression in other parts of the British Empire.

Initial attempts to enforce the Potlatch Law proved difficult.[28] Administrators and missionaries disagreed over the phasing of the implementation of the legislation. While some, such as Israel Powell, the Superintendent of Indian Affairs in Victoria, favoured a gradual and lenient enforcement of the law, others argued that a conciliatory approach would weaken the effectiveness of the legislation. A few Indian agents were reluctant to enforce a law that they believed would foster resentment towards them as authority figures and seriously impede their administrative duties. There was also disagreement between the federal and provincial governments over their respective responsibilities for the costs and the staff required to implement the terms of the Indian Act. This problem was partially solved in 1889 when the provincial government agreed to build lock-up centres and to provide constables as their contribution to the enforcement of the Act. For most agents, the lack of workers, combined with the difficulty of monitoring potlatches in the numerous communities located along miles of rugged coastline and in the equally remote hinterland, made the task of implementing the law extraordinarily difficult. In addition to these administrative difficulties, opposition from several sources also undermined the strength of the Potlatch Law.

Criticism of the law came from European-Canadian commercial traders, who profited by the sale of goods for potlatches, and from non-Christian Indians. The reaction of the potlatching households assumed several forms. While some insisted on holding their potlatches in defiance of the law, others agreed to desist from potlatching once their households had been allowed to hold one more ceremony to pay back their debts. In fact, Indian Agent W.H. Lomas proposed that enforcement be postponed until "each band could be allowed a special licence to hold just one 'returning potlatch' with the distinct understanding that no additional property [should] be lent."[29] Such proposals were based on a commonly held misconception that the potlatch was merely a creditor-debtor relationship similar to that in Western capitalism. Lomas's recommendation clearly failed to take into consideration the notion that the very intent of the potlatch was to perpetuate a state of indebtedness in order to confirm and maintain a hierarchical lineage system. The "once and for all" potlatches would have worked to the disadvantage of all the hosted communities who would not have been permitted to reciprocate to change their statuses. Therefore, the prohibition against potlatches would have fostered a more rigid stratification among the ranked families. Government officials and missionaries opposed Lomas's approach on the grounds that such permissiveness would only encourage potlatching.

Several Indian petitioners demanded the repeal of the legislation, but their requests were not seriously considered by the Department. The first arrest under the Potlatch Law was made in 1889. This test case is historically important since it led to a re-evaluation of the wording of the law.[30] A Kwakiutl chief of the Mamalillikulla band by the name of Hamasak was convicted by the Alert Bay Indian Agent, R.H. Pidcock, and sentenced to six months' imprisonment.[31] The case was appealed after Hamasak's supporters applied for habeas corpus. Apparently Hamasak had also been committed for trial in Victoria and could not be tried for the same crime twice. In his report of the case, Chief Justice Sir Matthew Begbie suggested that the potlatch itself was not illegal unless "liquor, rioting, and debauchery" were involved, since there were laws in place to address these matters.[32] Begbie believed that until the Statute defined what specific acts constituted a potlatch, the defendant should not be expected to know when an offence had been committed. During the next six years, potlatching became an issue for public debate. A number of settlers feared that the use of force would lead to violence, resulting in an "Indian Mutiny on a smaller scale, the murder of outlying settlers, and useless shedding of innocent blood."[33] Arthur Vowell, the new superintendent at Victoria, and the majority of Indian agents expressed the opinion that many potlatches were harmless in nature and their celebration would eventually disappear under the influence of Christianity. In addition, it was felt that the implementation of any further regulations would be difficult to enforce in the Northwest Coast villages and would only serve to further antagonize potlatchers. For these reasons, Vowell cautioned the government against enacting further legislation related to ceremonial activities.[34] Indian agents such as R.H. Pidcock, who worked in an agency where potlatching traditions remained strong, particularly among the Kwakiutl, continued to lobby for legislation. In the end, the Potlatch Law was rewritten and was passed as an amendment to the Indian Act on July 22, 1895. The revised regulation was incorporated into Section 114.

This new piece of legislation contained a definition of illegal activities associated not only with the potlatch but also with other ceremonies. In their historical analysis of the 1895 amendment, historians Douglas Cole and Ira Chaikin suggest that the revision of the Potlatch Law occurred as a reaction to the objectionable features of prairie Indian ceremonies and not to the potlatches of the Northwest Coast.[35] In a brief accompanying the amendment, reference was made to objectionable activities practised by Indians residing in the prairie region:

As there is a similar dance to the Potlach celebrated by the Indian Bands in the North West Territories known as Omas-ko-sim-moo-wok or "grass dance" commonly known as "Giving away dance," and there are, no doubt, Indian celebrations of the same character elsewhere, all of which consist of the giving away, parting with or exchange of large quantities of personal effects sometimes all that participants own, it is considered better to prohibit all giving away festivals.[36]

Other reasons given for this prohibition were the "extravagance," the "loss of time" associated with the ceremonies, and a concern for the attendant "evils" that were believed to occur at such gatherings of large numbers of people.[37]

In a memorandum written by J.D. McLean, Secretary to the Minister of the Department of Indian Affairs, economic concerns appeared to be foremost in the minds of the framers of the amendment. The new legislation was viewed as a means to prevent the "impoverishment" of Indians who were judged to be incapable of controlling their improvidence at ceremonies.[38] Accordingly, the 1895 amendment to Section 114 (c. 35, 58–59 Vict.) of the Indian Act was reworded to read:

Every Indian or other person who engages in, or assists in celebrating or encourages either directly or indirectly another to celebrate, any Indian festival, dance or other ceremony of which the giving away or paying or giving back of money, goods, or articles of any sort forms a part, or is a feature, whether such gift of money, goods or articles takes place before, at, or after the celebration of the same, and every Indian or other person who engages or assists in any celebration or dance of which the wounding or mutilation of the dead or living body of any human being or animal forms a part or is a feature, is guilty of an indictable offence.[39]

The term of imprisonment for those convicted of these offences was set at a minimum of two months and a maximum of six months. It is significant that the amendment made the giving and receiving of prizes at agricultural exhibitions an exception to the giving-away prohibition.[40] The reference to the "wounding or mutilation of the dead or living body of a human being" was directed towards outlawing the performance of the Hamat'sa or "cannibalistic-related" rituals performed by certain Northwest Coast Indian religious societies. Animal sacrifices such as those practised by the Nutlam Society, who celebrated the power of the Wolf Spirit by ritually consuming dog flesh, were also forbidden.[41] Whether this latter section of the amendment was intended to terminate self-mortification at Sun Dances and the ritual offering and consumption of dogs at plains and woodland ceremonies cannot be determined from the available documentation.

The revised version of the Potlatch Law enabled the Indian agent to apprehend offenders and to initiate prosecutions. This power, however, was tempered by official departmental directives that urged agents to proceed with caution and discretion by "exhausting every means of bringing the Indians to abandon the custom, through moral suasion, before instituting prosecution."[42] There were two major reasons for this cautionary advice. First, government officials and missionaries were convinced that subsequent generations, schooled in Christian beliefs, would eventually forsake these "unprogressive" and "morally degrading" customs. Secondly, administrators were particularly reluctant to use force to suppress the larger public communal ceremonies where face-to-face confrontations could lead to violence. The cautionary statements issued by the Department to its field employees regarding the implementation of this new legislation reveals that officials were aware that they were intruding into a sensitive and highly valued area of people's privacy. There also was the fear that undue force would lead to reprisals that would endanger the lives and property of European-Canadian settlers.

Despite protests from Indian petitioners, Section 114 of the Indian Act was not repealed and was used to suppress similar forms of indigenous religious expression in the prairie region.[43] As in the case of the Northwest Coast experience, Victorian colonists believed that the forms of worship practised by prairie Indians were nothing more than pagan superstitions, having no divine basis or practical function other than to meet the self-serving ends of greedy medicine men.[44] Worship through dancing, singing to the accompaniment of drums, rattles, and whistles, the use of sacred materials such as medicine bundles, and the ceremonial application of facial and body paint were, at worst, considered to be forms of "devil worship." At best, these expressions of spirituality were mistaken as recreation or amusement rather than means of sacred communication. The apparent lack of permanent religious structures or recognizable written religious codes also contributed to the belief that indigenous religious systems were simplistic and meaningless.

Of all the ceremonies performed by the plains peoples, the Sun (or Thirst) Dance was the most publicized and misunderstood. As the largest outdoor summer gathering of the ceremonial year, the Sun Dance was highly visible to White observers because of the large number of participants, the construction of a sacred lodge, its relatively lengthy performance, and the fact that Whites were allowed to attend the ceremonies. Colonists were fascinated and awestruck by the ritualized "drama" of the ceremony while, at the same time, repelled by some of the rituals and the custom of "giving away" goods. The ritual of self-mortification, or "piercing" of the flesh especially, became the focus for descriptions contained in missionary reports, Department correspondence, and press coverage.

With few exceptions, missionaries openly condemned all forms of indigenous worship such as the Sun Dances, and made no attempt to integrate traditional practices into Christian forms. The performance of the Sun Dance was considered to be clear evidence of the destructive work of the "devil" among unenlightened "pagans," "heathens," and "savages." An example of this attitude can be found in a description of the Blackfoot Sun Dance written by Archdeacon William Tims:

I can hardly describe the feelings that came over me when first I made the acquaintance of the Blackfoot. . . . I arrived in the month of July when that great heathen festival, the Sun Dance, was in full swing – when every Indian on the reserve almost was, willing or unwilling, obliged to attend that gruesome spectacle, the torturing of the body and the tearing of the flesh, as the victim danced before the Medicine Pole to the beating of the tom-tom and weird singing of a thousand voices. The fantastic costumes of the people, the paint and feathers, the then to me foreign tongue, made my heart sink within me, and if I ever felt the hopelessness of a task set me to do it was then.[45]

Noted for his intolerance of indigenous cultures, Tims alienated the Blackfoot with his dogmatic approach to religious matters. As his biographer explained, Tims' ethnocentrism made it impossible for him to consider "the idea of compromise, either in salvaging some of the native symbols and customs or in tailoring Christian ceremonies to meet native needs."[46] His successor, Reverend H.W. Gibbon Stocken, while supportive of Blackfoot-initiated economic programs, was likewise intolerant of indigenous religions.

Other firsthand observations were equally ethnocentric. In 1881, a North-West Mounted Police officer described a Plains Cree Sun Dance at Cypress Hills as the "strangest sight" he had ever witnessed and noted that the ceremony's main purpose was to "make braves or warriors" through self-torture.[47] Even empathetic

Department employees such as Farm Instructor Robert Jefferson of the Battleford Agency associated the dance with barbaric practices, as indicated in his description of the dance: "With the gree[n] of the boughs [of the lodge] enlivened by vari-colored prints, the gifts of votaries, the grotesque get-up of the dancers, and the general barbaric surroundings, the scene is one to be long remembered."[48]

European Canadians had little understanding of the profound meaning of the Sun Dance. Their interpretations of the purposes of the ceremony were generally uninformed and simplistic. These misconceptions found their way into the scholarly literature and popular writings of the day. While some writers associated the Sun Dance with the propitiation of "bad spirits" or regarded it as a form of "devil worship," others claimed that it was an ancient form of "sun worship." Fasting, continuous dancing and singing, and the performance of other forms of self-mortification were thought to be extreme types of behaviour and similar in purpose to "initiation rites" imposed to test a man's courage in other non-Western societies. Therefore, most early commentators would have agreed with historian Amelia Paget in her description of the Sun Dance as "a time for the making of braves, or, rather, an opportunity for the test of courage and endurance."[49]

Some nineteenth-century observers, however, were astute enough to recognize other important aspects of this ceremony. For example, Paget wrote that the Plains Cree version of the ceremony was "primarily a thank-offering to the Great Spirit, Kichie Manitou, for the re-awakening of all nature after the silence of winter," for mourning the departed, and "a time of petitions through their Pow-wah-kuns [spirit helpers] for future blessings and love."[50] Indian Agent Robert Wilson contradicted the public notion of piercing when he wrote:

Much misunderstanding exists among white people regarding the nature of the torture rite. It is generally thought that its purpose is the making of braves, and much nonsense has been written in that line, such as "it admits the young man into the noble band of warriors." It admits him into nothing. Many of the bravest men and most noted fighters in the blackfoot tribes have never undergone the ordeal; while other individuals who could not be persuaded to face an armed foe, have gone through the so-called "brave-making" year after year, until their breasts carry a group of scars on each side.[51]

The ceremonial redistribution of goods (giveaways) at Sun Dances and other ceremonies was also misunderstood and condemned as an excessive form of behaviour. Much like the potlatches of the Northwest Coast, the giveaway was seen as an impediment to material progress and was used to explain the existence of poverty on reserves. Very rarely were giveaways equated with one of the major requisites of Christian behaviour, that is, the charitable distribution of one's goods for the benefit of the less fortunate.

Giveaways were consistently referred to in negative terms, and in the opinion of Department officials and missionaries the condition of Indian farmers would not improve unless the practice were eradicated. In 1889, Superintendent Colonel S.B. Steele of the MacLeod District claimed that the Sun Dance itself had degenerated into "a gathering merely for the purpose of using up presents of tea, tobacco, etc., given them by their agents or begged from their white neighbours."[52] This Sun Dance was probably no different from others celebrated at the time, but the police superintendent was obviously struck by the practice of distributing goods, particularly when commercial items and government rations were involved. One of the few exceptional observers of giveaways was Robert Jefferson, who openly criticized the Department's rationale for banning them, claiming that "inasmuch as what one gave, another got and the aggregate of possession remained the same."[53] In general, however, the custom of distributing material goods as spiritual offerings was condemned as intolerably wasteful, and there is at least one documented instance of local Catholic nuns taking cloth offerings from the Sun Dance lodge and recycling them into clothing for the school children.[54] Equally offensive to European Canadians were the payments of goods to healers and shamans for treatments that were denigrated as forms of "quackery" and charlatanism.

Ceremonial distribution practices also created havoc with the Department's efforts to account for its expenditures on material aid and to promote assimilation through individual material progress. Considered by Indian families to be communal property, government-issued food rations, cash, horses, and wagons were passed along through the kinship networks within and between communities. The practice was equally bothersome to missionaries such as Reverend John McDougall, who reflected the general consensus of Department employees and missionaries when he insisted that "tribal communism has always been hurtful to individuality, and without this no race of man can progress."[55]

During these early years of the implementation of Indian policy in the prairie region, the Department's objective was the total transformation of the individual person, and most administrators and missionaries believed that there was little of value in these cultures worth saving – even their religious beliefs. Therefore, the government's assimilation program was very supportive of the objectives of the Christian churches. The material and spiritual rewards of this combined effort on the part of "Christian politicians" and "political Christians" included "a new affection in the Indian heart, changed modes of thinking, a new religion of higher and nobler import, training for the intellect, surer means of support, and a more useful and happier life."[56] The author of this statement, the Reverend John Maclean, was one of the few missionaries who believed that the plains indigenous people were very spiritual in their world view. However, he believed that indigenous customs were too antagonistic and combative to be incorporated into Western society. For Maclean, any acceptance of traditional forms of worship and value systems on the part of "civilized" societies would be retrogressive, and for this reason he refused to consider the possibility of encouraging the survival of plains cultural systems.[57]

In keeping with the popular theory of social Darwinism, which was used to explain the evolution of societies, Maclean, among other Christian social reformers, attributed racial characteristics and religious behaviour to the environment and to subsistence patterns.[58] He postulated that the "place of residence begets its own peculiar kind of labor, which acts upon the mental power of the individual, and upon his morality."[59] According to this logic, the Indian cultures were indifferent to the Christian message not because they may have had their own religion, but rather for environmental, cultural, and historical reasons. For instance, Maclean noted that the Plains Cree were less interested in Christian "religious matters" than were their northern Swampy Cree neighbours. He attributed this indifference to the relatively greater abundance of provisions supplied by the buffalo, which made life comparatively easier for prairie peoples such as the Plains Cree, Blackfoot, Blood, and Peigan. He observed that the "excitement of the chase" was generally followed by "feasting," "revelry," "idleness," and "warring with neighboring tribes"; a lifeway, that is, "camp-life," that debased "the intellect and morals."[60] The increase in White colonists, mission sectarianism, and tribal conflicts only served to exacerbate their debased lot in life. That the process of cultural transformation would exact a high price in Indian lives was accepted by the missionaries as a necessary evil. As Maclean explains, "Despondency takes possession of their hearts, the oppressive feeling that they are a conquered race presses heavily upon them, and, like the wild caged birds, they sicken and die."[61]

Representations of Plains Indians as barbaric and unprogressive became part of the consciousness of Canadians. Exhibitions such as the Wild West shows dramatized the military subjugation of "Plains Indians" by the Whites – visually re-affirming for White audiences the belief in the inferiority of indigenous peoples and the inevitable triumph of "civilization" over "barbarism." For Indian participants, the display of traditional outfits, housing, beadwork, and horsemanship was a way to communicate a pride in their culture, but these demonstrations also served to reinforce European-Canadian notions of the "barbaric nature" of indigenous peoples. Similarly, in Canadian museums, the material culture of the Plains Indians was displayed within a context of an evolutionary scheme that provided evidence to the public that Indian societies were less developed than their own. Most exhibits depicted Plains peoples through popularized warrior imagery achieved by displaying "fierce or stoic-looking mannequins surrounded by their war paraphernalia such as lances, clubs, knives, shields, bows and arrows, and scalp locks."[62]

Sacred materials, generally exhibited out of context and with little or no explanation, were reduced to exotic curios, leaving the uninformed public to project a fantasized opinion on the possible functions of such items. These popularized stereotyped treatments of Plains Indian cultures confirmed the validity of the concept of the social theory of the day that labelled Indian cultures "primitive" and contributed to public support for the government's assimilation programs.

Another major source of popularized negative imagery was the missionary whose fundraising lecture tours and published reports served to rally support for the repression of indigenous religious expression. For example, in 1896, Monseigneur Albert Pascal, Vicar-Apostolic of Saskatchewan, reported that "western Indians [were] very ferocious and blood thirsty . . . the cruel tortures of the War Dance or Sun Dance being evident of their state of savagery."[63] Missionary writings such as the works of John Maclean and John McDougall contained similar descriptions of the Sun Dances.[64]

One other major source of information on ceremonies was the newspaper. Reports of ceremonies and dances performed at stampedes appeared in both eastern and western publications. Highly sensationalized descriptions were guaranteed to win the attention of readers and to satisfy their curiosity for the exotic. Media coverage served to confirm suspicions regarding the state of savagery existing in western Canada. In 1883, *The Regina Leader* headlined a story about a Sun Dance held in the Broadview area, "Frightful Cruelties at the Manufacture of Braves: A Sun Dance, Revolting Scenes."[65] An eastern newspaper, the *Ottawa Evening Journal,* in 1896 claimed that Indians were dying as a result of their religious practices. The accompanying headline read, "Indians Perishing: Dying from the Practices of their Heathen Religion," and was followed by a description of a "war dance" that was claimed to have occurred twice a year, and during which participants were "cruelly tortured."[66] In its coverage of an 1894 Sun Dance attended by some 1,000 people from the Piapot, Muscowpetung, and Pasqua reserves, *The Regina Leader* reported that, while no "making of the braves" (piercing) had occurred, still "the savage was there in all his glory, painted in vermillion and bedecked with feathers, gaudy coloured cloth, in pristine splendour."[67]

Finally, the involvement of certain plains groups in the Saskatchewan Uprising of 1885 and rumours of the spread of the messianic Ghost Dance religion in the early 1890s heightened the European-Canadian intolerance of indigenous forms of religious expression.[68] After the Sioux Outbreak of 1890 and the Battle of Wounded Knee in the United States, Canadian officials, police, and settlers cast a wary eye in the direction of Dakota communities. Indian agents reported that a Sioux Dance was one of the war dances of the Plains Cree and had been observed at Poundmaker, Sweet Grass, and Thunderchild reserves. Concern was expressed over the effect of the dance on Indian farmers, and one report claimed that Indians worked themselves into "a complete frenzy" at these dances and consequently were unfit for work for a period of time.[69] While it is possible that the authorities associated this dance with the Ghost Dance movement, they would have been wrong. In his description of the Sioux Dance performed by the Plains Cree, anthropologist David Mandelbaum stated that the dance was often held during Pow-wows and was not directed against White colonists.[70] However, because the dancers pantomimed "scouting, aiming, shooting, and scalping," it is understandable that White observers would have become alarmed by the content.[71]

The shift in European-Canadian attitudes towards Plains Indian societies after the Saskatchewan Uprising of 1885 is significant. Before 1885, the press tended to portray Indians as "nuisances," "vagrants," "docile and harmless beings," or "members of a dying race," whereas, after the Uprising, they were viewed as a threat to the property and lives of White settlers.[72] Consequently, news reporters not only supported the efforts to civilize Indians but also expected the Department to take measures to guarantee the safety of White communities.[73]

Large communal ceremonies such as the Sun Dances were suspect as "hot beds" for civil disorder. In part, this distrust of communal ceremonies resulted from the political nature of the Sun Dance held near the Little Pine and Poundmaker reserves on the eve of the Saskatchewan Uprising of 1885. Rather than being mere social or recreational gatherings, these tribal ceremonies were now perceived as having a political function. As such, they were seen as forums for the expression of dissatisfaction with government policy. They obviously had the potential to mobilize large numbers of people who otherwise would have assembled in smaller gatherings. Farm Instructor Robert Jefferson observed that the Plains Cree Sun Dance was held annually until the year of the Rebellion of 1885 but was opposed by authorities "since it brought the Indians together, and increased the chances of massed insubordination."[74] White observers who had attended the Sun Dances had heard not only the recounting of sacred teachings and personal histories but also the glorification of past war records and impassioned criticisms of government policies. Father Joseph Hugonnard, Principal of the Qu'Appelle Industrial School, warned administrators about the political aspect of ceremonies when he drew a connection between the "regression" of school children from "civilizing" influences and the ceremonies "where speeches usually against those in authority over them were one of the main features."[75]

Attendance at ceremonies was also opposed because it interfered with government programs for Indian agriculture. Ceremonial time and space were traditionally determined by seasonal hunting, fishing, and gathering cycles. These patterns were incongruent with the agricultural cycle, the need to be permanently located on farms, and the European-Canadian concept of a six-day work week with a single day of religious observance on Sunday. Furthermore, some ceremonies were not necessarily localized affairs (as in the case of community church worship), and participants were often required to travel considerable distances off reserves to attend ceremonies at designated sacred sites.

These ceremonies also involved lengthy periods of time ranging from a few days to a number of weeks. According to Department officials and missionaries, indigenous religious cycles of movement precluded the successful transition to an agricultural economy based on a permanent settlement pattern and the constant care of property. In the opinion of one Indian agent, Hayter Reed of the Battleford area, Indians would be forced to abandon their "heathenish rites and ceremonies" once they adopted farming practices and needed the time to tend to their fields.[76] The conflict between ceremonial and agricultural time was also raised by Father Hugonnard in 1903:

> I know a case this Fall where Indians have been called and went to these dances in the midst of harvest, leaving their binders standing idle in the fields when their surrounding white neighbours were cutting night and day; they commenced dancing at noon, and in consequence of their neglect of work part of their crop was frozen.
>
> It is common for Indians to travel from fifty to a hundred miles the round trip to attend these dances, neglecting their stock during the two or three days they are absent from home.[77]

Yet another reason for the suppression of ceremonies was their role in the transmission and perpetuation of indigenous cultures. Ceremonial and ritual leaders were held directly responsible for undermining the training received by children in the schools. The powerful influence that ceremonies had on children was a particular concern of one teacher, Austin McKitrick, who described at some length the emulative behaviour of his young charges after they had returned from a Sun Dance on the Piapot Reserve.[78] Instead of playing at "gopher feasts" or hide-and-seek and tag, the children acted out the behaviour that they had witnessed at the Sun Dance:

> They came to us for pins and thread or twine. They fixed up a small dancing pavilion of slender trees with one strong pole. They bent the pins to be stuck through the flesh of their little breasts and tied by string to the centre pole. They asked us to come and watch them dance as they drummed on an old tin . . . oil can for music. Round and round, and to and fro, they danced to the hi-yi song, then with a miniature yell the boy dancers broke out the little piece of flesh where the pin had caught under the skin and a small drop of blood oozed out. . . . In mixed Cree and English they insisted that the sun dance was the right and good way to worship the Great Spirit and that our way of saying "Our Father which art in Heaven" was no good.[79]

Although Department administrators, Indian agents, and missionaries shared the conviction that indigenous cultural practices should be discouraged, there were differences of opinion as to how this should occur. The use of force was the most contentious issue. In 1889, Father Albert Lacombe denounced the Sun Dance as "that ugly feast" and "barbarian show," which interfered with agricultural pursuits, and he urged the minister of Indian Affairs, in his capacity as "the friend and tutor of the Indians," to "put a stop" to the ceremony.[80] The Deputy Superintendent of Indian Affairs, Lawrence Vankoughnet, supported Lacombe's request in a report to Indian Commissioner Edgar Dewdney, wherein he insisted, "The time has now arrived when the great obstacle to the civilization and advancement of the Indians, viz. the Sun Dance, should be abolished by statutory enactment."[81] Similarly, Reverend Tims, then stationed at Gleichen, Alberta, believed that his Indian charges were coerced into attending the Sun Dances. Tims asked Commissioner Hayter Reed to provide protection for those who chose not to attend the ceremony. Reed's response to Tims in 1891 indicated the future direction of policy decisions in the matter of ceremonial repression. The commissioner pointed out that the Indians had been informed to refrain from "making braves" and that agents were attempting to stop all dances. There were indications, he said, that dancing had ceased in many areas as a result of pressure from the agents.[82]

Not all objectors to indigenous religious practices, however, condoned the legislation and use of force. Methodist minister Reverend John Maclean wrote that the process of civilizing Indians did not mean the "compulsory acceptance" of Western culture, but rather the "transformation of the whole man" to be achieved by "undermining the customs of the Indians by giving them a superior religion, grander and purer customs, and a nobler civilization."[83]

There is evidence for only one attempt to prosecute Sun Dance celebrants under the terms of the original Potlatch Law of 1884. In 1893, the Hobbema Indian Agent, D.L. Clink, reported that a Sun Dance lodge had been destroyed and that ritual leaders were arrested. The ceremony had been held in a "Half-breed" settlement on the Battle River and involved people from Hobbema, Saddle Lake, and Stoney Plains, and a number of "Half-Breeds."[84] The Indian agent had been under the impression that the potlatch and the Sun Dance were essentially identical ceremonies. At this time, Clink was advised by his superiors that Section 114 of the Indian Act was not applicable and was warned to exercise "extreme caution" in making arrests in connection with this regulation.[85]

The integration of Indians into Canadian society was an objective shared by both the federal government and Christian missionaries. This goal clearly implied the transformation of indigenous peoples in order to facilitate their participation in a new socio-economic order based upon Western capitalism, the Christian religion, and European-Canadian values and behaviour. This transition entailed the acceptance of a lifeway in which material goods and property were the "measures of a man's worth" and prerequisites for citizenship status.[86] It was a system in which an individual's success could be achieved only through the disciplined application of Western notions of self-reliance, self-sufficiency, industry, temperance, and thrift.

The suppression of indigenous cultural systems was part of a larger design for the creation of a Canadian social order, an order firmly grounded in the doctrine of uniform social evolution rather than in a concept of political and cultural pluralism. Convinced of the ability of non-Western peoples to attain and enjoy the benefits of "civilization," Victorians undertook to destroy the cultural underpinnings of prairie Indian societies. The coincident depletion of bison herds and other game, and the move by eastern Canada to annex the western territories, created a fertile ground for the application of these tenets by missionaries.

Regulating Sun Dances and Giveaways: 1896 to 1914

5

Section 114 of the Indian Act had been introduced only in 1895, but its intentions had already been foreshadowed by an Indian agent's actions in the Battle River Sun Dance incident of 1893. Those who had been arrested in connection with holding Accasianent's Sun Dance had been released with a reprimand, and the ceremonial lodge had been torn down by the authorities.[1] In his 1895 annual report, Assistant Indian Commissioner A.E. Forget issued his concern that some reserves in the central and eastern regions of the Territories were returning "to the observance of their ancient rite of sun-dancing, accompanied, to a limited extent, by the practice of making 'braves' and its concomitant acts of torture."[2] An attempt to hold a Sun Dance at Touchwood Hills had been prevented, and only the Piapot Reserve had been able to hold its ceremony.[3] With the exception of a "mild type" of Sun Dance held in the western reserves, no others were reported.

With the passage of Section 114, the repression of ceremonial life became an integral part of the implementation of Indian policy in the prairie region. While formulation of policy and decision-making were the responsibilities of Department of Indian Affairs officials in Ottawa, the implementation of the Indian Act fell to the commissioner, Indian agents, and farm instructors. The distance from Ottawa and the need to react quickly to changing local situations provided the commissioner with some degree of latitude in carrying out departmental instructions. Moreover, the commissioner's office was the channel through which Ottawa received information regarding the conditions on reserves and Indian reactions to government programs. In general, politicians believed that the commissioner was in the best position to determine Indian policy since he dealt directly with Indians. The commissioner communicated his observations to his superiors in Ottawa on a regular basis through correspondence and annual reports. On occasion, the commissioner also introduced proposals for amendments to the Indian Act itself. Most important, he played a major role in determining how the Indian Act regulations were interpreted and to what degree they would be administered.

The commissioner based his decisions not only on his own observations but also on regular reports received from agency personnel, especially the Indian agent. It was the Indian agent who had the most contact with local people and was expected to implement government policy and programs on a day-to-day basis. His responsibilities included supervising Indian schools, distributing annuities and food rations, providing guidance for agricultural development, supplying medical aid, monitoring Indian and European-Canadian movements and behaviour on and off reserves, collecting statistical information, preparing budgets and reports, dispensing justice, and reporting particular problems to supervisors.[4] Within this broad mandate, Indian agents were expected to enforce the provisions of the Indian Act.

Although the Indian agent enjoyed a certain degree of discretionary power in the daily administration of reserves, he was obliged to refer judgements on any question of policy to the commissioner. In general, agents were expected to enforce the terms of the Indian Act with "firmness," "moderation," and "good judgement."[5] The extent to which these prerequisites of Indian management were operative depended upon the particular agent's political convictions, racial attitudes, field experience, personality, and professional commitment to the Department's objectives. These directives were especially relevant to enforcing the terms of Section 114. Indian agents were initially advised to proceed gradually, allowing time for the passing away of the older generation and for the assimilation programs to take effect. Legal sanctions were to be used to terminate only the "worst features" of the ceremonial life.[6]

In recognition of the sensitive nature of suppressing a highly valued and private aspect of indigenous life, the Department suggested the use of a pragmatic approach towards the prosecution of offenders. And, while agents were not expected to turn a blind eye to designated "illegal" activities, they were warned against the use of either force or imprisonment to discourage practitioners. This policy was spelled out in a directive issued by Indian Commissioner Frederick Paget to Agent J.A. Markle, who had attempted to prevent the occurrence of a Sun Dance on the Waywayseecappo Reserve in Manitoba in 1896. At that time, Paget advised Markle:

(i) to be guided in deciding what action you will take in the matter entirely by the circumstances and the nature and the extent of the opposition likely to be put forth should anything approaching force be resorted to . . . ;

(ii) the law be not resorted to until every other method of dissuading the Indians from holding the dance, has been tried and failed.[7]

According to these official guidelines, the repression of ceremonial life was left to the discretion of the Indian agent and was largely dependent upon his abilities to influence his charges. In short, the policy was ambiguous.

There was also some question as to whether the monitoring of ceremonies fell within the jurisdiction of the Indian agents. Some agents expressed the view that the spiritual well-being of unconverted Indians was more appropriately the concern of the churches. For example, after failing to prevent the File Hills Cree from holding their Sun Dance in 1896, a frustrated Indian agent, A. McNeill, wrote to the commissioner that although he would do his utmost to prevent the dance from being held, in his opinion the abolition of "heathenish customs" was dependent upon the Christian conversion of Indians, which was "more within the province of the missionaries than the Agents."[8] In this instance, McNeill succeeded in persuading the ceremonial sponsor, Cheepoostatin, to refrain from holding the dance. Participants from other reserves already camped on the ceremonial grounds, including nine lodges of Assiniboin and one lodge from Piapot's reserve, were then escorted back to their homes by the North-West Mounted Police. While no confrontation had occurred, a deliberate show of force from the police had nevertheless been necessary to disperse the celebrants. As McNeill commented, "Had it not been for their presence I no doubt would have failed to stop the dance, as the Indians were quite determined to have it."[9]

Department officials were naïve in expecting that personal suasion could stop the ceremonies. Many Indian agents, as representatives of an alien and civil authority, were not well received on reserves. Furthermore, even well-liked Department employees such as Farm Instructor Robert Jefferson soon discovered that talk was futile. His description of his own endeavours to undermine the influence of "medicine men" is revealing:

I – from a height, of course – have tried every way to combat these foolish beliefs, especially the blind acceptance of impudent bluffers at their self valuation. I have tried argument, I have tried ridicule; I have tried pity and I have tried disgust; and the result has been to undermine rather the Indian's estimate of my perspicacity than the faiths that have been accepted without question by generations of his forefathers. Time probably, and the rubbing against the white man are the only things that will effect change.[10]

Department officials generally attributed the ineffectiveness of the policy of persuasion to the inability of individual agents to exert their authority. When a number of celebrants from the Swan River, Crooked Lakes, File Hills, and Touchwood agencies had gathered at Yorkton for a Sun Dance in 1898, J.D. McLean, Secretary to the Department, observed: "It seems somewhat strange that the Agents concerned do not at this date possess sufficient influence and control over their

Indian charges to prevent such a retrograde step."[11] The number of Indian representatives who had deliberately by-passed the local bureaucracy to petition Ottawa officials was yet another indication that Indian agents had not yet firmly established their credibility on reserves. A petition sent to Ottawa by Chief Thunderchild and Charles Fineday of the Battleford Agency for permission to hold a Sun Dance in 1907 illustrates their agent's lack of authority. The assistant Indian commissioner was clearly perturbed that the request had been sent directly to Ottawa, and advised that, "if the Indians insist upon reference to higher authority, it is for the Agent to write himself and not to have the Indians communicate direct."[12] The assistant commissioner suggested that the petition would never have been sent if the Indian agent had followed instructions and had explained "very clearly and forcibly" that the Department was against the performance of such dances.[13] The persistence of ceremonial life and the problems encountered in discouraging participation led the Department to consider other methods of suppression that went beyond the prohibitions specified in Section 114.

According to the wording of Section 114, only specific types of religious expression were illegal. Ceremonies in general, including the Sun Dance, were not prohibited by the Act. As Indian Commissioner David Laird counselled Indian Agent James Wilson of the Blackfoot Agency, those Sun Dances that had been modified through the deletion of objectionable features did not fall under the provisions of the Act.[14] Provided that Sun Dance ceremonies were performed without the ritual of "piercing" or giveaways, the Indian Act could not be invoked.

These limitations on the application of Section 114 also affected the Department's efforts to use the police to monitor ceremonial activities. For example, in 1900, Bull Shield, Calf Shirt, and Eagle Ribs from Alberta received permission from the local police detachment at Fort Macleod to hold a Blood Sun Dance. This police "interference" was viewed as a serious challenge to the Indian Department's authority. The Agent, James Wilson, informed the headmen that the Indian Department rather than the police had jurisdiction over Indian affairs and that the Department was the "only one able to give them instructions and . . . Indian agents were appointed for the purpose of letting them know the law."[15] This problem of overlapping jurisdiction, which partly arose from the historical protective relationship that had developed between the police and Indian peoples, was apparently resolved in 1901. In an exchange of correspondence between Police Comptroller Fred White and the Indian Department, it was agreed that police officers would not discuss or become involved in the internal matters of reserves unless formally requested to do so. White emphasized that the North-West Mounted Police would not take a position on dances and would only disperse those gatherings where the law had been clearly violated.[16] He requested that the Indian Department clarify which ceremonies and dances were permissible.

Therefore, in 1900, the Gleichen detachment in Alberta provided a patrol "night and day" to prevent the Blackfoot and their Cree neighbours from Battleford and Bear Hills from holding a Sun Dance at which "three braves" were to be made (by piercing).[17] Some ten years later, Pyakwutch (Clean Earth, or Harry Brown) and Tootoosis from the Poundmaker Reserve requested permission to hold a Sun Dance from the police officer stationed in Cutknife. The officer received instructions from Ottawa to forbid the ceremony, but nevertheless informed Pyakwutch and Tootoosis that they could have the ceremony between the Poundmaker and Little Pine reserves.[18] In this manner the celebrants could not be arrested for trespassing on one another's reserve. Some police officials opposed any intervention in ceremonies. Colonel James Macleod, Commissioner of the North-West Mounted Police, had delivered a "scathing rebuff" to members of the force for arresting Sun Dance celebrants and insisted that, despite the "barbaric" nature of the ceremony, "what they had done was akin to making an arrest in a church."[19]

The cooperation of the police was essential if the strategy of "persuasion and moderation" was to be effective in reducing the occurrence of ceremonies. Even if officers refused to make arrests, their very presence during ceremonies was often sufficient to reinforce the Indian agent's authority. Towards this end, the police were frequently called upon to investigate "suspect" ceremonies. The arrival of the Indian agent accompanied by members of the local police detachment not only served to interrupt proceedings, but also intimidated participants. People were interrogated about the details of the rituals, and off-reserve "trespassers" were identified. In some instances the Sun Dances were supervised by the police, and in this way the Department was able to discourage the performance of objectionable rituals. Occasionally, celebrants were also persuaded to discontinue the ceremony and return to their homes.[20]

In addition to monitoring ceremonies, the Department adopted other measures to discourage people from attending Sun Dances, to undermine ritual leadership, and to dismantle the ceremonial complex itself. The pass system, for instance, limited off-reserve movement; it was used to restrict participation in ceremonies held away from the home reserve and to disperse celebrants who had not obtained a pass to travel off their reserves. These certificates of travel (passes), were issued by the Indian agents and were intended to control "troublemakers" as indicated by a notation on the pass for permission to bear firearms.

While the pass system was introduced to control Indian crossings over the international border, to protect settlers' property, and to deal with problems related to the alcohol trade and prostitution, it was also seen as an effective means to discourage attendance at Sun Dances.[21] Following the Saskatchewan Uprising of 1885, Hayter Reed, then Assistant Indian Commissioner for the North-West Territories, informed his superior, Edgar Dewdney, that all people in the Battleford area would continue to require passes. Even though he knew that this action was not supported by legislation, Reed advised: "We must do many things which can only be supported by common sense and by what may be for the general good."[22] Not everyone agreed with what was in effect a policy of containment. Colonel A.G. Irvine, the Commissioner of the North-West Mounted Police, contended that the enforcement of the pass system was a breach of treaty rights since treaty provisions neither compelled Indians to live on reserves, nor deprived them of the freedom to travel for "legitimate hunting and trading purposes."[23]

After 1885, the system was also used to prevent Indian farmers from leaving their reserves, particularly during the agricultural season. In 1889, travel related to family visits to other reserves, including trips to American reservations, was similarly scrutinized. The system was also employed to discourage frequent journeys made by parents to visit their children in residential schools. The general official attitude towards the off-reserve socializing with relatives and friends was aptly summarized by Indian Agent James Wilson of the Blood Agency in 1902, who stated that "the less visiting an Indian does the better. It makes them restless and unsettled, and they no sooner return from one trip than they start upon another."[24] From the Department's perspective, the larger the gathering of people, the greater potential there was for the development of a unified movement against unpopular regulations. As a case in point, the presence of several off-reserve Assiniboin and Piapot's Cree followers at a ceremony in File Hills prevented the agent from convincing people to forego their Sun Dance. In his report, Indian Agent A. McNeill wrote that the File Hills Cree appeared to be "more defiant and determined" upon the arrival of off-reserve celebrants, and that he would have been able to stop the ceremony if the "strangers" had not been there for support.[25]

The pass system was used to repress Indian ceremonies in the Battleford area until at least 1918 and was generally implemented in the Treaty Four and Treaty Six regions perhaps as late as the mid-1930s.[26] The documentary record on this practice is scanty, but sufficient hints are available in Department correspondence and in Indian oral testimonies to sustain such a conclusion. Verification of the use of the pass system is made more difficult by the fact that some agents confused it with the issuing of permits. As a mechanism for regulating people's movements, the system provided the Department with yet another means to undermine "legal" ceremonies. The major shortcoming of this form of social control was that legitimate "on-reserve" ceremonial attendance could not be restricted. By insulating the reserve populations from one another, however, the use of passes did curtail contacts between kinship groups and served to weaken social, economic, and political ties. Still another common method for controlling ceremonial attendance was the use of trespass regulations contained in the Indian Act (c. 30, 54–55 Vict.).[27]

The Department adopted several other tactics to discourage ceremonial practices. The Giveaway Clause of Section 114 could also be used to undermine the customary method of transferring spiritual knowledge, responsibilities, and associated ritual objects from one ritualist to another. In 1898, the Blood Chief, Red Crow, became involved in a confrontation with authorities on this issue. Although Red Crow had cooperated with the government by encouraging his people to practise agriculture and to send their children to White schools, he was nevertheless determined that indigenous religious practices should continue without interference.[28] When Red Crow became ill, his wife, Singing Before, made a sacred vow to assume the leadership of the Motokix Society (a sacred women's society) from Heavy Shield's wife. In return for the transfer of these spiritual responsibilities, specialized knowledge, and a medicine bundle containing sacred objects, Singing Before was required by customary law to give away fifteen horses. According to Section 114, however, the exchange of goods was being performed within the context of a ceremony. If the exchange did not occur, on the other hand, Singing Before would be unable to assume the leadership of the Motokix Society. Although the transfer had been prohibited by the Indian agent, Superintendent of Police R.B. Deane intervened to permit the exchange on the condition that only horses would be involved in the transaction and that no Sun Dance would accompany the ritual.[29]

In a second case, Heavy Shield's wife made a vow on her deathbed to become a member of the Medicine Pipe Society and wished to purchase a holy medicine pipe from Red Crow's wife.[30] The woman had recovered and, in order to fulfill the vow, four distinct dances over an eleven-day period had to be performed. Unfortunately, arrangements for the transfer of the medicine pipe were being made at haying time, and Indian Agent Wilson arrested Running Wolf, Big Rib, and White Man's Wife for holding the Medicine Pipe Ceremony.[31] In this instance, Wilson did not press charges but nevertheless expressed his opinion that such ceremonies should be discouraged, especially with the return of greater numbers of school children to their home reserves. For their part, those arrested agreed to refrain from requesting more Sun Dances and to exchange only the required amount of property needed for the transfer of the pipe.

Other Blood leaders also confronted their agent over the Sun Dance when their use of beef tongues (originally bison tongues) for ritual food was restricted. During the Blood version of the Sun Dance, whole beef tongues were ritually cut by a Holy

Woman who then distributed the pieces to the dancers. Realizing that whole tongues were required for this ritual, Indian Agent Wilson ordered that all the tongues given to the Blood as part of their beef rations be cut in half. As a result, no Sun Dance was held for three years, and the year 1895 was remembered in Blood winter counts as the time "Indian Agent James Wilson stopped the Sun Dance Lodge."[32] Eventually, Wilson's strategy was foiled by Blood scouts working for the North-West Mounted Police, who received whole tongues for their rations and passed these on to ceremonial leaders. Furthermore, Blood threats to slaughter government cattle herds to procure the necessary tongues finally curtailed Wilson's efforts.[33]

The Plains Cree experienced similar types of interference. By the late nineteenth century, commercial foods, tobacco, clothing, metal goods, and other articles were important components of ceremonial offerings and of redistributive activities. The use of material goods in this manner was adamantly opposed by the Department because it not only was considered wasteful, but it also sustained the indigenous economy and political structure. In addition to the more general prohibition of the slaughter of government-issued cattle for ceremonial food redistribution, there is at least one documented case of government intervention in the exchange of commercial goods related to ceremonies. In 1895, Agent E. Yeomans claimed that untimely credit arrangements between the Hudson's Bay Company and the Touchwood Hills Cree interfered with his attempts to suppress the Sun Dance. Yeoman's superior, Hayter Reed, wrote on his behalf to the Company's commissioner, pointing out that the Hudson's Bay Company officer in charge of the Touchwood Hills post was promoting the performance of the Sun Dance by allowing Indians to purchase goods and by even providing them with "presents" to be used in the ceremony.[34] The officer, Mr. Cooper, was accused of supplying the Cree with the red cloth used as one of the major offerings in the Sun Dance Lodge, and of donating "gifts" such as flour, which was either redistributed in its raw state or used as a staple in the large communal meals. Ultimately, Cooper was fined for supplying liquor to the Cree, but the Company refused to be pressured into withdrawing its support for its Indian clientele or for Cooper. Clearly, the Company wished to continue its traditional pattern of provisioning the Plains Cree and other prairie groups. Donations of goods at ceremonial time were important expressions of the Company's good will and a formal acknowledgement of a trading partnership.

Another method used by the Department to restrict Indian access to material goods for ceremonies was the withholding of agency food rations. This strategy, however, was not deemed wise, for, as Indian Agent Yeomans of the Peigan Agency reported, the "simple withholding of rations" would not deter determined followers of the Sun Dance, and, moreover, he would not support the withdrawal of rations from the "deserving and self-supporting."[35]

Still another form of interference in indigenous ceremonial traditions was the disturbance of sacred offerings and ceremonial lodges. According to one report, Roman Catholic nuns had removed sacred cloth offerings from abandoned Sun Dance poles and had recycled the material to make clothing for school children.[36] Customary sacred law required that these cloth offerings to the Creator be left to the elements. Therefore, such use of sacred cloth would have been sacrilegious to Indians. This demonstration of religious insensitivity only served to indicate to indigenous traditional religious leaders that their counterparts in the Christian religious tradition, like the Department's administrators, had little understanding of, or tolerance for, their customs. In addition to cases where Sun Dance lodges were dismantled, some reserves had been prevented from building traditional dance houses or were ordered to dismantle such structures. The Dakota of the Standing Buffalo Reserve in Saskatchewan were instructed by their new Indian agent, William Graham, to destroy their dance lodge in 1901.[37]

The Indian Department regarded conservative traditional ritual leaders as major impediments to the assimilation process. Consequently, officials were committed to using every possible means to divest them of their spiritual and secular power. Towards this end, the Department proceeded with the arrest and imprisonment of some prominent leaders and took away the official status of others. Due to the absence of local records in the existing Department files, the frequency of arrests and the number of convictions are difficult to determine. In his ethnography of the Plains Cree, Mandelbaum noted that "many Cree had been sent to jail every year for participating in the [Sun Dance] ceremony."[38] Those cases that have been recorded are worthy of attention in order to clarify the use of Section 114 and the circumstances surrounding the arrests and convictions.

The summer of 1895 witnessed not only the adoption of Section 114 but also one of the first recorded arrests among the Saskatchewan Cree when Indian Agent Wright succeeded in stopping a ceremony in progress in the Touchwood Hills area.[39] One individual from Touchwood, named Matoose, was arrested, retained in custody for five days with a $200 surety, and "bound to keep the peace" for three months for "inciting the Indians to commit a breach of peace."[40] Although the agent's actions were commended by his superior, Hayter Reed, the wisdom of interfering in the ceremony after it had started was seriously questioned.[41] The issue of employing extreme measures, that is, arrests and convictions, was also raised in 1896. In that year, Kah-pee-cha-pees of the Ochapowace Band in Saskatchewan was arrested and sentenced to two months of hard labour for sponsoring a Sun Dance. After consultation with the superintendent of Indian Affairs, Commissioner Hayter Reed concluded that the Indian agent had exceeded his jurisdiction as specified in Section 114.[42] In the commissioner's opinion, the punishment was excessive; nevertheless, he upheld the conviction, arguing that the incarceration of Kah-pee-cha-pees would serve as a warning to other Sun Dance sponsors. Moreover, he contended that the sentence would not in any way harm the accused and suggested that the incarcerated might "be benefitted" by the experience.[43]

In the case of Kah-pee-cha-pees's conviction, the agent had taken it upon himself to act as an *ex officio* justice of the peace by using his authority to evaluate the infraction. Such power was not within the agent's mandate. In his defence of the accused, a local police officer reported that Kah-pee-cha-pees "looked upon this as a religious matter" and insisted that "God himself had given him these Rites with a view of saving his own Soul."[44] For Kah-pee-cha-pees, his only crime was expressing his freedom to worship.

The published recollections of Abel Watetch, a nephew of Chief Piapot, provide a rare detailed account of the circumstances surrounding the arrest and incarceration of this renowned headman.[45] His reputation for performing powerful Sun Dances prompted some twenty young men to approach Piapot in the late 1890s with a request to arrange a piercing ritual. Piapot agreed to include the ritual in his Rain Dance (a version of the Sun Dance), and the men were pierced by a medicine man who had the spiritual prerogative to perform the ritual. The Indian Department authorities were informed about the illegal ritual, and, despite his age, Piapot was arrested, convicted, and imprisoned in Regina. It is significant that the official charge was not recorded as an infraction of Section 114; rather, the notice outside Piapot's cell stated that he had been arrested for "drinking." Apparently Piapot was unaware of this charge until he was visited by Harry Ball, a young schoolboy from the Piapot Reserve who was attending the Presbyterian Industrial College in Regina at the time. Upon hearing the official indictment, Piapot defended himself to the young student by stating that he never drank and that he knew that he was convicted "because of the Rain Dance and the piercing of the boys."[46]

Piapot's age and his some fifty years of leadership did not prevent the Department from removing him from his position as chief. In addition, his role in persuading Indian leaders in the southeastern section of the Northwest Territories to remain loyal to the British Crown during the Saskatchewan Uprising of 1885 was not considered sufficient reason for leniency. His biographer, Abel Watetch, notes that the Department's treatment of Piapot was a traumatic experience for both the leader and his followers, and "it broke the old man's spirit. He returned to the reserve, humiliated and sad."[47] In protest, members of the Piapot Reserve refused to elect another chief until after Piapot's death.

As in the case of Kah-pee-cha-pees, the general issue was the freedom of religious expression. For the Canadian government and missionaries to disapprove of indigenous forms of religious expression and presume to interfere in spiritual matters to the point of criminalizing their forms of worship was inconceivable to the various Indian nations. Piapot's own religious convictions and his skillful attempts to reason with the Department authorities are revealed in his conversation with the Assistant Indian Commissioner, A.E. Forget:

Forget: Ask him, Peter [Hourie, the translator], why, when he knew that it was contrary to the policy of the Department, he allowed a Sun Dance to be held.

Piapot: (Rising to his feet, dropping the blanket from his shoulders and holding it on his out-stretched arm in the gesture of the great Indian orator.) When the Commissioner gets up in the morning he has many varieties of food placed before him, and if he doesn't like what is in one dish, he has a number of others from which to choose. He does not know what it is to have an empty belly. My people, however, are often hungry and when they cannot get food, they pray to God to give it, and their way of praying is to make a Sun Dance.

Forget: He has an argument there. Tell him, Peter, that we are two big chiefs here together. I ask him as one big chief speaking to another, not to make any more Sun Dances.

Piapot: Very well, I will agree not to pray to my God in my way, if you will promise not to pray to your God . . . in your way.

Forget: By Jove, he has me there. The old rascal should have been a lawyer.[48]

Other chiefs and councillors were also removed from office. In 1902, David Laird, Indian Commissioner for Manitoba and the Northwest Territories, notified Ottawa that one chief and several headmen had been removed from office as part of a vigorous campaign to suppress illegal dancing on reserves.[49] A strong supporter of Section 114, Laird instructed Indian agents to notify all headmen that they were expected to set an example in their communities by discouraging the performance of ceremonies. Persistence in such activities would be considered unprogressive and irresponsible. Thus, in his reaction to a report of a Sun Dance in the Onion Lake area in 1910, J. McLean, Secretary of the Department of Indian Affairs, questioned "whether the Department is justified in allowing any Indian to hold the office of Chief or Councillor, who remains so ignorant or indifferent to the real welfare of those under his guidance."[50]

A number of people, including some headmen, were also charged for infractions against the Giveaway Clause in Section 114. In 1897, five men, including the Cree chief Thunderchild, Bran, Wa-pa-ha, Patty, and O-kan-ee, were convicted for holding a giveaway following a complaint registered with the police by Indian Agent P.J. Williams and the farm instructor of the Battleford Agency. All were sentenced to two months' imprisonment.[51] Department officials also took this opportunity to confiscate Chief Thunderchild's treaty medal. Determined to make an example of the influential elder, Williams claimed that Thunderchild was the "most guilty of the lot."[52] Williams had found the situation all the more intolerable because he had taken "particular pains to explain the law to him [Thunderchild]," and "from time to time" had made arrests in the hope that the offenders would honour their promises to refrain from practising giveaways.[53] Because of their youth, Patty and O-kan-ee were released on a suspended sentence. The commanding officer also recommended the release of the remaining offenders three weeks after they had commenced serving their terms. Although the leader, Thunderchild, was an elderly man at the time, it was felt that imprisonment, as long as it did not entail hard labour, would not be harmful to him.[54] Both the commanding officer and the magistrate indicated that they would have preferred to give a lighter sentence to these first-time offenders; however, they refrained, in order to deliver a "death blow" to giveaways and dancing in general. This decision was also meant to lend legal support to the authority of the agent, who, despite his "strenuous efforts," had not been able to stop Indian farmers from abandoning their fields and livestock to attend dances or ceremonies.[55]

In the same year, four men from the Sweet Grass Reserve were tried for the same infraction. In a report dated January 25, 1897, J. Cotton, Superintendent commanding "C" Division, Battleford, arrested Pas-ke-min, Baptiste, Sake-pa-kow, and Ky-ass-i-kan. All were released except Ky-ass-i-kan, who was given a two-month sentence. Because the convicted was elderly and weak, Cotton recommended that Ky-ass-i-kan receive a suspended sentence of three weeks.[56] Also in 1897, Yellow Bird was accused of being the leader of several File Hills Indians who were attempting to build a dance lodge on the Okanese Reserve against the orders of Agent William Graham. Yellow Bird was arrested, charged with encouraging giveaways, and was sentenced to three months in the Regina prison. The heavy sentence was perhaps a reflection of the stormy relationship that had developed between Yellow Bird and Graham. Yellow Bird was accused of using "threatening language" against the Indian agent, who had refused his request for rations.[57] In addition, Yellow Bird was considered to be a troublemaker by the police. Constable T. Hoskin had reported: "'Yellow Bird' is a bad Indian and has been a source of trouble to the Indian Agent for some time and has been warned and threatened until he has grown defiant."[58]

In 1901, Chief Piapot was arrested for a second time along with six other members of his reserve for participating in a Give Away Dance. Five of the accused were allowed to go free on suspended sentences, and a sixth was sentenced to six months of hard labour. Piapot, described as "the ringleader in inciting them to resist arrest," was sentenced to two months' imprisonment in Regina despite the fact that he was quite elderly.[59] Department officials felt that Piapot's incarceration would deter the initiation of similar ceremonies. The situation was considered particularly serious because the two arresting police officers experienced resistance from the gathered celebrants and were obliged to travel to Regina for reinforcements. On their return trip to the encampment, they had brought a warrant for Piapot's arrest, charging him "with interfering with an officer in the discharge of his duties."[60]

In 1903, there were at least three significant court cases involving infractions against the giveaway prohibition. These cases indicate the lack of uniformity in the treatment of offenders in addition to the various factors that came into play when sentences were handed down. The conviction of Wanduta in 1903 involved a Dakota ritualist from Manitoba.[61] In this instance, a number of Oak River Dakota had been paid by some members of the White community in Rapid City to perform a Hay Dance, or Grass Dance, in 1902. The public were charged an admission fee of fifteen cents by the White organizers, and a number of Dakota had been paid with provisions such as meat, sugar, and tobacco as well as $43 in cash. Wanduta was charged with hosting a dance involving the giving away of merchandise and a number of horses. He was also accused of inducing school children to participate. To make matters worse, the Department had been informed that Wanduta was intending to sponsor similar dances at Brandon and other nearby locales.

Described as the "ring leader" of the "discontented" at the Oak River Reserve, Wanduta was tried and sentenced to four months of hard labour by the magistrate at Griswold, Manitoba.[62] An appeal was made by the legal firm of Caldwell and Coleman, but the decision was upheld. In their correspondence with the minister of the interior, Wanduta's barristers insisted that their client had not been properly informed of his rights and that Wanduta's case had been unfairly biased because of his bad relations with the local Indian agent.[63] As in Piapot's case, this was clearly an attempt by the Department to break the power of traditional ritualists. According to anthropologist Wilson Wallis, who had interviewed Wanduta, this ritualist was a member of the sacred Clown Society, and it was his custom to "announce after the War dance held by the Dakota who assemble at Brandon, Manitoba, each year during the week of the exposition, the number of spirits that he had seen during the dance."[64] He was also able to forecast the number of deaths for the coming year. Following his incarceration, Wanduta continued to carry out his sacred obligations as a member of the most powerful of Dakota medicine (healing) societies.

Another, related, well-publicized court case occurred in the same year. In *The Queen* versus *Etchease of the Muscowpetung Reserve* in Saskatchewan, the Giveaway Clause, Section 114 of the Indian Act, was also challenged. Etchease was a Plains Ojibway from the Muscowpetung Reserve who had initiated a dance while the Indian agent was absent from the reserve; he was also conducting other Circle Dances throughout the File Hills Agency. Until this time, the agent had been able to prevent dancing for over two years; and, on the neighbouring reserves of Piapot,

Pasquah, and even among the Dakota, public dancing had not been recorded for eighteen months.[65] The Acting Indian Agent, William Graham, ordered Etchease arrested for giving away goods at a Circle Dance. One witness testified that, during a speech made at the Circle Dance, Etchease announced that he obtained money to hire a lawyer if he got "into trouble" for having the dance.[66] On the advice of Mr. Dickson, an advocate at Qu'Appelle Station, Etchease proceeded to hold a Circle Dance at which the only instances of giveaways included food and tea provided by a number of people to the guests.[67] Approximately thirty people from three different reserves were in attendance.

The assistant police commissioner accused Etchease of deliberately initiating the dance in order to test Section 114. The news media, such as *The Globe* of Toronto, publicized the case as a "crafty effort" on the part of Indians to evade the law.[68] In fact, *The Globe* report accused Etchease of substituting the Sun Dance for the Circle Dance on the Piapot Reserve. Etchease was initially acquitted of the charge. The court's decision was formally protested by Father Hugonnard, the Principal of the Qu'Appelle Industrial School and a fervent opponent of all forms of indigenous ceremonies. In the retrial, the decision that the distribution of food at ceremonies was not a contravention of the Giveaway Clause was reversed. In the opinion of the presiding magistrate, Justice Richardson, "the acts complained of exceeded the acts of ordinary hospitality" and he saw no reason why "tea and bannock or soup should be an exception to the goods or articles the giving away of which makes a dance illegal. . . . The value of the articles does not matter at all."[69] As a result, Etchease was sentenced to three months' imprisonment.

For Indian leaders who followed their traditional religious practices, the original decision in Etchease's case was a victory. They interpreted Etchease's acquittal as an official and formal recognition of their "legal" forms of "dancing."[70] On the other hand, Department authorities and missionaries reacted strongly to this challenge and argued that the decision had weakened the strength of Section 114. The assistant Indian commissioner saw Etchease's actions as a premeditated move against the government's Indian programs. He claimed that the motivation behind the test case had not been the assertion of the right of Indians to participate in "ordinary social intercourse," but rather to encourage the revival of obstructive "old-time gatherings and dances."[71] For their part, churchmen, including the archbishop of Saint Boniface, Reverend Dr. Sutherland of the Methodist Church, and Reverend Dr. Hart, Convener of the Indian Missions for the Presbyterian Church, actively campaigned for the conviction of Etchease. The initiator of the appeal, Father Hugonnard, was especially disturbed by the apparently successful attempt by the Indians to use the justice system to "circumvent" regulations contained in the Indian Act:

Indians unless punished in some visible way when justly arrested, consider their release a victory over the NWMP and Government authorities as there have been three cases lately, covering horse stealing, larceny, forgery and the test case dance, in all of which the Indians were guilty, but has retained lawyers, to which they ascribe the fact that they were not punished, as they know they were guilty; the effect is to greatly lessen their respect for the law, for the NWMP and for those in authority over them. Clemency in their eyes is a sign of weakness.[72]

When comparisons are made with the treatment of Shave Tail, a Cree accused of violating this same clause, and who was charged, found guilty of "enticing the Indians to dances," and released with a "severe reprimand," one suspects that there were other reasons for Etchease's imprisonment.[73] After his Circle Dance, similar ceremonies were held on nearby reserves, including those held by Shave Tail. Etchease was accused of encouraging these revivals of open dancing by his own example and by informing participants that the judicial system would protect them from prosecution. According to the testimony of one witness, Etchease had collected money from a number of people in order to pay legal fees.[74] Described in Department reports as a man having no property, only three government cattle, a pony, no implements, and an apathy towards farming, Etchease obviously exemplified for the Department the worst of the recalcitrant traditional elements.

A third recorded court case relating to giveaways occurred in Alberta following the arrest of two Peigan men, Commodore and Joe Smith.[75] Smith was accused of giving away twelve horses, a blanket, and other articles during a ceremony. Chief Justice Sifton found the prisoners guilty, but this was the first case he had tried of this nature. The prisoners were released on a suspended sentence with the warning that "the Indians were not to have any 'give away' dances in the future, and that he would be very severe with any that came before him again."[76]

Indian Department files recorded one other case of an arrest made in connection with Section 114. According to a newspaper report, an elderly man was arrested for attending a Sun Dance. However, the accused, from the Fishing Lakes Reserve, was probably attending a Midewiwin, or Medicine Society Ceremony. In early 1904, headlines in *The Telegram* declared "Injustice to Poor Old Indian. Nearly Ninety Years of Age He is Sent to Jail. No Wrong Meant – He Deserved Better Treatment From Canada."[77] The article was based on a letter to the editor from Edward Field, who was protesting the arrest of Elder Taytapasahsung for attending a Midewiwin ceremony at Nut Lake Reserve, Saskatchewan. The elder was sentenced to two months of hard labour, but C. Pearson Bell, the Assistant Surgeon for the North-West Mounted Police, had recommended his release. The prison register had described Taytapasahsung as being over ninety years old, "feeble, decrepit, and blind," and unable to take on the simplest of tasks.[78] Such negative publicity over the

Department's lack of good judgement undoubtedly tempered the occurrence of hasty prosecutions.

The total number of arrests that resulted from infractions related to Section 114 for the pre–World War One period is difficult to determine. Many arrests did not involve sentencing; in other cases those charged were released on suspended sentences. Furthermore, police reports of convicted "trespassers" do not always indicate if the offence resulted from off-reserve attendance at a ceremony. A survey of annual published police reports shows that, in 1900, there were two cases of "holding dances" with no convictions; in 1902 there were nine cases and convictions for "holding dances," and twenty-seven individuals were arrested for "engaging in a heathen dance" and released on a suspended sentence; one 1903 report noted that there were ten arrests for "holding dances" and nine convictions; and finally, in 1904, there were two arrests and two convictions reported for the Regina area.[79]

Indian Department officials were suspicious of several other forms of indigenous religious practices in addition to Sun Dances and giveaways. Shamans and healers were perceived as the keepers and purveyors of traditional values. In the opinion of the Deputy Superintendent General, Hayter Reed, they were "the guiders of thought and action and the inspirers of fear in all but the very boldest."[80] In the opinion of Department officials, missionaries, teachers, and Western medical personnel, shamans and healers were practitioners of medical "quackery" who were interested only in duping the naïve for their own material gain. Due to their age and "consequent fixity of ideas," medicine men were considered "beyond the reach of the elevating influences of civilization."[81] From a legal standpoint, both Indians and European Canadians were allowed to practise unlicensed medicine provided that the patient was unharmed and that no payment in money or gifts exchanged hands. The latter restriction was difficult to enforce, since most healing of this nature was conducted in private. Furthermore, traditional healers were often the only source of medical relief on reserves. According to customary law, payment and sacred offerings in the form of the reciprocal exchange of goods for healings was considered appropriate and even a necessary part of the healing process.

While the majority of Indian agency personnel were unsympathetic to the persistence of ceremonies, some did propose a more gradual approach to discouraging indigenous religious practices. Some Indian agents offered possible compromises to their superiors. They suggested, for example, that they might agree to refrain from interference with "legal" ceremonies; or they might permit abbreviated versions of the Sun Dance provided that the dance was devoid of features prohibited in the Indian Act; some agreed to permit the performance of the "harmless" dances; while still others made an effort to encourage Indians to replace their religious dances with European-Canadian sports activities and other forms of recreation.

As early as 1892, Hayter Reed reported that an Indian agent had promised the Cree on the Piapot Reserve that they could hold a Harvest Home Dance provided that they discontinue their Sun Dance.[82] In the following year, Indian Agent Clink of the Hobbema Reserve had gathered reserve residents together to celebrate the Queen's birthday with a community dinner. Interestingly, a fund of $40 was collected and given out as prizes for sporting events. In Clink's judgement, people enjoyed themselves at competitive sports "much better than I ever saw them do at a Thirst dance."[83] Sports days and community picnics were generally held on most reserves on Dominion Day following treaty payments, and at this time secularized versions of dancing, and foot and horse races, were permitted. These celebrations encouraged considerable visiting between reserves and provided opportunities for the incorporation of traditional ceremonies. Families also travelled from town to town following the popular horse-racing circuit, and one frustrated Indian agent, C. Paul Schmidt of the Duck Lake Reserve, requested that legislation be enacted to prohibit people from leaving their reserves without authorization.[84] This agent was obviously not enforcing the pass system, or the trespass law, and reported that some of the Duck Lake people were absent for over three weeks at a time.

With the growth of towns near reserves, sports days and fairs became events eagerly looked forward to by the Indians and Whites alike during the summer months. For White settlers, the presence of Indian families had become a money-making attraction. Much to the disapproval of the Department and of missionaries, Indian dances and parades in traditional outfits at these events were encouraged by local White organizers. A share of gate monies, food supplies, and monetary prizes for Indian participants did little to discourage their involvement.

Although there were indications that some Indian agents chose to exercise their discretionary powers by regulating ceremonial activities through cooperation and negotiated compromises, few officials or clergymen approved of this approach. Administrators in Ottawa and the regional offices continued to advise their personnel not only to enforce Section 114, but also to discourage *all* forms of dancing. This inflexible stance on the part of the government was evident in the careers of both Duncan Scott and William Graham. Before his appointment to the office of Deputy Superintendent of Indian Affairs in 1913, Duncan Scott had been one of the commissioners involved in the negotiation of Treaty Nine in the James Bay region. During a trip to the northwest, his attitudes towards indigenous religious expression became apparent in an incident at the Lac Seul Reserve. In response to a Dog Feast in progress at the time, Scott insisted upon meeting with the "conjurer," Neotamaqueb, and "lectured and warned" the people that they "would be watched in the future."[85] It is noteworthy that, following this encounter with Neotamaqueb, who was considered to be powerful in "driving out evil spirits," Scott became ill, and remained ill, until the next day of travel.[86] During a later tour to western Canada in 1909–10 as the Superintendent of Education, Scott issued a statement regarding his objections to the participation of Indians in White-sponsored agricultural exhibitions and fairs. His opposition to what he referred to as "senseless drumming and singing" was reflected in his policy towards dancing when he became Deputy Superintendent of Indian Affairs.[87] On October 15, 1913, he issued a directive entitled *General Instructions to Indian Agents in Canada,* reminding agents of their responsibilities associated with the implementation of Section 149 (the previous Section 114).[88] He advised that all gatherings "which tend to destroy the civilizing influence of the education imparted to Indian children at schools, and which work against the proper influence of agents and farming instructors," should be discouraged in "every way possible."[89] In conjunction with these directives, agents were also encouraged to work towards achieving at least a subsistence level of mixed farming in their agencies and instilling the "habits of thrift" in their charges.[90] This reference to "thrift" was explicitly directed at the indigenous economic system of redistribution.

Until 1914, the federal government passed no further amendments to the Indian Act that affected Indian "dancing" and attendance at White-sponsored exhibitions in traditional dress. It was possible, however, to invoke other laws to discourage such activities. Scott's predecessor, David Laird, had suggested that Section 208 of the Criminal Code prohibiting indecent exposure could be used against Indians who insisted on wearing traditional outfits; or the vagrancy law might be used to discourage people from gathering in and about White towns.[91] Some of the exhibition organizers themselves considered indecent exposure to be a problem with Indian events for, as the Cree historian Joseph Dion pointed out, "we were forbidden to even take our shirts off. All we were allowed to show was an arm, from under the blanket we used to cover with in our parades."[92]

Field administrators such as William Graham remained firmly committed to the Department's objectives of Indian economic self-sufficiency through agriculture and assimilation.[93] His professional career in the Department was long-lived, as he rose in the ranks from a young clerk in the Moose Mountain Agency (1885), to Clerk in the Commissioner's office (1895), to Indian Agent at File Hills (1897), and later to Inspector of Indian Agencies for the South Saskatchewan Inspectorate (1904). In 1920, Graham was appointed to the position of Indian Commissioner. As founder of the File Hills Indian farming colony, Graham continued to believe that the progress of Indians was possible only through their complete cultural transformation. His position on indigenous forms of religious worship was supported by the clergy, especially by his close ally, Father Joseph Hugonnard.

By 1914, it had become abundantly clear to administrators such as Scott and Graham that the policy of "moderation and compromise" not only had resulted in the inconsistent implementation of Section 149, but was also largely ineffective. While a number of factors undoubtedly contributed to this situation, the resistance of prairie Indians to the measures adopted to implement anti-ceremonial regulations was a major force in the government's decision to adopt more repressive measures in 1914.

Responses to Religious Suppression: 1896 to 1914

6

The correspondence files and official reports of the Department of Indian Affairs contain details of the reactions of a number of Indian individuals and communities to the implementation of Section 114. The degree of concern and the type of response varied from community to community. Some Indian leaders demanded a repeal of the legislation while others attempted to limit its implementation. When these efforts failed, other strategies were adopted, including open resistance and the modification of ceremonial life. The failure of the Plains Cree and other prairie leaders to obtain a repeal of Section 114 reflected their political powerlessness. As wards of the federal government, they were encouraged to depend upon the local personnel of the Department of Indian Affairs to act on their behalf. When this avenue of representation failed, they approached Ottawa directly. As British subjects, Indians also had access to the justice system but this was a costly and, for many people, still unfamiliar alternative. In the final analysis, resistance was a difficult and demanding matter; that the Indian communities persisted in their efforts to resist the regulations against their ceremonies was a measure of their commitment to their spiritual beliefs and cultural values.

Much of the correspondence sent to the agency offices involved written requests for permission to hold ceremonies. These letters, in turn, were usually forwarded to Ottawa for a response. Generally, such petitions were also accompanied by the Indian agent's evaluation of the local situation and, in some instances, his assessment of the petitioners themselves. Many of the earlier letters were written by leaders who had a poor command of the English language (the official language of communication), and this fact, compounded by the difficulty of communicating spiritual matters to unsympathetic officials, led the Department to take such Indian protests lightly.

Most of the petitions were requests to hold "legal" forms of ceremonies and dances. Some submissions challenged the legality of Section 114 on the grounds that it violated treaty rights. According to this view, the indigenous forms of religious expression were never part of treaty negotiations. Therefore, Indian agents were accused of exceeding their authority if they attempted to implement repressive measures against dancing and inter-reserve visiting. These petitions for the freedom of religious expression were part of an ongoing treaty-rights movement for more self-determination being initiated by the original signatories of the treaties.[1]

In 1907, two Plains Cree leaders, Thunderchild and Charles Fineday, protested the attack on their ceremonies as an abrogation of treaty rights. As one of the signatories of their joint petition pointed out, "I was present at the time the treaty was formed and I did not hear them stopping us the privilege of using our ceremonies or ways of rejoicing."[2] Their request for permission to hold a Sun Dance before the beginning of a local fair contained assurances that, in return for a positive answer, they would involve only those reserves in the vicinity and they would not interrupt their work or the children's schooling.[3] The Department refused to entertain the proposal. Similar objections were made by Joe Ma-ma-gway-see from the Sampson Band in Alberta, who defended the right of the councillors to hold a Sun Dance on the grounds of religious freedom. In his correspondence with the Department, Ma-ma-gway-see introduced another problem created by the implementation of Section 114.[4] The legislation against ceremonial activities, he claimed, was a direct challenge to customary laws. The dilemma of being forced to choose between those customary laws having sacred sanctions and a state-imposed secular law was causing trauma in the communities. Ma-ma-gway-see communicated this situation "in good heart" to the Department in 1908:

The law you make is of this world and we follow the law of God. If you stop everything we do we may as well go without the law of God. All of the councils beg of me to writ[e] to you because we like it [the Sun Dance] and it does no harm to the whites. . . . Everything will go well if every one does right according to the law of God. I have never seen him but it is in his command to us and you are trying to stop it.[5]

The contradiction between a state-imposed law and customary law was raised by other petitioners. For example, in 1914, an identical submission was made by Chief Thunderchild, who challenged the local agent's refusal to allow travel to other reserves for Sun Dances. According to Thunderchild, "customs" had not been negotiated away upon the signing of the treaties:

When the law was first made here I listened to the true law. The man that I made the bargain with [was] the queen's servant. When he was first going to look over us he said, I show our God what

I am now doing it is true, there is no fooling about it. I am not going to stop your manners. You will have in your future you[r] dance. Your people around Battleford would like to assemble for a sundance and another thing that was said is your farming you will have your own food that is to say all the ... animals. I[t] makes all the Indians think very much of that as they are now forbidden to kill anything. I was told there is going to be a sundance in Poundmaker. The inspector told me that no people could go to it but them. You will let me know if this is true as soon as you can.[6]

That Thunderchild sent his petition directly to Ottawa is indicative of the mistrust that leaders had for local Department administrators. As a result of treaty negotiations, a formalized trusting relationship had been established with the Canadian government, and it was on this understanding that Thunderchild undertook to clarify the actions of local inspectors. This relationship of Indian headmen to senior administrators in the Department was described by Thunderchild using kinship terms equivalent to those for *father* (the government administrator) and *son* (an Indian headman). Inherent in such a paternalistic relationship were expectations that the administrators would respond to Indian concerns in good faith. When questioning the inspector's refusal to allow attendance at a Sun Dance on Poundmaker's reserve, Thunderchild based his appeal on this relationship in the following words: "You will let me know if this is true as soon as you can. . . . I would like you to tell me about it as I take you as a father and you took me as a son."[7]

A year later, in 1915, Thunderchild submitted yet another request for permission to attend a Sun Dance on the Little Pine Reserve. In this instance, it was the Indian Agent, J. Rowland, who appealed to his superiors to "severely reprimand" the persistent leader. Although Rowland had directed the agency's farming instructors to notify people not to leave their farms, and had personally warned people, he anticipated having "considerable trouble" over this dance since "quite a number" had decided to oppose his authority.[8]

In addition to believing that the Indian agents were unilaterally behind the implementation of Section 114, petitioners had other reasons for circumventing local administrators and corresponding directly with Ottawa. There was undoubtedly some question as to whether local officials were communicating Indian concerns to the government accurately and in good faith. One agent, for example, recommended that the secretary of the Department ignore Ma-ma-gway-see's petition. According to this agent, James Campbell, Ma-ma-gway-see's submission was "a somewhat gratuitous interference from an Indian of the 'Smart Alec' class"; and Campbell dismissed the request as nothing more than "the old begging whine for free rations."[9] Because of his unfamiliarity with the English language and his difficulty in communicating spiritual matters in writing, Ma-ma-gway-see's concerns were not taken seriously. Campbell undermined the character of the petitioner and his credibility in his evaluation of the petition: "The letter was a more or less wandering effusion, attributing the institution of the Sun Dance to the Almighty, and involving for reply the somewhat large questions as to the inspiration of the scriptures, and of interference with religious freedom, questions which it did not seem advisable to discuss, all the less when brought up in the manner and by such an Indian as above indicated."[10] Campbell's attempts to undermine this petitioner's integrity were representative of the attitude taken by most agents. One Indian agent, W. Grant of the Assiniboine Agency, went so far as to caution his superiors that Indian petitions were merely "schemes and plots" being devised by the "old people."[11]

Another type of petition addressed the suppression of *legal* forms of ceremonies, that is, those that did not involve specific features as outlined in Section 114. As early as 1898, Panapekesis of the Yorkton area consulted a law firm regarding the legality of the Sun Dance. Indian Agent J. Wright of the Crooked Lakes Agency reported not only that the lawyers informed people that there was no law against the ceremony itself, but also that one lawyer had even offered them monetary support ($10) and went so far as to suggest that ceremonial leaders charge a fee of twenty-five cents to White observers.[12]

Some headmen demanded the removal of their assigned Indian agents. In 1900, two headmen from the Pasqua Reserve in Saskatchewan asked for clarification of their agent's authority from the justice of the peace at Fort Qu'Appelle. A meeting with members from other reserves in the Muscowpetung Agency was held, and a petition demanding the agent's removal was drafted. In his defence, the agent insisted that he was acting within his mandate to suppress all dancing and that his actions were being questioned because many believed that he was personally responsible for initiating the policy.[13]

The argument of discrimination was also used by some petitioners who claimed that they were entitled to enjoy the same holiday activities as did European Canadians. In 1903, the chief and other members of the Côté Reserve in Saskatchewan wrote that they wished to "meet at one another's houses for music, dancing, and refreshments without violating the law."[14] Three years later, a number of people from the Assiniboine Agency wanted two days set aside for feasting, sports activities, and a "thanksgiving promenade," that is, "holidays exactly similar to those observed by white people on Dominion Day."[15] Well aware of the Department's disapproval of any off-reserve movement during the agricultural season, the petitioners proposed a compromise whereby they would agree to remain on the reserve during the summer months if their request was granted.[16] Since this proposal seemed to indicate that Indian farmers were willing to substitute Canadian celebratory events for their traditional ceremonies, the Department responded favourably. However, the Indian Agent, W. Grant, local clergy, and Inspector

William Graham were not supportive, fearing the people would take advantage of the Department's leniency and introduce traditional dances at these activities. Moreover, the Indian agent advised his superior that his wards were "inclined to smuggle in some of their old fashioned sports and call it a thanksgiving promenade. . . ."[17] He also suggested that the Indian leaders and ritualists would not have taken the trouble to consult with lawyers if they had no intention of defying the Department's directives against dancing.

Resistance to the implementation of Section 114 also took the form of official visits to the local and national offices of the Department of Indian Affairs. One of these official delegations was relatively successful in addressing the repressive measures that went beyond the letter of the law. In 1911, a number of elderly headmen who had witnessed the signing of the Qu'Appelle Treaty sent representatives to Ottawa to formally protest the violation of a number of treaty promises.[18] The petitioners demanded the fulfillment of treaty obligations, that Whites stop the harvesting of timber and hay on reserve lands, that more educational aid be given, and that the government discontinue the unilateral removal of chiefs and councillors. Loud Voice from the Cowesses Reserve and other representatives from the Piapot Reserve spoke out on behalf of the Sun Dance and other indigenous ceremonies.

In a verbal exchange between Interpreter Alex Gaddie and Frank Oliver, the Superintendent of Indian Affairs, Gaddie explained that the Sun Dance was the way that their forefathers had taught them to pray, and for that reason the ceremony should not be prohibited.[19] Furthermore, he insisted that the Sun Dance did not interfere with farm work since the ceremony was held after seeding time. However, Oliver made it very clear that the Department would continue to discourage dancing because it wasted time and was seen as having a bad influence on young people.[20] The minister even offered his own experience on the issue of dancing as a case in point when he explained: "When I was a boy we did not have any dance at all. . . . Not that we thought it was any harm or sin, but we thought it was a waste of time."[21] Despite his personal opinion that people were better off without their dancing, Oliver was forced to concede that according to the Indian Act, dances could be legally held as long as there was no giving away of property or mutilation.

Although this delegation was unsuccessful in obtaining the repeal of Section 114, the occasion marks the first time that a delegation of Plains Cree and Ojibway officially asserted their treaty rights with reference to "the right to their own culture."[22] A press report on the delegates' train ride back home revealed their high feelings and sense of accomplishment. The delegates had requested permission to sing on the train and reportedly composed songs that recounted how the "seniors of the bands went to headquarters, and how they brought back good news to please their people."[23] In this manner, the history of the event became incorporated into the oral tradition. Still another song indicated their eagerness to return to their homes and the words were more reminiscent of traditional songs sung by returning warriors: "I am going home with contented mind to my sweetheart who is looking out for me."[24]

Despite their inability to secure self-determination, this delegation from Crooked Lakes Reserve did return home with an official document that clarified the parameters of Section 114. On his return, the group's interpreter, Alex Gaddie, informed Indian Commissioner David Laird: "[I] explained the circumstances of the sun dance [to Ottawa officials] and we were assured that nobody would be put in jail on its account."[25] This official clarification of the regulation resulted in an increase in open dancing, much to the dismay of local administrators, Indian agents and missionaries. One police report of a Sun Dance on the Ochapowace Reserve in 1911 indicated that seven families from other Canadian reserves and four American families were in attendance.[26] In his statement, Superintendent J.D. Moodie pointed out that "some of the Indians who visited Ottawa last winter misinterpreted what was told to them there; consequently, they believed that they were acting within the limits of the law."[27]

The Christian churches were very concerned about the effect of the Gaddie delegation on their missionary work. When it was discovered that people were preparing to hold a Sun Dance in the Crooked Lake Agency, the Indian agent reported that the Presbyterian and Roman Catholic churches "gave every assistance to discourage the dance and to keep their people away."[28] Father Hugonnard was particularly vocal in his criticism of the Department's failure to discourage all ceremonial practices rather than simply clarifying the mandate of Section 114 with the Crooked Lakes delegation. He informed Ottawa that the people inferred from the Department's response to the delegation that "dancing is no more forbidden or it is at least tolerated," and, moreover, the authority of local agents was severely undermined because "the delegates carry the 15 page letter under their arm and recognize in it a precious document from the Great Chief at Ottawa over the head of agents."[29]

For both local administrators and missionaries, the Crooked Lakes delegation of 1911 was a setback in the sense that Ottawa officials had refrained from openly affirming the informal policy of denouncing *all* forms of indigenous dancing. The Department's refusal to issue a formal statement substantiating their directives against all ceremonies placed local officials and missionaries in a defensive position. Nevertheless, they continued to support the government's general policy of assimilation. While the 1911 delegation had not persuaded the Department to have the legislation repealed, it nevertheless had succeeded in calling into question the attempt to suppress the "legal" aspects of their ceremonial life. The subsequent movement to perform dances within the parameters of the law led to a renewed lobby on the part of the churches and local administrators for further restrictive amendments to the Indian Act.

The regulations against ceremonial practices were also challenged in the courts. The case involving Etchease of the Muscowpetung Reserve in 1903 indicated the commitment on the part of administrators and clergy to discourage all indigenous ceremonies, and in particular the "giving away" of goods on such occasions. Before he held a Circle Dance, Etchease had consulted with a lawyer on his rights. During the course of the dance, food was distributed to the participants. Because Etchease had spoken with a lawyer and had sponsored the dance at a time when the Indian Agent, William Graham, was absent, administrators and clergy argued that Etchease's actions were a deliberate attempt to test the validity of Section 114 in a court of law. Etchease was arrested and charged for violating Section 114, and although he was acquitted at his first trial, he was eventually sentenced to three months' imprisonment. The reversal of the court's opinion was due to an effective lobby mounted by the churches and Department officials who had succeeded in re-opening the case. According to Hayter Reed, the Assistant Indian Commissioner, the issue was not that Etchease had participated in illegal forms of "social intercourse"; rather, his action "represented an attempt to undermine the agent and revert to traditional practices which hindered self support," that is, by being absent from work and distributing goods.[30]

The involvement of Indian students in these more formal methods of protest is evident in at least two instances. In the 1903 trial of the Dakota, Wanduta, the defendant had raised travel money to allow him to plead his case in the accompaniment of his son, a student from the Brandon Industrial School.[31] Three years later, with the help of ex-pupil Daniel Kennedy, members of the Assiniboine Agency successfully petitioned the minister of the interior for permission to hold feasts, sports, and thanksgiving promenades.[32] The petitioners in this instance had also consulted a lawyer, who sent a covering letter with the petition. In this letter, Barrister Levi Thompson stated that the promoters of these events were "among the best educated and most intelligent of them [the Indians]."[33] In return for two days of celebrations, the petitioners offered to work hard on their reserves and to refrain from attending Sun Dances. While the support of ex-graduates undoubtedly lent an air of credibility to the promises made in these types of petitions, it did not eliminate official fears that even apparently harmless sports might lead to the revival of Sun Dances. In spite of the fact that the Department approved the Assiniboin sports days, administrators and agents protested that participation resulted in a considerable waste of time, money, and productive farm work – preparations had to be made for these events, household money was diverted to producing beadwork dancing outfits, and Indians from other agencies were prone to leave their farm work and attend such celebrations.[34]

According to Department records and accounts by Indian historians, opposition to Section 114 was consistently non-violent. When their ceremonies were interrupted, celebrants expressed their opposition verbally and demonstrated a reluctance to leave their ceremonial grounds. However, there were no physical confrontations with the authorities. Some groups did attempt to bargain by suggesting that they would be more receptive to federal programs if they could hold their ceremonies. For example, as early as 1897, Indian Agent G.H. Wheatley wrote to his superiors that Running Rabbit, White Pup, Big Road, and Many Shot of the Blackfoot Agency had approached him with a promise that they would cooperate in the education of their children in exchange for permission to hold a Sun Dance.[35] Furthermore, they promised that they would not move into a large camp until the "Service Berries are ripe" and that the camp would break up after five days in order that participants could return to their work on their respective reserves.[36] In this case, Indian Commissioner A.E. Forget agreed to the terms, provided that no one would be forced to attend ceremonies, that preparations would not interfere with farm work, that children would not be taken out of the schools, that existing schools would be filled to capacity, and that objectionable features would be deleted from the ceremony.[37]

In 1900, the principal headman of the Pasqua Band, along with supporters termed "unprogressives" by the Indian agent, refused to honour their agreement to negotiate a sale of a parcel of reserve land and also demanded the removal of the agent. The agent claimed that these demands were motivated by the suppression of giveaway ceremonies and other illegal dances.[38] By 1915, there were reports from the Blackfoot Agency that parents were threatening to keep their children out of school as a protest against departmental attempts to prevent them from visiting the Blackfoot Reserve to attend dances.[39] Some headmen such as the Cree chief Star Blanket used their contacts with influential European Canadians to obtain permission to hold legal dances. In 1910, the artist Edmund Morris was initially unable to persuade Star Blanket to sit for his portrait unless he personally agreed to allow them to have a dance.[40] Morris agreed to speak to Indian Commissioner William Graham and to Duncan Scott, the Deputy Superintendent of Indian Affairs, regarding the possibility of people holding dances on their respective reserves. Star Blanket might have mistakenly believed that Edmund Morris had the authority that his father formerly possessed in his capacity as the lieutenant governor of Manitoba and the Northwest Territories when the plains treaties were negotiated.

During this period, local European-Canadian support for indigenous forms of religious expression was virtually non-existent, but other customary practices were ironically supported and in fact promoted. The sponsors of agricultural exhibitions and local stampedes inadvertently contributed to the persistence of traditional customs and certain religious practices by inviting local Indian people to participate in parades wearing their traditional clothing, to sell traditional crafts, to set up tipi villages, and even to perform indigenous dances. Some exhibition sponsors criticized the Department's policy of discouraging Indian involvement at such events as overly repressive. This feeling is apparent in the defence of the Assiniboine Agency's petition for sports days in 1906. Local residents believed that if, at the very least, sports days were permitted, local reserve communities would be "more satisfied" with their lot and would be encouraged to make "better progress" on their farms.[41]

In general, the strategy adopted by elders and school graduates was one of compromise and reason. Assuming that government policy on ceremonial practices was based on a misunderstanding of indigenous religions, some petitioners undertook the task of attempting to correct such notions by drawing comparisons between their dances and Christian religious worship or European-Canadian social behaviour. The right of the Assiniboine Reserve to hold feasts, sports days, and thanksgiving promenades was argued on the grounds that petitioners would be enjoying activities that were no different from those experienced by White communities on Dominion Day.[42] In 1909, the Assiniboin bands of White Bear, Pheasant Rump, and Strip Blanket used the same defence and further contended that departmental policy on dancing was discriminatory:

We wish to know why we are stopped dancing we don't do any harm to any body, we are the same as white men. White men like dancing so we like dancing to.
    We have no other way to enjoy ourselves, we can not dance with the fiddle so we have to use the drum that is our own way. . . . Makes no difference; . . . supposing we go to work to stop the White people from dancing they wont like it too and when its time to work we go to work when we have nothing to do then we want to have a little pleasure in dancing. We will promise you to do more work every year & we will promise you not to eat dogs . . . we wont dance naked and we dont give our things.[43]

Similarly, Chief Musqwa's appeal for a joint celebration of an "old fashioned tea or council dance" on behalf of the Muscowpetung, Piapot, and Pasqua reserves pointed out that this dance was "more like an afternoon tea among the whites than anything else."[44]

As was noted above, some petitioners compared religious practices at the Sun Dances with Christian forms of worship.[45] Others contrasted their particular version of the Sun Dance with that of other groups that were held to be more extreme. For instance, in 1911, Little Bird and the Wandering Crees hoped to present their version of the Sun Dance in a more favourable light by indicating that it contained fewer objectionable features than did the Blackfoot variation. The Wandering Crees argued that their ceremony lasted for only three to four days compared to the weeks spent in such camps by the Blackfoot, and that, unlike the Blackfoot, they did not impoverish themselves, act out war activities, or discharge guns.[46] Such arguments failed to sway the opinion of Department officials on the issue of dancing. These men were reluctant to permit the celebration of seemingly more "innocent" dances because they were unable to predict "what features or practices may be introduced at such a dance."[47]

Ritualists also selectively and carefully modified their ceremonial practices in order to omit the prohibited forms of behaviour specified in the Indian Act regulations. On the surface, this initiative might be interpreted as an acceptance of the government policy of repression, but the intent was to preserve as much of the content and integrity of the ceremonies as possible and to leave the government with no basis for interference. In addition to altering ceremonial time, space, and content, they introduced new modes of religious expression. These adaptations can be illustrated with specific reference to the Sun Dance (Thirst Dance), giveaways, and several other indigenous ceremonies because the Department of Indian Affairs created specific files on some of these events. In addition, some early anthropological observations are available from this period.

The abandonment of public forms of piercing (self-mortification) was said to be the first of the compromises. Though many Indian agents reported this departure from traditional practice, it is difficult to assess the accuracy of their observations. Both the agent's disruption of ceremonies in progress and the performance of more covert forms of piercing suggest that the practice was not dead. One observer, Robert Jefferson, reported that, after the Saskatchewan Uprising of 1885, the Plains Cree held their dance in a "place where the unsympathetic eye of authority will not be offended."[48] Nevertheless, he added that "self-torture" (piercing) was dropped, "out of deference to the white man's more delicate susceptibilities."[49]

Willingness to forego objectionable rituals was expressed by several other leaders. As early as 1896, when Indian Agent J. Markle pressured Astakasic of the Waywayseecappo Reserve to order Sun Dance celebrants from the Crooked Lake, Valley River, and Rolling River reserves to return to their homes, Astakasic indicated that a shorter version of the dance might be held without giveaways, "tortures," or fasting.[50] In the same year, the Sakimay Band agreed to alter their Sun Dance, by abstaining from piercing, refraining from inviting members from other reserves to the dance, and limiting the ceremony to two days.[51] In 1898, She-sheep of the Crooked Lakes Agency appealed for permission to hold a Sun Dance, with the promise that his followers would delete all objectionable features from the ceremony. The Indian agent refused to allow the dance, and She-sheep was forced to perform an alternate ceremony.[52]

The last formally reported instance of piercing occurred on Piapot's reserve in the late 1890s and resulted in the leader's arrest and conviction. Piapot was imprisoned and then deposed as chief by the Department. Because the ritual of piercing was considered to be a test of courage and the major reason for the celebration of the Sun Dance, the government and the churches continued to be unwavering in their opposition. Among the Blackfoot, Indian Agent Magnus Begg reported as early as 1895 that the Sun Dance had been reduced to "a mere religious ceremony" since self-mortification was no longer practised.[53] None of the petitions to the Department contained appeals for permission to practise this ritual, and therefore it is difficult to determine through the correspondence the effect of the deletion of such activities on ceremonies.

In response to Department claims that the Sun Dance was a waste of productive agricultural time and personal resources, the ceremony was shortened on some Plains Cree and Plains Ojibway reserves. Thus, the actual performance of the four-day celebration was reduced to two or two and a half days. Once an inter-band and inter-tribal ceremony, the Sun Dance was now more localized. These changes were largely determined by the intensity of enforcement of the pass system and trespass regulation. Many endeavoured to circumvent restrictions on their ceremonial attendance by persisting in worshiping in the traditional manner despite the risk of being turned back to their homes while en route to another reserve or being forced to pay a fine that few could afford.

In addition to performing Sun Dances according to the terms of Section 114, participants also offered to abandon other "objectionable" rituals. For example, in 1909, the White Bear, Pheasant Rump, and Strip Blanket bands agreed to refrain from the ritual consumption of dog meat, dancing "naked," and giving away goods.[54] Similar petitions were received from the Pasqua Band (1911), Little Bird and the Wandering Crees (1911), and Blue Quill's band in Alberta (1913).

The role of the Sun Dance and other ceremonies as mechanisms for transmitting cultural knowledge from one generation to another was also undermined by efforts on the part of the Department and the churches to prevent school children from attending these events. Church officials attached great importance to this form of suppression. A petition sent to Bishop Legal by Father H. Grandin and eight other signatories in 1908 offers an insight into their position on the matter of the presence of school children at traditional celebrations. These clergymen wrote that the children were being raised in an environment that fostered a "hatred" of authority and a defiant attitude toward the Department's "protective or progressive" measures.[55] They attributed this state of affairs to the children's attendance at ceremonies where "the sorcerers make long harangues by which almost invariably they excite the young people to hatred of White people in general and of government in particular."[56] Although children could be kept away from ceremonies while they were attending off-reserve residential and industrial schools, there was little that could be done to prohibit their participation once they were home. The return of school children to their homes in a state of ill health was itself a reason for parents and relatives to seek out healers at vowed ceremonies such as the Sun Dance. Furthermore, parents persisted in taking their young children to ceremonies so that there was some exposure to traditional values and behaviour at a very early age.[57]

The ability of the Plains Cree and other prairie Indian communities to continue to celebrate the Sun Dance varied according to the proximity of the reserve to White communities and the degree of suppression applied by Department personnel and missionaries. Ceremonial life in those communities subjected to more intense surveillance was often disrupted. Participants were both angered and frightened by the on-site interference of the Indian agents and police. Many were undoubtedly emotionally traumatized by their inability to fulfill their sacred vows. Nevertheless, celebrants persisted; and, in spite of the obstacles, there is only one documented case when repression forced the Indians to substitute an alternate ceremony for the Thirst Dance. In 1898, She-sheep of the Crooked Lakes Agency performed a one-night Smoke Dance when he was prevented from holding a Thirst Dance. This ceremony was performed on a Sunday evening in order not to interrupt the work week, and was restricted in attendance to reserve members.[58]

The alteration of giveaway ceremonies during this period is more difficult to assess. Though agency reports indicate that such alterations did happen, it is also apparent that giveaways were held on many occasions and were simply not detected. Giveaways were conducted at the Sun Dances and at most ceremonial gatherings. Many of these were held during the winter months in traditional dance lodges, in European-Canadian types of recreational "dance halls," or in the privacy of homes where they escaped the notice of officials. Giveaways varied not only in time and location, but also in the amount of goods distributed; some were small localized affairs and might involve only the distribution of tobacco and food, while others, such as a giveaway at the Blood Sun Dance of 1913, involved the exchange of 300 head of horses over a six-week period.[59]

In addition to alterations in the Sun Dance and giveaways, some petitioners also indicated that they would be willing to consider regulated forms of other ceremonies or dances. Some Indian agents also proposed this solution as a method of avoiding discontent among their charges and at the same time maximizing productive agricultural time. In 1914, Indian Agent W. Dilworth of the Blood Agency informed his superiors that attendance at Sun Dances would not interfere with work if they were held during the last two weeks in June (between the end of farm work and the start of roundup).[60]

A small number of individuals from Saskatchewan reserves submitted their own proposals for alterations in traditional ceremonial patterns in an effort to negotiate an agreement regarding the terms under which their ceremonies could occur without interruption. For example, in 1911, the Pasqua Band presented a list of restrictions that they were willing to enforce in exchange for permission to conduct their dances.[61] The frequency of dancing was to be greatly reduced and timed according to the labour requirements of the agricultural cycle, with dancing to commence after threshing and to occur once a month until spring. Another dance would be celebrated between seeding and breaking the ground, with a second being held prior to treaty payments rather than during payments. The latter condition addressed the Department's concern over the fact that treaty money was being spent on dancing. It was further proposed that the ceremonies would close by 1:00 a.m. and that, while necessary refreshments would be provided, no feasting would occur. The band also agreed to exclude school children, half-breeds, and Whites from the dances. The younger children would be permitted to attend only the outdoor summer celebrations (as opposed to indoor dancing in crowded buildings). It was suggested that an officer from the Department might attend the dances in a supervisory capacity. Other proposed rules included the prohibition of liquor consumption and the use of facial or body paints and an agreement to refrain from performing dances off the reserve at fairs or in towns. While J.D. McLean, Secretary of the Department of Indian Affairs, responded by agreeing that the Pasqua Band would not be contravening any law if they danced according to these conditions, he nevertheless urged the agent to discourage *all* dancing, which he considered a "waste of time and energy."[62] As demonstrated in this 1911 petition, some bands were seriously addressing White prejudices against their religious practices and were actively seeking a compromise in the matter.

To what extent ceremonies were replaced or combined with secular activities is not apparent from the reports submitted by the Department's personnel. The history of the Thanksgiving Promenades of the Assiniboin and the Tea Dance of the Plains Cree still need to be researched further on a local level. Mandelbaum reported that the Tea Dance was popular among the Plains Cree in the first quarter of the twentieth century. The celebration involved dancing, socializing, and the consumption of strong tea to which were added berries and, sometimes, plug tobacco.[63] Moreover, White-sponsored stampedes, fairs, and agricultural exhibitions, and Department-approved sports days and Treaty Days also provided people with opportunities to visit and perhaps to participate in a variety of ceremonies. Because local Whites were willing to pay to see traditional dance performances, these occasions served to promote, rather than discourage, persistent traditionalists.

Local White support for traditional exhibitions evolved out of fascination with the idea of the "frontier primitive" rather than from any advocacy for religious freedom. Program organizers for these events capitalized on this curiosity by sponsoring Indians and their families to perform at these events. As early as 1891, the Department reacted to this unexpected development. In that year, Hayter Reed wrote to Reverend J. Tims: "One of our greatest difficulties . . . is the countenancing of these dances by white people, who, not only by their presence, but in other ways encouraged them."[64]

In his 1896 annual report, Indian Commissioner Amedee E. Forget also expressed concern over Indian involvement with exhibitions:

> I might draw attention to one of the most serious [impediments] encountered in our efforts to secure the final abandonment of heathen rites and ceremonies by the Indians. I refer to the encouragement given to the Indians on reserves adjacent to towns and settlements by that element of the white population which is ever ready to assist in the creation or maintenance of anything which panders to an appetite for the sensational and novel and to whom the resultant effect on the actors therein is a matter of perfect indifference. So long as such "shows" are patronized and supported by the gate-money of this class of whites, so long will the difficulty of securing a total abandonment of such continue.[65]

Forget went as far as to suggest that the country's press would provide a valuable service by directing the public's attention to this matter.[66] However, two years later the various bands of the Pelly Agency had not only received permission from their Indian agent to have a Sun Dance, but also been asked by the community of Yorkton to have the celebration there to coincide with their First of July sports days.[67] At least 2,000 Indians of various tribal affiliations were expected to gather at Yorkton for this event. Clearly, with the growth of White towns near reserves, this type of cooperative activity increased, and the "grand Indian Pow-wow" became a major prairie event.

For the performers of "traditional" dances at White events there were rewards other than the opportunity to congregate, socialize, and perform ceremonies. Economic returns came in the form of cash payments and prizes for winners in horse races and rodeo contests, and for successful contestants in best-traditional-dress competitions. Rations were also provided to those who camped on-site. Following his trip to a number of reserves to evaluate the progress of former students, Father Hugonnard reported in 1913 that dancing at fairs and celebrations had increased on all reserves with the exception of File Hills and Oak Lake. That commercialization of indigenous performances was becoming entrenched on the prairies was evident in the coloured posters advertising the 1913 Indian celebrations at the Moose Mountain and the Assiniboine reserves. Some 3,000 Indians and Whites had attended the three-day Assiniboin event. The stampedes in Calgary and Winnipeg, and the agricultural fairs in Regina and Brandon, were also great attractions for Indian communities.

For administrators and missionaries such as Father Hugonnard, the enthusiastic response to White-sponsored events was unacceptable. Hugonnard believed that such activities were responsible for an increase in immorality (drinking and prostitution) and the neglect of farms, and were a general waste of time for school graduates who took pleasure in devoting their energies to "the making of new and better dance costumes and to the painting of their faces in some new way for every dance."[68] In a lengthy letter written to the Department in 1913, Hugonnard laid part of the blame squarely on the shoulders of Department officials themselves, who invited Indians to be represented at celebrations, fairs, and stampedes. These cases arose when political dignitaries were visiting western Canada.

For reserve communities, such occasions continued to offer evidence that there was some degree of support for their indigenous practices – a form of support that was also an important source of capital. In addition to the material rewards, the opportunities to socialize and "act as Indians" provided on these occasions encouraged many Indians to incorporate the fair and stampede circuit into their economic and ceremonial cycle.

The only public support for Indians on the question of exhibitions came from a Methodist minister, Reverend John McDougall, whose position on indigenous religious practices clearly deviated from that of his counterparts. The development of a conflict between the Department and the Alberta Provincial Indian Commission of the Methodist Church over Indian involvement in the Dominion Exhibition of 1908 spurred McDougall to express his views publicly.[69] Although he did not approve of the piercing ritual of the Sun Dance, McDougall contended that Section 114 of the Indian Act and the methods used to suppress indigenous religions challenged the principle of religious freedom:

These Indians of the old faith have as much right to join in the sun dance, or the thirst dance, as a Methodist has to join a camp meeting. We fought hard for the privilege of civil and religious liberty, and the Indian is just as much entitled to religious freedom as the white man. . . . So far as the sun dances and the thirst dances . . . is concerned, my opinion is that the Indians should not be allowed to mutilate themselves, but if the Indians who cling to the old faith wish to continue these observances, they must be allowed to do so and there is no harm in them.[70]

When McDougall requested Department permission for an Indian camp meeting in the Peace Hills Agency, he was refused despite the fact that no objectionable features were involved. Officials pointed out that approval would contradict the informal policy of discouraging all dancing and would encourage a ceremonial revival on the prairies. In addition, they informed McDougall that they were unable to discern parallels between Christian camp meetings "founded on Christian doctrine, for worship, fellowship and mutual improvement, and the original Thirst meeting which was a pagan festival for the purpose of invoking some supernatural power to send rain."[71]

Although government officials continued to refuse to consider the deletion of Section 114 and of other directives intended to undermine ceremonies, they did recognize that regulations alone would not suffice to eradicate indigenous ideologies. Rather, Christian missions and schools were viewed as the most effective mechanisms for cultural transformation. They also argued that the official discouragement of all dancing would contribute to the process by subverting the power of the traditionalist leaders and by shaming or frightening school children and their parents. But the strength of indigenous religions in comparison to Christianity had been under-rated by both the government and the missionaries. In 1896, the agent for the Assiniboine–Crooked Lakes Agency had warned his superiors that "paganism is dying hard":

There is anything but indifference to religion. The old pagan Indian is very conservative about the sun dance, and takes it very hard that it is made illegal to hold them, and great firmness will be necessary to suppress the barbarous institution. The Christian religion does not seem to progress as quickly as one would suppose, taking into consideration the amount of persuasion employed by the different denominations at work. . . . Of course the schools will show a powerful influence in the future.[72]

This resistance to religious suppression prompted Indian Agent S. Swinford of the Assiniboia–Touchwood Hills Agency to comment in 1900 that the destruction of indigenous beliefs would only be achieved by educating the children in the Western school system. While many of the elderly and middle-aged held on to their traditions, he wrote, their children would "in all probability incline towards Christianity, and . . . will not know anything about their grandparents' beliefs."[73] In Saskatchewan, however, evidence of persistence even among former students was obvious from both the petitions and the reports of Indian agents for Assiniboia-Touchwood, Battleford, Onion Lake, Qu'Appelle, Thunderchild, and the Crooked Lakes agencies.

The wording of the regulations contained in Section 114 permitted Indian ceremonial ritualists and believers to adapt to the law without destroying the integrity of their ceremonies. That is, all ceremonies were subject to official disapproval and scrutiny, but, with the exception of the giveaway, the Sun Dances themselves and other ceremonies were never specifically mentioned in the legislation as offences. Furthermore, the fact that the regulations were not uniformly implemented from one area to another significantly undermined the effect and the credibility of the government. In particular, Manitoba and Saskatchewan petitioners were able to use these cases of inconsistencies to their political advantage, as was evident in their references to what they viewed as differential treatment in Alberta where indigenous peoples continued to hold their Sun Dances openly.[74] The consequences of the Department's policy of "moderation in implementation" were clearly apparent and were succinctly pointed out by one agent's experience with Ojibway Sun Dancers from Turtle Lake, Manitoba, in 1908:

The principal man who tried to get up the Dance then produced a letter from one of the Hobbema [Alberta] Indians saying that at that agency the Department had given permission to the Indians to hold a Sun Dance and that they did not see why they were allowed to dance at one Agency, and forbidden to do so in another; this view was also taken by several Newspapers, which reported that the Wetaskiwin Sun Dance was held by special permission from the Department: this of course put me in an awkward position.[75]

The combination of inadequate legislation, inconsistent implementation, and local accommodation to these factors by Indians resulted in the federal government's reassessment of Section 114 in 1914.

During the years from 1895 to 1914, the Plains Cree and other Indian peoples in the prairie region responded to the prohibition of their ceremonies in a number of ways. Representations were made through written petitions, delegations, legal consultation, and at least one judicial test case. The legislation contained in the Indian Act and the Department's implementation of a policy of total repression of dancing was viewed as a violation of treaty promises as well as discrimination. When these official avenues for redress failed to produce results, solutions to religious repression were initiated on indigenous terms, that is, through the modification of ceremonial behaviour. While some practices were abandoned or performed covertly, others were altered, officially supervised, and even secularized and commercialized.

Other Forms of "Objectionable Customs": 1914 to 1940

7

With the close of the first decade of the twentieth century, economic issues were foremost in the minds of Sir Wilfrid Laurier's Liberal government. For the Department of Indian Affairs this meant a further reduction in expenditures and a centralization of operations in Ottawa. Salaries of Department personnel were reduced, and some employees were dismissed. Agricultural lands for European-Canadian immigrants were becoming scarce, land values had risen, and the unfarmed portions of reserves were more than ever attracting the attention of local settlers. This factor, combined with the reduction of government expenditures on Indian economic programs, placed even greater pressure on the Department's administrators to foster a viable level of economic self-sufficiency.

The Department continued to support a program of self-sufficiency through agricultural production on individually owned family farms. All unfarmed, or what were considered to be surplus, communally held reserve lands were then to be reallocated to White farmers. These developments were also symptomatic of the increasing importance of agricultural products to Canada's exports. The rationalization of labour and land resources to meet these new demands, however, would be achieved at the expense of indigenous economies.

Following World War One, the Department renewed its commitment to "civilizing" Indians and undertook a number of steps to hasten the process through the introduction of Bill 14. In 1920, the governor-in-council was empowered to apply the annuity and interest of children's band funds toward the establishment of more schools, the maintenance of existing schools, and the transportation of children to schools (c. 50, 10–11 George II).[1] School attendance was made compulsory for all Indian children between the ages of seven and fifteen years, truant officers were hired, and penalties were put in place to implement this regulation. Another clause of the same bill involved compulsory enfranchisement for those status Indians who were judged fit to become Canadian citizens, but had not volunteered to make this transition.

The compulsory enfranchisement clause would have empowered the superintendent general to appoint a board consisting of two officers from the Department and a member of the band to which the Indian or Indians being considered for citizenship belonged in order "to make enquiry and report as to the fitness of any Indian or Indians to be enfranchised."[2] Indian leaders argued that the clause would destroy their special status as "Indians" and all the rights accruing to them from this status, terminate reserve holdings by imposing individual allotments, and undermine future land claims. The Liberal Opposition leader opposed Bill 14 on the grounds that Indians had not been consulted. After heated debates over the issue, the bill was passed, only to be modified after the fall of the Meighen Conservative government. At that time, an amendment introduced by Charles Stewart, Minister of the Interior and Superintendent General of Indian Affairs, stated that enfranchisement could be initiated only "upon the application of an Indian" (S.C. 1922, c. 26, 12–13 George V).[3] In 1933, the clause was further amended to protect individuals with rights owing to them through the treaties (S.C. 1933, c. 42, 23–24 George V).[4]

Other forms of control were also imposed upon Indian communities. On the Northwest Coast, people experienced renewed government efforts to suppress their potlatches, and in the prairie region, William Graham, well known for his opposition to indigenous dancing and ceremonies, was appointed to the post of Indian commissioner for the three prairie provinces in 1920.

The Department insisted that it did not intend to deprive its wards of "such harmless sports and celebrations as are indulged in by their white brethern,"[5] but any traditional activities that would "seriously demoralize" farming operations or were judged to be a "moral and physical detriment" to society in general were to be formally discouraged.[6] The view that dancing caused physical deterioration and mental instability was expressed by Frank Pedley, the Deputy Superintendent General of Indian Affairs, to the Indian agent at Carlyle, Saskatchewan, in 1902.[7] Pedley denounced indigenous dancing as being "inimical" to good work habits and self-reliance. He also suggested that the rise in the incidence of tuberculosis might be partially attributed to the exhaustion brought on by excessive dancing.

Similar opinions were offered by Christian Indian converts who, at times, petitioned the Department to take action against the performance of traditional ceremonies. One such petition was written by a Plains Cree from the Piapot Reserve who stated that he spoke with authority since he had been dancing for sixteen years and had attended twenty-four Sun Dances.[8] His description of Saturday dancing on the reserve assuredly confirmed the Department's suspicions of the negative effects of this practice:

A meal is given and invariably a barel of apples is distributed. . . . The indians Dancing neglect their work, do not farm or very little [and] use the little money they have to buy beaded suits for the dances for themselves, wifes and children [and] to buy foodstuff or apples for the dances. The ex-pupils cannot resist the temptation and fall in with the other indians for the dancing; their clean suits soon give up and are replaced by neglected and even raggy clothes, as soon as they have the money they buy dancing [outfits] and apples to give at dance. Even when pupils come home for vacation, they put on the dancing suit which has been kept for them by parents; . . . most parents keep their children at home several years before sending them to school in order to enjoy seeing them dancing, covered with beads from the age of three or even less; . . . some went this summer to a Sun Dance at Eagle Hills near Battleford and came back eager for dances.[9]

This petitioner further informed the Department that people from nearby reserves attended the dances and that these visitors were given presents by the host community.

Efforts were increased to control the occurrences of dances both on and off reserves. As early as 1902, Agent Wheatley of the Birtle Agency in Manitoba had suggested that all dancing be prohibited; and by 1908, Frank Pedley took measures to prevent the granting of government monies to White agricultural societies that encouraged Indian cultural exhibitions.[10] A description of a pageant published by a Calgary newspaper indicates the attraction that Indian displays, particularly "war parties," held for White communities.[11] At the pageant there were 600 Stoney, Blackfoot, Sarcee, Peigan, and Blood outfitted in "gaudy trappings . . . in war bonnets, buckskin, war paint, scalps and armed with every kind of weapon, from knife, tomahawk and muzzle-loader, to the modern repeater and revolver."[12] The outfits of the "war parties" or, rather, members of the various Warrior societies, were described as "fearfully wonderfully and truly made; some were even naked."[13]

Departmental reactions to such overt displays of traditional arms-bearing warriors and feigned aggressive behaviour were predictable. Indian agents claimed that participation in these events seriously interrupted farm work, promoted the regression of school children to traditional habits, and provided opportunities for the traditionally oriented to surreptitiously perform their dancing. Moreover, it was argued that the local White demand for these exhibitions was taken by participants as an indication of support in their struggle for cultural persistence. Finally, attendance at such events was also condemned because it increased the chances of contact with the more unsavoury elements of White frontier society, especially liquor traders.[14] Foremost in the minds of administrators and churchmen was the connection between these public shows and the revival of ceremonies. Father Hugonnard's correspondence over the years with Indian Commissioner Graham included several references to this correlation. Upon their return from the 1913 Winnipeg Stampede, for example, a number of individuals from the Qu'Appelle Agency informed Hugonnard that they had received official authorization from Ottawa to dance and had even proceeded to erect a new dance hall.[15]

While these exhibitions were enjoyed by Indian participants as social gatherings and entertainment, they had also become sources for provisions and cash income. At the 1913 Winnipeg Stampede, contestants received prize money for the best-decorated traditional outfits and for horse races. In order to attract the attendance of those individuals and their families from Alberta who most ostentatiously represented public notions of the "primitive Plains Indian," organizers offered not only to pay for transportation costs and to provide food rations, but also to award $25 per tent for up to twenty-five tents of families.[16]

In the absence of legislated measures against Indian attendance at these events, the Department decided to resort to other avenues of control. Some agents threatened to withhold rations in order to discourage people from leaving their reserves during the summer months. This tactic was undermined when exhibition organizers themselves offered provisions. Furthermore, the Department had already undertaken to reduce rations on a more general level, and thus a further reduction was not an effective deterrent. In 1908, one Indian agent from the Blood Agency reported that his practice of curtailing rations to all those who travelled to local fairs was unsuccessful because fair organizers would butcher six to eight steers for the Indians.[17] Such measures clearly obstructed the Department's endeavours to dampen enthusiasm for stampedes and agricultural fairs. Some stampede organizers decided to confront the Department on this issue. For instance, the officials of the 1913 Winnipeg Stampede, along with several Indian participants, consulted lawyers on the legality of government interference in private lives in this manner.[18]

By 1914, Department officials had concluded that their informal measures for regulating dancing were impossible to implement in a uniform manner. The increasing presence of Indian people at public fairs and similar events served as a continual embarrassment to Ottawa. The performance of ceremonial and even more secular forms of dancing had become symbols of the Canadian government's failure to assimilate its indigenous population. This is clear from comments offered by administrators such as Assistant Indian Commissioner J. McKenna, who remarked upon Indian participation in the Dominion Exhibition in Calgary in 1908:

The Indians in war-paint and feathers will be pictured in English and American journals, whose readers will be given the impression that the aborigines still wander wild over the plains of Alberta. I would go so far as to suggest that if there is to be anything in the nature of an Indian exhibit or show at this Exhibition, measures should be taken to have the Indians that appear there representative of the working Indians, and clad as the ordinary people of the Country are; and that articles put on exhibition should be the product of their civilized industry.[19]

An inquiry was conducted through the Ottawa head office in 1914 in order to determine the effect of exhibition attendance on agricultural productivity and morality, and to explore possible solutions to the growing popularity of these events among reserve populations. Opinions from fieldworkers were solicited, and briefs were presented by a number of organizations including the Alberta Conference of the Methodist Church and the Board of Control of the Dry Farming Congress.[20] Statements from inspectors and Indian agents claimed that exhibitions distracted Indian farmers from sowing and planting their crops, and that these events had a "demoralizing" effect on Indians by "exposing them to temptation arising during the excitement of celebrations."[21] Coordinating managers working for the stampedes were accused of unsettling Indian farmers with advance promises of support for their involvement, a situation that encouraged reserve families to put their energies into preparing for exhibitions rather than tending to their farms.

During this inquiry, the Sun Dances and other indigenous ceremonies were condemned for identical reasons. In addition, the spread of tuberculosis and other diseases was attributed to poorly ventilated and overcrowded dance lodges and halls.[22] As for the frequency of inter-reserve visiting, the Department repeatedly insisted that it had no intention of preventing visits *per se* and that its only concern was the frequency of visitations. Nevertheless, officials, guided by the reports sent to the head office by its field employees, concluded that Indian people were incapable of using good judgement in determining their "own best interests" and of preventing their festivities from deteriorating into "mere debauches."[23] Liquor consumption, promiscuity, and the spread of social diseases were concerns mentioned in some agency reports. Accordingly, it was agreed that the Department was obliged to play a more active role in protecting its wards not only from unscrupulous Whites, but also, and most importantly, from themselves.

The informal policy of regulating all off-reserve dancing was provided with legislative backing in 1914. The legislation itself was an amendment to Section 149 of the Indian Act. It prohibited the attendance of Indians at dances held on other reserves. It also stipulated that participation in indigenous forms of activities at White-sponsored events was subject to the approval of the superintendent general of Indian Affairs or his representative:

Any Indian in the province of Manitoba, Saskatchewan, Alberta, British Columbia, or the Territories who participates in any Indian dance outside the bounds of his own reserve, or who participates in any show, exhibition, performance, stampede or pageant in aboriginal costume without the consent of the Superintendent General of Indian Affairs or his authorized Agent, and any person who induces or employs any Indian to take part in such dance, show, exhibition, performance, stampede or pageant, or induces any Indian to leave his reserve or employs any Indian for such a purpose, whether the dance, show, exhibition, stampede or pageant has taken place or not, shall on summary conviction be liable to a penalty not exceeding twenty-five dollars, or to imprisonment for one month, or to both penalty and imprisonment.[24]

Well aware that federal legislation was being used to restrict freedom of movement and regulate individual rights, the Department nevertheless proposed an amendment that was not intended to prohibit *any* Indians from attending these celebrations, but rather "to authorize the attendance of those whose interests will not suffer."[25]

The Indian commissioner, the Department's field employees, and churchmen welcomed the amendment as a positive step towards curtailing "uncivilized" and unproductive behaviour. Some, however, argued that the legislation did not go far enough. These critics contended that on-reserve events such as the three-day celebrations at treaty time often resulted in the loss of a whole week's work. On-reserve dancing remained an unresolved and contentious issue. The Indian agent's only recourse was to use his power of persuasion to regulate these dances and to encourage their replacement with secular sports days at Treaty Days celebrations.

An unexpected negative reaction to the amendment came from a government branch within the Ministry of the Interior – the Anthropological Division of the Department of Mines. Since its inception in 1842, the Geological Survey of Canada had included descriptions of indigenous cultures in its scientific reports. A number of archaeological and ethnological objects had also been collected and were housed, along with natural history specimens, in the Geological Survey of Canada's museum in Ottawa. Under the Act of 1907, the Department of Mines was established, and the Geological Survey, as part of this department, was assigned a broader mandate, including the responsibility for ethnological investigation. One of the major reasons for this change was the realization that most ethnological investigations in Canada had been conducted by American scholars and that opportunities for scientific research would soon disappear as the indigenous cultures vanished under the influence of "civilizing" policies.[26] Government scholars were also involved in providing cultural information and supplying artifacts for the ethnological exhibits being planned for the new Victoria Memorial Museum in Ottawa opened in 1910. In 1909, pressure had been placed upon the federal government to conduct ethnological studies and to centralize the information and collections in a national repository. This lobby was led by the Royal Society of Canada, the British Association for the Advancement of Science, and the Canadian Branch of the Archaeological Institute of America.[27] By 1910, the Anthropological Division of the Mines Department had been formed under the headship of Dr. Edward Sapir, and within four years at least six fieldworkers had been hired to collect cultural information from Canadian Indians.

The Anthropological Division, which at the time was under the same minister as that for the Department of Indian Affairs, contended that the amendment to Section 149 would interfere with its scientific investigations. The Deputy Director of the

Geological Survey of Canada, Reginald Brock, informed the Department of Indian Affairs that he would not formally contest the amendment, provided that ethnological studies of indigenous religious practices were not obstructed. He agreed to support the amendment on the condition that the ethnology staff could "employ an Indian or Indians in a private performance of Indian rites or ceremonies for the purpose of securing such information."[28] Although the Deputy Superintendent of Indian Affairs, Duncan Scott, assured Brock that the legislation would not impede scientific investigations, Brock remained unconvinced. In correspondence with the Department, Brock pointed out that information regarding ceremonial practices was difficult to obtain "under the best of circumstances" and that "a suggestion that it was illegal . . . might absolutely stop the work."[29] He recommended that a provision for research might be added to the Indian Act in order to facilitate scientific studies. Such a provision, he argued, would not only exempt researchers from Section 149, but also have the benefit of exalting research in the eyes of indigenous peoples.[30] Brock's concern for scientific access to Plains ceremonialists did not imply that ethnologists were prepared to become political advocates by opposing the amendment to Section 149 as a breach of religious freedom. Ultimately, no special provisions were made to officially accommodate the work of the Anthropology Division, because Scott decided that field investigations could still proceed if the ceremonies were performed according to the letter of the law.

Once the amendment to Section 149 became law, the Department issued a circular to Indian agents on June 17, 1914, for a public reading on all reserves. The reaction of Indian communities was unexpected, for they interpreted the law to mean that the Department's "informal" policy of prohibiting *all* dances was at an end. Some even viewed this amendment as an official approval for the performance of ceremonies and dancing *within* the boundaries of each respective reserve, provided that the specified objectionable features were eliminated. Ironically, the amendment, designed to increase the power of Indian agents, only served to erode their authority in the eyes of their wards.

William Graham, at that time Inspector of the South Saskatchewan Inspectorate, vented his frustration at this turn of events in correspondence with Ottawa. He believed that the Department's refusal to legislate against the performance of all indigenous dancing had only made matters worse, since tradition-oriented Indians believed that they finally had "the sympathy of the officials higher up on this dance question and [were] continually bringing it up."[31] In fact, the circular was perhaps one of the first official statements clarifying the parameters of legislation pertaining to dances. The fact that the circular was read by local Indian agents without reference to the official general policy of opposition to *all* dancing, in principle, prompted

Graham to warn his superiors that the inadequacy of the new amendment was "sufficient to cut loose any strings that we had to partially control the dancing up to that time."[32]

In 1915, Graham's worst fears were confirmed as agent after agent reported the revival of open dancing on reserves. Missionaries from the Qu'Appelle Agency observed that nearly all the school graduates on the Piapot and Muscowpetung reserves had "retrogressed" to their old customs by "painting their faces" and "tying false hair on their head"; as a consequence, all farming and work had "gone to pieces."[33] These reports were taken seriously by the Department, and immediate steps were taken to remind agents that the officials had not abandoned their original intention to suppress *all* dancing. In response to Indian Commissioner Graham's critique of the new amendment, the assistant deputy and secretary of the Department assured him that this section in no way authorized anyone to participate in celebrations without first receiving approval from the proper authorities. The issue of what constituted harmful dancing activities was also addressed. Graham was informed that the Department would continue to support the suppression of dancing when it had a "demoralizing" effect, or took farmers from their work, but that it did not intend to prohibit "simple dances" held on home reserves.[34] In 1915, a second circular clarifying the Department's official stand on ceremonial dancing was issued to agents. In this document, Indian agents were instructed to use their "utmost endeavour to dissuade the Indians from excessive indulgence in the practice of dancing" and to allow only forms of "reasonable amusement and recreation."[35] The definition of *reasonable* was left to the judgement of local authorities.

Immediately after the 1914 amendment came into effect, a number of dance-related arrests were made. These "manifestations of the strong arm of the law" were most evident in the Saskatchewan prairie region and were intended to serve as cautionary warnings to those who defied the law.[36] Among those who would serve as examples to other recalcitrants were several Saskatchewan religious leaders, including the elderly headman Fineday. More arrests were made in June 1915, when some 2,000 people (predominantly Cree) had gathered at Whitefish Lake near present-day Wynyard to celebrate a Sun Dance sponsored by Charles Tott as a thanksgiving for the recovery of his ill child. Chief Joseph Kenemotayo was arrested for "permitting" the dance to be held; Charles Tott for leaving his home reserve at Sturgeon Lake and organizing the dance; and Seeahpwassum Kenemotayo for leaving his home reserve without permission and inducing people to attend the ceremony.[37] Because celebrants from the Mistawasis Reserve were present at Tott's invitation, the police were able to charge the three men with sponsoring an off-reserve ceremony. At a trial before the Indian agent, all three pleaded guilty and requested leniency in sentencing. Charles Tott was sentenced to thirty days' imprisonment, to be served at Prince Albert, Saskatchewan, and the other two men were fined $5 and $2.50 and costs to be paid at treaty payment time.

More celebrants were convicted in 1915. A Sun Dance on the Little Pine Reserve was attended by members of the Sweet Grass Reserve, including Chief Fineday. As at Whitefish Lake, the presence of participants from other reserves provided the agent and the Battleford police with the pretext to make a number of arrests. Of the twelve men who were apprehended, six were convicted, including Fineday, who had hired a lawyer to defend his right to attend a ceremony on another reserve. In this case, the Indian agent also felt obliged to hire a lawyer to represent the Department because, as he explained, he "was fighting a losing battle, and the Indian Act was not explicit enough on certain points."[38]

A number of other reserves had similar experiences, and many ceremonies were interrupted while in progress. Reports on the activities of the following reserves were made in the Department's files: Alexander, Buffalo Point, Edmonton Agency, Little Pine, Long Lake, Long Plain, Ochapowace, Onion Lake, Pelican Lake, Piapot, Poundmaker, Red Pheasant, Rocky Mountain House, Sakimay, Swan Lake, Thunderchild, and Whitefish Lake.[39] In 1919, the police were asked to investigate a Sun Dance at the Piapot Reserve and to monitor associated activities. They reported that no arrests were made since no "rites of the savage" (piercing) were performed.[40] Three years later, approximately 500 people were dispersed from a Sun Dance being held at the Red Pheasant Reserve, where at least two other reserves were represented. Participants were informed that they could not continue the ceremony, and they were eventually persuaded by the chief to return to their homes. In order to demonstrate visibly the Department's disapproval of such gatherings, the constable in charge chopped down the sacred Sun Dance pole.[41] This act of sacrilege was defended on the grounds that "Indians used to torture themselves in a barbarous manner at these sun dances, and there was always the possibility – albeit a remote one – that they might revert to the practice."[42]

The last recorded extensive series of prosecutions connected with the performance of a Sun Dance occurred in 1921. Leaders responsible for a Sun Dance held at Buffalo Point, Manitoba, were charged with engaging in a ritual of self-sacrifice by piercing. During this particular ceremony, approximately ten men underwent the forbidden ritual as an offering for the return of their health after being stricken with a severe form of influenza.[43] While some of the convicted were given a suspended sentence, the organizer of the dance, who had sponsored the ceremony to relieve the trauma caused by the epidemic, was sentenced to a prison term of two months.

Throughout this period, arrests and convictions were generally not viewed by the Department as the ideal ways of terminating communal ceremonial activity.

Police surveillance and the regulation against off-reserve dancing in combination with the intermittent use of the pass system were the typical means of regulating ceremonial attendance. As Commissioner Graham noted, the very appearance of the police was usually a sufficient deterrent.[44] In cases where dancing was legal, however, the commissioner could not depend upon any further action since the official directive to discourage all dancing was not backed by legislation.[45] But the police refused to interfere in legal ceremonies, as indicated by their refusal to interrupt a Blackfoot Sun Dance in 1922 when no offences against the Indian Act were evident.[46] Again, in 1923, upon a request from the Hobbema Reserve, the RCMP commissioner, on the recommendation of the local police detachment, formally supported the performance of a modified Sun Dance and even managed, much to Graham's consternation, to receive the approval of the deputy superintendent general of Indian Affairs.[47] In general, however, the police did respond positively to requests for the investigation of ceremonies on behalf of the Department. For example, in 1927, police were asked to look into a Sun Dance being held on the Poundmaker Reserve. Because of the presence of off-reserve participants, the police dispersed some 500 to 600 people who originated from several different reserves.[48] Although those responsible for the gathering (termed *ringleaders*) were brought to Battleford to appear before the Indian agent, no charges were laid and they were released after a lecture. These surveillances of larger ceremonies were common occurrences, as indicated by Superintendent G.L. Jennings in his annual report for 1927: "During the summer months we are often requested by Indian agents to attend Indian celebrations, sports, dances, etc. At times large gatherings from various reserves meet quietly at some central point for the purpose of carrying out a series of dances, against the orders or wishes of the Indian agents."[49] As late as 1938, police had attempted to prevent the putting up of a Rain Dance lodge at Onion Lake Reserve, but in this instance they were unsuccessful.[50]

The general reluctance by the local police detachments to act "beyond the law," and the accommodation by reserve communities to the letter, if not the spirit, of the legislation eventually convinced Graham that a moderate policy was unworkable. He believed that Indians would ultimately be forced to choose between cultural persistence or progress. As the commissioner informed his superiors, "No amount of talking or moral suasion can stop them . . . we will either have to give up farming and [allow] the Indians to carry on their dance, or stop the dances and carry on the farming."[51] Other agents shared Graham's critical evaluation of a moderate policy. For instance, in 1922, Indian Agent G. Gooderham of the Blackfoot Agency referred to reserve participation in Sun Dances and the Calgary Stampede in his agency as a "serious" situation and recommended the use of every means of "legal force to compel an able bodied Indian to do his work."[52]

To the extent that it was enforced, the pass system was also proving to be ineffective as a restraint. Graham pressed for a more careful scrutiny of applicants before passes were issued, arguing that people abused the system particularly when making requests to visit sick relatives. Invariably, the term *visiting* was broadly interpreted by Indians as a leave to attend ceremonies. Therefore, in 1921, Graham issued a directive to his agents to prosecute visitors to reserves who engaged in activities other than those specified in their pass.[53] From the perspective of members of reserve communities, this meant that visitors were prohibited from providing spiritual, emotional, and material support to relatives and friends during ceremonies. In spite of this obstacle, visitations for these purposes continued, as was indicated by Graham's 1921 report of an incident at Moose Mountain:

The Indian when asking for a pass to visit another Reserve from his Agent, is very careful not to mention that he has any knowledge that a dance will take place on the Reserve which he intends to visit, but will state that the object of his visit is to visit "Sick relatives." In the case under review, . . . the visiting Indians were permitted to remain owing to the fact that they had passes from their Agents; in no case did the pass state that they were for the purpose of attending an Indian dance – "visiting sick relatives" I am informed was the reason given for their visit in each case.[54]

Giveaways involving the ceremonial redistribution of goods, money, and labour also continued to be an important feature of reserve economies. They sometimes, but very rarely, ended in arrests. No such cases appear to be recorded for the Plains Cree. One young man from the Blackfoot Agency was given a suspended sentence for passing twenty-five cents to a woman during a dance in 1915.[55] Also in 1915, Big Chief Face was convicted by the Supreme Court of Alberta for making a presentation of two mares at a Blackfoot ceremony, and a resident of the Swan Lake Reserve in Manitoba was sentenced to two months in 1926 for giving away a buggy and other goods.[56] The fact that money was collected in support of the war effort during some of the giveaways held between 1914 and 1918 did not deter the Department from adhering to the legislation. Giveaways sponsored in support of projects that would have in themselves received approval from the Department were similarly discouraged. For example, the collection of funds for the construction of a church or to assist the needy was not considered an objectionable undertaking unless it occurred at a traditional dance. Such was the case of the Dakota from the Griswold area in Manitoba in 1917:

We help anyone with the money, and in that time they were going to build a church here on this reserve. So we had some money from the dancing and we [gave] help to the church. We give 225 dollars and that is the best thing we did. And when we have dances we always talk about the seeding and how the children are going. . . . When anyone cannot seed for himself, he tells it in the dances, and we can go and finished his seeding for him. . . . So anyone cannot find anything bad about the dances.[57]

This petition was written to protest the fact that the Indian agent had prohibited dancing for the previous five years. In order to present a stronger case for permission to resume dancing, the petitioners pointed out that they were raising money for the war effort at these gatherings.[58]

Information on the frequency of giveaways is not available, but this form of redistribution certainly did continue. In one Department report concerning Dakota giveaways submitted by Two Bears, information regarding the locale, sponsorship, and distribution of goods at twenty-three dances held in the Wahpeton Reserve near Prince Albert, Saskatchewan, in the winter and spring of 1916–17 were recorded.[59] Groceries, boxes of apples and oranges, and venison were distributed among the participants. One woman from the Sioux camp sold $75 worth of horses in order to make a cash contribution in support of the dance.

Another list of provisions redistributed in giveaways is available in documents associated with the arrest of Hotain, a Dakota, who had celebrated a giveaway near Oak Lake, Manitoba, in 1917.[60] In exchange for the Indian agent's permission to hold a memorial feast for the dead, Hotain had been asked to sign a statement agreeing to refrain from holding future feasts of this nature. However, he later held a giveaway and distributed shawls, guns, and cash to the participants. The collected money was to be used as a contribution towards the Patriotic Fund and to cover costs of sending a delegation of Dakota to the Department's office in Ottawa. Hotain was arrested and was forced to hire a lawyer for his defence. He was given a suspended sentence on the condition that he not hold any more dances.[61]

The Department's commitment to undermining indigenous forms of economic and political organization through ceremonial repression is also revealed in its activities among woodland communities. Ceremonies occurring along the east side of Lake Winnipeg and in the Interlake region of Manitoba were also investigated for infractions against Section 149. Giveaways held at the Bloodvein Reserve were interrupted in 1916. And in 1921, Joseph Black's giveaway drum from the Hollow Water Reserve was seized by the local police detachment. The police, in turn, destroyed the drum as a punishment for Black's part in a ceremony involving the exchange of "articles of every description."[62] In the same year, another giveaway drum was destroyed at the Jackhead Reserve after the police informed the keeper of the drum, Chief Councillor Travers, that giveaway ceremonies were prohibited in the Indian Act.[63] The Indian agent also recommended that Travers be removed from office because of his involvement with giveaways. Other police records demonstrate that giveaways were occurring at least once a week during the same period in the Manitoba Interlake region despite warnings from the Indian agents.[64]

Giveaways at ceremonies held by the Midewiwin, or the Grand Medicine Society, were also subjected to surveillance. In 1925, a number of Saulteaux from Craig Lake, Saskatchewan, were dispersed while attempting to conduct a Midewiwin Ceremony. Since the offering consisted of material goods, the ceremony was considered to be a breach of Section 149.[65] During the same year, two other men were arrested on a similar charge; both were found guilty but were released with a warning.[66] The last recorded interference in woodland ceremonies such as the Midewiwin resulted in the prosecution of George Gilbert of the Wabigoon Reserve, Ontario, in 1938.[67] Some fifty celebrants had gathered to pray for the healing of the chief's ill son. Chief Mark Shaboqua and Councillor Pitchenesse were each given two-month suspended sentences on the condition that they never perform another ceremony. Charges included the exchange of material goods such as clothing and the payment of supplies to the officiating medicine men.

These official interventions were comparatively fewer in the woodland region of the eastern interior than in the agricultural belt. This was partially due to the logistical problems inherent in conducting police and departmental surveillance of sparsely populated, widely scattered woodland reserves, which were barely accessible without great effort and expense. Furthermore, the perceived need to transform Indian populations was a greater priority in the prairie region since, ideally, unworked or "surplus" Indian lands could be released only once the privatization of property had been entrenched among nuclear families. Once this stage in development had been reached, enfranchisement would naturally occur and people would be expected to assume their rightful place in the nation-state as Canadian citizens.

In order to further discourage giveaways, the Department introduced another amendment to the Indian Act (S.C. 1918, c. 26, 8–9 George V) in 1918 that provided Indian agents with greater power. Before this date, self-mortification rituals and giveaways had been indictable offences; that is, the agent was allowed to press charges for infractions of the Indian Act. However, he was not permitted to preside over the hearings of specific cases. Thus, the legal cases had to be heard by another official of the court. Under the 1918 amendment, the word *indictable* was replaced with the term *liable* and the process of *summary conviction*.[68] As the assistant deputy minister explained to George Race, the Indian Agent at Edmonton, agents now had the power to try cases under the provisions of Section 161 of the Indian Act as well as infractions against Sub-section 2 of Section 149. However, the Department continued to recommend that preventive measures with regard to dancing and giveaways were preferable to "prosecution."[69]

Another amendment to the Indian Act was proposed in 1934 by the Assistant Indian Commissioner, Charles Perry, in order to further control potlatching activities among the Northwest Coast peoples. If passed, the amendment would have had implications for the suppression of giveaways. Perry had recommended that the Indian agent and police be authorized "to seize and detain any goods and supplies, in excess of immediate family needs, accumulated by an Indian and reasonably believed to be intended for potlatch purposes."[70] The Indian agent at Alert Bay suggested that other restrictions to potlatching activities be instituted, including the arrest of everyone who attended potlatches and even the owners of traditional potlatch-related paraphernalia. While the Department refused to support these measures, the seizure-of-property clause was officially recommended. The seizure amendment was tabled in early 1936 but was reversed largely due to the efforts of a former Indian agent, A.W. Neill, who was now the Independent member for Comox-Alberni.[71] Efforts to terminate the potlatch system, particularly in the Kwakewlth Agency at Alert Bay, continued. While some officials went as far as to admit that indigenous economies might have had a useful function in the past, they maintained that holding potlatches was "wholly unsuited to modern conditions."[72]

In addition to strengthening existing regulations on the performance of dances and providing agents with more power through the "summary conviction" process, the Department employed several other means to check ceremonial persistence. As in the pre-1914 period, pressure was brought to bear on local indigenous leaders to support federal Indian policies and the Indian Act. In 1916, Secretary McLean responded to a request submitted by Cree Chief Thunderchild and Councillor Okanee of the Thunderchild Reserve to hold a Sun Dance by warning them that they were expected to support their Indian agent's efforts to "advance the Indians towards the adoption of the customs of civilization and to exert their influence in that direction."[73]

In 1917, Walter Ochapowace, the hereditary chief of the Ochapowace Reserve in Saskatchewan, was removed from office by Graham on the grounds of incompetency. Ochapowace had forwarded a request to the Department to hold a Tea Dance and to allow inter-reserve gatherings on the Kahkewistahaw and Ochapowace reserves. In addition, Ochapowace asked for permission for his people to gather socially at schools and churches on the condition that they not "mutilate" their bodies or "give anything away unless it be something on the table to eat and [in] friendship."[74] His concluding query regarding the official restrictions on his movement off the reserve was a powerful commentary on the personal hardships and frustration brought on by such controls: "Can I not go with my wife and visit my wife's people on the other Reserve without being guilty of an offense."[75] In a second petition, Ochapowace had also asked the Department to consider the unification of his reserve with Kahkewistahaw under the administration of one farm instructor, school, and church.[76]

Another Cree headman, Thunderchild of the Thunderchild Reserve, received similar treatment from his Indian agent. In 1922, Agent S. McDonald, in an effort to check the rising incidence of pow-wows on the Stoney, Red Pheasant, and Thunderchild reserves, warned the headman that he would lose his "Gold Braid" (the braidwork appearing on a chief's treaty outfit) if he continued to support ceremonies.[77] This act would have symbolized the loss of Thunderchild's official status as a chief. His record of loyalty evident through his successful efforts in leading his own band and a segment of Big Bear's followers into treaty negotiations did not temper the Department's threat.

With the expansion of federal medical services to reserve communities, the Department subjected another class of people to closer scrutiny. Attacks against those referred to as medicine men (shamans and healers) were forthcoming from missionaries and medical professionals who believed that indigenous healers were responsible for the physical, moral, and spiritual deterioration of Indian communities. A statement that typified this attitude was contained in a report submitted to Ottawa by the nursing field matron at the Cree reserve of Little Pine. The medicine men were accused of being the "laziest" men on the reserve, who used their cunning for their personal gain "by working on the credulity and ignorance of their brethren."[78] The medicine men were also blamed for the reluctance of the relatives of the sick to allow the Department's medical officer to visit them.[79]

Since no federal legislation referred to indigenous medical practitioners, agents had little recourse other than personal influence. This approach had limited effect for a number of reasons. In the first place, most healing ceremonies were not overtly practised and thus escaped detection. In the second place, adequate federal medical facilities and medicines were simply not readily available to reserve populations. Like many European immigrant groups who had settled in the prairie region, Indian communities continued to depend on their own resources for dealing with illness. At this time, the Department could not resort to provincial medical acts since Indian healing activities were not illegal as long as they were practised within reserve boundaries. In the absence of prohibitive legislation, officials resorted to "informal" methods to discourage healers and their patients. These methods included the withholding of government rations and opportunities for government employment, the denial of more general types of aid, and "vaguer threats of official sanction."[80]

Because indigenous forms of religious expression were viewed as recreational activities, the substitution of secular alternate activities for ceremonial dances was considered a culturally appropriate solution to complaints about the severity of the government's repressive measures. Initiatives taken by Indian agents to replace ceremonies with European-Canadian versions of recreation were supported by Deputy Superintendent Duncan Scott, who officially approved of any "endeavour to substitute reasonable amusements for this senseless drumming and dancing."[81] In 1917, the Blood Reserve Indian Agent, W. Dilworth, recommended that a Department grant be allocated for the purchase of prizes for fairs and sports meets. They would be offered, of course, only for competitions in European-Canadian forms of activities.[82] This request was in keeping with a program of Indian agricultural exhibitions that had been introduced in the late 1880s. The Department had awarded funds to the territorial agricultural societies in order to provide prizes for outstanding examples of Indian farm products, livestock, and a variety of home-made household items and farm equipment. These monetary rewards were intended to raise levels of individual productivity by encouraging a "healthy spirit of competition" among reserve farming families.[83] Therefore, from an official perspective, not only did these exhibitions and sports days provide Indians with "reasonable amusements," but they also served to put in place a system of rewards for those individuals who adopted the dominant society's value system and lifestyle. Seriously considered to be replacements for large public ceremonies such as the Sun Dances, these secularized gatherings received the Department's blessing through the early twentieth century.

Commissioner Graham, supported by Father Hugonnard, never wavered in his commitment to the policy of repressing traditional behaviour and practices. Of particular concern to these men was the participation of school graduates in ceremonies. Not only did they regard such activity as morally and spiritually detrimental, but they saw its persistence as evidence of the failure of the Indian school system. In opposing a petition made by the Swan Lake Reserve Indians in Manitoba for a Sun Dance, Graham reiterated his stand against Indian dances and used the opportunity to impress upon the Department the negative consequences of moderation. Graham reported that the graduates from Swan Lake and other parts of the Portage la Prairie Agency encouraged the older Indians to perform the Sun Dance and travelled from town to town attending picnics and horse races that took place within a radius of a hundred miles of their reserves.[84] Graham trivialized the efforts of tradition-oriented graduates to re-learn and practise their indigenous customs, noting that they "dress up like old time Indians and are the laughing stock of the white community around, who know perfectly well that they have been through our schools."[85] Although some Indian agents suggested that reserve agricultural productivity would increase if such ceremonial and recreational activities were permitted on a regulated basis, Graham refused to believe that Indians were able to refrain from what he perceived to be self-indulgence and excessive forms of behaviour. Graham believed that his wards had "no idea of moderation with regard to the pursuits of pleasure"; he insisted that they became easily excited and unsettled and, unlike White people, were not capable of settling down to farm work after such activities.[86]

Overriding all these objections was Graham's determination to promote agricultural development and to release unfarmed reserve lands to European Canadians. Throughout his career, the commissioner had been committed to these goals. This explains his initiation of the File Hills colony for former students, his actions as supervisor of the Greater Production Scheme during and after World War One, and his aggressive promotion of new legislation to facilitate the release of "unused" portions of Indian lands to White farmers. For Graham, the persistence of indigenous forms of behaviour, especially ceremonial dancing and communal economic relations, remained a major obstacle to Indian economic self-sufficiency. In his view, traditional customs and values, rather than ineffective government programs, were partially responsible for economic troubles. The attraction of traditional forms of cultural practices for school graduates left Graham perplexed. In 1931, he was appalled by reports from Indian agents that boarding-school students were so easily persuaded to "revert to these pagan customs" and, in some cases, actually became ceremonial leaders themselves.[87] Even graduates from his beloved experimental colony at File Hills were known to have attended the occasional traditional dance. As one former colonist, Eleanor Brass, has explained, their founder considered fiddle dances, Pow-wows, and all forms of ceremonies to be hindrances to "progress." Brass recalls attending a fiddle dance with her sister and parents "secretly" and that "everyone seemed to enjoy themselves very much – possibly the more so because they had been forbidden."[88]

The regression of young people once they returned home from school was largely responsible for Graham's demand for more restrictive legislation and a firmer hand in administering existing regulations. The specific targets for more repressive measures were those "unprogressive traditionalists" who were accused of undermining economic programs by encouraging ex-pupils "to neglect their work and revert to the Pagan standard of living."[89] Graham was equally concerned about the rapidly disappearing game resources and the impoverishment of those families who continued to resist farming as an alternative to hunting and casual labour. The commissioner's most comprehensive statement on the situation was written in 1921:

If we do not prevent these objectionable customs, we will only be marking time, and our efforts towards making material progress will be futile ... in many instances the Indians will take up more than a reasonable amount of time in the pursuit of pleasure, but it is hoped that by earnest effort and cooperation, we can prevent them from leaving their Reserves in a body, as they have been in the habit of doing at the time of the year when they should be engaged at working on their summerfallow, which practice has resulted in badly prepared land, with the consequence that in many instances instead of getting a return of at least twenty bushels of wheat per acre, they have only been getting eight or nine bushels. We have a very short season in which to prepare the land and the Indian cannot hope for success, if he wastes this valuable time.[90]

For Graham, there would be no "Indian problem" if Indian farmers took only a single day, like their White neighbours, to attend a local celebration.

That the appropriate "measures of discipline" needed to enforce the terms of Section 149 were not forthcoming from the Indian agents was evident in Graham's criticisms of lenient field employees. As a case in point, in 1915, the commissioner was disturbed by reports that the Star Blanket and Little Black Bear bands of the Assiniboine Agency in Saskatchewan had taken advantage of Indian Agent Thomas Donnelly's permissiveness and had insisted on holding their dances. During the same time, another Saskatchewan agent had allowed the celebration of ceremonies in the Balcarres area and at Standing Buffalo. For Graham, this type of leniency was unacceptable, and the agent was accused of not possessing the "force of character" needed to control the Indians.[91]

Until his retirement in 1932, Graham remained unwaveringly opposed to policies of moderation. The discrepancy between Graham's and his superior's position on policy implementation was illustrated in an incident arising from the Hobbema Sun Dance of 1923. After his tour of the west in 1922, Deputy Superintendent Duncan Scott had witnessed firsthand the persistence of indigenous dances but continued to support the Department's policy of "persuasion" and "compromise."[92] To this end, Scott was amenable to the idea of allowing the performance of ceremonies such as the Sun Dance, with the provision that their duration be greatly reduced and that prohibitions contained in Section 149 be respected.[93] This compromise was negotiated in 1922 and 1923 with the Blackfoot and Cree of the Hobbema Agency.[94] While he was unable to keep the Blackfoot in the Hobbema Agency to their promise of shortening their Sun Dance from ten to three days, Scott was more successful with the performance of a shortened and supervised Cree Thirst Dance in the same agency. Graham, who received the backing of the missionaries in the area, was deeply perturbed by Scott's seeming disregard for his authority and expertise in the field of Indian affairs. Graham openly criticized the Department for its moderate position and pointed out that the inconsistency in policy between Ottawa officials and field staff would only serve to encourage the revival of dancing. Moreover, he argued that his own campaign against dancing would be seriously compromised if people became aware that his superior did not support his informal measures to discourage ceremonies.[95] In 1931, he once again requested Scott to refrain from officially sanctioning "legal" dances throughout western Canada.[96]

Throughout his career, Commissioner Graham also remained opposed to Indian participation in fairs, exhibitions, and stampedes, and he continued to advise Ottawa to turn down all White requests for Indian involvement. Other activities, such as

Wild West shows and film-making that featured traditional clothing and behaviour, were similarly discouraged. In 1914, two requests for filming Indians in their traditional settings were officially denied.[97] The first submission, made by the British and Colonial Photographic Company, requested permission to film ceremonies and dances on western reserves. The second was a petition made by the Reverend John McDougall on behalf of a small group of Indians for their participation in a film on location in the Wainwright Buffalo Park.

Graham's continued protest against Indian involvement in these events was welcomed by most Indian agents and regional administrators. J.A. Markle, Inspector of Indian Agencies and Reserves for the Alberta Inspectorate, claimed that the lack of economic progress on his reserve was due to the fact that his charges were "often enticed away from their homes and their work to take part in so called Wild West Shows."[98]

Despite Department regulations and personal efforts of administrators like Graham and his field staff, local fairs, exhibitions such as Banff Indian Days, and rodeos like the Calgary Stampede continued to draw families away from their reserves. While the persistence of important aspects of Indian cultures, the loss of productive agricultural labour and time, and exposure to unsavoury White influences were obvious motivations behind government policy, some astute observers were also concerned about the new role models who seemed to be having an effect upon the children. Specifically, the hard-working Christian farmer and rancher were being challenged as role models by a new hero – the free-spirited rodeo star. Using the example of the Calgary rodeo hero, Tom Three Persons, Indian Agent W. Dilworth wrote:

The fact that Tom Three Persons, a Blood Indian won the belt and championship at the Calgary Stampede in 1912, has been responsible for the condition, that every boy on the Blood reserve between the ages of 17 and 23 wished to be a second Tom Three Persons, and all they think about is saddles, chapps, silver spurs, Race and bucking horses, etc., a full equipment of the above accoutrements makes him a hero in his own eyes, and in the eyes of the admiring young women on the reserve.[99]

Between 1914 and 1919, the Department withheld official approval of Indian participation in fairs and stampedes, but, by the 1920s, the battle had been lost. In the opinion of historian Brian Titley, the growth of the Calgary Stampede as "one of the leading 'wild west' shows on the continent" was partially responsible for the failure of the Department's policy of cultural suppression.[100] In 1919, organizers of the stampede defied both Scott and Graham by sending invitations to Indians to participate. And in 1923, Scott's opposition to a formal request was duly subverted when the organizers appealed directly to Superintendent Charles Stewart, who had once been premier of Alberta.[101] In the following year, a compromise was reached and Graham was directed to make the appropriate arrangements for Indian involvement. It was agreed that Indians could attend the Stampede provided that the Department's officials were allowed to supervise their charges and that organizers would exhibit school work and handicrafts.[102] In exchange for these conditions, some thirty lodges would be set up in the fair grounds and a number of Indians would be permitted to ride in the parade in traditional outfits.

Despite the fact that the regulations contained in the Indian Act were proving to be ineffective, there was no move at this time to introduce further restrictions. This cautionary policy can be largely credited to Scott, who persisted in advocating "moderation," claiming that the approach had been effective in the administration of eastern-Canadian Indians. Scott continued to insist that "persuasion" and an "appeal to reason and experience" would be successful once more Indians were self-supporting, educated in the ways of the European Canadian, and able to enjoy "free contact with a civilizing environment."[103] And, while Scott might have shared Graham's opinion that dancing and participation in White-sponsored summer events could be controlled only if the pass system was legislated as an amendment to the Indian Act, he was doubtful about whether he could convince Parliament to endow the Department with this power.[104] Thus, the pass system was never backed by legislation.

By 1931, perhaps as a result of pressure from Graham, Scott was having second thoughts regarding the efficacy of the Department's policy of "firmness and moderation." In correspondence with his superior, Scott expressed his frustration with the failure of legislation in discouraging indigenous cultural practices. Scott indicated that he was rendered "powerless" by a "feeble" and "inoperative clause" in the Indian Act, and that he was hopeful that Parliament would give the Department "the power to control aboriginal customs and native restlessness."[105] In Scott's opinion, the government's objective to create self-supporting Indian farming operations would never be realized if the Department could not prevent Indians from "squandering their time."[106]

In response to Scott's appeal for greater departmental control over tradition-oriented Indians, some modifications were made to provisions of the Indian Act. In 1933, the words "in aboriginal costume" were deleted from Section 149, now 140 (S.C. 1932–33, c. 42, 23–24 George V), which meant that *any* participation – not only that involving special dress – in off-reserve pageants, shows, dances, exhibitions, or other performances was punishable by a penalty of $25 and/or one month's imprisonment.[107] Indian attendance at these events was permitted only if the approval of the superintendent of Indian Affairs or the agent was obtained beforehand.

Although the successors of Graham and Scott did not lobby for further restrictions, other amendments to the Indian Act did affect the implementation of Section 149. In 1927, Section 92 (S.C. 1926–27, c. 32, 17 George V) empowered the superintendent general to "make regulations governing the operation of pool rooms, dance halls and other places of amusement on Indian reserves."[108] Section 185 (S.C. 1930, c. 25, 20–21 George V), passed in 1930, authorized band councils, with the approval of the superintendent general, to control or prohibit "participation in, or attendance at, public games, sports, races, athletic contests or other such amusements on the Sabbath."[109] The only concession given to indigenous religious practices was an amendment to the Indian Act that presumed to protect certain aspects of cultural heritage. In March 1927, Section 106 of the Indian Act was amended to permit the prosecution of individuals who disturbed certain cultural materials located on reserves:

No title to any Indian grave-house, carved grave-pole, totem-pole, carved house-post or large rock embellished with paintings or carvings on an Indian reserve, shall be acquired by any means whatsoever by any person without the written consent of the Superintendent General of Indian Affairs, and no Indian grave-house, carved grave-pole, totem-pole, carved house-post or large rock embellished with paintings or carvings, on an Indian reserve shall be removed, taken away, mutilated, disfigured, defaced or destroyed without such written consent.[110]

Violations to this provision carried a penalty of a maximum fine of $200, seizure of said materials, and three months' imprisonment in default of payment.

Throughout the 1930s, federal policy on indigenous ceremonies remained consistent with the strategy adopted in the late nineteenth century. The Department attributed the lack of agricultural productivity and the absence of economic self-support among prairie Indians to their refusal to abandon traditional cultural practices and values. This was articulated in a 1932 report on the continuation of Indian ceremonies in the southern Saskatchewan agencies of File Hills, Carlton, and Qu'Appelle by Inspector J. Murison. Insisting that Indians had "no idea of the value of time," the Inspector stood firm in his condemnation of ceremonies, particularly those involving the attendance of people from outside the "sponsoring" reserve community.[111]

With the exception of potlatch activities on the Northwest Coast, there is no evidence to suggest that officials confiscated or destroyed ceremonial objects *en masse* as a means to control ceremonies. There is, however, one file dealing with the Department's attempts to investigate the use of peyote in connection with worship in the Native American Church. Peyote, a hallucinogenic plant, was being transported into Canada from the United States; and, since it was relatively unknown by authorities and not listed as a narcotic, possessors of peyote could not be prosecuted under the provisions of the federal Narcotics Act. In 1941, the Department endeavoured to control its entry into the country by requesting police surveillance of known users and by investigating the possibility of prosecution under the Customs Act or the Drug and Food Act.[112] Police monitoring was considered the most effective means of control, since its use was limited to a few reserves.

At this time, there was little knowledge regarding the plant's role in a ritual context, and adherents of the Native American Church (generally referred to as a cult) were accused of participating in clandestine peyote "parties" or "orgies."[113] An article published in *The Winnipeg Tribune* as late as 1954 entitled "Devil's Brew or Sacred Potion?" publicized the official discussion concerning the consumption of peyote among the Long Plain Dakota and Ojibway of Manitoba.[114] While some anthropologists defended its use as an aspect of religious freedom, churchmen, local White farmers, and the Pharmaceutical Association condemned the drug. Other than these incidents, prairie Indians, unlike their counterparts on the Northwest Coast, were not subjected to massive dispossession of their ceremonial materials.

Historical evidence in the form of government reports, anthropological fieldwork, and Indian petitions indicates that, although ceremonial life was interrupted by official repression, some form of the ritual complex persisted in many communities. This situation was perhaps predictable given the fact that the sons and daughters of the tradition-oriented parents of the 1870s had already been inculcated with indigenous values at home by the time the government-directed assimilative programs had been firmly established through the federal Indian school system. What the Department had not anticipated was the continued relevance of indigenous values and associated behaviour for even this generation of school children who had been removed from their cultural milieu through the mechanism of the off-reserve boarding school. Moreover, it was from this group of graduates that a new form of political leadership eventually emerged – but it was one that insisted upon the perpetuation of "Indian" cultural identity, values, and the freedom of worship.

Persistence, Reason, and Compromise: 1914 to 1940

8

Despite the voluntary enlistment of Indian men in the armed forces and their contribution to Canada's efforts in World War One (the Saskatchewan Cree had an especially high enlistment rate), the treatment of indigenous peoples did not change significantly in the years that followed. The fundraising activities sponsored by numerous reserves were lauded by Ottawa and received commendation in popular journalistic coverage. But even the returning Indian war veterans received little acknowledgement or support for their efforts. While they were provided with an opportunity to become enfranchised, to obtain land allotments on reserves, and to receive emergency loans under the provisions of the Soldier Settlement Act of 1917, the government's dealings with these veterans were defined according to the terms specified in amendments to the Indian Act rather than through the Soldier Settlement Board established for non-Indian veterans.

The political marginality of Indian communities was further entrenched during the period between 1914 and 1945 when the federal government introduced greater restrictions on personal and property rights. And new amendments to the Indian Act were created so that the Department (now the Indian Affairs Branch) might exert even greater control over indigenous political and economic life as well as religious and cultural forms of expression.

The war effort, however, did spark the beginnings of a national sense of Indian political self-awareness. While fighting alongside their counterparts from other areas of Canada, the Indian soldiers, who had known only their own reserve community and district, had discovered "that a person's race or religion seemed unimportant when they had to fight to stay alive."[1] They also developed a strong sense of brotherhood with soldiers from other Canadian indigenous cultures. In his study of the effect of the World War One experience on Indian soldiers, Brian Titley has observed that the "seeds of pan-Indian consciousness" were sown during the war and "an awareness of common grievances was created which led naturally to a perceived need for political action on a national scale."[2]

In 1919, this brotherhood and consciousness-raising experience found political expression through the creation of Canada's first national Indian organization, the League of Indians of Canada. Under the leadership of its president, Fred Loft, a war veteran from the Upper Mohawk Reserve in Ontario, the membership grew to embrace many reserves. On the prairies, grievances were discussed at formal meetings of the League held in Elphinstone, Manitoba (1920), the Thunderchild Reserve in Saskatchewan (1921), and on the Samson Reserve in Alberta (1922) where some 1,500 Blackfoot, Peigan, Stoney, and Cree met to demonstrate their support for the League's platform.[3] Although the League was weakened by surveillance on the part of the Department and the police (as was all political activism suspected of anti-government and "Bolshevist" motives during the period), the lack of funding, the difficulty of effectively communicating with reserves across Canada, and its leader's poor health, the roots of cross-cultural indigenous political organization took hold in western Canada.[4] As in eastern Canada, the voices of the elders and the first generation of Indian school graduates were now reinforced by men who believed that they were in a stronger position to bring their concerns before the government. Among the League's many demands was the right to retain indigenous values and the various forms of cultural identity and customs.

Petitions sent to the Department during this period attest to the fact that prairie Indian leadership was becoming more openly critical of the Indian Act. The issue of "human rights," notably the right to religious freedom, was central to many of their written protests. A plea for religious tolerance delivered by Plains Cree Chief Thunderchild is perhaps the most definitive documented statement on the issue. As translated by the Reverend Edward Ahenakew, Thunderchild declared:

Can things go well in a land where freedom of worship is a lie; a hollow boast? To each nation is given the light by which it knows God, and each finds its own way to express the longing to serve him. It is astounding to me that a man should be stopped from trying his own way to express his need or his thankfulness to God. If a nation does not do what is right according to its own understanding, its power is worthless. I have listened to the talk of the white men's clergy, and it is the same in principle as the talk of our Old Men, whose wisdom came not from books but from life and from God's earth. Why has the white man no respect for the religion that was given to us, when we respect the faith of other nations? . . .

The white men have offered us two forms of their religion – the Roman Catholic and the Protestant – but we in our Indian lands had our own religion. Why is that not accepted too? It is the worship of one God, and it was the strength of our people for centuries. I do not want to fight the white man's religion. I believe in freedom of worship, and though I am not a Christian, I have never forgotten God. What is it that has helped me and will help my grandchildren but belief in his message.[5]

The spirit of this statement was reflected in other petitions. In 1925, elders from Lizard Point, Manitoba, protested the suppression of "legal" Medicine Dances, contending not only that these practices were exempt from the law, but also "that religious thought both Christian and heathen is a personal matter and not restricted by law."[6] During the same year, the Swan River Reserve had been actively challenging Section 149 on the grounds that it was discriminatory. Support was even forthcoming from White residents who insisted that, as Canada's earliest inhabitants, Indians had an inherent right to their ceremonies, particularly when no one was being "harmed."[7] In 1932, Chief Red Dog of the File Hills Reserve attempted to negotiate the repeal of Section 149 by offering the Department an explanation of the importance and spiritual context of ceremonial dancing from a Cree perspective; that is, rather than being a form of recreation, dancing was an important aspect of religious expression and prayer.[8] When the local police detachment investigated a ceremony on the Piapot Reserve in 1931, it was informed by Indian school graduate Harry Ball that the celebration was "just a religious service, like any church service that they held once a year, and that there would be no trouble of any kind."[9]

A number of spokesmen stressed the point that several types of Indian dances were as secular in nature as those being enjoyed by the White community. For example, Red Dog of File Hills stated that the Cree Circle Dance and Tea Dance were comparable to European-Canadian dances.[10] When Dakota members of White Bear's band from Carlyle, Saskatchewan, protested their Indian agent's decision to "shut down" their dances in 1929, they reminded the Department that Whites in the area entertained themselves at dances almost every day at the Carlyle Lake resort.[11] Petitioners from the Qu'Appelle Reserve minimized the traditional content of their dances by emphasizing their participation in European-Canadian forms of social activities. As their legal representatives, barristers Miller and Wilson wrote in 1928 that the Qu'Appelle people wished to hold "ordinary dances" consisting primarily of "imitations of white mans dances which they learned at school, also some jiggs and marches"; musical instruments were also listed – a drum, fiddle, and gramophone.[12] Despite this attempt to "Anglicize" their dances, Ottawa officials, after due consultation with Commissioner Graham, advised the Qu'Appelle Reserve that it was in their "best interests" that the request be refused.[13] In 1929, Graham took a similar position when Indian Agent E.W. Stephenson recommended that people in the Wood Mountain Agency be allowed to hold secularized dances. Stephenson argued that certain amusements should be allowed at the "discretion" of the agent and that this power would provide the agent with a means "to induce the Indians to perform their work at the proper time – permission to hold dances or other amusements could be given or withheld according to conditions."[14] Much to the dismay of Graham, the acting assistant deputy and secretary agreed with this proposal.

Several other types of arguments were put before Ottawa officials by a number of communities that had participated in the war effort. Between 3,500 and 4,000 Indian men had voluntarily enlisted in the armed forces, and this contribution became an important political argument in the lobby for religious freedom.[15] As a counter-argument to the Department's claim that dancing and giveaways were a waste of time and property, petitioners hastened to point out that these same dances facilitated the collection (through the redistribution of cash) of significant amounts of money for the National Patriotic Fund. Saskatchewan reserves alone had raised approximately $17,000 through their dances and might have made an even greater contribution if the Department had not discouraged large public dances.[16]

Traditional dances, and particularly the Pow-wows, were also important venues for honouring and blessing those who had enlisted in the war effort. In an appeal to the Department in 1932 by Henry Two Bears of the Indian Temperance Union Society in Alberta, the performance of a Pow-wow at the Prince Albert Exhibition was defended on the grounds of both its affinity to White dances and its patriotic intent. Two Bears explained the meaning of one of the Pow-wow songs that had been composed in honour of Indian war veterans in these words: "Germany declared war but we don't want her to pull down Canada's Flag."[17] In addition, a Canadian flag had been requested for use at this Pow-wow. On the recommendation of Inspector W. Murison, who feared that his approval would establish a precedent for performing indigenous dances at exhibitions, the Department withheld its approval of the event.[18]

Several other petitioners specifically addressed the clause of the Indian Act that prohibited the wearing of traditional clothing at White-sponsored events. Of particular note was a letter of concern forwarded in 1931 by the elders of the Sakimay Reserve in Saskatchewan, who had hired a lawyer to present their case. In a covering letter accompanying an appeal to wear traditional clothing and to dance at sports days, their barrister wrote: "Many of the Indians on these Reserves are now getting old and are desirous of these sports days to keep alive their old dances."[19] A similar stand was taken by sixty-year-old Blackbird and other elders of the Côté Reserve in Saskatchewan, who were prevented from holding their Treaty Days celebration in the customary manner in 1933:

We were not allowed to wear our head-dress or the special costume which all Indians enjoyed, and the public, we believe, attend in great numbers for the purpose of seeing the Indian regalia. . . . In order to maintain the proper spirit amongst the younger members of the band, they should be brought up to reverence our ancient customs and to learn them.[20]

A number of petitions concerning the Sun Dance were sent to the Department between the years 1920 and 1933. Among the reserves that petitioned were: Roseau

Rapids, Manitoba (1920, 1924); Hobbema, Alberta (1920, 1923, 1925); Rolling River, Manitoba (1925, 1926); Swan Lake, Manitoba (1925, 1926); Broadview, Saskatchewan (1928); and reserves from the Edmonton Agency (1926). Three petitions involved requests for the Rain Dance: Loud Voice, Saskatchewan (1929); Okanese, Saskatchewan (1931); and Fishing Lake, Saskatchewan (1932). The Loud Voice petition claimed that the Rain Dance was being allowed at other reserves such as Moose Mountain, Piapot, and Touchwood. Two of these requests appealed for an expansion of ceremonial privileges. In 1920, Chief Ermineskin of Hobbema wished to "enlarge" the Sun Dance through the participation of younger men.[21] In yet another petition submitted jointly by four reserves in the Crooked Lakes Agency, members asked to be allowed to celebrate a Rain Dance on an inter-reserve level. Their lawyer argued on their behalf that "the lines between each reserve is imaginary insofar as general customs and activities . . . are concerned."[22] Permission was denied in both cases.

As in the pre-1914 period, advocates of religious freedom continued to consult with local lawyers. For their part, a number of barristers wrote letters of support on behalf of their clients. Others were not as empathetic and felt that they were being placed in a compromising position by being asked to represent clients against a federal government department. One barrister, A. Messner, stated that he was well aware that the legal system was being used by his clients to circumvent the Indian Department's regional bureaucracy. In this instance, his clients were Sun Dance celebrants from the Swan Lake Reserve in Manitoba. In spite of his recommendation that the Sun Dancers approach their Indian agents and the commissioner, the petitioners insisted that Messner translate their demands into English and communicate them in writing directly to Ottawa.[23] Throughout this period, legal representation continued to be important for those petitioners who challenged the Department's implementation of the more informal policy of prohibiting "legal" dances.

A few communities also sought support for their cause from local police detachments and other sympathetic Whites. In 1920, the Hobbema Cree used their long-standing favourable relationship with the Hudson's Bay Company to persuade the manager of the Edmonton store to intervene on their behalf. Over the years, these Cree had continued to hold their "legal" forms of Sun Dances under the watchful eye of the police. While the presiding Indian agent had tolerated the ceremony, the Cree feared that his replacement would be less tolerant. Desiring to maintain good relations with the Plains Cree, the Company's manager, F. Harker, forwarded an appeal to the Department with an explanation that the Hobbema Cree and others "frequently call upon us to help them, and as far as it is within our power we endeavor to act as intermediaries for them."[24] After consulting with Graham, Scott refused to give his consent on the grounds that an official sanction in this case would lead to a revival of dancing on other reserves.[25]

Another potential source of support for ceremonial practices appeared when American anthropologists began to conduct their fieldwork on the Canadian prairies in the first half of the twentieth century. The interest demonstrated by anthropologists who undertook to understand and document traditional forms of ceremonies was sometimes perceived by Indian leaders as a form of empathy. For instance, in 1932, Chief Matoose of Swan Lake, Manitoba, sent a request for support to the anthropologist Donald Cadzow with a copy forwarded to the Department.[26] In the letter, Matoose appealed to Cadzow to intercede on their behalf for the right to hold a Sun Dance. The situation on this reserve was extremely tense, since one woman's death had already been attributed to the agent's refusal to allow the ceremony:

> This winter one woman was sick and we appealed to our religion the Sun-dance. And when we told Mr. Waite the Indian Agent about having the dance, he said, no, the Indian Department doesn't allow it. When this was told to the woman she was very sorry as she put her trust in getting well in joining the dance. She grew worse after then and finally pass[ed] away on the 10th. of this month. And we are asking you kindly to please, make arrangement with our Canadian Government to allow us the freedom to have our Sun Dance, and our religion.[27]

Cadzow wrote to Scott on behalf of Matoose indicating that the community was "very unhappy" because of the "severe methods" of their Indian agent and suggested that the Sun Dance, which had been reduced to a "harmless" affair, would do much towards raising their morale.[28]

A similar appeal was made to anthropologist David Mandelbaum by the Little Pine Cree in 1935. During his attendance at a Sun Dance at Little Pine, the young anthropologist was informed that he had been allowed to record the Sun Dance because he was deemed to be a "worthy man" and was advised to not be "ashamed of the way" he had acted while attending the ceremony since everything people did on this occasion was "given to manito."[29] In his fieldnotes, Mandelbaum stated that the Plains Cree assumed that he had influence and would be able to defend their religious practices, particularly against missionaries who not only kept children from these ceremonies but, more important, it seemed, "because they invoked police power to stop the ceremonies."[30] In addition, while at the Sun Dances, Mandelbaum was continually informed that "no evil" or "any evil name" had been invoked, leading him to conclude that these reassurances resulted from "the missionaries thundering about the native ceremonies being the work of the devil!"[31] Mandelbaum also wrote that he assured his hosts that he "should do all I could."[32]

Instances of direct confrontation with local officials were rare. One case from the Piapot Reserve which serves to illustrate the futility of this form of protest was recorded by Plains Cree historian Abel Watetch. The reserve wished to honour those who had died in World War One and to celebrate the safe return of its veterans by holding a Sun Dance. In order to obtain official clearance for the ceremony, one of the veterans went to Regina beforehand to confer with the "Big Boss."[33] The "Big Boss," better known as Commissioner Graham, was quoted as having responded that the Indians had been forbidden to hold Sun Dances and, furthermore, "It's part of the Indian religion and it's no damn good."[34] In his defence, the veteran argued that the fact that he had offered his life in the war effort was reason enough to receive approval. As he informed Graham, "I fought for you and I fought for all those who sat in this office during the war. I have the right to ask you to give us back our Sun Dance."[35] That summer, the Sun Dance was held despite Graham's warnings, and a number of participants from other reserves joined in the event. Local Department officials notified the police, who dispersed the visitors and allowed the performance of only a shortened version of the ceremony.

The predominant means of resistance against Section 149 was, as in the earlier period, persistence. While some may have been motivated by the principle of religious freedom, a deeper, spiritual commitment and the personally devastating conditions of reserve life continued to draw people to the ceremonies. The two decades after 1918 were extremely stressful for most prairie reserve communities. In addition to the fact that the government was assuming ever greater control over nearly every aspect of their lives and lands, there was also intense physical and emotional suffering. Not only had inadequate government economic programs resulted in a state of under-development on reserves, but also the population was being decimated by waves of epidemics. The deputy superintendent general of Indian Affairs had reported that the occurrence of tuberculosis was five times higher among Indian populations than among European Canadians, and it was anticipated that at least fifty percent of children attending boarding schools would contract the illness.[36] War casualties and the influenza epidemics that swept through Canada during the 1918–19 period also took their toll. Medical records indicate that the Saskatchewan Cree were particularly susceptible to the deadly Spanish flu, and that in 1919 as many as twenty-six deaths were reported on one Cree reserve alone.[37] It was not until 1927 that the Office of the Medical Director was established to address Indian health problems. In the interim, traditional methods of healing, especially the powerful Sun Dances, continued to provide relief on a physical, emotional, and spiritual level for "traditionalists" and Christian Indians alike.

In order to illustrate the types of ceremonial persistence that occurred in this period, I examine a number of cases found in Department files and anthropological studies. These examples are the most fully recorded occurrences of ceremonial continuity. Though they are presumably a small percentage of the total number of ritual activities, they nevertheless provide an insight into the nature of ceremonial persistence and accommodation within the context of the implementation of Section 149 of the Indian Act.

In 1919, residents of the Onion Lake Reserve in Saskatchewan petitioned Duncan Scott for a two-day Sun Dance. Petitioners stated that the ceremony was needed because of the "Great Epidemic," "the Great War," and the fact that they "have been in very poor circumstances this last few years."[38] When Indian Agent William Sibbald refused permission, Kanipitataw insisted on holding the ceremony. The events as they unfolded after the arrival of Sergeant Howard and Constable Pratt at the ceremony attest to the strength of the elders' religious convictions and their willingness, albeit reluctantly offered, to acquiesce to police authority. The incident was reported by Pratt:

We went into the tent . . . where some ceremony was being held. Canipotato, Robert Chief, Peter Thunder & Joseph Quinney and many other Indians were there. Sgt. Howard spoke to Canipotato urging him not to proceed with preparations but he was as obstinate as ever and went as far to say that the sgt. might put a bullet through his brains – if he liked that was the only thing [that] would stop him – I suggested to the Sgt. that we give him 1/2 an hour to consult with his colleagues . . . and before the time was up we were called to the tent and Robert Chief (chief) told us the dance would not go on and asked that they might conclude some ceremonies they were intercepted in and have a smoking [tent?] in the evening and if this was not objectionable the people would disperse the following morning.[39]

The Blackfoot and Cree of the Hobbema Agency caused the most controversy within the Department over their Sun Dances in 1923, because, contrary to previous policy, Deputy Superintendent General Duncan Scott had given his permission for the performance of the ceremonies. During his tour to the prairie provinces in 1922, Scott had been approached by Blackfoot representatives for permission to hold a Sun Dance and, in a spirit of "compromise," agreed to a shorter, three-day version of the ceremony. However, in the summer of 1923, the longer, ten-day version was performed.[40]

In 1921, the Indian agent and the police had stopped the performance of a Cree Sun Dance south of Wetaskiwin in the same agency and had been unsuccessful in persuading M. Christianson, the Inspector of Indian Agencies, to allow them to have a ceremony.[41] Therefore, Chief Ermineskin of the Ermineskin Band and John Curry of the Montana Band turned to the RCMP for support and were able to have a letter sent on their behalf to the Department requesting an abbreviated, supervised, "legal" version of the Sun Dance.[42] Despite Graham's and Christianson's objections, Scott permitted the ceremony to be held. The ceremonial grounds were located on the Samson Reserve just southeast of Hobbema and were open to a number of Whites, including police, the Indian agent and inspector, the farm instructor, the Edmonton manager of the Hudson's Bay Company (who distributed tea and other gifts to the headmen), and a journalist (who was allowed to film and report the event). Graham's reaction to the headlines of the *Edmonton Journal*'s coverage of the event can be well imagined. The headline – "Sun Dance of the Crees at Hobbema by Special Permission of Government" (with sub-headlines "Red Men Observe Weird Ceremony" and "Scene in Hall Where Indians Dance Continuously for Forty-Eight Hours Beggars Description: Former Barbarous Custom of Initiating Braves Left Out") – indicates the level of media sensationalism surrounding the event.[43]

The Piapot Reserve was more successful in celebrating a Sun Dance to honour its war veterans. The dance, attended by people from other reserves, was performed in spite of Graham's opposition.[44] Similarly, in 1925, several hundred people chose to disregard the Department's orders and once again gathered at the Hobbema Reserve for worship at a Sun Dance. This ceremony occurred without incident because the Indian agent had only requested the police to serve a warning and had not insisted that arrests be made.[45] And in yet another incident, four bands belonging to the Crooked Lakes Agency had a joint Rain Dance without referring the matter to the Department.[46] The police were notified and a number of participants were summoned to appear at the agency office. The charges were withdrawn when hired lawyers successfully argued that there was not sufficient evidence to lay charges against the accused.

The Indian Department, wishing to avoid confrontational situations, felt that the ideal way to prevent the occurrence of large communal ceremonies such as the Sun Dance was through early detection by monitoring people's movements as they prepared to attend these gatherings. In a response to a report that a Sun Dance was imminent at the White Bear Reserve in Saskatchewan in 1921, police were able to disperse some forty Dakota, Assiniboin, and Cree who had arrived from North Dakota to attend sports days. An additional fifty men, women, and children who were en route to White Bear from the Crooked Lakes Agency were also turned back. When an effort was made to resist the order to return to their homes, the corporal in charge reported that he was "forced to take the leader's team and start them back," and to provide a police escort to place the Indians on the road to their reserve.[47] Three years later, after receiving legal advice, approximately 1,500 people who had gathered for their treaty payment at the Saddle Lake Reserve in Alberta planned to stay on for a Sun Dance. The sponsor, Albert Stony, had intended to hold the ceremony in spite of the Department's opposition and a visit from the police. One report stated that, in fact, the dance was not held; this was probably the case, since off-reserve participants were present from Hobbema, Long Island Lake and Big Island Lake.[48] In at least one instance, the inconsistent implementation of Section

149 resulted in a "hostile" verbal exchange between the police and the chief of the Big River Reserve in Saskatchewan in 1932. Since other reserves were known to have celebrated their ceremonies, the police experienced "considerable difficulty" in dispersing some 300 people from Big River, Sturgeon Lake, and Sandy Lake who had congregated for a Sun Dance.[49]

The type and degree of confrontation varied among communities. In 1932, Indian Agent G.A. Dodds had notified police regarding the construction of a Sun Dance lodge on the Okanese Reserve in Saskatchewan. A number of off-reserve participants "refused outright to move [their] tents as instructed, stating that they had come to worship god the same as other religions."[50] Chief Red Dog, Cotasse, Adelard Starblanket, Allen Starblanket, and Buffalo Bull were arrested, but whether they were convicted is not confirmed in the available documents. However, charges were laid against leaders of a Rain Dance on the Sakimay Reserve in Saskatchewan in 1933.[51] While Indian Agent J. Ostrander had been successful in persuading the "better class of Indians" to remain at home, Rain Dance celebrants continued to make preparations. As a precautionary measure against interference, they invited a lawyer to attend the ceremony. Since people from Moose Mountain and the Qu'Appelle Agency were present, the Indian agent was provided with a justification to disband the worshipers. Although he received backing from the police, a number of participants refused to return to their homes. After consultation with his superior, the agent arrested those responsible for holding the ceremony. The charged celebrants were successfully defended by their lawyers and were subsequently released with a stern lecture.

Not all such confrontation tactics were related to Sun Dances. In 1934, when one of the Indian agents attempted to stop a Fiddle Dance being held in the community house, the participants "firmly sat him down near the door and held him there until the dance was over."[52] Their intent was not to harm the agent, but rather to demonstrate the limits of the Department's powers to both the agent and to Graham, who had issued the order for interference.[53]

The importance of ceremonial continuity to the physical and cultural survival of the Plains Cree communities was emphasized time and again at large communal gatherings. During these orations, leaders reiterated the spiritual power of their ceremonies, the strength in "community," and the need to follow sacred customary laws in order to relieve personal and community suffering. The message of resistance to religious suppression contained in these orations was evident in three speeches recorded by Mandelbaum at a Sun Dance on the Little Pine Reserve in 1935.[54] A chief and councillor advised the worshipers at this Sun Dance to persist in their faith despite possible obstruction from the authorities. The chief stated:

There is some talk going around that the Farm Instructor from Red Pheasant is coming to chase the R.P. [Red Pheasant] people back to the reserve. Do not listen and do not be scared. Let us just go at this [Sun Dance] hard. If he comes I am the one that will have to face him and I will take the blame. I will meet him and see that nothing goes wrong. The counsellor said "We have gone thru much trouble to get this dance going. . . . We take a pipe here and ask for good things. If we have faith nothing will go wrong. So much do I believe in this that I don't expect anything to go wrong. It looks a lot better to keep on singing and dancing."[55]

A second elder, Alec Tootoosis, reiterated this commitment:

We have thought much of this ceremony. Today our father has given us (the blessing) to us to reach it. Any person who wants to stop us had better desist. Boys and girls should obey the old people [in following the old ways?]. I won't force you to go at this but it is very close to the finish now. Thirty three years ago my father told me something good and I am following it yet.[56]

At another Sun Dance held at the Little Pine Reserve in 1935, a speaker urged his people to hold on to their faith in the power of the Sun Dance for, as he explained, "a lot of us had a hard time last winter. We should be thankful today to meet each other here. And let us try from now on to see this sun dance pole next year. . . . All of us – from all the reserves are poor and we are all related let us be good friends.[57]

Following the First World War, a number of communities modified their ceremonial cycle and content in response to both the continual attempts by the Department to disrupt the Sun Dance and the socio-economic realities of reserve life. Some individuals even adopted new forms of worship as alternatives to their traditional forms of worship and Christianity. Certain aspects of these historical changes have been documented in Department correspondence, Indian petitions, and anthropological reports.

By the 1920s, there were no official reports of the public performance of the piercing ritual at the Sun Dances. In the Department's files for this period, there is only one record of arrests made in connection with the practice. In 1921, a form of the Sun Dance had been introduced to the Ojibway residing at Buffalo Point, Manitoba, by a "dance maker" from the "west."[58] The sponsor, Jim Kubinase, had received the teachings to perform the ceremony through a ritualist from the Roseau River Band. At Buffalo Point, approximately ten men took part in a ritual that involved the piercing of shoulders. Although the dance was held during the night in a secluded area, the ceremony had been detected and police were notified. In his defence of his participation, one celebrant, Mayzenahweeshick, testified to the healing powers of the Sun Dance and claimed that he had been cured of rheumatism since he had taken part in the ceremony.[59] Mayzenahweeshick and another man, Blackbird, were arrested and charged under the provisions of Section 149.

In reporting the persistence of this ritual among the Plains Ojibway, anthropologist James Howard observed that, although it was no longer practised, the Sun Dance had been performed covertly during the inter-war years.[60] Howard was informed that the Plains Ojibway of southern Manitoba would travel to the Turtle Mountain area of North Dakota to celebrate the Sun Dance with their relatives. Here, the ritual of piercing was performed in the "early pre-dawn hours" to avoid detection by either Whites or the Metis. Similar published evidence is unavailable for the Dakota; however, anthropologist Wilson Wallis noted in 1914 that piercing had been last practised at Portage la Prairie, Manitoba, some fifty years before.[61]

Some Plains Cree communities had deleted the traditional form of the ritual of piercing but retained its meaning in a symbolic manner. One of Chief Piapot's relations, Abel Watetch, explained that "symbolically the same dance [Sun Dance] was performed with the dancers fastening ribbons to their clothing and tying the ends to the lodge pole."[62] The same observer reported that the intent of personal sacrifice made through the piercing ritual might have been replaced by a greater obligation on the part of the young men to make material offerings. Thus, the offering of scarce material goods became an even more important component in the Sun Dance. Other forms of personal offerings – such as prolonged periods of fasting without food or water, and sustained periods of dancing – also persisted. Ceremonial fasting was not understood as a form of prayerful offering by officials or missionaries and appears to have been rarely detected.

In addition to the deletion of certain forms of self-mortification, some communities decided to open their ceremonies to public scrutiny by admitting European Canadians. The few respectful sincere White participants were not included in this category of observers because anyone who sought help from the Sun Dance was not generally denied access to its powers. In order to prevent the interruption of this important ceremony, both the Indian agents and the police were invited to monitor the activities. During the period between 1920 and 1928, petitioners from Hobbema, Alberta (1920), Roseau River, Manitoba (1924), Swan Lake, Manitoba (1925, 1926), Rolling River, Manitoba (1926), and Little Pine, Saskatchewan (1928) indicated that either such monitoring was already in effect or that they were willing to allow this form of surveillance.[63] Another reason given by petitioners for the presence of European-Canadian authority figures at these ceremonies was the need to control liquor consumption and to prevent disorderly conduct.

At least two reserves in Manitoba – Roseau River and Swan Lake – suggested that European Canadians would be welcome at their Sun Dances, the latter proposing that curious observers be charged an attendance fee to provide revenue.[64] The Department rejected this suggestion since it was felt that a White presence would only serve to encourage and legitimize the performance of these ceremonies.

One Indian agent, W.J. Dilworth, even attempted to prevent curious White observers from viewing Blood ceremonies by ordering the construction of a fence on the Macleod side of this Alberta reserve. This action prompted one irate citizen to write a letter to the local newspaper, contending that Macleod citizens could not understand the harm they could do since few were able to make any sense out of what they were witnessing.[65]

The potential number of celebrants and the locale for Sun Dances were also affected by the regulations. The pass system, trespass law, and the prohibition of off-reserve dancing severely restricted communal participation on a large scale. Some reserves whose borders abutted one another were able to circumvent this obstacle. For example, in the 1920s, the Poundmaker and Little Pine Cree constructed their Sun Dance lodge on the borderline of the two reserves.[66] And Mandelbaum reported that in 1934 the Crooked Lakes Agency dance was held on the border between the Ochapowace and Kahkewistahaw reserves.[67] The more common, smaller, localized performances of the Plains Cree and Ojibway Sun Dances (and those of other groups) during this period can be directly attributed to restrictive measures contained in the Indian Act.

Another major modification of the Sun Dance was the continued reduction in ceremonial time to two, or one and a half, days from at least a four-day period. This time period did not include preliminary ceremonies and associated personal rituals, which would have been held at specific times throughout the ceremonial year prior to the Sun Dance proper. This abbreviated version of the Sun Dance was commonly known among the Plains Cree as the Rain Dance. This new name was possibly derived from a popularized term attributed to the ceremony by local Whites due to the tendency of rainfalls to occur during the dance. But the Sun Dance was also referred to as a Rain Dance in Indian petitions, and this possibly reflected an effort to disassociate the new form of the Sun Dance, at least in White minds, from the more controversial version. As one of the elders explained to Abel Watetch, a Piapot Cree, the Rain Dance was a shorter version of the Sun Dance – "like low mass and high mass. We performed the Rain Dance on one day instead of three days. . . . The white man never knew it was the same ceremony."[68] By the late 1920s, the term *Rain Dance* was consistently being used in correspondence received from several Saskatchewan reserves, including Loud Voice, Moose Mountain, Touchwood, Piapot, Grenfell, Sakimay, Ochapowace, Okanese, File Hills, and reserves in the Crooked Lakes Agency.[69]

This separation of the Rain Dance from the Sun Dance (at least through nomenclature) and giveaways was unsuccessful in convincing the Department that the Rain Dance should be tolerated. A petition from Chief Day Walker of the Okanese Reserve in 1931 to perform a Rain Dance was denied even though assurances were given that "the giving away of goods" and "mutilation" would not be performed.[70] Day Walker insisted only that "traditional outfits" be worn by the participants. One year later, a similar request made by members from the Fishing Lake Band in Saskatchewan was also turned down.[71] Although the Department continued to oppose the Rain Dance as an acceptable alternative to the Sun Dance, other groups in the prairie community apparently were more supportive. During the drought years, White farmers had frequently observed that rain fell during this ceremony; and much to the Indian agent's dismay, people from Fishing Lake, Ochapowace, and the Sakimay reserves were being encouraged to perform the Rain Dance. Indian Agent Ostrander wrote in his 1933 report to the Department:

I believe the Indians receive a great deal of encouragement in this connection from the white farmers in the district, who, whether they profess Christianity or not, are so anxious to see rain after two dry years that they are inclined to try anything. Naturally the Indians need little encouragement in this case as they have always been glad for an excuse to hold one of their aboriginal dances.[72]

In his 1967 interview with Felix Panipekeesick, an eighty-three-year-old medicine man from the Sakimay Reserve, Koozma Tarasoff was informed that Felix had made thirty-nine to forty Rain Dances and had received support from local farmers during the Depression years.[73] During the particularly dry years of 1938 and 1939, farmers collected between thirty-five and forty dollars to help this medicine man to hold a Rain Dance.

Some types of changes evident in Plains Cree ceremonial life were recorded by Mandelbaum when he documented the Sun Dances on the Ochapowace (1934), Kahkewistahaw (1934), and Little Pine (1935) reserves. As was typical of this era of ethnographical recording, he was primarily interested in detecting survivals of the more "traditional" aspects of Indian cultures, and thus devoted little attention to the analysis of ceremonial modification either in terms of ideology or ritual content. Nevertheless, Mandelbaum's field observations do provide us with insights into the nature of Plains Cree responses to pressure imposed upon them by the Department to terminate their ceremonies.

In his comments on the frequency of Sun Dances in the Crooked Lakes Agency in 1934, Mandelbaum noted that the dances were no longer annual affairs because of government prohibitions. In 1911, his predecessor, Alanson Skinner, had reported that one leader, Four Clouds, had attempted to hold the ceremony but was stopped by authorities; the unfinished lodge remained standing at the time of Mandelbaum's visit. Apparently, the Sun Dance had been performed over the previous three or four years, but only on a localized level.[74] Mandelbaum's interpreter informed him that the trespass law was still being enforced and that even he had been arrested and fined for attending a Sun Dance at Goose Lake in 1933.[75]

According to Mandelbaum's notes, approximately six tipis and twenty-five tents of people attended the 1934 dance held in a pasture bordering the Ochapowace and Kahkewistakaw reserves. Tepaw'tath, or Calling Man, had sponsored this ceremony in fulfillment of a vow to obtain the recovery of his ill daughter.[76] That the celebrants were under considerable pressure from the Department is evident from the fact that a lawyer had been hired to prevent interference by the Indian agent or Christian Indians. One of the singers, Harvey King, showed Mandelbaum two letters from their lawyer that stated that he was looking after their interests.[77]

While it is difficult to ascertain the extent or details of ritual change or loss from Mandelbaum's notes, one of his field helpers, Harvey Kenny, did explain to the anthropologist that celebrants could not complete all of the associated rituals, since the Sun Dance had been reduced from four to two days.[78] Mandelbaum was also provided with some evidence for changes in the Little Pine Sun Dance. These modifications included the deletion of piercing, the tendency of some dancers to break their fast and take a drink of water when they left the lodge unescorted, and the absence of the practice of climbing into the Thunderbird's nest located at the apex of the sacred pole.[79]

At the Crooked Lakes Sun Dance, a new element, consisting of a small Christian service, had been incorporated into the proceedings. Participants in the service were members of the audience, Sun Dancers, and the headman, Harry Fauch, who was "standing beside Mr. Ross [the missionary] as one of the pillars of the Church."[80] Surprised at this intrusion by the missionary, Mandelbaum recorded the event as follows:

Much to my amazement, the principal of the church school at Round Lake was there with Mrs. Taryon, the matron, [and] Mr. Taryon. They had brought with them about twelve of the school girls in blue skirts, brown stockings, brown sneaks, and faded middy blouses. The singing and dancing stopped and some of the spectators and dancers went outside to the place just south of the lodge entrance where Mr. Ross was to conduct the services. I asked Michael if the people resented it and he emphatically stated that they did not at all. . . . First the school girls sang a hymn. Then Mr. Ross read the 45th Psalm, "Sing unto the Lord with thanksgiving". Then Mr. Ross gave a short sermon. . . . After the sermon the girls sang "Jesus loves me, this I know, because the Bible tells me so." Then the dancing began again.[81]

The minister's sermon was directed towards the more traditional members of the congregation, who were reminded that the Christian God and Jesus were "disappointed" in the way they worshiped.[82]

Some observations of a more general nature were also made by Mandelbaum. In addition to participation by men and women, children were involved in the Sun Dance. A four-year-old boy had fasted for half a day and was dancing, "his eagle bone whistle just barely clearing the booth fence."[83] Food was distributed daily to celebrants who had not vowed abstinence; and while not referred to in this set of Mandelbaum's notes, giveaways undoubtedly occurred. Mandelbaum was also concerned with documenting the introduction of European-Canadian goods into the dance and accordingly reported any substitution of traditional items and clothing.[84]

In 1935, Mandelbaum attended the Little Pine Thirst Dance where some 100 to 120 tents of people were pitched. As in the case of the Crooked Lakes dance, there was a great deal of local anxiety over rumours that the farm instructor from Red Pheasant was intending to break up the gathering. As was noted previously, the chief personally assumed responsibility for any trouble with the Indian agent.[85] A number of public orations made during the ceremony referred to the "hard times" that people were experiencing, and the Shouter advised celebrants to continue in their faith in the power of the Sun Dance and to be mutually supportive of one another.[86] The latter message specifically referred to the necessity of maintaining the traditional form of society based upon kinship and friendship networks. After this particular ceremony had finished, some twenty tents of people moved to another location, where a Medicine Tipi Ceremony was held by one Blind Kennedy, who had vowed to build the lodge as a propitiation for relief from illness. Food was distributed, sacred mementos of deceased relatives were honoured, and handgames were played.[87]

Children were encouraged to participate in other ways at the Little Pine ceremony. A ten-year-old girl relieved an adult female dancer and a three-year-old boy helped to distribute the first drink to fasting dancers. Having been cured from his illness, this was the little boy's way of demonstrating "his kindness" to the Sun Dance sponsors.[88] Many of the children in camp were wearing sacred facial paint for the duration of the ceremony. Thus, at both Sun Dances attended by Mandel-baum, parents were not heeding Ottawa's warnings to refrain from allowing their children to participate in the ceremony.

Despite the prohibition against giveaways, offerings of goods continued to be an important part of Sun Dances, and, while Mandelbaum was not prevented from witnessing these exchanges, precautions were taken. The anthropologist was asked by his sponsors to refrain from making notes, taking photographs, or mentioning these activities in his forthcoming monograph. In one instance, the leader of the Sun Dance refused to allow Mandelbaum's interpreter to accompany him into a lodge where a number of offerings were being given. As a further precaution, the anthropologist was assured that there was "no evil" associated with what he was about to see. Material offerings included blankets, clothing, flour, and horses, the latter being symbolized by a distribution of "twigs." Mandelbaum, as a demonstration of good faith, added his own sweater to the offerings.[89]

In his published monograph dealing with the Sun Dances, Mandelbaum notes that a general gift-giving also occurred at the conclusion of the Little Pine Sun Dance and that these goods were distributed to relatives and visitors. The social and economic implications of the giveaway were apparent in his observation that, while the goods were formally acknowledged as "offerings to the supernaturals," the gifts brought both blessings and prestige to their donors.[90] Muskwa, the eldest man residing at Little Pine at this time, informed Mandelbaum that about twenty years previously, horses were popular giveaway items but they were rarely given now because of their scarcity.[91] As a variation of the Sun Dance, the Rain Dance also included numerous giveaways.[92]

The persistence of the Sun Dance as late as the 1930s attested to the continued relevance of Plains Cree religious ideology in changing times and led Mandelbaum to conclude that it remained an "active force" in Plains Cree life.[93] Sponsoring a Sun Dance was still considered to be the "most difficult vow to fulfill and hence, the one most likely to bring about the desired result."[94] For Mandelbaum, the importance of the Sun Dance was revealed in the many requests he received from the Plains Cree to become personally supportive in their fight against the repressive activities of the churches.[95] While conversion to Christianity undoubtedly precluded the attendance of some, many Plains Cree perceived little inherent contradiction in combining their traditional spirituality with the precepts of Christianity. Mandelbaum observed that at least one Catholic Indian from the Poundmaker Reserve refused to attend the Sun Dances, but this religious separation was not generally practised by others. At a 1934 Sun Dance, for example, Jim Kacucimau (One Who Rattles) was dancing in fulfillment of a vow but also had previously vowed to join the Anglican Church if he was cured of his illness.[96] In addition, Christian Indians were often present at Sun Dances, if only to provide support for their more traditional relatives.

The predominant reasons for the sponsorship of the Sun Dance were health-related. That is, an individual was either seeking a cure for illness or offering a thanksgiving for a cure that had been received during the year. This concern for health was central to most Sun Dances, as indicated in Mandelbaum's documentation of a history of the dance performed by Fineday on the Sweet Grass Reserve. Fineday's first Sun Dance was vowed upon the illness of his son, and six subsequent ones were sponsored as offerings for spiritual aid in the curing of his grandchildren. Having vowed a total of eight dances in his lifetime, Fineday informed Mandelbaum that the final one would be used for his own salvation: "The only time I'll use that last one is when I am dying or afraid like that. I have done it only when there is some sickness going on among my grandchildren. That is what we give to the children. But I nearly starved to death when I was getting the power. I was weak for a long time."[97] The importance of the Sun Dance as a healing ceremony and the traumatization of fearful believers by the Department's prohibitions were substantiated by anthropologists working among other prairie Indian groups. During the summer of 1914, Wilson Wallis was conducting research among the Dakota and questioned a number of people in the Griswold and Portage la Prairie areas regarding the reason for their participation in the Sun Dance.[98] In order to avoid detection, these Indians were performing shortened versions of the dance during the night. The trauma brought on by fear of government intervention was related to Wallis in one case study of a man who believed that his own illness and the loss of his six children were attributable to an unfulfilled vow.[99] In this instance, the man refused to dance during the daylight hours "because it was against the law to have the Sun Dance," and when he danced at night, "the white people would not be apprised of it."[100] He was also convinced that the "wakan," or spirit beings, would not be offended by this shorter version because of their knowledge of the law. In a second case study, a man suffering from illness and the loss of two children firmly believed that his death would be imminent if he could not dance. In an announcement to those present at his dance, in 1901, he explained the importance of fulfilling sacred customary law:

I had been told to do this by the thunders more than a year ago. Now it is too late to profit much by performing it for my boy is dead and my girl is dead. . . . Yet, I wish to save my own life. I would have done it at the time appointed a year ago, but for the fact that it is now against the law and I was afraid to do it. But now I must do it. If I have to go to jail it will not matter for I shall save my life and I shall feel better when it has been done.[101]

No piercings were reported for the Sun Dances recorded by Wallis.[102]

One common message that leaders of the Sun Dances communicated to the anthropologists was that the fulfillment of a sacred vow to perform the Sun Dance was a serious matter. It was a question of life and death itself. Like their Dakota neighbours, the Plains Cree were deeply disappointed if they were unable to fulfill their religious vows. This fact was not appreciated by administrators and missionaries who remained oblivious to the spiritual depth of indigenous ceremonies. According to one report, the wife of the Plains Cree leader, Fineday, was "stunned" upon hearing the news that the Department had prohibited her husband's Sun Dance and "went into a state of complete shock, 'as though she had been shot.'"[103] In an interview with Mandelbaum, another Plains Cree elder, Coming Day of the Sweet Grass Reserve, described two disasters that he attributed to his failure to complete a Thirst Dance.[104] His account is noteworthy because, in this instance, spiritual retribution for the non-fulfillment of a Sun Dance vow was not exclusively an Indian experience. After having been prevented from holding a Sun Dance some years previously by a police officer, Coming Day's wife died ten days later and the policeman's own horse rolled over the offending officer. According to Coming Day, the punishment was insufficient, since "the one who sent the policeman should have had the evil on him but it didn't turn out that way."[105]

Persistence in the belief in the Sun Dance ideology as a strong regenerative force is attested not only by its continued performance by groups such as the Plains Cree, Blood, Blackfoot, and Plains Ojibway, but also by its more recent adoption by other cultures such as the Buffalo Point Ojibway of Manitoba. The Buffalo Point Sun Dance involved illegal piercing. Approximately ten men were pierced during the ceremony, the sacred skewers being passed through the shoulders rather than the chest; these skewers were in turn attached to ropes suspended from the central sacred pole.[106] In a police report, Mayzenahwegeshick of the Manitou Reserve testified that the dance was new to the area and had been secretly performed during the night in a secluded area in an attempt to avoid detection. William Oshie and Tom Lightning of Gull Bay, Lake of the Woods, testified that the dance witnessed at Buffalo Point was similar to the Sun Dance practised many years ago by western Indians, and in fact the presiding ritualist had been described as a "tall middle-aged Indian from the west."[107]

While the need to deal with higher rates of illness among reserve populations partially explains the popularity of the Sun Dance, the major reason for its survival stemmed from the fact that its ideology of world and personal renewal and regeneration continued to have relevance. Before the disappearance of the bison herds, the reproduction of these animals and their natural environment – the prairie grass, sun, and rainfall – figured prominently in the symbolism and the ritual content of the ceremony. The regeneration of the earth was equally necessary for struggling Indian agriculturalists who also depended upon favourable environmental conditions. Accordingly, prayers were frequently offered at Sun Dances for abundant crops. In a letter written by Reverend James Donaghy, a missionary working on the Swan Lake Reserve in Manitoba in 1928, this correlation between the celebration of the Sun Dance and agricultural productivity was discussed at some length:

> The Manitou ordered them to keep up certain ceremonies, and if they failed to do so their crops would fail. The old folks firmly believe this and it makes it difficult to influence them to accept Christianity. The Sun Dance was one of these old ceremonies, and they felt very sore when the Government ordered it to be suppressed because of the ordeal they had to go through [piercing]. . . . At Indian Springs when we went there they told us that for seven years they had no Sun Dance, and for these seven years their crops had dried out; then they began again and the rain was sent by Manitou. This change just came when we went to that Reserve, and they held two of these dances, then they were forbidden. They are out for good now. But the fact that by a coincidence wet seasons returned the year they re-established the dance convinces them of the reality of the order issued by Manitou.[108]

Despite the fact that Sun Dances could be celebrated in their legal form within the boundaries of a reserve as long as the celebrants were from that particular community, pressure from Indian agents and missionaries did not end. While some communities chose to conduct their ceremonies in secrecy, others, depending on the local circumstances, abandoned the Sun Dance. In his interviews with the Canadian Dakota, James Howard was told that the Sun Dance had not been practised on Canadian Dakota reserves after 1910.[109] There are reports, however, of Dakota attending Plains Cree Sun Dances. For their part, the Plains Cree often travelled to secluded areas on their reserves to avoid being interrupted in their more traditional forms of public worship. For example, an investigation of a Sun Dance held on the Thunderchild Reserve in 1929 revealed a gathering of some one hundred off-reserve celebrants camped in a deep coulee in the northeast corner of the reserve.[110] This type of gathering probably occurred frequently and escaped the notice of Indian agents and missionaries, particularly on those reserves that were distant from administrative centres or were difficult to reach by road.

Some reserves succumbed to government pressure on their Sun Dances more quickly. In a story collected by Alexander Wolfe from an Ojibway elder, Standing Through the Earth, the circumstances under which the last Rain Dance was held by the Goose Lake people in Saskatchewan are worthy of note.[111] This ceremony had been attended by members of the North-West Mounted Police and government officials. Despite the warnings given by the elders to refrain from piercing, one Sun Dancer, Osowwahshtim (Brown Horse), who was from another reserve, insisted on fulfilling his vow to perform the ritual so "that the whiteman present should know the spiritual strength of the Indian."[112] Osowwahshtim was pierced, and, as he broke away from the rawhide ropes fastened to the sacred tree of life, he fell at the feet of one of the officials. The ceremony was halted immediately; several men were arrested, placed in bonds, and forced to walk behind the authorities' buggies to jail. Standing Through the Earth stated that, as a result of this performance, "a ban was put on all Indian ceremonies which was to last many, many years," and that, "because the traditional ceremonies and rituals were no longer practised, many of [the Indian] people do not know their language or the value life gives to everyone."[113] While the Goose Lake people continued to take part in other dances, this was the last Rain Dance to be sponsored for many years.

It is evident that giveaways were very much a part of ceremonial life throughout the early decades of the twentieth century. Mandelbaum noted that the distribution of goods and material sacrifices or offerings was a feature of all ceremonies that he witnessed. The Give Away Dance in particular was an important aspect of the winter ceremonial cycle. Mandelbaum observed its performance on the Little Pine Reserve in 1935 in spite of the fact that it was "secretly held lest the Department got wind of it."[114]

Although the major giveaways traditionally occurred on an inter-band and inter-reserve level, the prohibition against their performance in Section 149 tended to make the practice more localized and more private. During the summer months, however, giveaways did occur whenever large gatherings of people were permitted, such as at Treaty Days celebrations or at local agricultural fairs. In 1917, Indian Agent James Macdonald reported that the Dakota from Griswold held giveaways while attending the Brandon Fair; both giveaways and other ceremonies were held prior to and after exhibition hours. Among the items exchanged at these events were horses, buggies, and "things of value," many of them being distributed to relatives and visitors residing in the United States where they were difficult to trace by the authorities.[115] Throughout the same year, Henry Two Bears reported that the Round Plains Dakota in Saskatchewan were holding dances in the Presbyterian missionary's residence and the schoolhouse where giveaways of property and money took place![116] Other forms of exchanges, such as of horses, occurred among the Plains Cree as well as other groups, but were difficult to detect. In the case of the Cree, the transfer of ownership of a horse was often indicated by the passing of a marked stick to the new owner. The actual exchange took place after the ceremony.

Giveaways were also an integral part of the Midewiwin ceremonies that were held by both the Ojibway and Cree. In a petition sent to the Department by the members of the Midewiwin at Wabigoon in Ontario, this redistribution of goods was explained by comparing it to offerings made in Christian churches. The gifts of blankets, prints (cloth), cooking pots, and food brought by initiates who were learning traditional medicines and healing practices were described as "thank offerings to the Great Spirit."[117] These goods were distributed among the ceremonial participants – a practice, it was claimed, not unlike donations received and distributed in Christian churches. In addition, the value system and appropriate behaviour upheld by Midewiwin Society members were equated with the Ten Commandments, and thus the petitioners could not understand "why any objection could be raised by the white Father to such a ceremony."[118] These arguments for the repeal of Section 149 by the Midewiwin leaders at Wabigoon echoed those of their counterparts in the prairie region.

In order to reach a compromise with the Department on the issue of giveaways, some Alberta Indians suggested certain modifications to their ceremony. In correspondence signed by over fifty people, Peigan headman Bull Plume proposed in 1915 that a differentiation be made between "Indian goods" and "non-Indian goods," and that a money limit of $2 be imposed upon cash distribution.[119] Indian goods included items produced in the home, such as dance outfits, coats, moccasins, beaded belts, beaded neckwear, stone pipes, tobacco, and "things we can do without such as pocket knives, handkerchiefs and blankets"; non-Indian goods were identified as wagons, harnesses, rigs, saddles, horses, cattle, furniture, and stoves.[120] In other words, home-made items and those associated with the commercial fur-trade economy were being categorized differently from those obtained through government-controlled agricultural programs, which were associated with a European-Canadian lifestyle. This line of reasoning was not seriously considered by the Department, since any level of giveaway would only serve to perpetuate the indigenous aspects of the economy.

Even the redistribution of goods on Christian occasions of celebration was suspected as a clandestine attempt to hold giveaways. In 1915, Arthur White Elk of Gleichen, Alberta, asked for permission to hold a Christmas Tree Dance, contending that Indians had the same right to celebrate Christmas gift-giving as the European Canadians.[121] This request was denied on the grounds that the wording of Section 149 did not permit Indians to give gifts to friends during "any Indian festival, dance or ceremony." This was the most extreme instance of the application of the giveaway prohibition. In the same year, Daniel Little Axe, a Blackfoot from the same community, informed the Department that the Gleichen Blackfoot would refuse to recognize the validity of regulations against giveaways.[122] In an earlier petition, Little Axe had attempted to make a case for the more lenient implementation of the pass system, a move that would have facilitated the expansion of the reciprocal exchange network among the Blackfoot, Peigan, and Blood.[123]

While certain Plains ceremonies were modified and persisted at least into the 1930s, others were no longer celebrated. Among the Plains Cree, for example, Mandelbaum listed the continuation of the Sun Dance, the Smoking Tipi ceremony, giveaways, the Masked Dance, or *wîhtikôhkânisimowin*, the Prairie-Chicken Dance, the Round Dance, and the Midewiwin. In the early twentieth century, new forms of dances were also adopted. One such ceremony was the *pîcicîwin*, or Moving Slowly Dance, actually a regional variation of the Omaha, or Grass, Dance. A further modified version of this dance came to be known as the Pow-wow. Introduced to the Plains Cree by the Assiniboin around 1885, the *pîcicîwin* had, by the 1930s, replaced many traditional elements of ceremonialism. Its more secularized form provided "the most common social activity of reservation life."[124] The more "traditional" version of the Pow-wow was formally organized, and it incorporated the ceremonial redistribution of goods on several levels. In his study of this type of Pow-wow, Mandelbaum noted that dance halls had been constructed on each Plains Cree reserve for the winter performance of this ceremony. This communal dance was hosted by a "dance chief" in cooperation with resources and labour donated by a hierarchy of officials (crier, servers, whip owners, drum leg owner, and a tobacco handler) and their relatives. As in the earlier period, traditional ceremonies, spiritual prerogatives, and personal roles in this new dance were partially derived from the acquisition of special status through public demonstrations of liberality such as the distribution of food and tobacco. The transfer of spiritual prerogatives and functions associated with hierarchical positions also involved ceremonial exchanges to publicly affirm the transition from one status to another.

Other forms of gift exchanges also were important elements of the Pow-wow. They validated one's social, economic, political, or spiritual status, served to identify and reinforce kinship networks, and established new relationships. As in the case of more traditional forms of Plains Cree ceremonies, this dance embodied the essence of indigenous political, economic, and social values. One's position within the kinship network and society in general was re-affirmed through customary law in that the range of partners for specific types of dances was regulated.[125] While not common, these "partner dances" reinforced the indigenous system of obligatory kinship responsibilities (the foundation of economic production) and served to indicate which families enjoyed a greater access to strategic resources. It was through the redistribution of these resources that kin were acknowledged and status and prestige were acquired. In his interpretation of the dance to Mandelbaum, Solomon Blue-horn explained how this system functioned:

If you consider yourself to be a worthy man (i.e., one of some status) you can choose a woman and dance next to her. You give her something valuable. Then her husband tells her to invite you (to dance) and to give you something in return. . . .

There are some women with whom everyone is afraid to dance. Their husbands are well off and both husband and wife are brave. If you touch her with gifts she'll give back much more than she gets. When a woman thinks that a man can't keep up with her in gift giving, she won't dance with him any more.

To cut in, you follow the woman around the circle for a few steps. The person dancing to the right of her will hesitate a bit and you step right in. But, if the person to the right is the woman's mother, or her father's sister, or her sister, a man cannot cut in. And a man cannot cut in to dance with any of his woman relatives except his *nitcimus* (female cross-cousin) or *nitim* (sister-in-law). After the dance the man gives the Shouter the gift. The Shouter stands in the middle and announces who gave what to whom.[126]

Because both men and women were prohibited by customary law from dancing with potential parallel female kin relatives (non-marriageable partners), the restriction of partners reinforced the norm of cross-cousin female-male relations.

The Pow-wow has evolved into a variety of forms in the present day. New dance societies and songs have been introduced.[127] In many areas, a highly secularized version of the Pow-wow, which features a commercial program of dance competitions and monetary prizes, has become common.

Two other dances were introduced during the post-1914 decades. The Tail Wagging Dance was brought to Saskatchewan by those Plains Cree who had fled to the United States after the Saskatchewan Uprising of 1885. Men and women danced as partners in a style very similar to that of European Canadians, and gift exchanges were made between those who danced together out of respect for one another.[128] The Tea Dance involved the social consumption of a drink made from berries and tobacco mixed with tea. Mandelbaum wrote that this dance was popular among the Plains Cree in the early twentieth century.[129] Other groups also adopted new dances. For example, anthropologist James Howard recorded the introduction of the Grass Dance (or Pow-wow), the Night Dance, Dragging-foot Dance (or Round Dance), and the Kahomni (or Turnabout Dance) among the Canadian Dakota.[130] As in the case of the Plains Cree, these new dances also retained the feature of gift exchange.

Religious syncretism, a blending of indigenous and Christian forms of worship, was also evident. In 1924, barristers Trotter and Company wrote to the superintendent of Indian Affairs on behalf of some twenty "leading" Indians from the Muscowpetung, Piapot, and Pasqua reserves for permission to hold a joint "revival meeting."[131] The superintendent was reassured that the meeting was neither a Sun Dance nor a giveaway. Its purpose, the petitioners claimed, was to "revive the spirit of Christianity among the younger element whose present indifference to prayer causes their elders considerable concern" and to pray for "abundant and successful harvests."[132] The barristers also commented that their clients felt that their own traditional ceremonies had been successful in procuring relief from misfortune.

Sensitive to the possible objections that would be raised by the Department, these petitioners provided a detailed description of activities for this joint revival meeting.[133] The meeting was to be led by four elders who would spend the first two days conducting a "prayer ceremony" in a tent holding forty to fifty people. On the third day of the four-day celebration, Cree hymn books were to be used in the service. The singing was to be accompanied by numerous addresses on "right living." In order to avoid accusations of extreme behaviour, the Department was given assurances that no "endurance tests" (piercings) would occur and that no excessive dancing would be tolerated. To emphasize this point, the petitioners stated that, contrary to traditional forms of worship, "trained and instructed volunteers [representing a choir, will] rise in their places in the front circle and sing songs of praise and thanksgiving. While they sing they will keep time to the tunes with their feet. There will be no jumping about, however. This singing will last four or five minutes at a time."[134] Accompanying this petition was a covering letter from the barristers who supported the request on the grounds that the petition was motivated by "a desire to satisfy religious instinct rendered stronger by times of stress."[135] Despite the obvious syncretic nature of this Sun Dance, Graham refused to grant his permission when the matter was referred to him by his superiors in Ottawa.

A small number of Indian people in Manitoba, Saskatchewan, and Alberta left their indigenous religious practices and joined the American Indian Peyote religious movement (later known as the Native American Church).[136] While there is reason to believe that some Canadian groups were already familiar with the properties of peyote, its use in the performance of rites associated with the Peyote religion was apparently unknown to officials until the 1930s. Howard recorded the presence of the Peyote religion in the late 1930s on a number of Dakota reserves in Manitoba, including Sioux Village, Sioux Valley, Oak Lake, and Long Plain.[137] Permission for the use of the hallucinogenic plant in a ritual was requested by followers of the movement from Griswold, Manitoba, in 1941.[138] Subsequent departmental inquiries into the practice revealed that its use was confined to southern Saskatchewan and Manitoba Dakota reserves, with concentrations of adherents in the Griswold and Pipestone areas of Manitoba.[139] In 1952, the ritual consumption of peyote related to the activities of the Native American Church was reported among members of the Cree band led by Louis Sunchild. Sunchild had received his formal spiritual training among the Rocky Boy Cree in Montana and had a following of some fourteen members of his band.[140]

The growth of the Native American Church movement in the prairie region is difficult to document. However, correspondence monitoring Sunchild's activities indicates that he visited the North Battleford area in Saskatchewan in 1954 and that he and George Necotine of the Red Pheasant Reserve had hired a lawyer to apply for a legal charter for the Church.[141] The Native American Church, with forty to fifty members on the Red Pheasant Reserve, was officially incorporated under the Saskatchewan Benevolent Societies Act in 1954. Other reserves mentioned in connection with this movement were the Mosquito and the Grizzly Bear's Head.[142]

To what extent the rise of the Native American Church was related to the repression of traditional forms of public worship is not discernible from the available information. Its presence, nevertheless, suggests that some prairie Indians, including the Cree, viewed this indigenous church as a viable alternative to both indigenous and Christian forms of public worship. For others, however, little if any differentiation was made between the various religious practices. In other words, one could follow the Peyote Road and still maintain allegiance to both traditional spirituality and even Christianity. Such was the case for one Plains Cree leader who participated in the Native American Church while visiting relatives in Rocky Boy, Montana. When queried on the subject of religious allegiance by anthropologist Verne Dusenberry, this leader responded:

There are no conflicts in religion. . . . Since we are all the children of one God, whether it is Ki-sei-men'-to or the God of the white man, it's all the same thing. So a man can be a Catholic and a leader of the Spirit Lodge or the Smoke Lodge or the Sun Dance. He is just following the instructions of the Creator in different ways. He can also be a leader of the peyote church, for here again, one is just following the Creator who had put all his power in Peyote. You see, he can take part in all three of these ways of doing things, for all the prayers lead to the same place in the end.[143]

During the period from 1914 to 1945, Indian leaders were not successful in obtaining the repeal of Section 149 of the Indian Act. This was due to their relative political powerlessness and general marginalization within the Canadian state. Attempts to organize on a national and even at the local level were subverted by government monitoring of their meetings. During this time, even European-Canadian political activism, such as the socialist-oriented movements of the Co-operative Commonwealth Federation (CCF) and the Social Credit Party, were regarded as suspect by the federal government. In the prairie region, Commissioner Graham of the Indian Affairs Branch was equally opposed to political rallies not only because he wished to prevent open criticism of federal Indian programs but also because, like the Sun Dances, these meetings interfered with agricultural productivity by drawing men away from their farm work during the summer months.[144]

When formal political and legal avenues for redress proved ineffective between 1914 and 1940, Indian people adopted a number of alternatives to deal with religious suppression. These involved alterations in ceremonial time, space, and content, and they ranged from the persistence of indigenous practices to syncretic modes of worship in which aspects of Christianity were blended with traditional ideologies. For groups such as the Plains Cree, the more successful solutions to government interference in their public forms of religious worship were pragmatic adjustments to the realities of reserve life and to "being Indian" within a White-dominated Canadian society. This reality was one of social upheavals, poverty, high mortality rates, racial discrimination, and political impotency. It was within this context that the healing and regenerative powers of the collective rites of the Sun Dance continued to have cultural relevance. Similarly, the indigenous ideology of communally based reciprocal relations persisted as a practical strategy for survival on the economically under-developed reserves.

By the 1930s and the 1940s, the more traditional individuals living in reserve communities were more than ever concerned about the loss of cultural values and practices. Their fears of an alienated younger generation were being realized; the Indian Act regulations and Indian schooling were producing the feared effect. The fear of imminent cultural disappearance and, indeed, of indigenous nations as distinct societies, led to a concerted move to repeal the repressive aspects of the Indian Act in the late 1940s.

A Matter of Religious Freedom:
1940 to 1951

9

By the 1940s, criticisms of the Canadian government's treatment of indigenous populations were more evident in political spheres and in the media. Several Indian leaders, such as the Reverend Edward Ahenakew, began to use their positions in the churches and Indian political organizations to publicize the conditions of their people. In his many public addresses and newspaper articles, Ahenakew appealed for an end to the government's wardship system. His writings contain several references to the detrimental effects that paternalistic "humanitarian" programs had on the Cree, and he called for an end to this approach to Canada's Indian policy:

A time comes in a child's life when he begins to ask the reasons for the actions of his father; a time comes when he wants to know the "why" of things. That may be a source of trouble and annoyance to the father, but not if he is wise, for he will know that it is the nature of development and should be welcomed; he will do his best to guide this newly acquired curiosity. To check it is to hinder natural development.[1]

But throughout the inter-war years, this need for change was not realized and the Department of Indian Affairs continued to operate on the philosophical tenets that had influenced policy throughout the nineteenth century. Historians of Canadian Indian policy have concluded that the Depression years were the "high water mark of government regulation and interference in the daily lives of the Indian population" and that any changes in policy until at least 1985 were not substantive and were simply adjustments to new circumstances.[2] The general lack of criticism by politicians of the Department's activities was partly due to its relatively low bureaucratic profile within the federal structure and the "mystique" surrounding Indian Affairs because of the "unique aspects of its tasks."[3] It was assumed that those who administered to the needs of Indians were in the best position to understand them and, indeed, to do well by them. As Harold Hawthorn has pointed out, this bureaucratic isolation from voters, politicians, and from the Indians themselves, led to an "inward-looking parochialism" and a "grass-roots pattern of career mobility" that removed the Department from further accountability.[4] At the same time, however, the Department's peripheral status had minimized its political power and its funding base.

Continuity in policy also existed because of the long political careers of Department administrators such as Deputy Superintendent of Indian Affairs Duncan Campbell Scott, Department Secretary J.D. McLean, and Indian Commissioner William Graham. While these administrators were often embroiled in power struggles over their relative authority in policy formulation and implementation, they rarely disagreed about the ultimate objectives of Indian policy. Their commitment to protecting a "dependent race in its land, monies and its contact with the community" remained the driving force behind any reconsideration of departmental policies in the inter-war years.[5] In the opinion of Department administrators, the Indians would continue to be best served by the special regulations that offered the necessary protection and guidance for their adjustment to the Canadian reality.[6]

Not all Canadians accepted the Department's evaluation of the Indian situation. Some of the critics were in a position to view firsthand the human cost of the Department's policy, and the criticism they formulated provided the basis for a movement seeking an official enquiry into the Indian Act in the immediate post-1945 period.

Following a renewed but unsuccessful effort to discourage the potlatch on the Northwest Coast in the 1920s, Deputy Superintendent General Duncan Scott had persuaded Canadian anthropologist Marius Barbeau to investigate the history of the implementation of Section 149 in that region. Barbeau, who was in the employ of the Anthropology Section of the Department of Mines at the time, prepared a report largely based on his notes and materials from the Department of Indian Affairs. The opinions of colleagues such as Dr. Franz Boas, Charles Hill-Tout, Harlan I. Smith, and Dr. Edward Sapir, and those of local "experts" including Indian Agent E.K. DeBeck, the manager of the Alert Bay Cannery, and Dr. C.F. Newcombe, a "local ethnographer," were solicited by Barbeau. The Kwakiutl, however, who had originally lobbied for an investigation of Section 149 by the federal government, were not consulted. While the report contained no specific recommendations, it apparently took the place of a costly royal commission of inquiry which had been demanded by prosecuted potlatchers.[7]

Barbeau's expert witnesses concluded that the potlatch laws had contributed to a general demoralization among the Northwest Coast Indians. The existing social malaise, it was claimed, was caused by the Indians' loss of traditional customs and their failure to discover or to take advantage of European-Canadian alternatives. Dr. Sapir went as far as to recommend greater tolerance for indigenous activities and suggested, "White men are not doing the Indians much of a favour by converting them into inferior replicas of themselves."[8] Barbeau closed his report with a citation of Boas's cautionary remark of 1897, which advised governments to refrain from suppressing potlatching. Boas had not only insisted that European Canadians misunderstood the potlatch but also warned that suppression should not be attempted without "making provision for the gradual transition from the old system to a new one."[9]

Others were also critical of the legislation as an unnecessarily harsh measure. Historians dealing with the Potlatch Law have cited the comparatively empathetic views of political representatives, Department personnel, and even some missionaries. The Department was perhaps most alarmed by its traditional allies in the matter, the missionaries. Of particular concern to the Department were the writings of Anglican clergyman Reverend John A. Antle, founder of the Columbia Coast Mission. Antle believed that coercive policies were unacceptable. For instance, in a 1931 issue of the Anglican journal, the *Log of Columbia*, he suggested that potlatching would die out in time. He warned that "the big stick never yet advanced the cause of Christ," and that the law would only "outrage and embitter a people whose only crime is to love their own people."[10] In addition to supporting appeals made by Indian spokesmen like Chief Johnnie Scow, Antle pointed out that "the Indian has borne with a great deal of patience an outrageous attack on his liberty, scarcely equalled in the annals of British colonialism."[11] Shortly after this statement was published, articles supporting a revision of the anti-potlatch regulation appeared in the *Log*. Such critiques of government policy were not shared by Anglican Church leaders in British Columbia who refused to re-evaluate their position on potlatching as late as the 1935 synod.[12]

For its part, the Department continued to press for further restrictions on potlatching, and by 1938 the House of Commons was informed of this intention. The restriction took the form of a proposed amendment that condoned the seizure of property (confiscation) associated with giveaways and imposed a penalty of six months' imprisonment. The suggested amendment was subverted by Independent Member of Parliament for Comox-Alberni A.W. Neill (a former Indian agent), who served as a spokesman on behalf of enfranchised Indians. In a debate on the issue of greater restrictions during the 1936 session of Parliament, Neill clashed with J.S. Taylor, the Member of Parliament for Nanaimo.[13] Taylor contended that objectionable marriage practices associated with potlatches could be discouraged only through greater controls. Neill countered this argument by claiming that his opponent's representations of the potlatch were outdated and used this opportunity to question the humanity and relative effectiveness of policies of "forced" cultural transformation.[14] Along with the support of others, such as J.S. Woodsworth, the CCF Member of Parliament from Winnipeg, Manitoba, and a number of British Columbia CCF supporters, Neill managed to make his point, and the new superintendent of Indian Affairs, T.A. Crerar, was forced to withdraw his support for the amendment.[15]

While the outcome of the debate on the seizure amendment was viewed as a victory by those who practised the potlatch, the proponents of the regulation remained unconvinced that potlatching was harmless. In 1940, for example, Anglican Church representatives and government officials met at Kingcome Inlet, Kwawkewleth, with Indian representatives to discuss the contemporary potlatches.

During the early 1940s, other European Canadians spoke out against the regulations. In 1941, anthropologist Frank Speck, from the University of Pennsylvania, published an article in the *Crozer Quarterly* entitled "An Ethnologist Speaks for the Pagan Indians."[16] In this statement, a copy of which still lies in the Department's files, Speck defended the validity of the Iroquoian Long House religion and condemned White intolerance of indigenous forms of worship, denominational warfare over Indian converts, and "oppressive missionization." For Speck, the price paid by the Indian communities for this aggressive form of interference in their lives was typified by the demoralized condition of the Iroquois. Their only solace was to be found in the strength that they derived from their own traditional belief systems. In this published critique of government Indian policy and professional declaration of support for the preservation of indigenous forms of worship, Speck indicated that he was only one of several anthropologists who intended to "defend the religious liberties of oppressed and over-propagandized people."[17] The impending demoralization, Speck claimed, would be characterized by the "loss of the will to live," "moral irresponsibility," "mental then physical sickness," and the "loss of social coherence."[18]

In addition to support from scholars, popular writers of the day were beginning to show signs of support for a re-evaluation of government policy. In his historical review of Canadian journalism on Indians, Ronald Haycock characterized the period between 1930 and 1960 as a transitional era when "social humanitarianism" was slowly replaced by "humanitarian awareness and guilt."[19] Some writers argued that the adoption of Western social and moral values was not necessarily predicated on the acceptance of Christianity, and thus "the Indian could achieve acceptable life standards without ever becoming a Christian."[20] This emerging social consensus led to a greater tolerance in certain circles for non-Christian religious traditions.

One example of this shift in the journalistic reporting on Indian cultures was Maude Bridgman's 1945 report of a revival of a Cree ceremony held at Roche Percée to commemorate World War Two veterans.[21] Bridgman, unlike her predecessors, refrained from being judgemental in her description of this event. Some journalists attempted to promote a more positive image of Indian people by portraying them as Canada's "natural conservationists," while still others wrote exposés correlating the impoverished conditions of reserve life with inadequate government economic support. One such writer was Richard Finnie, who had been commissioned by the government to prepare a report on the economic condition of northern Indians and to recommend policy changes. Another popular author, George Stanfield Belaney (Grey Owl), provided the Canadian public with a positive, although greatly romanticized, view of Canadian Indian cultures.[22] As Haycock has pointed out, this popular journalism resulted in a heightened public awareness of the colonial position of Indian communities within Canada. By the 1930s, the realities of Indian poverty, disease, and community stress began to have an effect on a once "unreceptive and uninformed" public.[23]

Impoverished reserve conditions were largely attributed to the negative effect of European Canadians upon Indian societies. Popular historians like Philip Godsell, a fur trader, while emphasizing the important role that Indians played in the development of the fur-trade economy, also condemned their treatment by European-Canadian traders. Other writers challenged the historical depiction of Indian leaders involved in the 1885 Saskatchewan Uprising as "uncivilized" rebels who unreasonably opposed the federal government's attempts to bring law and order to the West. Mary Weekes described Poundmaker as a leader who was forced to participate in the Uprising because of government oppression of his people.[24] Another author, Al Cooper, presented the public with an unprecedented pro-Indian account of Almighty Voice's "one-man rebellion against White civilization."[25] In his survey of popular literature, Haycock discovered that at least half the articles dealing with contemporary Indian issues were in fact supportive of a "new deal" for the Indians.[26] This "new deal" included provisions for better education, less government bureaucracy, and more opportunities for community-initiated programs. The wardship system was equated with "second class citizenship" rather than "special status," and writers called for the full enfranchisement of Indians. Control over education by Christian churches also came under attack. For instance, political news commentator and former editor of *Maclean's Magazine* Blair Fraser partly attributed the economic marginality of Indians to the outmoded, poorly operated, and under-funded denominational school system created by a penny-pinching government.[27]

Canada was not alone in undertaking a re-appraisal of its relations with indigenous peoples. Under the administration of John Collier, the Commissioner of Indian Affairs from 1933 to 1945, the United States had initiated a number of reforms that were implemented through the Indian Reorganization Act of 1934, including the repeal of repressive legislation against religious practices. In 1940, Collier himself chaired the North American Committee at the First Inter-American Conference on Indian Life, held in Mexico. The objectives of the conference delegates were to establish avenues of consultation for indigenous populations on both continents and to provide a clearing house for information and problem-sharing.[28] Canada was invited to send a delegate, but declined the invitation. Department files indicate that administrators were aware of policies relating to indigenous populations in other areas of the world. These files include materials pertaining to New Zealand, South Africa, the United States, the International Labour Office, and the United Nations Educational, Scientific and Cultural Organization.[29] The shift in power between European colonial states and indigenous populations on the international scene after World War Two also provided the government with an impetus to reassess Canada's situation. As the European hold on colonies in Africa and Asia diminished and the British Commonwealth became an institution over which non-Whites exerted control, "the salience of race" was questioned in international affairs and in the domestic relations of both Britain and Canada.[30]

In the 1940s, the Canadian government began to respond to concerns regarding its own relations with its indigenous populations. In his analysis of the intellectual and political climate responsible for this trend, Harold Hawthorn emphasizes the shift from a *laissez-faire* attitude to one that advocated a more active role on the part of the federal government in the "regulation of the economy" and the "welfare of its citizenry."[31] Following World War Two, the failure of the government's "custo-dial" approach towards Indians was being re-evaluated. The Department of Indian Affairs found itself in a dilemma:

It was staffed with few professionals; its financial appropriations were inadequate; many Indian children did not go to school; much of the existing schooling was undertaken by religious orders which provided only half-day teaching for their Indian pupils; the Act governing the administration of Indian Affairs had been devised in the previous century and had undergone few amendments; the Act contained a repressive attitude to Indian cultures.[32]

Still, there was little in the way of public debate on federal Indian policy. This situation has been attributed by some historians to the "apolitical context of Canadian Indian administration" and the "British traditions of reticence, of letting well enough alone, or hushing up 'scandals,' of trusting officials."[33]

The various Indian political organizations were largely ineffective in altering their relations with the state during the inter-war years. However, a number of individuals in the prairie region emerged publicly as serious critics of Canadian Indian policy. Products of the government's assimilation programs themselves, these men utilized various forums to express their concerns and to raise the consciousness of the general public. Though these individuals played important roles in publicizing the circumstances of Indians, they have received little recognition from historians. Three such individuals were Mike Mountain Horse, Reverend Edward Ahenakew, and Joseph Dion.

Mike Mountain Horse was a Blood Indian who had attended St. Paul Mission School and the Calgary Industrial School as a child. Before 1907 and following World War One (in which he served overseas), Mountain Horse had worked in the local police detachment. In 1933, he left this job and dedicated his life to writing and lecturing about the culture and history of his people. In 1943 he returned to employment as a locomotive labourer for the CPR and in 1959 he served on the Blood Tribal Council.

Encouraged by Canon S. Middelton, Principal of St. Paul's School, Mountain Horse began to submit articles to the *Lethbridge Herald* in the late 1920s. By 1936, he had completed a manuscript entitled "Indians of the Western Plains." However, lack of public interest and the economic exigencies of the Depression prevented it from being published until it was rescued from the archives by historian Hugh Dempsey.[34] Through his writing, Mountain Horse hoped to reverse the negative stereotypes of Indians held by the European-Canadian public. In an attempt to achieve a balanced history, he not only dealt with the destructive aspects of Indian-White relationships, but also documented the progressive achievements of his own nation. While admitting that some government programs had benefited the Blood, Mountain Horse attributed the ability of the Blood to adapt to historical changes and negative experiences to their own efforts.

For Mountain Horse, "progress" was manifested through the Blood's willing adoption of new economic activities and good citizenry. Progress was visible in successful stock-raising and agricultural ventures, the good rate of school attendance, the building of modern homes, the use of modern transport, and the participation of the Blood in the war effort:

By the 1930s our women folk no longer served as servile drudges; every Sunday the churches on the various reserves were filled with well-dressed Indian couples who, in most cases, drove to worship in modern, up-to-date cars, some equipped with radios. Some of our young ladies were serving as qualified registered nurses in many of the hospitals throughout Canada. . . . We are not looking forward to the time when the buffalo shall return. Nor are we anticipating a time when the white man shall disappear from the continent. We are scanning the horizon for further chances of advancement and further opportunities of proving ourselves true and loyal subjects of the British Empire.[35]

In his manuscripts, Mountain Horse addressed the issue of religious freedom, and, although he refused to condone the practice of certain rituals, he defended the right of his people to worship in the religion of their choice. He also undertook to create a greater understanding of Blood forms of indigenous worship by explaining the meaning of certain practices. For instance, piercing was discussed in terms of a personal offering made to the supernatural world on behalf of an ailing relative rather than as a ritual for "making braves."[36] A noteworthy historical observation is the discrepancy between the description of traditional forms of worship in Mountain Horse's original manuscripts and the published version. The negative-sounding adjectives pertaining to certain practices were edited out of the published version by Hugh Dempsey, who was personally acquainted with Mountain Horse. As Dempsey explained, negative qualifiers were used by Mountain Horse to appeal to a White audience who persisted in viewing the Indians as "bloodthirsty individuals, yelling, whooping, and seeking to destroy."[37] As a result, Mountain Horse, a member of the Salvation Army but supportive of the Blood's own beliefs, tended to be publicly apologetic for his people's religious and "warring practices."[38]

In comparison, Reverend Edward Ahenakew's message to the Christian public was more critical and less optimistic than that of his Blood contemporary.[39] Born on the Cree reserve of Sandy Lake, Saskatchewan, in 1885, Ahenakew was educated at the mission school and later attended the boarding school at Prince Albert. He taught school for a brief period before undertaking theological training at Wycliffe College in Toronto and Emmanuel College in Saskatoon. At the age of thirty-five, he was accepted into the Faculty of Medicine in Edmonton as a student, but ill health prevented him from pursuing a medical career. It was during this period of illness that Reverend Canon Edward Matheson of Battleford encouraged Ahenakew to collect the oral history of his people. Once his health was restored, he supervised Indian mission work in the northeastern section of the Battleford Diocese.

Ahenakew's political career involved extensive public lecturing and service as the western President for the League of Indians of Canada. Much of his energy was devoted to improving educational opportunities for his people, and he was success-ful in re-establishing the schools on the Little Pine and Thunderchild reserves. In 1932, he was appointed General Indian Missionary for the Northern Diocese of Saskatchewan, and a year later he became Honorary Canon of St. Alban's Cathedral in Prince Albert.

In an attempt to discover his own roots and to preserve Cree cultural traditions and history for posterity, Ahenakew collected numerous oral accounts from Chief Thunderchild. These, together with his own manuscript, entitled "Old Keyam," were formally collated in 1923. These writings offer valuable insights into the social, economic, and political conditions of the Cree. While the character Old Keyam is fictitious, he served well as a literary tool to personalize Ahenakew's opinions on Canadian Indian policy. The very name given by Ahenakew to his elder spokes-person was highly symbolic. As Ahenakew's biographer, Ruth Matheson Buck, explains, Old Keyam was "poor, inoffensive and genial" and his very name reflected the Indian condition.[40] According to Ahenakew, the term *keyam* meant "I do not care," an attitude adopted by an old man who had tried to accommodate change and the promise of a new life in Canadian society, but had been "defeated" and, in despair, withdrew and appeared not to care.[41]

Among Old Keyam's concerns was the repression of his people's religious beliefs and practices although he referred to many traditional beliefs as "super-stitious" and looked to the day "when the Christian Church would be strong on every reserve."[42] Freedom of worship was defended as a "British principle," and anti-ceremonial legislation was condemned. Ahenakew argued that the use of federal regulations to force Christian conversion and to suppress the Sun Dance would result in Indian opposition, thus "only keeping alive what would almost certainly die a natural death."[43] To answer criticisms of "extreme" forms of ritual behaviour, Ahenakew pointed out that self-mortification was also practised by certain Christian orders, and that travelling to Sun Dances was in essence equivalent to Christian pilgrimages.

During his ministry, Reverend Ahenakew delivered many sermons and lectures that were designed to enhance public knowledge of reserve conditions. His addresses were published in local newspapers and nationally distributed journals such as *The Canadian Churchman*. His messages also found expression through the Cree *Monthly Guide*, which he translated into syllabics, typeset, and distributed throughout the reserves at his own expense. He discussed a wide range of topics. An issue of the *Guide* in 1923 included articles on "agriculture, health, the Indian Act, the League of Indians of Canada, the work of the University of Saskatchewan, and world news."[44] Firmly convinced that "knowledge is power," Ahenakew was particularly vocal in advocating improved educational services for Indian children. His locally produced press coverage of Indian life served to expose the inadequacies of government programs and the need for change.[45]

A third and final example of prairie Indian leaders who strove to create a public awareness of reserve conditions was Joseph Dion.[46] Of Cree heritage, Dion was born on the Onion Lake Reserve located to the northwest of historic Fort Pitt in Saskatchewan, where he received his education at the Catholic Mission School. He farmed on his home reserve and, in 1916, at the age of twenty-four, became a teacher at the first school on the reserve. During the 1930s, he became politically active and was instrumental in the formation of l'Association des Métis d'Alberta et des Territoires du Nord-Ouest, later known as the Métis Association of Alberta. He was also involved with the Indian Association of Alberta.

Dion was intensely interested in recording information on the traditional aspects of Cree culture. He undertook this project by interviewing friends, relatives, and historically prominent Indian personalities. During the 1930s, he developed a means to communicate this heritage through a travelling lecture circuit and performances by a Metis dance troupe. Both Indian and Metis music and dances were incorporated into Dion's presentations. He spoke to his audiences of the difficulties encountered by the Cree as they struggled to adapt to "White Man's way of living" and their loss of customs and sacred traditions in the wake of assimilation programs. Moreover, Dion was convinced that understanding would lead to acceptance, for, as he explained to one audience at Bonnyville, "I am sure that when you understand my people better you will agree with me when I say 'long live the Indian.'"[47]

In his unpublished manuscript entitled "Index to Dances and Societies," Dion listed a number of Cree dances that persisted into the 1930s and 1940s as well as those that had been discontinued. In his accompanying commentary, he was especially concerned about the opposition to the Sun (or Thirst) Dance expressed by both converted Indians and Whites. He was also distressed by what he perceived as a growing lack of spirituality among his own people. Thus he observed,

What a change time has brought. Some of the Indians now are neather white nor red. They go to church for the fun of it, the sun dance is nothing but a farce. They will waylay the poor old fellows and steal the offerings as soon as they are hung up. These men and women will openly laugh at the church and at the Indian belief. They are what we call "civilised." Why not let the old people who still cling to the old style – practice it at will, it's better than no belief. . . . The old system is going anyway. Why hasten its demise.[48]

Several other notations in the manuscript reveal Dion's true feelings about the narrow-mindedness of European Canadians towards traditional customs. On the issue of their reaction to "nudity and dancing," he noted, "We were forbidden to even take our shirts off. All we were allowed to show was an arm, from under a blanket we used to cover with in our parades. What about the nudists among the Palefaces of today."[49] Dion also came to the defence of traditional healers, particularly those who were associated with the Mite-wikamik (or Medicine Lodge) Society. He commented that, although Whites might deny the power and efficacy of Indian "doctoring," he knew otherwise.[50] At the conclusion of his description of Cree dances, Dion succumbed to a moment of despair with regard to Whites ridiculing Cree traditions. "Poor overbearing Paleface," he wrote, "you have much to learn from the Indian, had you taken the trouble . . . to come off your high horse."[51]

The loss of a number of Cree values as a result of the breakdown of traditional economic relations was also discernible in Dion's description of the giveaway. In his comparison of the role of generosity and sharing in contemporary giveaways with those of the past, he observed that few men of prestige were now able to resist the "temptation" of withholding material offerings from further redistribution and preferred to augment their own surpluses.[52] According to customary law, these men and their families would have been responsible for ensuring that material goods were distributed beyond their immediate households.

All three men – Mountain Horse, Ahenakew, and Dion – had been educated in the White system; and, while recognizing the strengths of the Western world, they were nevertheless repelled by the demoralizing effects brought about in the implementation of government programs. Despite their obvious Christian bias, all three condemned state interference in indigenous forms of worship, particularly through the use of force.

The personal efforts of these three leaders were reinforced by the growth of Indian political organizations on the prairies. In the late 1920s, the Pasqua, Piapot, and Muscowpetung reserves in Saskatchewan collaborated to form an organization known as the Allied Bands. This united political front emerged in response to the immediate problem of Indian land policies as they were being implemented by Commissioner Graham under the mandate of the Soldiers Settlement Act. Ignoring a warning received from the Department, a delegation from this group had travelled to Ottawa in 1928 to demand Graham's replacement, the creation of a royal commission to inquire into the administration of Indian affairs, and the establishment of reserve schools "so that the Indian way of life could survive."[53]

Other forms of political activity were also evident during this period. In 1929, at the Onion Lake Reserve in Saskatchewan, a number of delegates representing Treaty Six reserves formed an offshoot of the League of Indians of Canada known as the League of Indians of Western Canada.[54] The members of the western branch of the League adopted a number of resolutions that addressed the residential school system, the alienation of Indian lands, religious freedom, and the right of League officers to travel and have their meetings away from their home reserves. Notably, delegates asked for the freedom to hold the Sun Dance, a ceremony "dear to us for centuries and . . . still dear to us."[55] In addition, a memorandum of resolution passed by the chiefs, councillors, and members of the various bands attending a League of Indians Conference in 1933 included a statement on religious freedom. Concerned in particular with the celebration of Sun Dances, the resolution declared that since Canada espoused the principle of the freedom of religion, the signatories were petitioning the government "to worship in our own way" and "according to our past customs."[56]

During the late 1930s and early 1940s, a number of other bands began to organize formally into political groups, including the Indian Association of Alberta (1939), the Saskatchewan Indian Association (1944), and the North American Indian Brotherhood under the leadership of Andrew Paull (1943). Three other organizations evolved on the prairies in direct response to the need for Indian representation in the inquiry conducted by the Special Joint Committee of the Senate and House of Commons, which met during the period between 1946 and 1948 to review Indian policy. These were: the Protective Association for Indians and their Treaties, the Saskatchewan Indian Association, and the Queen Victoria Protective Association (later known as the Federation of Saskatchewan Indians).[57] By 1946, under the impetus of the newly formed CCF government led by Tommy Douglas, the three separate Saskatchewan organizations re-aligned as the Union of Saskatchewan Indians with John Tootoosis as its president.

Prompted by international developments and lobbying on the part of a number of interest groups including "social organizations, churches, and veteran's associations,"[58] the Canadian government in 1945 appointed a joint committee of the Senate and House of Commons to review the Indian Act and its administration. Eight specific areas of concern fell within the mandate of the committee: the fulfillment of treaty rights and obligations, band membership, taxation, enfranchisement, voting privileges, the encroachment of Whites on Indian lands, Indian education, and "any other matter or thing pertaining to the social and economic status of Indians and their advancement."[59]

Historians dealing with the development of Canadian Indian policy have concluded that the major objectives and general conduct of the Joint Committee reflected an adherence to the nineteenth-century philosophy of paternalism and represented yet another effort toward "assisting the Indian to assist himself" in achieving equality in Canadian society.[60] With the exception of Andrew Paull, the President of the North American Indian Brotherhood, who was invited to appear before the Joint Committee in 1946, no other Indian representatives were asked to play a role in its initial deliberations. And, in fact, a motion by Joint Committee member B.H. Castledon for the creation of a national Indian committee of five members to monitor the proceedings was soundly rejected on the grounds that such a process would hamper rather than facilitate the Joint Committee's work.[61] However, pressure for representation on the part of Indian organizations resulted in delegates being allowed to appear before the Joint Committee midway through 1947 after the hearings were well under way. One historian, Ian Johnson, suggests that the Department might have made a deliberate effort to undermine Indian representation because bands were prohibited from using their funds to sponsor representatives to travel to Ottawa.[62]

That Indian representatives were not involved in setting out the agenda or defining the mandate of the Joint Committee is evident in the proceedings and written briefs. While the Joint Committee assumed that a continuation of assimilative objectives was still in the best interests of Indians, most representatives at the hearings lobbied for a greater recognition of treaty and Indian rights, increased political power through self-government and national representation, more local control over band financial assets, and a decrease in the unilateral authority of the agent and the Department in the internal affairs of the bands. Some also requested a more formal definition of the political relationship between treaty Indians and the provincial governments.

Few submissions raised the question of religious freedom. This may not indicate a lack of concern, but rather it may reflect the Joint Committee's terms of reference. Moreover, the attainment of self-government would have allowed for the internal settlement of religious matters by the band councils. This interpretation is sustained by an important brief submitted to the government by the Protective Association for Indians and their Treaties in September 1945.[63] Tracing its origins to the Allied Bands, the Association represented five to six thousand Indians residing on eighteen reserves in four Saskatchewan agencies. The first item of their presentation was entitled "The Freedom of Conscience and Religious Worship":

This freedom should assure the Indian of freedom to his religious beliefs, and the right to practice his religion according to ancient tradition, without prosecution for the performance of rituals, so long as they do not offend against the general criminal or civil law of the land. It assures freedom to the Indian from the arbitrary imposition of foreign religious beliefs upon him, through parochial schools, or through the undue influence elsewhere, of any particular church or religious creed.[64]

Religious freedom was identified with other civil liberties, such as the freedom of "speech" and "expression," "peaceful assembly," "equality of opportunity," and the "protection of rights of minorities."[65] Another section in this brief, entitled "The Indian Religion," dealt with "civilization and tradition" and contained a defence of "Plains Indian" religious beliefs. Petitioners argued that Plains Indians "were never pagans but had a religion of their own which they practice in many cases with a great deal of devoutness."[66]

The suppression of the Sun Dance was singled out as an instance wherein the law was based upon misconceptions of indigenous religious practices. In this 1945 brief, the Sun Dance was described as a major religious healing ceremony which was performed to effect the recovery of sick children.[67] The Protective Association for Indians and their Treaties defended the use of traditional forms of healing and admitted that, while Indian healers did use "mummery" in their rituals, they were able to achieve "remarkable cures" and had a "remarkable knowledge of pharma-copoeia" that amazed European-Canadian doctors.[68] One other related concern voiced by the Association was the regulation of the movement of people off their home reserves and the use of the permit system. The Association noted that "at one time they were practically prisoners on the land that had been allotted to them."[69]

All Indian submissions to the Joint Committee demanded an end to cultural intolerance and coercive measures used to implement assimilation programs. This was the message that Chief Yellowfly, a Blackfoot witness for the unaffiliated Indians of Alberta, brought to Ottawa. Yellowfly announced that the time had come for the treatment of Indians as "fellow Canadians" rather than as a "bunch of savages who must be subjected and regimented in order to get them to do anything."[70] The Joint Committee was particularly surprised by Yellowfly's statement that parents enjoyed the freedom of religion only if they chose to affiliate with a Christian church, a condition often necessary for the enrolment of their children in schools. Yellowfly's testimony claimed that this policy was discriminatory and forced parents into a hypocritical situation:

That regulation overlooks the fact that some Indians very definitely have a religion of their own, which to them contains deep beauty and consolation. If an Indian is adherent to his native religion, what are you going to do with his children? In a country that advocates freedom of religion, are you going to force that Indian to become a hypocrite by assuming a veneer of either of the religions mentioned in the Act, particularly if he is a better Indian by respecting the sanctity of his real belief?[71]

Ultimately, it was the relationship between religious freedom and the Indian education system that motivated the Joint Committee to consider the issue of regulating ceremonial life. When questioned about the persistence of traditional beliefs, Yellowfly replied that even the converted continued to have faith in their indigenous ceremonies. He also pointed out that the ideologies of traditional Indian religions were "exactly the same" as those held by Christians.[72]

Similar appeals were presented to the Joint Committee by the Indian Association of Alberta and the Union of Saskatchewan Indians.[73] The similarity of wording in the presentations indicated that there must have been some collaboration between the two groups. In addition, a brief submitted by the United Farmers' Organization of the Stablo Tribe from Sardis, British Columbia, also called for the freedom of religion, assembly, and social gathering.[74]

While religious freedom was dealt with in the representations made by the various Indian political organizations, the Joint Committee did not formally discuss the issue until it unexpectedly surfaced during sessions related to the secularization of education and other social services. It was apparent from the reactions of the Joint Committee members that they were unprepared for the forceful verbal attack that was launched against denominationally operated boarding schools. They were equally astonished upon hearing that parents were forced to declare an official affiliation with a particular Christian denomination not only to receive education for their children, but also medical aid and other forms of relief distributed through the churches. Indian witnesses before the Joint Committee also testified that some of their people deliberately repressed their true beliefs in order to receive these benefits.

These criticisms were also part of the formal presentation submitted by the Protective Association for Indians and their Treaties, which made the case that denominational schools not only had a negative effect upon Plains Indians but also served as mechanisms for religious repression. Specific reference was made to the terms of the Qu'Appelle Treaty (Treaty Four), which obligated the federal government to assume responsibility for Indian education but in no way stipulated that Christian conversion was a condition for receiving an education.[75] The Protective Association for Indians and their Treaties expressed its appreciation for efforts made by Christian religious organizations to meet the needs of Indian education, but condemned the practice of making such benefits "contingent upon the acceptance of one or other of the white man's faiths."[76] In fact, the Association recommended that "all social work, including educational, relief, and other ameliorative work proceed among Indians on a non-denominational basis."[77]

In its interviews with the Saskatchewan Indian delegates in 1947, the Joint Committee questioned the relationship between religious affiliation and accessibility to government services. One witness, Joseph Dreaver, former President of the Saskatchewan Indian Association, testified on this matter. He reported that many families were formally associated with specific denominations in order to have their children educated but nevertheless attended Indian ceremonies.[78]

Both Dreaver and John Tootoosis, President of the Union of Saskatchewan Indians, claimed that the denominational school system was responsible for factionalism among their people. (Chief Dreaver had a Presbyterian affiliation, and John Tootoosis had a Roman Catholic background.) Their statements regarding the divisive nature of denominationalism reveal its disruptive effect on communal cooperation and kinship relations:

Mr. Dreaver: One of our Indians at the meeting held in Saskatoon pointed out although he belonged to the Roman Catholic faith he had friends and relatives on many different reserves in that territory whose children were being taught in schools run by different denominations. He said that when those children come out of school they do not mix well. He said, "Why should that be? Why can we not have a school where our children would be brought up together so that there would not be any feelings between the various churches on the reserve?" . . .

Mr. Tootoosis: In my experience trying to organize the people in every band I go to I insist on having a meeting with them, and in each band where there are two denominations and one school they have an awful time to get together. There is a difference there because they are brought up in different schools. It seems like the preachers and the Catholic priests are pulling me this way and that way. They make us fight. This is the chief difficulty in getting co-operation amongst the Indians. With proper co-operation you will get better living conditions because they will co-operate in every scheme they want to take up.[79]

The Joint Committee also solicited opinions from the "scientific community," including Diamond Jenness, Dominion Anthropologist with Mines and Resources, and T.F. McIlwraith, Professor of anthropology and the Head of the Department of Anthropology at the University of Toronto. Jenness, in his evaluation of Canadian Indian policy, compared the plight of the Indians in Canada "to the concentration camps of Nazi Europe."[80] Although he was very supportive of the Department's assimilation policy, Jenness believed that this objective could be achieved only when true social and political integration occurred and a separate political status for "treaty Indians" was abolished. Jenness's testimony clearly impressed the members of the Joint Committee as it was referred to as "one of the finest" talks in the hearings.[81]

McIlwraith specifically dealt with problems arising from the retention of indigenous forms of socio-economic values and ceremonial practices. He attributed the failure of government programs to undue expectations and the social phenomenon of "culture lag." He argued that the lack of progress was inherent in the ongoing struggle of "the old and the new" and reminded the committee that "it took a long time for our ancestors in Europe to become adjusted to modern life."[82] Believing that indigenous social systems were incompatible with personal advancement, McIlwraith claimed that traditional social relations of production and distribution that bound kin to one another through reciprocal obligations were partially responsible for the lack of material progress. To illustrate his point, McIlwraith cited one case involving a student who was forced to abandon his education in order to help his brothers, and he referred to other examples where attempts at private entrepreneurship had been hindered by kin obligations:

An Indian will start up a little store or a garage or something of that nature and somebody will come in and ask for some tobacco. Well, he had not got any money but, well, he is somebody's second cousin, therefore the storekeeper advances him credit and the next thing you know the storekeeper is ruined – ruined by his own relatives or by the claims of his own fellows. The Indian is not as hardboiled as the white man in terms of economy or industrial life. Now that means that we have a slow progress.[83]

McIlwraith also expressed the opinion that indigenous religious practices were disruptive to material progress. The Sun Dance was described as a ceremony that distracted young people from their studies. McIlwraith explained that "it interfered with their studies and their thoughts" even when children overheard their parents speaking about the ceremony.[84] Despite his testimony regarding the negative correlation between Indian "progress" and ceremonies, McIlwraith cautioned the Joint-Committee members against being over-critical of these interruptions in the children's education or their parents' advancement, and warned that, "after all, we permit plenty of things to interfere with our activities."[85] Although Jenness and

McIlwraith were well intentioned in their presentations to the Joint Committee, their opinions no doubt confirmed in the official mind that the dismantling of the indigenous economy and ceremonial life was a precondition to Indian progress and integration into Canadian society.

In the end, the Joint Committee refrained from making any specific recommendations pertaining to the issue of religious freedom. In a section of their report entitled "Other Cognate Matters," Joint-Committee members proposed that the question of the legitimacy of marriages performed on reserves according to "tribal custom and ritual" be placed on the agenda for the next provincial-federal conference.[86] The more repressive regulations contained in the Indian Act were simply removed. Thus, those sections prohibiting ceremonial practices, attendance at rodeos or agricultural fairs, and the sale of one's produce without prior approval from the Indian agent were dropped when the 1951 version of the Indian Act was drafted.

In its brief to the Joint Committee, the Protective Association for Indians and their Treaties had successfully argued that any school system that coerced parents and their children to submit to Christian teachings and conversion to the detriment of their own belief system was "a contravention of the most elementary right of freedom of religious belief, a freedom of worship and freedom of conscience, which are basic in every British Country."[87] It was this concern over the rights accorded to British subjects rather than a tolerance for indigenous religious practices that motivated the Joint Committee to recommend the removal of the ban on potlatches, giveaways, and other rituals. While the Joint Committee's report concluded that most sections of the Indian Act be amended or repealed, the first revision of the Indian Act tabled in 1950 as Bill 267 retained the section on the ban on potlatches. A subsequent version of the Act as Bill 79 was passed in 1951 with all regulations dealing with potlatches, dances, giveaways, and the "mutilation of flesh" being dropped. As Douglas Cole and Ira Chaikin have pointed out in their analysis of the reaction of the Northwest Coast Indian leadership to these revisions, the new draft left out these provisions in an effort to respond to the Joint Committee's recommendations rather than to the objections raised by Indian representations to the Joint Committee.[88]

In a document issued in November 1952, *Regulations Governing Indian Schools*, parents were released from the obligation to declare a Christian denominational affiliation as a condition of enrolling their children into schools. It stated: "A pupil shall not be required to receive instruction in the faith of any religious denomination contrary to the desire of such pupil's parent or legal guardian."[89] However, little had changed in the minds of officials regarding the fundamental principles guiding the nature of the relationship between the Canadian government and indigenous peoples. Indeed, in 1950, the Minister of Indian Affairs, W.E. Harris, confirmed the continuity of the assimilative objective of Canada's Indian policy and the necessity of retaining "special treatment and legislation" in order to achieve this goal.[90]

It was evident from the testimony provided by both the Saskatchewan and Alberta Indians that indigenous ceremonies would continue to have meaning in reserve communities. Ironically, the circumstances under which the Blood Indians discussed and drafted their formal submission to the Joint Committee were symbolic of the role of ceremonial gatherings in secular life. Their submission had been prepared while members of the Blood Indian Band had congregated for their annual Sun Dance on July 15, 1946.[91]

Despite the lobbying by Indian representatives, anthropologists, and a number of other European-Canadian supporters including representatives from the Christian ministry, the revised Indian Act of 1951 brought few meaningful changes. Most important, the underlying notions of wardship and paternalism that had been the basis for the development of British imperial relations with indigenous colonials remained intact. As Harold Hawthorn has indicated in his examination of government Indian policy during the inter-war years, the revisions in the new act were symptomatic of a "spill-over of changed citizen government relationships in White society."[92] They represented "the domestic reaction to the demise of a world in which White skins and the possession of power were tightly correlated" rather than a change of attitudes towards the Indian peoples.[93]

The decision of the Joint Committee to recommend deletion of those clauses in the Indian Act that contradicted the principle of human rights was a pyrrhic victory. Indian activists were disappointed in their failure to secure political support at either the provincial or federal level. This weakness had severely undermined the process of consultation in the Joint Committee and had ruined its potential in their view. However, Indian leaders continued to press for greater political representation and were now developing organizations based upon European-Canadian structural models. This movement required time and patience, and it did not bear fruit for another two decades. Only in 1968–69 did it win national attention in connection with the efforts of Indian leaders to oppose the Liberal government's proposed legislation to terminate the "special and separate" status governing the relations between Canada and status Indians (the White Paper).

The government regulation of plains ceremonial life and the forced conversion of many Indian children who attended church-run schools have become important historical symbols of colonial repression for Canada's indigenous peoples. Moreover, the devastating effect of this history still remains deep in the hearts of many who are only now becoming more open about their own spiritual beliefs and ceremonial practices.

Summary and Conclusions

The period from the early 1870s to the turn of the century was a watershed for prairie Indian peoples. They were forced to come to terms with a series of major ecological, social, economic, and political changes in a relatively short period of time. The reduction of natural food resources and, in particular, the demise of the bison brought an end to highly productive economies based upon the harvesting of natural resources for both domestic use and commercial markets. Moreover, Indian communities were significantly diminished in number and weakened because of their exposure to new diseases, the abuse of alcohol as a trade item, and an increase in territorial conflicts as groups competed for access to resources and commercial markets. While coming to terms with these changing conditions, indigenous nations also had to address the political and economic ambitions of the Canadian nation.

With the decline in the commercial fur trade, Indian lands rather than their labour or fur and provisions resources now became the focus for development. The Canadian acquisition of Indian lands was achieved through formally negotiated treaties arranged between the British Crown and representatives from the various Indian nations. It is important to note that the Indian signatories of these treaties did not intend to surrender control over their internal affairs or their cultural integrity. The subsequent imposition of legislated regulations contained in the Indian Act and the extensive administrative powers of a newly created Department of Indian Affairs in 1880 were major changes in the political relationship between Indians and European Canadians. The elaboration and consolidation of federal regulations governing Indians, their lands, and the relations between Indians and European Canadians through the introduction of the Indian Act of 1876 and its amendments was intended to further support and accelerate assimilation. Government officials assumed that, as in eastern Canada and in other White settlement colonies through-out the British Empire, indigenous cultures would disappear as they conformed to the mores of the dominant society and became incorporated into the Christian capitalist nation-state system. Until Indians proved themselves "worthy of all the privileges of the white men,"[1] they would be treated as wards of the Canadian government. This wardship, or tutelage relationship, was considered to be the most humanitarian means of "uplifting" those who were considered to be lower on the evolutionary scale of human development. Government officials argued that what was in the best interests of the nation-state would best serve the Indians. A European-Canadian education, Christian conversion, and a shift to an economy based upon subsistence and commercial agriculture would not only provide opportunities for tribal peoples to become self-supporting and "civilized," but also ensure the maintenance of peace and order during some difficult adjustments.

While the permanent settlement of indigenous peoples on reserves provided them with a land base, the management of these lands was controlled by the federal government. The reserve system also effectively separated Indians from Canadian society, but officials saw this as a brief transitional phase leading to "civilization." The process of "civilization" meant, in this context, the elevation of Indians "to the moral and intellectual level of the white men and preparing them to undertake the offices and duties of citizens."[2] When the assimilative programs were not as successful as the Department had anticipated and voluntary applications for enfranchisement were not forthcoming, steps were taken to hasten the process. Therefore, in the 1920s and 1930s, amendments to the Indian Act involved compulsory education and forms of both voluntary and compulsory enfranchisement. These steps were in keeping with the policy of the Department under Duncan Campbell Scott who supported an end to "the state of tutelage" for Indians: "Our object is to continue until there is not a single Indian in Canada that has not been absorbed into the body politic, and there is no Indian question, and no Indian Department. This is the whole object of this Bill."[3]

There was little change in the more general objective of assimilation in the revised Indian Act of 1951 with the exception that the term *integrated* was now used rather than *assimilated*. The Indian Act went beyond the regulation of relationships between "status Indians" and Canadian society. In effect, the Act enforced patterns of social, economic, and political behaviour that were consistent with those of the ruling majority in the Canadian nation-state.

The repression of indigenous religions and other forms of cultural expression was perceived as being fundamental to the transformation of individuals into European Canadians. While several Christian denominations assumed the responsibility for religious and cultural assimilation, these efforts were supported by the federal government through funding and, after 1884, by special legislation. The decision of Victorian government officials to control indigenous traditional forms of religious expression was motivated not only by their abhorrence of certain types of non-Christian religious expression but also by the liberal humanitarian impulse to "better" their fellow human beings. Evidence presented in this study suggests that the Canadian government supported a general policy of religious suppression because European Canadians were able to comprehend the dynamics of Indian cultures sufficiently to recognize the connections between religious ideology and expression and the survival of Indian groups as distinct societies. In parallel studies of Central and South American colonialism, social historians have pointed out that such "coercive practices" by colonial governments are not merely occurrences of "social abuse or aberration"; but, rather, these practices "underwrote ongoing social relations of production and exchange and formed the very basis of a labor system."[4]

The colonial experiences of prairie Indian nations in western Canada were similar to those of the original inhabitants of other British temperate-climate settlement colonies such as Australia, New Zealand, British Columbia, and eastern Canada. While these colonial experiences varied during the earlier phases of contact, a familiar pattern of formal and informal relations can be traced. In general, a turning point in economic and political relations occurred when indigenous resources were commercially over-exploited, or when indigenous methods of production were no longer of value to the survival of a European colony. This situation usually developed once White settlers had established a viable economic base. This form of colonialism – that is, economic development through White settlement – resulted in the land itself being transformed into a commodity for exchange and eventually led to the separation of indigenous societies from their resource base. As the negative effect of colonization on indigenous populations became apparent, the non-military aspects of British Native policy consisted of strategies to integrate the colonized into the new political economy. For societies based on hunting-and-gathering subsistence activities, this integration involved major socio-economic and political changes, as populations were encouraged to become agriculturalists and labourers in a state-directed, market-oriented economy.

The use of religious repression as a means of incorporating indigenous peoples into Western nation-states deserves more attention by researchers than has been the case so far. Australian researchers, such as Erich Kolig, are beginning to examine relationships between religious transformation and national economic development policies.[5] From the general histories on colonial policy in Australia and New Zealand, it is evident that administrators were concerned about the role of tribal elders, ritualists, and customary laws in the preservation of indigenous cultural values and practices. Often referred to categorically as "local customs," or "superstitions," indigenous religious practices were subjected to controls because they offended moral sensibilities, posed a possible threat to lives of colonists by serving to unify people, and interfered with the government's desire to transform indigenous economies and loyalties. The Tangi, a communal funerary rite, and political religious movements such as the Hau Hau religion have been cited as examples of religious expression that colonial governments discouraged.

The Canadian approach to the suppression of indigenous religions was most comparable to the policies instituted by the United States government. By 1883, a system of tribal police and the Courts of Indian Offences had been established on the U.S. Indian reservations. Although this administrative arm of the federal government had no legal basis, the Rules for the Courts of Indian Offences outlawed the Sun Dance ceremony and the Scalp Dance on the grounds that their performances interfered with the "civilization" process and were "repugnant to common decency and morality."[6] By the mid-1880s, Wild West shows and similar commercialized exhibitions that glorified "savagery" and exposed Indians to the more "unsavoury" elements of White society also came under attack. While no specific legislation was introduced, in 1889 the Commissioner of Indian Affairs, John Oberly, instructed his agents to use "every legitimate means" to prevent Indian involvement in such shows.[7] In 1892, on the recommendation of officials in the Bureau of Indian Affairs, Commissioner Thomas Morgan introduced a regulation designed to discourage the performance of specific ceremonies (the Sun Dance, the Scalp Dance, and other similar feasts). First-time offenders were to be denied their rations for ten days, and subsequent offences were punishable by the further withdrawal of rations for a period of ten to thirty days or by imprisonment for the same duration.[8]

As White settlers advanced into the northern plains and increased the pressure on Indian lands, more regulations were enacted as part of the civilization program. In 1901, the infamous "short-hair order" was issued by the commissioner of Indian Affairs to force European-educated males to cooperate with administrators and to reject their traditional lifestyles.[9] Additional measures were adopted against ceremonies performed in the Southwest. In 1922, Circular 1665 was issued at the same time as the passage of a bill to open Pueblo tribal lands to leasing companies and White squatters. This circular instructed agents to intervene in all ceremonies that included self-mortification, snake-handling, explicit sexuality, and giveaways.[10] In particular, the initiation rites of the Pueblo groups were targeted for suppression.

The colonial experience of the Plains Cree mirrored that of other non-Western societies who were forced to deal with White settlement. Following the signing of the treaties and the selection of reserves, the federal government introduced a number of measures to destroy Cree political independence and cultural integrity.

Foremost among these were the attempts to replace the communal kinship-based system of cooperative production and distribution with the social relations characteristic of the individualized competitive structure of capitalism. This was to be accomplished by undermining traditional collective land-use patterns and encouraging the concept of individualized property ownership. Attempts were also made to dismantle traditional political structures, particularly after the Saskatchewan Uprising of 1885. Uncooperative leaders were deposed; hereditary forms of leadership were attenuated through forced elections or simply by the non-recognition of local leaders; and formerly independent Indian nations became subject to federal and provincial laws.

The government-imposed controls were directed towards the young adult population and their parents. It was felt that the assimilation process would actually begin once children were socialized and educated in the Western tradition. An Indian school system, initiated by the government and virtually controlled by the Christian churches, was created to prevent the Cree and other prairie Indian societies from culturally reproducing themselves. Through this system, the traditional role of the parents, relatives, and elders as producers and transmitters of culture and ideology was undermined. The destruction of the indigenous language, a crucial factor in the communication of any culture's ideology, particularly one that stresses socialization through oral tradition, also served to undermine Cree culture. The residential school system, which involved the physical removal of the child from the influence of his or her home environment, was favoured by the Canadian government.

The government decision to suppress certain forms of religious expression and ceremonies can be partially attributed to contradictions inherent between capitalism and the indigenous kinship-based methods of producing, distributing, and consuming goods. Neither the Victorian objection to indigenous religious customs nor the fact that "religion was a part of the larger cultural complex"[11] fully explains this policy. Rather, one must emphasize that religious beliefs and practices were very much a part of indigenous economic, political, and social life. That this relationship between ceremonialism and the perpetuation of communal forms of production and consumption was recognized by officials is evident in the Potlatch Law and in the Giveaway Clause of the Indian Act. The practice of distributing moveable property through ceremonial channels was considered by administrators and missionaries to be a major factor in Indian poverty and explained the lack of Indian material progress. Furthermore, ceremonial offerings of material goods to the spirit world were condemned as wasteful and impoverishing. As noted in the discussion on the relationship of religious beliefs and ceremonial practices to other aspects of Cree life, one's worth in both the physical and spiritual worlds (these were not separated) was based upon one's ability to produce surpluses for redistribution beyond one's own use. Both moral and spiritual obligations to one's kin and community motivated individuals and their families and served to reinforce traditional obligations. One's personal welfare was assured only through the well-being of the whole community.

Traditional forms of ceremonial time, space, and content inherent in Plains Cree religion impeded the Westernized version of productive labour.[12] Initially, communal ceremonies were synchronized with the natural cycles of subsistence activities and, in particular, with the early summer bison hunts. Thus, the period of late spring through early fall was the most important time not only for food-gathering but also for celebration, socialization, and inter-band visiting. Locations for public communal ceremonies were pre-determined by the availability of game sufficient to support larger numbers and the sacred nature of specific locales. With the demise of the bison herds and the subsequent introduction of agriculture in the 1870s, it became evident to administrators that the continuation of ceremonial rounds to these sacred grounds hindered not only the establishment of permanent Indian settlements, but also the transition to labour cycles that were necessary for field cultivation and the raising of livestock. It was felt that the traditional ceremonial round would result in the neglect of crops and livestock and would compromise the attainment of economic self-sufficiency.

Ceremonial content was also a major concern to administrators and, in particular, to missionaries. Some public rituals often involved self-mortification, the ritual sacrifice and consumption of dogs, dramatized aggression, sexuality, and nudity. These aspects of ceremonial life offended Victorian sensibilities. Dancing as a form of spiritual communication was perceived as "devil worship" and, at best, a form of recreation. In response to a strong lobby by missionaries and certain administrators, some rituals were defined as offences in the Indian Act. The inclusion of giveaways (within ceremonial contexts) in the regulations clearly demonstrated the government's recognition of the role played by these ceremonies in the political, economic, and social life of the Plains Cree.

The social and political functions of large communal ceremonies such as the Sun (Thirst) Dances were also referred to by administrators and missionaries in their justification of religious suppression. Such gatherings were correctly recognized as occasions for the transmission and reinforcement of cultural values. The relationship between attendance at ceremonies and the "regression" of school children and graduates was a particular concern for the Department. The attendance of students at ceremonies undermined the assimilative purposes of the Indian education system and also represented a waste of public monies. Finally, communal gatherings were feared as potential vehicles for mobilizing reactionary political movements. Departmental field reports indicated that administrators and missionaries were aware that their policies were discussed and criticized at these ceremonies. Thus, efforts were made to control this customary method of mobilizing political and military power by instituting the pass system to contain people within the boundaries of their respective reserves and by supervising "legal" ceremonies. Other measures consisted of deposing uncooperative headmen (many of whom were also spiritual leaders) and generally exerting pressure on celebrants through warnings.

The Canadian government's regulation of ceremonial life was also based upon a number of erroneous notions about prairie Indian religious practices. Significantly, the misinterpretation of the intent and meaning of the Sun Dance resulted in an amendment to the Indian Act that prohibited self-mortification but failed to make the performance of the ceremony itself an offence. Viewing it as a rite to publicly test and validate the courage of young men as warriors, officials assumed that the dance would disappear once the self-mortification ritual and inter-tribal raiding activities were outlawed. However, Indian peoples themselves regarded the dance as a ceremony devoted to world regeneration and healing through prayer and personal sacrifice. It was not simply a means of "making braves," as officials believed, but also "to maintain the order of one's world and the meaning in one's way of life."[13]

The use of discretionary controls in combination with legislation against the most objectionable religious practices indicated that the government was aware that ceremonial repression would be met with opposition and might even result in concerted forms of resistance. The preferred policy of "moral suasion" placed a heavy responsibility on the administrative and personal skills of the Indian agents. On the Northwest Coast and also in the prairie region, the task of monitoring the movement of people to their sacred grounds was nearly impossible.[14] Those agents who were successful in forcibly containing their wards only undermined the confidence of the community in the Indian administration. Yet, from the government's perspective, an agent's inability to discourage ceremonies was seen as an indication of a lack of professional backbone and an inability to influence communal decisions. Administrators such as William Graham generally attributed the failure of ceremonial repression to the shortcomings of the Indian agents rather than to the weaknesses inherent in the legislation and the impracticality of its enforcement.

The inadequacy of the policy of discretionary regulation led to the implementation of extra-legal forms of ceremonial repression. The use of non-violent methods to suppress ceremonies, and dancing in general, can be partially ascertained from the Department's correspondence files. These included the intimidation of participants, interference in ceremonies, the withholding of rations from celebrants, the destruction or confiscation of sacred objects, and the refusal to allow the construction of "dance halls." In addition, headmen were pressured not to lend their support to traditional ritualists. In some cases, administrators attempted to limit access to commercial goods for ceremonial redistribution by discouraging local store managers from selling supplies to Indians at ceremonial time. The pass-system trespass law and the use of police to supervise ceremonial proceedings were two of the more common methods of repression. Finally, the replacement of ceremonies and secular forms of dancing with substitutes derived from European-Canadian culture, such as sports days and agricultural exhibitions (but accompanied by prohibitions against Indian performances at White-sponsored agricultural exhibitions and stampedes), represented one last "endeavour to substitute reasonable amusements for . . . senseless drumming and dancing."[15]

This policy of "moderation" with "firmness" was reflected in the number of arrests and convictions. With the exception of a few cases, which were intended to serve as cautionary warnings, most arrests resulted in suspended sentences with fines or releases after a stern lecture from the presiding judge. Arrests related to a Sun Dance were usually made under the terms of the Indian Act clause that prohibited off-reserve dancing.

Throughout the period under consideration, the Department remained inflexible on the issue of ceremonies, although it did defer to the Indian agent's judgement about how and when to intervene. This strategy led to inconsistencies, a fact that undermined the effect of the legislation. However, this was counteracted in the prairie region by Indian Commissioner William Graham, who, until his retirement in 1932, demanded that his agents rigorously enforce the law. Despite his entreaties, the Department refused to consider further restrictive amendments to the Indian Act. This was consistent with its strategy of "moderation and suasion" and, above all, indicated its faith in the long-term power and wisdom of the wardship system. The Department reasoned that time was on its side and that perhaps its initial expectations regarding Indian material progress were unreasonably optimistic. Such beliefs motivated the Deputy Superintendent General of Indian Affairs, Duncan Scott, to refuse to initiate legislation to enforce the pass system. His only concession to Graham and other lobbyists was the deletion in 1932 of the phrase "in aboriginal costume" in relation to off-reserve attendance at exhibitions and stampedes.

From the evidence available in the files of the Department of Indian Affairs and elsewhere, the intensity of repressive measures, and forms of Indian responses, varied from reserve to reserve. While the aggressiveness of local administrators and missionaries was certainly a factor, it is apparent that those communities that were geographically isolated from White settlements were less vulnerable to repression than reserves located on agricultural lands or in areas designated for public works. In the latter cases, Department correspondence and personal testimonies reveal that Plains Cree leaders undertook every means short of violence to ensure the preservation of their traditional forms of religious expression.

Indian signatories of the treaties believed that government repression of their religion violated the intent of those agreements. They constantly challenged the new regulations as contravening their rights. They believed that local administrators and Indian agents were directly responsible for unilaterally introducing these regulations without Ottawa's knowledge, not realizing that religious control was a major component of the assimilation program. Few Indian people at this earlier stage were even aware of the contents of the Indian Act.

As wards of the state, devoid of any political power through provincial or federal representation, there were few official channels through which leaders could present their case. Moreover, according to Ottawa's directives, all matters pertaining to Indians were to be handled through one department. Therefore, working through the official channels available to them, leaders such as Fineday and Thunderchild forwarded letters of protest to local agents and commissioners and, when possible, directly to Ottawa. Their unfamiliarity with the English language tended to reduce the effectiveness of their message; however, with the aid of school graduates and hired White lawyers, this difficulty was gradually overcome. Once people knew more of the actual legislative wording and were able to critically evaluate the legality of informal forms of repression, they began to challenge administrators by using local lawyers and the courts. This was particularly true after the return of the Crooked Lakes delegation from Ottawa in 1911.

In general, written and personal representations to the Department were discredited as the work of uneducated "unprogressives" or "traditionalists" whose power would soon be undermined by a White-educated leadership. The only alternative employed by Indians was the use of the legal system to challenge administrators and Indian agents who went beyond the law. However, as the two court decisions of 1903 (Wanduta and Etchease) demonstrated, the Department and church representatives were successful in securing judgements against the resisters.

Some leaders sought other means to compensate for their political powerlessness. While they were few in number, there are documented instances of attempts to gain political leverage by threatening to oppose other government programs such as the education of children or the leasing of reserve lands for public works. Another method used to enhance their political power and to legitimize protests was the recruitment of White supporters. Although they were not significant in number, sources of White support for Indian resistance included local political representatives, town councils, agricultural fair-and-stampede organizers, Hudson's Bay Company store managers, anthropologists, and even the occasional Indian agent.

The non-violent strategy of opposition to anti-ceremonial regulations also included attempts to correct European-Canadian misconceptions of indigenous religious practices. Thus, some petitioners undertook the task of putting forth the argument that their religious ideology was equivalent to the Christian religion. They drew parallels between the Sun Dance and Christian forms of worship. Elders continue to point out these similarities today:

> The forked centre post with a bundle of brush fastened to the top, and considered to be the "nest" of the Thunderbird, is no other than the symbolic Jesus when he was on the cross, wearing a crown of thorns. The red streamers symbolize his blood. And those gathered in the Rain Dance lodge are people who come to pay tribute to their prophet. The smoking of tobacco and the burning of Sweetgrass is . . . no different from the [use of] incense that burns in many churches. . . . The giving of Indian names to young children is said to have a parallel to the baptism ritual of the Roman Catholic church. . . . The feast which follows the Rain Dance, a wake, or a Sweat Bath is no other . . . than that of the communion that people share in church. . . . The self-torture . . . was interpreted as no other than the Christian custom of suffering as the Biblical Jesus had done.[16]

The giveaway was defended on the grounds that, as a means for the distribution of goods that ensured that the less fortunate were materially cared for, it fulfilled the Christian values of sharing and generosity to other human beings. And, in fact, for Indian elders, being a "free-giver" and participating in giveaways was highly valued and viewed as an important distinction between Indians and Whites. One elder, Elizabeth Ogle from the Wood Mountain Reserve, observed in the early 1970s that "the white man saves his money and puts it away – that's their life; they like to pass it on" while the "Indian way" stipulates that, when "somebody comes, you feed them."[17] More secular forms of dancing were compared to social events enjoyed by White neighbours.

With greater strictures against dancing and participation in White-sponsored exhibitions from 1914 through to the 1930s, some petitioners expressed concern over the connection between religious suppression and cultural loss. In these years, the issue of cultural disintegration was increasingly addressed by Indian war veterans and school graduates. In addition to arguing that anti-ceremonial legislation was a contravention of treaty rights, they contended that such regulations were also a denial of the freedom of religion that they were to have as British subjects. These new leaders, more knowledgeable in the ways of the White world, now began to assert their power by adopting European-Canadian methods of political organization in order to unify the locally initiated and often largely ineffective protest groups. The issue of religious freedom was included in the platforms of the various Indian political organizations that were founded after World War One.

While attempts to force the government to reverse its policy of religious suppression through the use of bureaucratic and legal channels were unsuccessful, ceremonial leaders challenged the government more effectively by continuing to hold ceremonies. In effect, the persistence of ceremonies was a form of resistance, and its effect can best be measured by the continual struggle by administrators such as William Graham and the Christian churches to have more repressive measures enacted. Depending upon the type and degree of repression that occurred on particular reserves, religious persistence assumed a number of variations ranging from open and surreptitious performances of the dances; the modification of ceremonial time, space, and content; and, in a few instances, the adoption of a new religion such as the Peyote religion.

I have used the Plains Cree experience in particular in my research to examine ways in which the features of the ceremonies were deliberately modified in response to government regulations. The deletion of the public versions of self-mortification, or piercing, was one of the more obvious accommodations to the legislation. According to Plains Cree historian Abel Watetch, some religious leaders created a new ritual, in which the physical act of piercing was replaced symbolically by a greater offering of material goods.[18]

The location, timing, and attendance at large communal ceremonies such as the Sun Dance were affected by the prohibitions against off-reserve dancing and the implementation of the pass system. As a consequence, Sun Dances became more localized and of shorter duration, and they were attended by fewer participants. In his 1960s study of the Plains Cree Sun Dance, Lloyd O'Brodovich attributed the limited local version of the ceremony to the fact that the Plains Cree were not politically integrated into a tribal structure of society but, rather, retained the characteristics of localized bands. Evidence presented here suggests that the local performances were a reaction to travel restrictions and regulations against the celebration of inter-community ceremonies.[19] Only contiguous reserves were able to maintain a degree of inter-reserve participation by celebrating the ceremony along their borders. More frequently, however, communal ceremonies were held in secluded portions of the reserve, thus allowing some protection for off-reserve celebrants.

The length of the Sun Dance was reduced to accommodate the "civilized" work week and to meet the objections that it was a "waste of time." The exigencies of the agricultural cycle itself and the labour-intensive demands of working the land during the early summer and fall were responsible for an abbreviated version of the Sun Dance and associated ceremonies. On some reserves, a shorter version of the Sun Dance, now devoid of the self-mortification ritual, was known as the Rain Dance. It was celebrated for a period of one and a half to two days. As one contemporary researcher has noted, the modification of the Sun Dance into a Rain Dance (if only in name and ritual exclusion) transformed the original ceremony into "a kind of respected Indian church."[20]

In order to ensure the survival of their Sun Dances, some communities invited the monitoring of their ceremony by the police and Department officials. This outside presence of authority was at times welcomed by celebrants as a means of controlling the distribution and consumption of liquor. A number of reserves also permitted the attendance of White observers, presumably as a public validation that "illegal" practices were not being performed. At least two reserves felt that this situation might work to their economic advantage and charged admittance fees for non-Indians.

Other forms of accommodation were also adopted to meet White objections to ceremonial practices. Some petitioners, for example, offered to refrain from the ritual consumption of dog meat and the distribution of goods, and to observe European-Canadian notions of decency by not dancing naked. There was only one documented instance of ceremonial substitution for the Sun Dance, and this occurred under duress at the Crooked Lakes Agency in 1898 when a one-night Smoke Dance was used to fulfill a Sun Dance vow.[21]

From descriptions of ceremonies in both historical and anthropological documents, it is evident that giveaways persisted. However, there is little discussion of the ceremony in Department reports except for the few files related to specific arrests. In the early years, when the Giveaway Clause of Section 114 was enforced closely, one of the government's major concerns had been the movement of Department-issued goods (goods for use rather than ownership) such as wagons and horses between reserves and to neighbouring reservations in the United States. Some groups may have attempted to negotiate terms of redistribution with the government. For example, in a petition submitted by the Peigan leader Bull Plume in 1915, it was proposed that only "Indian made goods," that is, domestically produced goods and commercially purchased goods of small value (including small amounts of cash), be allowed to change hands during ceremonies. The lack of documentation on giveaway practices was largely due to the ability of celebrants to keep such activities away from the prying eyes of officials, missionaries, and even anthropologists. Unlike the potlatches of Northwest Coast cultures, the majority of prairie giveaways appear to have escaped the notice of White observers. Many community giveaways were held during the winter, a time during which most agents would have found it difficult to monitor ceremonies. Other giveaways may have involved the distribution of goods in the privacy of homes after a ceremony. In addition to modifying their Sun Dances and perhaps the giveaways, some bands attempted to synchronize the timing of their ceremonies with the agricultural cycle and also agreed to refrain from consuming alcohol, feasting, using body and facial paint, and allowing the attendance of school children.

Finally, the persistence of indigenous ceremonies was facilitated by the incorporation of a number of rituals into more secular events at which people naturally gathered – Treaty Days, sports days, White agricultural exhibitions and rodeos, for example. During the Dominion Day and annual treaty celebrations, members from numerous reserves gathered not only to collect treaty monies and to socialize, but also to perform communal ceremonies. Among the dances performed were the Tea Dance, the Prairie Chicken Dance, the Whitiko Dance, the Bear Dance, the Elk Dance, and the Horse Dance. With the passage of amendments limiting the performance of dancing to the reserves, this avenue for ceremonialism was open only to those who were willing to travel the exhibition circuit despite government regulations.

While a number of rituals were either discontinued or reformulated, the general ceremonial complex was paradoxically enriched during this period of repression. One outstanding example is the adoption of the Grass Dance and its later development into a traditional (non-commercial) Pow-wow. When it was introduced to the Plains Cree in the earlier part of the twentieth century, the Pow-wow provided yet another avenue for perpetuating indigenous political economies and concomitant values. Both secular and sacred forms of the Pow-wow are still practised. Other newly introduced dances that can be traced to this period included the Tea Dance, the Round Dance, the Tail Wagging Dance, and the Kohomni (or Turnabout) Dance (the latter occurring among the Dakota).

There were also many recorded local revivals of ceremonies and dances, the timing of which was generally related to periods of official relaxation or of Indian challenges to the law. There is evidence for the existence of at least one major attempt to initiate a syncretic indigenous and Christian movement by the Muscowpetung, Piapot, and Pasqua reserves in the mid-1920s. As explained by several petitioners, the purposes of their meetings were to offer prayers for abundant crops, to relieve illness, and, most important, to heighten the awareness by the younger generation of the spiritual precepts through which they could live a better life.[22]

In addition to the modification of indigenous religious practices, many Indian men and women did convert to Christianity. While some left their indigenous practices behind following their conversion, others combined their traditional beliefs and practices with Christian doctrines and forms of religious expression. For many, the Sun Dance and the Christian churches were all part of the same spiritual path. There were others who rejected all these alternatives and became members of the Peyote religion or Native American Church. Primarily consisting of individuals of Dakota affiliation in Manitoba, members could also be found among the Cree bands of Louis Sunchild, Red Pheasant, Mosquito, and Grizzly Bear's Head.

To the extent that scholarly research exists in the area of religious suppression on the northern plains, there is evidence that the Cree experience was shared by other groups. The fact that repression drove ceremonial practices underground and caused participants to be cautious renders documentation difficult. In his study of the Canadian Dakota, anthropologist James Howard records that most Dakota reserves ceased to perform their Sun Dances by 1910.[23] The historical relationship of Dakota communities with the Canadian government is often cited as a reason for their reticence in discussing indigenous forms of worship:

The refugee Dakota in Saskatchewan made a real effort to acculturate, knowing that only the goodwill of the Canadian authorities enabled them to remain in their new homes. The Cree were not under such pressure to acculturate, and to this day have conserved much of their traditional culture, more than even their relatives in Montana have retained.[24]

The Blackfoot are reported to have discontinued many of their Sun Dances by the 1940s. Historian Hugh Dempsey has observed that since 1920 there have been no overt attempts by the government to suppress Blackfoot ceremonies and that it was the "apathy of their own people in the post-war years that resulted in the decline and loss of a number of ceremonies."[25] However, he acknowledged that Blackfoot Indian forms of "doctoring" persisted.[26]

Anthropologist Margot Liberty suggests that legislation against the performance of the Sun Dance in the United States was responsible for its disappearance among the Teton Sioux in 1883, the Kiowa in 1890, and the Wind River Shoshone in 1911.[27] However, Liberty cautions that more scholarly case studies would need to be undertaken in order to verify this information. Her research on religious suppression among the Cheyenne illustrates the survival of the Sun Dance in a situation where there was relatively little government opposition.[28]

The extent to which indigenous ceremonial practices among the Plains Cree declined as a direct result of government intervention can be answered only through studies of the various reserves. Certainly the fear of imprisonment and the imposition of fines on a cash-poor people must have deterred some celebrants. Other forms of trauma are unmeasurable but can be perceived in the emotional oratory of the elders to this day. The inability to fulfill one's sacred vows because of the pass system or the interruption of ceremonies would have placed individuals and their families under considerable stress. In his interview with anthropologist Alice Kehoe in the early 1960s, Harry Brown (Pyakwutch, or Clean Earth) stated that, because of the general fear of arrests in the early twentieth century, people "did not yet dare to hold Sun Dances annually on most reserves."[29] In some cases, sacred objects were lost. Two Midewiwin leaders from Manitoba passed their sacred scrolls to the anthropologist Alanson Skinner for safekeeping in the Museum of the American Indian in New York.[30] Other sacred materials were purchased by non-Indian collectors and are still held in private collections and in public museums. The extent of the confiscation or destruction of sacred objects cannot be determined from the Department's records, with the exception of the giveaway drums that were confiscated in Manitoba.

For those who chose to retain their indigenous beliefs and practices (at times combining them with Christian practices), ceremonial life continued to provide physical, emotional, and spiritual support. But, for many, this path was not an easy one. Elderly healers, shamans, and ritualists interviewed in the 1960s suffered not only from Department repression but also from ostracism by those Christian relatives who refused to associate with traditionalists.[31] As late as the 1960s and 1970s, some elders still believed that they would be arrested for performing their ceremonies openly.[32] At times, those who had taken on spiritual commitments performed their ceremonies with little community support and in secret; but, according to one Manitoba elder, as long as one person assumed these responsibilities and learned the appropriate teachings from the elders, there was an opportunity for the preservation of sacred knowledge."[33]

New lifestyles also affected one's ability to meet sacred commitments in the traditional manner. For families supporting themselves through seasonal labour, and by hunting and fishing, meeting ceremonial obligations was relatively less stressful. However, for those who chose to farm and adopt the Western work week and Sunday as a religious Sabbath day, the fulfillment of ceremonial commitments, especially those that involved time-consuming off-reserve travel, became increasingly difficult.

As in the pre-reserve period, ceremonial life continued to provide a means for the re-affirmation of ethnicity, the attainment of status and prestige, and the redistribution of goods. Gifts to and from ritual leaders and their helpers, as a kind of payment for their services, enabled these keepers of religious knowledge to perform their spiritual duties and to support their families. Although the circle of kinship appeared to be attenuated by government restrictions on inter-reserve movement in certain areas and perhaps by new regulations on residency and band membership, the system of kinship-based reciprocal obligations was retained as a means through which the social relations of production and distribution were organized. According to Department reports and observations made by researchers, even Christian relatives who refrained from attending the ceremonies were induced to provide a share of the material support needed to sustain such communal ceremonies as the Sun Dance and giveaways.[34]

The impact of government controls on traditional forms of leadership that had been legitimized through the acquisition of spiritual power warrants further research. In the state-imposed political system, the affairs of the secular world were increasingly separated from the sacred world, and, as a result, a new leadership emerged. These new leaders were not necessarily knowledgeable in game management, nor were they respected because of their spiritual power (as were Piapot and Fineday); rather, they were often accorded status because of their success at accumulating wealth or property as farmers, or because of their ability to act as conduits between the reserve community and the Department of Indian Affairs. They were the young male adults who had received their education in government schools and who knew more of the White system than did their parents or elders. These were indeed the new "warriors" whose battles would be fought not only on the European front in the two world wars, but also in the offices of the Department of Indian Affairs.

To what extent the political role of ritual leaders and the elders was reduced deserves to be re-examined. It is evident, however, that their displacement by the Department may not have terminated their customary power. In the Hankses' study of Blackfoot ritualists, for example, it is suggested that, while traditional leaders were not formally involved in decision-making, they offered advice when invited to do so.[35] Considering the Department's efforts to encourage "non-traditional" people to run for office, the role of traditional leaders would undoubtedly vary from community to community. Certainly the loss of indigenous spirituality among the new leaders could have led to a situation where the elders were ignored. Today, on local, provincial, and federal levels, the elders are officially included in decision-making, and the connections between the secular and the sacred are once again evident.

The impact of religious repression on the process of assimilation must also be considered within the context of other government programs that were simulta-neously being introduced to the prairies. In his historical overview of the 1920s and 1930s, Plains Cree historian Stan Cuthand describes the convergence of genera-tional, religious, economic, political, and social changes in that period. Cuthand depicts the 1930s as a period of increasing conflicts between the "older generations" and the educated members of the "new generation":

Family-arranged marriages were opposed by the youths, and they often ran away to be married elsewhere. The younger generation refused to accept the traditional role of submitting to the wishes of their fathers and tended to question such traditional customs as giving away horses to visitors. The more educated Indians scoffed at Indian rituals and refused to participate. They danced square dances and quadrilles. They would speak English rather than their native tongue. The more traditional families ignored this and continued to show their Indianness. No matter how far removed they may have been from their hunting, fishing, and food-gathering ancestors, and in spite of opposition from the Indian Affairs policies, the elders continued to renew themselves at the sweat lodges and feasts. They restored relationships and kinship ties at the sweat lodges and feasts. When sun dances were completely suppressed by the government, Indians met at exhibitions and fairs to meet each other and renew friendships and strengthen kinship.[36]

Similar observations were made by agents and missionaries such as Reverend James Donaghy of the Ojibway Swan Lake Reserve in Manitoba, who wrote in his journal:

The young are already tiring of some of these customs, and leave them to the old folks. . . . At one of their annual picnics the old people put on a pow-wow in an enclosure, while the young men had a series of baseball games to manage. The old folks ordered them to help within the pow-wow, but the ball players told them they were too busy playing ball to dance pow-wow. The old men felt that their superior position had been challenged.[37]

These same developments were reported among the Blackfoot in the 1940s and the Fringe Saulteaux on the Côté Reserve in Saskatchewan. And many elders who have been interviewed or have given workshops on "Native awareness" invariably express the fear that the younger generation will no longer care for their cultural ways.

The residential school system, which isolated children from their families for prolonged periods of time, disrupted the socialization of the younger generation in indigenous values and religious expression. Responsibility for education that once resided with grandparents, parents, and other relatives was now assumed by European-Canadian teachers. Because the traditional means of learning involved oral communication, based upon a linguistic-bound world view, the loss of language at school significantly undermined ceremonial continuity. Indigenous cultural learning through direct observation and practical experience was also an important aspect of training that was not available to school children. Ceremonies were conducted in the indigenous language, and many school graduates, not knowing their language or the appropriate ceremonial behaviour, often remained peripheral to ceremonial life or refrained from attending, believing that these practices were innately "bad" or "evil." The performance of ceremonies in secrecy undoubtedly enhanced these perceptions.

For those school graduates who chose to resume indigenous forms of worship, the years of spiritual training that had been lost had to be addressed by their parents and elders. To this day, elders are still concerned about religious persistence, particularly about the need for candidates who will be able to assume responsibility for the spiritual and material welfare of the community.[38] Plains Cree elder Abel Watetch expressed this fear in the 1950s about the continued performance of the Sun Dance:

The history of the Sun Dance, even in its modern form of the Rain Dance, is almost over. There are few left to carry on the tradition. The youths who once learned the ethics of the Crees in various steps of participation are no longer in training in sufficient numbers to maintain the tradition. It is almost impossible to find young men of the necessary quality. They are contaminated by their contacts with the worst side of the White man's culture before they are of an age to begin their training. The Indian, even when he is corrupted by his contacts outside the reserve, has great respect for tradition. He will not try to carry on an empty form if he has not the true qualifications for attempting his communion with the Great Spirit. The Crees will not feed on the husks of ancient rituals. No man will attempt to sponsor a Rain Dance if he knows he lacks the spiritual capacity. Moreover, the Rain Dance demands powers of endurance and self-discipline which few will possess when the present elders are gone.[39]

To what extent the threat of ceremonial loss was circumvented by the "reversion," or "retrogression," of school graduates is difficult to determine. However, contemporary researchers do suggest that this process was a factor in ceremonial survival. Alice Kehoe noted that among the Plains Cree the age of forty was a time when many men educated in the European-Canadian tradition would assume an active ceremonial role. A similar situation was recorded in detail by Hanks and Hanks, who interviewed young Blackfoot men who had chosen to follow a "traditional" lifestyle after being unsuccessful in the White world:

> Every year brings the young men closer to the circumstances of the caricatured old Indian. Then as he gives up his hard-earned symbols he comes to question the values for which he has been striving. If his child dies, his faith in the protection of white medicine and Christianity is shaken. If his livestock dies of disease, he wonders whether he has not made some great mistake. At first he may vow to give money to the church in order to ensure a good crop. He may vow a pilgrimage to a shrine so that his child may recover from the measles. But should these fail, the entire set of values is questioned. Indeed, his success, as defined by continued good crops, health for his children, and increase in livestock is almost unattainable. The vagaries of Alberta weather, the high rate of infant mortality, and the difficulty in controlling disease among animals combine to draw most Indians back to their old way of life.
>
> After a series of failures a typical transition occurs. One man lets his hair grow; a second joins a sacred society; another appears at the Sun Dance camp with a painted tipi; a fourth vows to cut the rawhide strips that hold a rafter to the Sun Dance lodge; a fifth summons a Medicine Man to cure his sick child instead of going to the hospital.[40]

Hanks and Hanks astutely point out that this acceptance of traditional ceremonial behaviour and its inherent ideology is not viewed as a "degrading experience" or as an indication of failure, but rather as a path of personal redemption, renewal, and strength for those forsaking or otherwise not seeking to emulate the White way.[41] One must be cautious, however, not to assume that all who have turned back to their indigenous religion have been "unsuccessful" in the White world. Their return might equally represent a public expression of ethnicity and a re-assertion of cultural heritage and values.

In sum, to the extent that they did persist, the various forms of indigenous-modified ideologies and ceremonial practices continued to be relevant within the context of Indian life. The Thirst (or Sun) Dances and their associated rituals such as giveaways continued to fulfill a variety of basic needs for reserve populations. Of particular note was the continuing importance of the collective public ceremony as a powerful source for physical, emotional, and spiritual well-being. The flexibility of the Sun Dance as a ceremony, which accommodated a number of changes (in time, space, and content) while retaining and even perhaps enhancing its value as a regenerative power, is evident in its emergence as one of the most potent healing ceremonies in Canada and the United States during the reserve period. The lack of effective medical services (until the 1940s in Canada), impoverished living conditions, under-nourishment, and disease (especially the post–World War One influenza epidemic and tuberculosis) undoubtedly contributed to the persistence of those indigenous ceremonies that were believed to have significant healing powers.

In Canada, the increasing importance of the Sun Dance as a healing ceremony is attested to in its adoption (including piercing) by the Buffalo Point Ojibway in 1921 to counteract the devastating effects of the influenza epidemic. In the 1940s, the Nibagoimung, or Rain Dance (a version of the Sun Dance), was adopted by the Saulteaux in the Côté Reserve area. This group apparently had refrained from practising their collective ceremonies since 1904. According to researchers Shimpo and Williamson, this version of the Sun Dance was taken up as a "re-integrative" religion by the elders in an attempt to counteract the disintegration of their culture. In addition to emphasizing the need to retain indigenous values, the elders re-introduced kinship-based reciprocity through the performance of giveaways and other rituals at the communal Rain Dance.[42]

The Sun Dance has been revived or adopted by contemporary Indian communities in the United States for similar reasons. In his analysis of the Sun Dance "religion" as practised by the Indians of the Great Basin area, Joseph Jorgensen noted that, with the exception of the Wind River Shoshone, the Sun Dance was a post-reservation phenomenon.[43] This development has been attributed to a flexibility in the ideology of the world-renewal ceremony whereby the focus "was changed from insuring successful bison hunts and warfare to an increased concern over illness and community misery."[44] Described as a nativistic redemptive movement, the Sun Dance "religion" now offers its adherents, through collective forms of worship, an opportunity to re-affirm their cultural identity within a positive framework (that is, Indian). In addition to serving a healing function, the Sun Dance and other collective rituals such as the giveaways persisted because of the political and economic marginality of most reserves. While more specific studies of reserves are required to test this relationship, a pattern does seem evident.[45]

In its historical overview of the economies of the Indian reserves in the Saskatchewan prairie region, the Hawthorn/Tremblay Report of the 1960s described these communities as under-developed and depressed. Although some of the bands, such as the James Smith and Piapot bands, held large amounts of agricultural land, the report concluded that these holdings were "too small to sustain the population on the basis of the large-scale farming operations required for optimum efficiency."[46] Furthermore, off-reserve economic opportunities were also relatively unrewarding. Other than low-paying casual labour, there were few employment prospects near reserves. Thus, most Indian workers had to leave their homes on the reserve, where they received valued community support, in order to participate in the cash-market economy. This economic alternative, however, also had its limitations due to their lack of education and technical skills, the racism that prevailed in the wider community, and the under-development of the prairie region in general. As the Hawthorn/Tremblay Report points out, limited industrial development in the area further worked to the disadvantage of Indian workers due to "the existence of an already over-surplused, under-employed White population and excessive competition for jobs in cities and towns."[47]

Contrary to the consensus of non-Indian opinion at the time, the Hawthorn Report attributed the lack of economic progress in Indian communities to a state of under-development that resulted from the wardship, or "caretaking," role assumed by the Department. Government repression, said the Report, not indigenous patterns of socio-economic and religious behaviour, was responsible for Indian poverty. The Report further argued that a more positive approach to economic development, including adequate training and capital investment, would have produced more viable communities in the prairie region. Although no direct correlation was made between the observation that prairie Indians maintained "widespread" kinship networks and obligations *and* the state of under-development, the Report did suggest that, "as among other depressed and dependent low-income groups," the persistence of the kinship-based system of support was "a result, rather than a cause, of poverty."[48]

Ironically, it was the very system that had been developed to eliminate Indian cultures that ensured at least some degree of ideological persistence. The reserves, which reinforced Indian collectivism, allowed the communities to survive physically, emotionally, and spiritually in their "neocolonial, satellite niches."[49] As Noel Dyck has indicated, "Prior to 1970 there were relatively few Indians in Saskatchewan who had not lived the greater part of their lives within the confines of more or less strict variants of this 'reserve experience.'"[50]

A comparison of the Plains Cree and Blackfoot reactions to their experience with economic under-development shows that both were participating simultaneously in two types of economy. To ascertain at what point these economies intersected would require an extensive study of individual reserves. On the one hand, the Cree and Blackfoot lived within a national market economy. On the other, they participated in a reserve economy. This reserve economy, or the marginal economy of under-development, has been characterized by Hanks and Hanks as one built upon reciprocal obligations rather than acquisition, money, and property:

The one is the indigenous system where goods and services flow on a basis of reciprocal obligations between members of a common group of kinsmen. Though the prestige-gaining treasures of the system required a fee on entering an age-graded society, subsistence was based on reciprocal obligations. The poor were either not poor in this basic sense or were isolated individuals without kinsmen. The other economy, the White system, places even subsistence on a fee basis and dissolves the community of obligations within most groups beyond the family. On the reserve services for a fee have entered; dealings with whites are necessarily on such a basis, and between Indians this pattern is also found occasionally. . . . However, the mechanisms of distribution within the reserve and the relation of Indian employer to employee are still based on reciprocal obligations.[51]

As Hanks and Hanks point out, lifestyle cannot necessarily be correlated with religious practice. For, whether hunter, trapper, seasonal worker, farmer, or professional, if an individual continues to fulfill his or her sacred and social responsibilities within the structure of kinship reciprocity, one is being Plains Cree, Blackfoot, Assiniboin, Ojibway – not White. This philosophy – "know your relatives and you will know who you are" – continues to have relevance to this day.[52]

The piecing together of today's Aboriginal spirituality is very much part of the contemporary struggle for empowerment through self-determination and self-government. In effect, the Aboriginal peoples are "re-appropriating" their cultures, their histories, and their very identities. This struggle has not been an easy one, and many forms of persecution still exist. For example, the performance of indigenous forms of religious worship in penitentiaries has gained limited acceptance only in recent years, and the transportation of sacred materials across international borders continues to be a problem. The use and preservation of traditional sacred sites and environments that are located off reserve lands and are threatened by development projects are other contentious issues. Access to religious materials and burial remains held by museums and universities is an issue now being addressed by cultural institutions across North America.

The revitalization of Aboriginal tradition-oriented forms of worship has been a difficult one for the younger generations raised in the residential school system. Their search is conducted in written texts and oral histories left behind by elders and anthropologists, and in artifacts now housed in museum storage areas and the holdings of private collectors. The answers they seek ultimately reside with those elders who have assumed the responsibility of learning their traditions and who keep this knowledge in trust for future generations. Today, many sacred offerings of tobacco are being taken by the younger generation to their elders as they seek to maintain and – yes – to restore, through spiritual teachings and ceremonies, the "ties that bind."

Appendix

UNTITLED POEM

Reverend Edward Ahenakew

I've tasted of the boasted fount
Of knowledge that the Whiteman's is,
Its waters ripple in the sun,
Fit place for gods to drink is this.

Its waters sparkle radiantly
They glitter so in colored light,
–But simple life and simple truth
Seem gone forever with the night.

Nought but the complex things remain,
Men boost the good which they defy,
Each other's blood they freely shed,
Whil'st they the Christ re-crucify.

Why should we take the path they tread
And leave our own approach to God
Exchanging our own humbler way,
For that along the bloody sod?

Oh! surely Christ will not despise
The winding trail our fathers trod
With simple steps and faithful hearts
With loyal minds to reach their God?

Can we not then in "heathen" rites,
As ritual, serve the Crucified?
Mayn't He in dances, reverent, pure,
As truly then, be glorified?

Why ape the race whose stated creed
Seems not to lie plumb with their deeds,
Why follow that which is not ours,
Nor which doth satisfy our needs?

Ah! Spirit that o'er Indian lands
Wouldst fain reclaim thine olden sway,
Thy children are upherded sheep
Pushed north by even those who pray!

Thy children yearn for what is past
Nor yearn for what in future lies,
Perception of thy Presence now,
Draws forth from them regretful sighs.

In Sun-dance, where the Indian soul,
Excels itself in striving might
To reach the sphere from whence he may
Absorb a ray of godly light.

In this old rite the Whiteman sees
That which he holds should be erased,
Whil'st winking at his turkey-trot
And other things that are debased.

"Sun-dancing is against the faith
of Him, Whom Christian nations serve!"
–Ah! Christian nations hold the path
From treading which they should not swerve.

Two thousand years of Christian faith
and Knowledge's progress unsurpassed
and Wisdom delving deep, for Truth
And adding to what was amassed,–

These mark the height of aerial flight
To which immortal mortals soar,
–But what of Truth and simple good,–
Should not these plain things come before?

If pride of Knowledge gains the world
And homely Goodness' lost for aye,
What vantage gains the human soul
With pride that lasts but for the day?

"Religious freedom in the land?"
–Then leave us to our peaceful ways,
What boots it that we should depart
From ancient rites of by-gone days?

You'd force your way to God on us,
Therein is blood and much deceit,
'Twere better that we stayed behind
Than do that which seems counterfeit.

Our fathers groped where darkness was,
And found that which has served the race,
An Indian rite wherewith to serve,
A Sacrament, a means of grace.

Next day . . .

I sense the soul of Indian days
It hovers in the glooming air,
Which, pregnant with the Presence, felt,
A cloister in the hour of prayer.

I sense the soul of Indian days
As spreads the night in solitude,
My soul responding to the touch
Took on a humbler attitude.

It feels the touch of its own kind,
It senses there a sympathy,
The outward paste of white veneer
Falls as if in antipathy.

(Saskatchewan Archives R-1, Reverend Edward Ahenakew Papers)

Notes

PREFACE

1 In this book, the terms *Indian, Aboriginal,* and *First Nations* are used to refer to Canada's indigenous populations. The term *Indian* was the operative term applied by the Canadian government and Canadian society to indigenous peoples, and I have used the term in this historical context.

INTRODUCTION

1 The Indian Act has regulated almost "every aspect" of the lives of men, women, and children and still has "the force of the Criminal Code and impact of a constitution on those people and communities that come within its purview" (see J. Rick Ponting and Roger Gibbins, *Out of Irrelevance: A Socio-Political Introduction to Indian Affairs in Canada* [Toronto: Butterworth and Company Limited, 1980], 9).

2 William Simmons, "Culture Theory in Contemporary Ethnohistory," *Ethnohistory* 35, no. 1 (1988): LO. See also: James Axtell, *The European and the Indian: Essays in the Ethnohistory of Colonial North America* (Oxford: Oxford University Press, 1981); and Bruce Trigger, "Ethnohistory: The Unfinished Edifice," *Ethnohistory* 33, no. 3 (1986):253–67.

3 These relationships are often described in anthropological literature, but in many cases they are not fully understood and have generally been explained according to the "theory of the day" from a Western "scientific" perspective.

4 I am indebted to the earlier works of Jacqueline (Gresko) Kennedy, including Jacqueline Gresko, "White 'Rites' and Indian 'Rites': Indian Education and Native Responses in the West, 1870–1910," in *Western Canada Past and Present,* ed. A.W. Rasporich (Calgary: McClelland and Stewart West, 1974), 163–81; and Jacqueline Kennedy, "Qu'Appelle Industrial School: White 'Rites' for the Indians of the Old North West" (Master's thesis, Carleton University, 1970). For a history of the government's anti-ceremonial policy under Scott, see Brian Titley, *A Narrow Vision: Duncan Campbell Scott and the Administration of Indian Affairs in Canada* (Vancouver: University of British Columbia Press, 1986). Keith Regular, in "'Red Backs and White Burdens': A Study of White Attitudes towards Indians in Southern

Alberta, 1896–1911" (Master's thesis, University of Calgary, 1985), and "On Public Display," *Alberta History* 34, no.1 (1986):1–10, discusses aspects of the legislation against ceremonies and Indian participation in stampedes and agricultural exhibitions in Alberta.

5 Forrest LaViolette, *The Struggle for Survival: Indian Cultures and the Protestant Ethic in British Columbia* (Toronto: University of Toronto Press, 1973); and Douglas Cole and Ira Chaikin, *An Iron Hand upon the People: The Law against the Potlatch on the Northwest Coast* (Vancouver: Douglas and McIntyre Limited, 1990).

6 In addition to Titley, *Narrow Vision,* see J.R. Miller, "Owen Glendower, Hotspur, and Canadian Indian Policy," *Ethnohistory* 37, no.4 (Fall 1990):393–96.

7 For example, see the following: David Aberle, "A Note on Relative Deprivation Theory as Applied to Millennariun and other Cult Movements," in *Millennial Dreams in Action*, ed. S.L. Thrupp (The Hague: Mouton and Company, 1962), 209–14; Joseph Epes Brown, *The Spiritual Legacy of the American Indian* (New York: Crossroad Publishing Company, 1982); Joseph Jorgensen, *The Sun Dance Religion: Power for the Powerless* (Chicago: University of Chicago Press, 1972); Ralph Linton, "Nativistic Movements," *American Anthropologist,* n.s., no. 45 (1943): 230–40; Omer Stewart, "Origin of the Peyote Religion in the United States," *Plains Anthropologist* 19, no. 65 (1974):211–33; Anthony Wallace, "Revitalization Movements," *American Anthropologist* 58, no. 2 (1956):264–81.

8 See the following published ethnographies: Donald Cadzow, "Mr. Cadzow's Field Trip of 1925," *Indian Notes,* Museum of the American Indian 3, no. 1 (1926):48–50; Donald Cadzow, "Peace Pipe of the Prairie Cree," *Indian Notes,* Museum of the American Indian 3, no. 2 (1926):82–94; Donald Cadzow, "Expedition to the Canadian Northwest," *Indian Notes,* Museum of the American Indian 4, no. 1 (1926):61–63; Donald Cadzow, "Smoking Tipi of Buffalo Bull the Cree," *Indian Notes,* Museum of the American Museum of Natural History 4, no. 2 (1926):271–80; Pliny Earle Goddard, "Notes of the Sun Dance of the Sarsi," *Anthropological Papers of the American Museum of Natural History* 16 (1919a):271–82; Pliny Earle Goddard, "Notes on the Sun Dance of the Cree in Alberta," *Anthropological Papers of the American Museum of Natural History* 16 (1919b):295–310; Alanson Skinner, "Political and Ceremonial Organization of the Plains-Ojibway," *Anthropological Papers of the American Museum of Natural History* (1914a):475–512; Alanson Skinner, "Political Organization, Cults and Ceremonies of the Plains Cree," *Anthropological Papers of the American Museum of Natural History* 11 (1914b):513–42; Alanson Skinner, "The Sun Dance of the Plains-Cree," *Anthropological Papers of the American Museum of Natural History* 16 (1919a):283–94; Alanson Skinner, "The Sun Dance of the Plains-Ojibway," *Anthropological Papers of the American Museum of Natural History* 16 (1919b):311–15; Wilson Wallis, "The Sun Dance of the Canadian Dakota," *Anthropological Papers of the American Museum of Natural History* 16 (1919):319–85; James Vanstone, *The Simms Collection of Plains Cree Material Culture from Southeastern Saskatchewan,* Fieldiana Anthropology, n.s., no. 6 (1983):1–57. Another anthropologist, Douglas Leechman, travelled to the Canadian prairie region in 1936 and collected material for the Victoria Memorial Museum; however, there is no public record of his fieldnotes. The Canadian Museum of Civilization houses the artifacts that he collected.

9 Marius Barbeau, "The Potlach among the B.C. Indians and Section 149 of the Indian Act," Canadian Museum of Civilization, Archives, Native Ethnology Section, VII-X-46. While a handwritten date of 1934 appears on the front page of the report, the information was collected in response to a request made by the Deputy Superintendent of Indian Affairs, Duncan Scott, to the Anthropology Division of the Department of Mines around 1920.

10 For relevant contemporary anthropological studies relating to aspects of the Sun Dance and change over time, see: Neils Winther Braroe, *Indian and White: Self-Image and Interaction in a Canadian Plains Community* (Stanford: Stanford University Press, 1975); Kennedy, "Qu'Appelle Industrial School"; Lucien Hanks and Jane Hanks, *Tribe under Trust: A Study of the Blackfoot Reserve of Alberta* (Toronto: University of Toronto Press, 1950); Jorgensen, *Sun Dance Religion*; Alice Kehoe, "The Ghost Dance Religion in Saskatchewan: A Functional Analysis" (Ph.D. diss., Harvard University, 1964); Margot Liberty, "Suppression and Survival of the Northern Cheyenne Sun Dance," *Minnesota Archaeologist* 27, no. 4 (1965):120–43; Margot Liberty, "The Sun Dance," in *Anthropology on the Great Plains*, ed. W. Raymond Wood and Margot Liberty (Lincoln: University of Nebraska Press, 1980), 164–78; Thomas Mails, *Sundancing at Rosebud and Pine Ridge* (Sioux Falls: The Center for Western Studies, 1978); Lloyd O'Brodovich, "The Plains Cree of Little Pine: Change and Persistence in Culture Contact" (Master's thesis, University of Saskatchewan, 1969); Mitsuru Shimpo and Robert Williamson, *Socio-cultural Disintegration among the Fringe Saulteaux* (Saskatoon: University of Saskatchewan, 1965); and Koozma Tarasoff *Persistent Ceremonialism: The Plains Cree and Saulteaux*, Canadian Ethnology Service, Paper no. 69, Mercury Series (Ottawa: National Museums of Canada, 1980).

11 In response to a formal request made to David Mandelbaum by the Canadian Plains Research Center in Regina, copies of fieldnotes and photographs are now in this Canadian repository for study. While much of Mandelbaum's data has been published in his monograph on the Plains Cree, unpublished materials in the area of kinship are invaluable. Having been one of the first researchers to utilize the fieldnotes, I am deeply indebted to David Mandelbaum for making this information available to the Plains Cree and Western scholars. Mandelbaum's monograph is entitled *The Plains Cree: An Ethnographic, Historical and Comparative Study* (Regina: Canadian Plains Research Center, 1979).

12 Edward Ahenakew, *Voices of the Plains Cree*, ed. Ruth Buck (Toronto: McClelland and Stewart Limited, 1973); Stanley Cuthand, "The Native Peoples of the Prairie Provinces in the 1920s and 1930s," in *One Century Later: Western Canadian Reserve Indians Since Treaty 7*, ed. Ian Getty and Donald Smith (Vancouver: University of British Columbia Press, 1978), 31–42; Joseph Dion, *My Tribe the Crees* (Calgary: Glenbow-Alberta Museum, 1979); Mike Mountain Horse, *My People the Bloods*, ed. Hugh Dempsey (Calgary: Glenbow-Alberta Institute and Blood Tribal Council, 1979); Norma Sluman and Jean Goodwill, *John Tootoosis: A Biography of a Cree Leader* (Ottawa: The Golden Dog Press, 1982); John Snow, *These Mountains are Our Sacred Places* (Toronto: Samuel Stevens, 1977); John Tootoosis, "Modern Indian Societies," in *Proceedings of the Plains Cree Conference*, Fort Qu'Appelle, October 24–26, 1975 (Regina: Canadian Plains Research Center, 1979), 74–78; Abel Watetch, *Payepot and His People* (Saskatoon: Modern Press, 1959); Alexander Wolfe, *Earth Elder Stories* (Saskatoon: Fifth House, 1988).

13 Saskatchewan Indian Cultural College, *Kataayuk: Saskatchewan Indian Elders* (Saskatoon: Saskatchewan Indian Cultural College, 1976); and Saskatchewan Indian Cultural College, *Enewuk* (Saskatoon: Saskatchewan Indian Cultural College, 1979).

14 In the United States, the American Religious Freedom Act of 1978 has addressed some of these issues, but it has not proved to be an effective means for asserting rights, particularly where court cases are concerned. In Canada, access to cultural heritage collections and sacred materials has been addressed by a special task force, which was organized by the Assembly of First Nations and the Canadian Museums Association. See *Turning the Page: Forging New Partnerships between Museums and First Peoples,* a report jointly prepared by the Assembly

of First Nations and the Canadian Museums Association, Ottawa, 1992. I was a member of this task force.

PIAPOT'S STORY

1 See W.P. Stewart, *My Name is Piapot* (Maple Creek: Butterfly Books Limited, 1981); and Watetch, *Payepot and His People,* for biographical treatments of Piapot. While biographer Abel Watetch stated that Piapot was born around 1816, the Department of Indian Affairs recorded that he was born in 1833. Indian Commissioner William Graham claimed that Piapot was fifty-five in 1901 when he was arrested for participating in a giveaway (see James Dempsey's Introduction in William Graham, *Treaty Days: Reflections of an Indian Commissioner* [Calgary: Glenbow Museum, 1991], 88). This estimate was inaccurate, as Piapot was elderly when he died in 1908. In *Treaty Days,* Graham states that Piapot passed away in 1918, whereas his death actually occurred in 1908 (see *Manitoba Free Press,* May 4, 1908, 3).

2 The spelling of Payepot's name was anglicized to Piapot, and this is the version used in my study.

3 Isaac Cowie, *The Company of Adventurers* (Toronto: William Briggs, 1913), 389–90. There have been varying opinions regarding this event. W.P. Stewart believes that Piapot was mocking the pretentiousness of the Hudson's Bay Company (*My Name is Piapot,* 34). Cowie viewed it as "immodest" and "blasphemous" (*Company of Adventurers,* 390). Of interest is an observation on the use of the word *lord* offered by Henry Youle Hind in the late 1850s. In his commentary on the employment of the word *lord* by a local Indian healer, Hind noted that the word did not imply a "supreme master" but rather "an idea of independence and individual power, and is better expressed in English, as the half-breeds informed me, by the word *gentleman* (Henry Youle Hind, *Narrative of the Canadian Red River Exploring Expedition of 1857 and of the Assiniboine and Saskatchewan Exploring Expedition of 1858,* vol. 2, rpt. [Edmonton: M.G. Hurtig Limited, 1971], 127–28).

4 Sarah Carter, *Lost Harvests: Prairie Indian Reserve Farmers and Government Policy* (Montreal and Kingston: McGill-Queen's University Press, 1990).

5 Stewart, *My Name is Piapot,* 75. Men of rank generally had two or more wives. According to Mandelbaum, women were married three or four years after puberty, but men generally did not marry until their mid-twenties (*Plains Cree,* 148). The women would have provided the labour necessary for Piapot to process game and hides for the support of his following and for commercial trade.

6 Hugh Dempsey, *Big Bear: The End of Freedom* (Lincoln: University of Nebraska Press, 1985), 60.

7 Sarah Carter, "The Genesis and Anatomy of Government Policy and Indian Reserve Agriculture on Four Agencies in Treaty Four 1874–1897" (Ph.D. diss., University of Manitoba, 1987), 242.

8 Graham, *Treaty Days,* 86. In his memoirs, Graham commented that Piapot never forgot this incident and "declared to the day of his death that it was a put up job to try to get rid of him."

9 Stewart, *My Name is Piapot,* 79. Scaffolding was a traditional method of burial whereby the wrapped dead and selected belongings were placed on platforms located in trees.

10 Dempsey, *Big Bear,* 113.

11 *Ibid.*

12 Stewart, *My Name is Piapot,* 68.

13 John, son of Piapot, was a witness to these negotiations, which occurred between his father and the railway officials (Stewart, *My Name is Piapot,* 68). For a critical treatment of this event, see David Lee, "Piapot: Man and Myth," *Prairie Forum* 17, no. 2 (Fall):251–62. The incident is not well-documented in the historical records and was over-sensationalized by White journalists and historians to the point of "myth-making."

14 Mr. Z. Hamilton, Saskatchewan Historical Society, to Mrs. A.L. O'Farrell, December 8, 1945 (SA, Manuscript Collection SHS-49, Piapot file 1,344), 12–13.

15 *Ibid.,* 14.

16 *Ibid.*

17 Graham, *Treaty Days,* 85.

18 Stewart, *My Name is Piapot,* 145–46. (All quoted material throughout this volume is cited as it appears in the original.)

19 Watetch, *Payepot and His People,* 39.

20 Watetch states that the arrest was made around 1899. In his report for the year 1895, A.E. Forget, Assistant Indian Commissioner, Regina, reported to the Superintendent General of Indian Affairs that "torture" or "making braves" was being practised in the central and eastern portions of the Territories but that only on Piapot's Reserve was the dance held "successfully" (A.E. Forget, Regina, to the Superintendent of Indian Affairs, Ottawa, September 20, 1895 [Canada, *Sessional Papers,* no. 14, 59 Victoria, A. 1896]).

21 Watetch, *Payepot and His People,* 39.

22 Annual Report of Inspector J.O. Wilson, Commanding Regina District, North-West Mounted Police, District Office Regina, December, 1901 (Canada, *Sessional Papers,* no. 28, 1–2 Edward VII, A. 1902), 91. Five of the arrested were released on suspended sentence, while a sixth was sentenced to six months' imprisonment "with hard labour" in the Regina prison guard room.

23 Graham, *Treaty Days,* 87.

24 Mr. Z. Hamilton, Saskatchewan Historical Society, to Mrs. A.L. O'Farrell, December 8, 1945 (SA, Manuscript Collection SHS-49, Piapot file 1,344), 13.

25 *Ibid.,* 15.

26 Watetch, *Payepot and His People,* 22.

CHAPTER 1

1 David McNab, "Herman Merivale and Colonial Office Indian Policy in the Mid-Nineteenth Century," in *As Long as the Sun Shines and Water Flows: A Reader in Canadian Native Studies,* ed. Ian Getty and Antoine Lussier (Vancouver: University of British Columbia Press, 1983), 100.

2 Rita Bienvenue, "Comparative Colonial Systems: The Case of Canadian Indians and Australian Aborigines," *Australian-Canadian Studies: An Interdisciplinary Social Science Review* 1 (1983):30; Robin Fisher, *Contact and Conflict: Indian-European Relations in British Columbia, 1774–1890* (Vancouver: University of British Columbia Press, 1977), 1–14; Wilbur Jacobs, "The Fatal Confrontation: Early Native-White Relations on the Frontiers of Australia, New Guinea and America – A Comparative Study," *Pacific Historical Review,* no. 40 (1971):283–309; and Paul Sharp, "Three Frontiers: Some Comparative Studies of Canadian, American and Australian Settlement," *Pacific Historical Review,* no. 24 (1955):369–77.

3 Beverley Gartrell, "Colonialism and the Fourth World: Notes on Variations in Colonial Situations," *Culture* 6, no. 1 (1986):9.

4 Bernard Porter, *The Lion's Share: A Short History of British Imperialism* 1850–1970 (New York: Longman Group Limited, 1978), 23.
5 J. Little, "Legal Status of Aboriginal People: Slaves or Citizens," in *Racism – The Australian Experience: A Study of Race Prejudice in Australia,* vol. 2, ed. F.S. Stevens (New York: Taplinger Publishing Company, 1972), 85. Commenting upon this middle-class group of reformers known as the Clapham Sect, Jean Usher (Friesen) noted that members such as William Wilberforce and James Stephen, longtime Secretary of State for the Colonies, commanded enough authority to influence Native policy. The sect was noted for its support of benevolent activities, its opposition to the slave trade, and its promotion of world-wide missionization through the founding of the Church Missionary Society, the British and Foreign Bible Society, the Religious Tract Society, the Sunday School Society, and the social reformist schools of Bell and Lancaster and Hannah More (see Jean Usher, "William Duncan of Metlakatla: A Victorian Missionary in British Columbia" [Ph.D. diss., University of British Columbia, 1968], xii).
6 Little, "Legal Status," 82–83.
7 Usher, "William Duncan," 31.
8 Phillip Curtin, *The Image of Africa: British Ideas and Action, 1780–1850* (Madison: University of Wisconsin Press, 1964), 259.
9 *Ibid.*
10 Ronald Robinson and John Gallagher, *Africa and the Victorians: The Official Mind of Imperialism* (London: The Macmillan Press Limited, 1978), 2–3.
11 *Ibid.*, 2; Usher, "William Duncan," 34.
12 Usher, "William Duncan," 35.
13 John Galbraith, "The Humanitarian Impulse to Imperialism," in *British Imperialism: Gold, God, Glory,* ed. Robin Winks (New York: Holt, Rinehart and Winston, 1963), 2.
14 Leslie Upton, "The Origins of Canadian Indian Policy," *Journal of Canadian Studies* 8, no. 4 (1973):59.
15 Douglas Lorimer, *Colour, Class and the Victorians: A Study of English Attitudes towards the Negro in the Mid-Nineteenth Century* (New York: Holmes and Meier, 1978); George Stocking, *Race, Culture, and Evolution* (New York: Free Press, 1968); and George Stocking, *Victorian Anthropology* (New York: Free Press, 1987).
16 Lorimer, *Colour, Class and the Victorians,* 149.
17 *Ibid.*, 148.
18 Christine Bolt, *Victorian Attitudes towards Race* (London: Routledge and Kegan Paul, 1971), 20.
19 *Ibid.*, 27.
20 John Bodley, *Victims of Progress* (Menlo Park: The Benjamin/Cummings Publishing Company, Inc., 1982), 9.
21 Robinson and Gallagher, *Africa and the Victorians,* 2.
22 Bolt, *Victorian Attitudes towards Race,* 120.
23 Marvin Harris, *The Rise of Anthropological Theory* (New York: Thomas Y. Crowell Company, 1968), 200–01.
24 Bolt, *Victorian Attitudes towards Race,* 120.
25 Harris, *Rise of Anthropological Theory,* 201.
26 *Ibid.*
27 Edward Tylor, *Primitive Culture: Researches into the Development of Mythology, Philosophy, Religion, Language, Art and Custom* (London: J. Murray, 1871).

28 Harris, *Rise of Athropological Theory*, 203.
29 Jacob Pandian, *Culture, Religion, and the Sacred Self: A Critical Introduction to the Anthropological Study of Religion* (Englewood Cliffs: Prentice-Hall, Inc., 1991), 35.
30 Sir James Frazer, *The Golden Bough: A Study in Magic and Religion* (London: Macmillan and Company Limited, 1960), 16.
31 Stocking, *Victorian Anthropology*, 80. Ethnographers used the written observations of colonial administrators such as George Grey; Methodist missionary Thomas Williams; gentleman-explorer Francis Galton; and scientific traveller Alfred Russell Wallace.
32 Frazer, *The Golden Bough*, 347.
33 *Ibid.*
34 *Ibid.*, 119.
35 *Ibid.*, 72.
36 *Ibid.*, 115.
37 *Ibid.*
38 *Ibid.*, 46.
39 Harris, *Rise of Anthropological Theory*, 207–08.
40 *Ibid.*, 208.
41 *Ibid.*, 212.
42 *Ibid.*, 229.
43 Lewis Henry Morgan, *Ancient Society* (New York: World Publishing, 1877).
44 David McNab, "The Colonial Office and the Prairies in the Mid-Nineteenth Century," *Prairie Forum* 3, no. 1 (1978):21.
45 *Ibid.*, 27.
46 *Ibid.*, 24.
47 *Ibid.*, 27 and 35.
48 Bodley, *Victims of Progress*, 104.
49 McNab, "Herman Merivale," 92.
50 Herman Merivale, *Lectures on Colonization and Colonies* (London: Oxford University Press, 1928), 502–03.
51 Bamber Gascoigne, *The Christians* (London: Jonathan Cape Limited, 1977), 239–40.
52 Bolt, *Victorian Attitudes towards Race*, 123.
53 Bodley, *Victims of Progress*, 116.
54 Bolt, *Victorian Attitudes towards Race*, 168.
55 *Ibid.*, 161.
56 *Ibid.*, 160.
57 *Ibid.*, 162.
58 Bodley, *Victims of Progress*, 106–07. For instance, in her analysis of the suppression of certain Fijian ceremonies by the British colonial governments, Martha Kaplan concluded that "to be found 'custom' in the colonial eyes," Fijian practices and institutions had to show social utility in relation to colonial goals and purposes. A ceremony such as the Luve Ni Wai (performed to create supernatural invulnerability among male youth undergoing a transition to a warrior status) was considerd to be obstructive to progress and a threat to the law and order of the colony (Martha Kaplan, "Luve Ni Wai as the British Saw It: Constructions of Custom and Disorder in Colonial Fiji," *Ethnohistory* 36, no. 4 [1989], 359).
59 C.D. Rowley, *The Destruction of Aboriginal Society: Aboriginal Policy and Practice*, vol. 1 (Canberra: Australian National University Press, 1970), 24–25.

60 *Ibid.*, 103. See also T. Long, "The Development of Government Aboriginal Policy: The Effect of Administrative Changes, 1829–1977," in *Aborigines of the West: Their Past and Their Present*, ed. Ronald Berndt and Catherine Berndt (Nedlands: University of Western Australian Press, 1979), 357–66.
61 Rowley, *Destruction of Aboriginal Society,* 19.
62 *Ibid.*
63 *Ibid.*, 20.
64 *Ibid.*, 126.
65 Pauline Turner Strong, "Fathoming the Primitive: Australian Aborigines in Four Explorers' Journals, 1697–1845," *Ethnohistory* 33, no. 2 (1986):184.
66 Rowley, *Destruction of Aboriginal Society,* 134.
67 A. Elkin, "Aboriginal-European Relations in Western Australia: An Historical and Personal Record," in *Aborigines of the West: Their Past and Their Present,* ed. Ronald Berndt and Catherine Berndt (Nedlands: University of Western Australia Press, 1979), 291.
68 *Ibid.*, 294.
69 Bienvenue, "Comparative Colonial Systems," 35.
70 Rowley, *Destruction of Aboriginal Society,* 139.
71 Keith Sinclair, *A History of New Zealand* (London: Oxford University Press, 1961), 54.
72 *Ibid.*, 59.
73 Kenelm Burridge, *A New Heaven New Earth: A Study of Millenarian Activities* (New York: Schocken Books, 1967), 19–20; and Guy Turvey, "The New Zealand Maori and the Process of Acculturation: An Historical Perspective," *Na'pao* 12 (1982):26–34.
74 Turvey, "Process of Acculturation," 33.
75 See Alan Ward, *A Show of Justice: Racial "Amalgamation" in Nineteenth Century New Zealand* (Canberra: Auckland University Press, 1974) for the history of Native policy in colonial New Zealand.
76 Raymond Firth, *Elements of Social Organization* (Boston: Beacon Press, 1951), 117.
77 *Ibid.*, 117.
78 *Ibid.*, 118.
79 Peter Cumming and Neil Mickenberg, eds., *Native Rights in Canada* (Toronto: Indian-Eskimo Association of Canada, 1972), 13–23. For example, as early as 1629, the British government had instructed Governor Endicott of Massachusetts Bay colony to purchase Indian title to land.
80 George Stanley, "Introductory Essay," in *As Long as the Sun Shines and Water Flows: A Reader in Canadian Native Studies*, ed. Ian Getty and Antoine Lussier (Vancouver: University of British Columbia Press, 1983), 5.
81 *Ibid.*, 7.
82 *Ibid.*
83 John Tobias, "Protection, Civilization, Assimilation: An Outline History of Canadian Indian Policy," *The Western Canadian Journal of Anthropology* 4, no. 2 (1976):13–30, 40. See also J. Douglas Leighton, "The Development of Federal Indian Policy in Canada, 1840–1890" (Ph.D. diss., University of Western Ontario, 1975).
84 Cumming and Mickenberg, *Native Rights in Canada,* 26.
85 John Milloy, "The Early Indian Acts: Developmental Strategy and Constitutional Change," in *As Long as the Sun Shines and Water Flows: A Reader in Canadian Native Studies*, ed. Ian Getty and Antoine Lussier (Vancouver: University of British Columbia Press, 1983), 56.
86 *Ibid.*, 57–58.
87 *Ibid.*, 58.

88 Upton, "Origins of Canadian Indian Policy," 56.
89 John Webster Grant, *Moon of Wintertime: Missionaries and the Indians of Canada in Encounter Since 1534* (Toronto: University of Toronto Press, 1984), 81.
90 *Ibid.*, 82.
91 Upton, "Origins of Canadian Indian Policy," 56.
92 *Ibid.*, 57.
93 *Ibid.*, 59.
94 Jean Barman, Yvonne Hébert, and Don McCaskill, "The Legacy of the Past: An Overview," in *Indian Education in Canada: The Legacy,* vol. 1, ed. Jean Barman, Yvonne Hébert, and Don McCaskill (Vancouver: University of British Columbia Press, 1986), 5.
95 Upton, "Origins of Canadian Indian Policy," 59.
96 Tobias, "Protection, Civilization, Assimilation," 42.
97 Wayne Daugherty and Dennis Madill, *Indian Government under Indian Act Legislation, 1868–1951*, part 2 (Ottawa: Department of Indian and Northern Affairs Canada, 1980), 2.
98 *Ibid.*, 5.
99 *Ibid.*, part 1, 3.
100 McNab, "Herman Merivale," 86.
101 Gartrell, "Colonialism and the Fourth World," 8. See also Philip Mason, *Patterns of Dominance* (London: Oxford University Press, 1970), 105–06.
102 Ponting and Gibbins, *Out of Irrelevance,* 6.

CHAPTER 2

1 Dale Russell, *Eighteenth-Century Western Cree and Their Neighbours,* Archaeological Survey of Canada, Mercury Series, Paper 143 (Ottawa: Canadian Museum of Civilization, 1991), 215. Contrary to previous scholarly opinions regarding the origins of the Plains Cree, Russell argues that these groups were well established in the eastern parklands of Saskatchewan by 1715. Russell rightly points out that the nomenclature *Plains Cree* is misrepresentative since these Cree were more oriented to the parklands than to the plains. However, by 1820 they were adopting numerous cultural traits that were shared among several bison-oriented Plains cultures.
2 Arthur Ray, *Indians in the Fur Trade: Their Role as Hunters, Trappers and Middlemen in the Lands Southwest of Hudson Bay* (Toronto: University of Toronto Press, 1974). Ray notes that the gun was used primarily for military advantage and that the bow and arrow were preferred for hunting. Inferior and cumbersome firearms, ammunition requirements, the lack of tools for repairs, and the tendency for flintlocks to freeze in winter are reasons cited for the persistent use of more traditional forms of weaponry and hunting technology (75–76).
3 John Palliser, cited in Mandelbaum, *Plains Cree,* 3.
4 Mandlebaum, *Plains Cree,* 42.
5 *Ibid.*, 105.
6 See map, p. xv this volume.
7 *Ibid.* See also William Fraser, "Plains Cree, Assiniboine and Saulteaux (Plains) Bands 1874–84" (GA, M1190, TS, 1963), 5.
8 Susan Sharrock, "Crees, Cree-Assiniboines, and Assiniboines: Interethnic Social Organization on the Far Northern Plains," *Ethnohistory* 21, no. 2 (1974):95–122.
9 Isaac Cowie, cited in Sharrock, "Crees, Cree-Assiniboines, and Assiniboines," 112.
10 Mandelbaum, *Plains Cree,* 101.

11 *Ibid.*, 105.

12 *Ibid.*, 115–16. Mandelbaum noted that, "if a man evaded the Warriors and tried to make a kill before the proper time, they immediately advanced to the offender's tipi, slashed it to bits and destroyed all his possessions. This was also done to a hunter who had unintentionally stampeded the buffalo because of an unmanageable horse." If the transgressor remained calm throughout the punishment, the Warriors would provide goods from their own possessions after a period of four days as a form of restitution (*Plains Cree*, 115–16).

13 Alan Klein, "The Political-Economy of Gender: A Nineteenth Century Plains Indian Case Study," in *The Hidden Half: Studies of Plains Indian Women*, ed. Patricia Albers and Beatrice Medicine (Lanham: University Press of America, Inc., 1983), 143–73.

14 *Ibid.*, 155.

15 *Ibid.*, 110. Much of the theoretical orientation I've used to analyze the political and economic life of the Plains Cree was derived from the following works: Morton Fried, *The Evolution of Political Society: An Essay in Political Anthropology* (New York: Random House, 1967); Marshall Sahlins, *Tribesmen* (Englewood Cliffs: Prentice-Hall, Inc., 1968); Joan Townsend, "Ranked Societies of the Alaskan Pacific Rim," rpt. from *Alaska Native Culture and History*, ed. Yoshinobu Kotani and William Workman (Osaka: National Museum of Ethnology, 1980), 123–56; and Joan Townsend, "The Autonomous Village and the Development of Chiefdoms: A Model and Aleut Case Study," in *Development and Decline: The Evolution of Political Organization,* ed. H. Claessen, M. Smith and P. Vande Velde (South Hadley: Bergin and Garvey, 1985), 1–57.

16 Amelia Paget, *The People of the Plains* (Toronto: Ryerson Press, 1909), 130–31.

17 *Ibid.*

18 Horses, garments, and white-tanned bison hides were also traded with the Mandan. John Milloy states that "the contact of the Cree and Assiniboine with a source of firearms, the common Sioux enemy, and the Mandans' production of corn were the three legs of the tripod upon which the Cree-Assiniboine-Mandan Alliance rested" (John Milloy, "The Plains Cree: A Preliminary Trade and Military Chronology, 1670–1879" [Master's thesis, Carleton University 1972], 118).

19 *Ibid.*, 66–68.

20 John Ewers, *The Horse in Blackfoot Indian Culture,* Bureau of American Ethnology, Bulletin 159 (Washington, D.C.: Smithsonian Institution, 1955), 18.

21 Elizabeth Grobsmith, *Lakota of the Rosebud: A Contemporary Ethnography* (New York: Holt, Rinehart and Winston, 1981), 9.

22 *Ibid.*, 21.

23 Mandelbaum, *Plains Cree,* 62.

24 *Ibid.*, 78. Mandelbaum documented the ownership of pack dogs by women. The dogs were not a "freely circulating asset" or "inalienable" because, unless they were traded over a great distance, dogs would return to their first homes. Dogs did have exchange value and, while men negotiated these exchanges, it was necessary to obtain a woman's permission before her dogs could be bartered. Trade goods accruing from these transactions were considered to be a woman's property.

25 Colin Turnbull, *The Human Cycle* (New York: Simon and Schuster, 1983), 273.

26 Mandelbaum, *Plains Cree,* 108.

27 Eric Wolf, *Europe and the People without History* (Berkeley: University of California Press, 1982), 181.

28 Mandelbaum, *Plains Cree,* 108.

29 *Ibid.*, 107.

30 *Ibid.*, 108–10.

31 Certain dances, songs, and insignia were owned by the various societies, some having been acquired from the Dakota, such as the Buffalo Dancers Society. The following is Mandelbaum's list of each band's society. It should be noted that names and regalia frequently changed hands, thus this list may have been contemporaneous only with Mandelbaum's fieldwork or within the memories of his informants. The reported societies were: Rattler's Society (River People Band); Big Dog Society, acquired from the Paddling Men Band of the Stoney (Eastern Bands of Cree); Buffalo Dancers Society (purchased by the West, East and River People Bands); Prairie Chicken Society (Upstream People); Cold Society (House People Band); Ghost Lodge Society (Calling Band, River People Band); and the Kit-Fox Society (one of the western bands) (*Plains Cree,* 117).

32 *Ibid.*, 120.

33 Alvin Josephy, *Now that the Buffalo's Gone: A Study of Today's American Indians* (Norman: University of Oklahoma Press, 1984), 79–80.

34 I do not intend to imply that Aboriginal religions remained unchanged over time, but, rather, that religious ideology provided people with the basic spiritually sanctioned cultural "blueprint" for each generation to follow. The syncretism of Woodlands Cree religious ideology and expression with that of plains-oriented Aboriginal nations, and later with Christianity, are examples of the types of changes that occurred among the Plains Cree over time.

35 Mandelbaum, *Plains Cree,* 159–62; 177–78.

36 A vow is a sacred promise made by individuals who are seeking spiritual intervention in their lives for particular needs such as a healing or success in battle or hunting. Often great personal sacrifices or offerings are made in order to demonstrate the necessary humility and respect needed to obtain the Creator's pity and, hopefully, the fulfillment of the request. An unfulfilled vow was viewed as a very serious matter, which would have both material and spiritual ramifications for the pledgers and their relatives.

37 Pat Albers and Seymour Parker, "The Plains Vision Experience: A Study of Power and Privilege," *Southwestern Journal of Anthropology* 27, no. 3 (1971):206. See also Kathleen Dugan, *The Vision Quest of the Plains Indians: Its Spiritual Significance, Studies in American Religion,* vol. 13 (New York: The Edwin Mellen Press, 1985), 235.

38 Albers and Parker, "Plains Vision Experience," 206.

39 Mandelbaum, *Plains Cree,* 171. Sacred materials were carefully stored in hide and cloth wrappings and special containers. The name *bundle* is derived from this method of storage.

40 Hanks and Hanks, *Tribe under Trust,* 91.

41 Turnbull, *The Human Cycle* 273.

42 Mandelbaum, *Plains Cree,* 107.

43 Watetch, *Payepot and His People,* 37.

44 Mandelbaum, *Plains Cree,* 234.

45 Robert Jefferson, *Fifty Years on the Saskatchewan,* Canadian Northwest Historical Society Publications 1, no. 5, Battleford, Saskatchewan, 1929, 20; Mandelbaum, *Plains Cree,* 206–07. Jefferson was a teacher on the Red Pheasant Reserve and a farm instructor for the Poundmaker Reserve.

46 Pat Atimoyoo, *Nehiyaw Matow wena: Games of the Plains Cree* (Saskatoon: Saskatchewan Indian Cultural College, 1980), 6–9. In the teaching "The Youth Who was Pakakus," the spirit's gifts to humans are successful hunts and a long life.

47 Mandelbaum, *Plains Cree,* 206–07.

48 Dion, *My Tribe,* 51–52.
49 *Ibid.,* 52.
50 Ahenakew, *Voices,* 100.
51 Mandelbaum, *Plains Cree,* 206–07.
52 *Ibid.,* 207.
53 Jefferson, *Fifty Years,* 91.
54 Margot Liberty, "The Sun Dance," in *Anthropology on the Great Plains,* ed. Raymond Wood and Margot Liberty (Lincoln: University of Nebraska Press, 1980), 164.
55 *Ibid.*
56 Mandelbaum, *Plains Cree,* 343.
57 *Ibid.*
58 Dugan, *Vision Quest,* 123.
59 Liberty, "The Sun Dance," 167; and Mandelbaum, *Plains Cree,* 183–99. See Peter Nabokov and Robert Easton, *Native American Architecture* (New York: Oxford University Press, 1989), 168–71, for accounts of the relationship of the sacred architecture of the Sun Lodge to the cosmos.
60 David Mandelbaum, Plains Cree Notebook 2, June 27, 1935 (SA), 14.
61 *Ibid.,* Plains Cree Notebook 1, June 25, 1935 (SA), 22.
62 O'Brodovich, "Plains Cree of Little Pine," 95.
63 Mandelbaum, *Plains Cree,* 193.
64 Ahenakew, *Voices,* 137–38. The benefits of self-mortification were reified through oral tradition; one of the teachings described the trickster spirit, We-sa-ka-cha'k, and his introduction to the purposes of the Sun Dance. Upon being awakened abruptly from a "spell" of dancing and drumming, We-sa-ka-cha'k discovered that he had thrust his head into an old bison skull filled with ants. The skull is said to be the Sun Dance lodge itself. Because his face was swollen from ant bites, We-sa-ka-cha'k was unable to remove his head. Finally the force from a bolt of lightning that struck a nearby tree released him. Through this intercession by the Thunderbird spirit, who was sent by the Creator, the trickster spirit was freed from his suffering. This blessing is symbolized through the rainfall, for which dancers must pray in order to replenish the earth and themselves; (dancers are permitted to drink rainwater). Thus, Reverend Edward Ahenakew writes, just as We-sa-ka-cha'k mortified his flesh, "so must man sustain trials to open himself to the store of mercy that is Ma-ni-to [sacred power]" (138).
65 "Counting coup" involves obtaining honours by touching one's enemy with a "coup stick" without inflicting harm or being injured in the process.
66 Mandelbaum, *Plains Cree,* 197.
67 *Ibid.,* 198.
68 Arthur Amiotte, "The Lakota Sun Dance: Historical and Contemporary Perspectives," in *Sioux Religion,* ed. Raymond DeMallie and Douglas Parks (Norman: University of Oklahoma Press, 1987), 89.
69 Watetch, *Payepot and His People,* 39. Rainfall is considered to be a "blessing" that indicated that the prayers of the people had been heard.
70 Liberty, "The Sun Dance," 165.

CHAPTER 3

1 Arthur Ray, "The Northern Great Plains: Pantry of the Northwestern Fur Trade, 1774–1885," *Prairie Forum* 9, no. 2 (1984):275.

2 *Ibid.*, 275. At this time the Hudson's Bay Company still depended upon the York boat and canoe to transport supplies over comparatively greater distances to their posts and eastern outlets. The products of the plains were more effectively brought to closer American markets through the use of a land/river transportation system based upon the *bâteaux* and steamboat. Fur-trade historian Arthur Ray states that during the period from 1815 through to the 1860s the bison-robe trade in the Missouri River area numbered 20,000 to 200,000 bison robes annually, with half these originating from herds in the British-controlled western territories.

3 Gerald Friesen, *The Canadian Prairies: A History* (Toronto: University of Toronto Press, 1984), 131; Irene Spry, "The Tragedy of the Loss of the Commons in Western Canada," in *As Long as the Sun Shines and Water Flows: A Reader in Canadian Native Studies*, ed. Ian Getty and Antoine Lussier (Vancouver: University of British Columbia Press, 1983), 210. Spry documents attempts made by some Cree headmen, including Piapot, to exact payment for passage through their hunting grounds and for the use of resources.

4 Ray, "Northern Great Plains," 278.

5 Spry, "Loss of the Commons," 212–13.

6 John Milloy, in *The Plains Cree*, has presented these developments in detail. See also Friesen, *Canadian Prairies,* 131–32.

7 Morris Zaslow, *The Opening of the Canadian North, 1870–1914* (Toronto: McClelland and Stewart Limited, 1971), 23.

8 George Brown and Ron Maguire, *Indian Treaties in Historical Perspective* (Ottawa: Department of Indian and Northern Affairs, 1979), 33. The Hudson's Bay Company was paid 300,000 pounds sterling for its assets, allowed to retain posts in the North-West Territories, and was given the option of selecting "a block of land adjoining each Post outside of Canada and British Columbia." Further options for land acquisition were contained in a provision for a claim up to fifty years after settlement of "1/20 of the land set apart for settlement in the Fertile Belt (bounded on the South by the United States, on the West by the Rocky Mountains, on the North by the North Saskatchewan River, on the East by Lake Winnipeg, the Lake of the Woods and the water connecting them)."

9 John Tobias, "Canada's Subjugation of the Plains Cree, 1879–1885," *Canadian Historical Review* 64, no. 4 (1983):520. A number of "outside" provisions had been negotiated and were not included in the text of the treaties. In a memorandum forwarded to Ottawa, Treaty Commissioner Wymess Simpson had promised the eastern Ojibway farm animals, horses, wagons, farm tools, and equipment.

10 Richard Bartlett, *The Indian Act of Canada* (Regina: Native Law Centre, University of Saskatchewan, 1988), 17–18.

11 Provencher, cited in Brown and Maguire, *Indian Treaties in Historical Perspective*, 35.

12 Bodley, *Victims of Progress,* 11–12.

13 Friesen, *Canadian Prairies,* 139–40.

14 Alexander Morris, *The Treaties of Canada with the Indians of Manitoba and the North-West Territories*, 1880 reprint (Toronto: Coles Publishing Company, 1971), 169–71.

15 Tobias, "Subjugation of the Plains Cree," 521.

16 To this day, the meanings associated with the terms of the treaties and "outside promises" are still a matter of strong debate between Aboriginal leadership and the Canadian government. The situation has arisen partly from the fact that representatives involved in the negotiations came from very different cultural and historical backgrounds. In addition, the varying languages and the cultural understandings inherent in the meanings of particular words and concepts, especially surrounding the definitions of land ownership and use, also contribute

to present-day allegations on the part of First Nations that the federal government has not fulfilled its promises in "good faith."

17 Dempsey, *Big Bear*, 57.

18 Spry, "Loss of the Commons," 211.

19 Morris, *Treaties of Canada,* 353.

20 *Ibid.,* 354.

21 Dempsey, *Big Bear,* 74. The interpreter for these conversations had mistakenly thought that Big Bear was alluding to corporal punishment by hanging. According to Dempsey, the correct term was *ay-saka-pay-kinit,* which translates as "lead by the neck" rather than *ay-hah-kotit* or "hung by the neck." After the death of Sweet Grass, Big Bear became the leader of the Fort Pitt Cree.

22 Tobias, "Subjugation of the Plains Cree," 524.

23 *Ibid.,* 523.

24 Friesen, *Canadian Prairies,* 137. After the Battle of Little Big Horn in 1876, Sitting Bull led his people into the North-West Territories. In May 1877, 135 lodges of his followers joined other Tetons camped in the Wood Mountain area.

25 Tobias, "Subjugation of the Plains Cree," 526.

26 At the 1876 negotiations, Chief Seenum of Whitefish Lake had requested a "large area" to be set aside for those Woodlands and Plains Cree who had not accepted the terms of the treaty at that time. His request was refused. See Peter Erasmus, *Buffalo Days and Nights,* ed. Irene Spry (Calgary: Glenbow-Alberta Institute, 1976), 260. See also John Tobias, "Indian Reserves in Western Canada: Indian Homelands or Devices for Assimilation," in *Approaches to Native History in Canada,* Papers on a Conference held at the National Museum of Man, October 1975, edited by D.A. Muise (Ottawa: National Museum of Canada, 1977), 93.

27 Tobias, "Subjugation of the Plains Cree," 537. Edgar Dewdney, the Indian Commissioner (appointed in 1879), prevented the territorial concentration of the Cree by rejecting a proposal by Big Bear, Poundmaker, Lucky Man and others to have a reserve at Buffalo Lake and a subsequent request made by Big Bear, Little Pine and Lucky Man for reserves near Poundmaker's.

28 *Ibid.,* 538.

29 *Ibid.*

30 See Friesen, *Canadian Prairies*; Tobias, "Subjugation of the Plains Cree"; and Blair Stonechild, "The Uprising of 1885: Its Impacts on Federal Indian Relations in Western Canada," *Saskatchewan Indian Federated College Journal* 2, no. 2 (1986):81–96.

31 See Dempsey, *Big Bear,* 93, for an excellent examination of the growth of factionalism between the young warriors and their leaders.

32 Jefferson, *Fifty Years,* 132.

33 John Tobias, "The Origins of the Treaty Rights Movement in Saskatchewan," in *1885 and After: Native Society in Transition,* ed. F. Laurie Barron and James Waldram (Regina: Canadian Plains Research Center, 1986), 245. There were a number of reasons for limited participation in the uprising by Indian leaders. In the Qu'Appelle region, Piapot remained loyal but was subjected to a strong military presence on his reserve. The Blackfoot Confederacy also refused to take up arms due to the pacifying efforts of elderly headmen such as Crowfoot and the generally weakened state of the southern prairie nations.

34 Jefferson, *Fifty Years,* 160.

35 Daugherty and Madill, *Indian Government,* 6.

36 Legislation governing Canada's relations with Aboriginal nations was extended to Manitoba, British Columbia, and the North-West Territories in 1874. The Indian Act of 1876 was a consolidation of previous acts, and its initial purpose was to manage lands and property.

37 Hayter Reed was the "architect of Indian policy" in the North-West Territories in the decade following the aftermath of the events of 1885. He was born in Prescott County, Ontario, and received much of his training in military schools. In 1871, he arrived at Fort Garry as a recruit with the Provincial Battalion of Rifles. In 1872 he was called to the Bar of Manitoba but did not pursue a legal career. A year before his retirement from the military in 1881, he accepted a position as chief land guide for the Department of the Interior. In 1881 he became an Indian agent at Battleford, and was promoted to the position of Assistant Indian Commissioner in 1884, Commissioner in 1888, and Deputy Superintendent of Indian Affairs in 1893. See Carter, "Indian Reserve Agriculture," 287–88, and *Lost Harvests*, 141–58, for a discussion of his policies directed against indigenous tribal systems.

38 Daugherty and Madill, *Indian Government,* 29.

39 *Ibid.,* 58.

40 *Ibid.,* 57.

41 Hanks and Hanks, *Tribe under Trust,* 129.

42 Alan Beals, *Culture in Process* (New York: Holt, Rinehart and Winston, Inc., 1967), 245.

43 D.J. Hall, *Clifford Sifton: A Lonely Eminence, 1901–1929,* vol. 2 (Vancouver: University of British Columbia Press, 1985), 46. See also Sarah Carter, "Agriculture and Agitation on the Oak River Reserve, 1875–1895," *Manitoba History,* no. 6 (1983):2–9; and Carter, "Indian Reserve Agriculture."

44 "Annual Report of the Department of Indian Affairs" (Canada, *Sessional Papers,* no. 12, 1889), 165.

45 Carter, *Lost Harvests,* 20.

46 *Ibid.*

47 Jefferson, *Fifty Years,* 38.

48 Carter, "Indian Reserve Agriculture," 179–80.

49 *Ibid.,* 180.

50 Jefferson, *Fifty Years,* 106.

51 Sluman and Goodwill, *John Tootoosis,* 32.

52 Noel Dyck, "An Opportunity Lost: The Initiative of the Reserve Agricultural Programme in the Prairie West," in *1885 and After: Native Society in Transition,* ed. F. Laurie Barron and James Waldram (Regina: Canadian Plains Research Center, 1986), 126. Dyck views the early reserve period as "an opportunity" lost for the creation of "self-governing" and "self-supporting" Indian communities owing to the "lack of commitment on the part of government officials to these objectives" (121). See also: Carter, "Agriculture and Agitation"; and Carter "Indian Reserve Agriculture."

53 Douglas Leighton, "A Victorian Civil Servant at Work: Lawrence Vankoughnet and the Canadian Indian Department, 1874–1893," in *As Long as the Sun Shines and Water Flows: A Reader in Canadian Native Studies,* ed. Ian Getty and Antoine Lussier (Vancouver: University of British Columbia Press, 1983), 113.

54 Tobias, "Origins of the Treaty Rights Movement in Saskatchewan," 246.

55 John Mitchell to the Superintendent General of Indian Affairs (Canada, *Sessional Papers,* "Annual Report of the Department of Indian Affairs," no. 14, 1900), 166.

56 *Ibid.* In 1899, John Mitchell reported that this was the case in the Qu'Appelle area.

57 Hayter Reed, cited in Carter, "Agriculture and Agitation," 5.

58 See F. Laurie Barron, "The Indian Pass System in the Canadian West, 1882–1935," *Prairie Forum* 13, no. 1 (Spring 1988):25–42; and Sarah Carter, "Controlling Indian Movement: The Pass System," *NeWest Review* (May 1985):8–9. The Department of Indian Affairs introduced a pass system during the time of the Saskatchewan Uprising of 1885 to regulate off-reserve movement. Any person wishing to leave their home reserve was obliged to obtain a pass from their Indian agent stating the purpose and duration of their leave. The pass system had no legal basis. In general, most people were able to evade the system, but they did risk being arrested for "trespassing" if caught.

59 Ponting and Gibbins, *Out of Irrelevance,* 21.

60 Ahenakew, *Voices,* 148.

61 Dion, *My Tribe,* 134.

62 *Ibid.*

63 *Ibid.*

64 "An Act to Amend the Indian Act" (S.C. 1911, c. 14, 1–2 George V) in *Indian Acts and Amendments, 1868–1950,* Indian and Northern Affairs Canada, compiled by L. Van Hoorn (Ottawa: Department of Indian and Northern Affairs, 1981), 130.

65 *Ibid.* (S.C. 1918, c. 26, 8–9 George V), 134. Costs accrued from improvements were to be deducted from the rental payable for the lease.

66 John Taylor, *Canadian Indian Policy during the Inter-War Years, 1918–1939* (Ottawa: Indian and Northern Affairs Canada, 1984), 16–17.

67 *Ibid.,* 32; Duncan Scott to Honourable Arthur Meighen, December 1, 1919 (Canada, *Sessional Papers,* "Annual Report of the Department of Indian Affairs," no. 27, 1920), 10.

68 Sluman and Goodwill, *John Tootoosis,* 120.

69 S.D. Grant, "Indian Affairs under Duncan Campbell Scott: The Plains Cree of Saskatchewan, 1913–1931," *Journal of Canadian Studies* 18, no. 3 (1983):28–29. Compensations for these rights were arranged through the Superintendent of Indian Affairs.

70 Barman, Hébert, and McCaskill, "The Legacy of the Past," 6.

71 Nicholas Davin, cited in Gresko, "White 'Rites' and Indian 'Rites,'" 169.

72 *Ibid.,* 171.

73 Kennedy, "Qu'Appelle Industrial School," 96.

74 *Ibid.,* 101.

75 Hall, *Clifford Sifton,* 126.

76 Barman, Hébert, and McCaskill, "The Legacy of the Past," 9.

77 Star Blanket, cited in Sluman and Goodwill, *John Tootoosis,* 162.

78 Cuthand, "Native Peoples," 36.

79 Tootoosis, cited in Sluman and Goodwill, *John Tootoosis,* 109.

80 See E. Brian Titley, "W.M. Graham: Indian Agent Extraordinaire," *Prairie Forum* 8, no. 1 (1983):27.

81 David Mandelbaum, Plains Cree Notebook 6, August 27, 1934 (SA).

82 Dominion of Canada, *Annual Report of the Department of Indian Affairs, March 31, 1933,* Report, Harold McGill to Thomas Murphy, August 31, 1932, 7.

83 *Ibid.*

84 Cuthand, "Native Peoples," 38–39. Seneca root was gathered, dried and sold to dealers. It was used commercially in cough medicines for its expectorant quality.

85 H.W. McGill, Report of the Department of Mines and Resources for the Fiscal Year Ended March 31, 1940, Indian Affairs Branch (Canada, *Sessional Papers,* no. 41, 1941), 184.

86 Cuthand, "Native Peoples," 38–39.

87 David Mandelbaum, Plains Cree Notebook 6, September 4, 1934 (SA), 65.

88 Palmer Patterson, *The Canadian Indian: A History Since 1500* (Don Mills: Collier-Macmillan Canada, 1972), 175.

89 Tobias, "Origins of the Treaty Rights Movement in Saskatchewan," 247.

90 *Ibid.*

91 *Ibid.*

92 Taylor, *Canadian Indian Policy,* 181. The penalty for the offence ranged from a fine of $50 to $200 or a maximum prison term of two months.

93 *Ibid.*, 182.

CHAPTER 4

1 Friesen, *Canadian Prairies,* 162.

2 Titley, *Narrow Vision,* 11.

3 Department of Indian and Northern Affairs, *The Historical Development of the Indian Act* (Ottawa: Department of Indian and Northern Affairs, 1975), 42–43.

4 Friesen, *Canadian Prairies,* 157–58.

5 See Cole and Chaikin, *An Iron Hand,* for an excellent study of the history of the Potlatch Law in British Columbia.

6 Fisher, "Contact and Conflict," 176.

7 *Ibid.*, 123.

8 *Ibid.*, 127–28; see also Usher, "William Duncan."

9 Fisher, "Contact and Conflict," 169.

10 *Ibid.*, 66–67.

11 *Ibid.*, 155.

12 Cole and Chaitkin, *An Iron Hand,* 14–15.

13 Fisher, *Contact and Conflict,* 178.

14 Philip Drucker, *Cultures of the North Pacific Coast* (New York: Harper and Row Publishers, 1965), 55; and see 55–56 for a discussion of the various types of potlatches. The term *potlatch* originates from the Chinook trade language and means "giving."

15 Alice Kehoe, *North American Indians: A Comprehensive Account* (New Jersey: Prentice-Hall, Inc., 1981), 411.

16 Drucker, *Cultures of the North Pacific Coast,* 64.

17 Mary Lee Stearns, *Haida Culture in Custody: The Masset Band* (Seattle: University of Washingon Press, 1981), 289.

18 LaViolette, *Struggle for Survival,* 33.

19 *Ibid.*, 33–34.

20 *Ibid.*, 39–40.

21 Grant, *Moon of Wintertime,* 137–38.

22 Cole and Chaikin, *An Iron Hand,* 16.

23 LaViolette, *Struggle for Survival,* 38.

24 *Ibid.*

25 Department of Indian and Northern Affairs, *Historical Development of the Indian Act,* 95.

26 *Ibid.*

27 *Ibid.*, 95–96.

28 LaViolette, *Struggle for Survival,* 56; and Cole and Chaikin, *An Iron Hand,* 25–39.

29 LaViolette, *Struggle for Survival,* 46.

30 *Ibid.*, 59.

31 Cole and Chaikin, *An Iron Hand*, 35.

32 *Ibid.*, 60.

33 *Ibid.*, 68. The reference here is to the mutiny of native troops from the British army in India in 1857.

34 Cole and Chaikin, *An Iron Hand*, 36–38.

35 *Ibid.*, 43.

36 Indian Affairs Branch, Department of Mines and Resources, "Brief on the Bill to further Amend the Indian Act," in "Amendments to Indian Act 1895" (document is indistinct) (NAC, RG10, vol. 6,808, file 470-2-3, part 1), 7.

37 *Ibid.*

38 "Memorandum for the Minister" in "Re: Proposed Amendment of the Indian Act," 1897 (NAC, RG10, vol. 6,808, file 470-2-3, part 4).

39 Indian and Northern Affairs Canada, *Indian Acts and Amendments, 1868–1950* (Ottawa: Department of Indian and Northern Affairs Canada, 1981), 95–96.

40 *Ibid.*, 96.

41 See Drucker, *Cultures,* 162–63, 165. See also Jay Powell, Vickie Jensen, Vera Cranmer, and Agnes Cranmer, *Yaxwattan's* (Alert Bay: U'mista Cultural Society, n.d.).

42 LaViolette, *Struggle for Survival,* 75.

43 Titley, *Narrow Vision.* An overview of the history of the suppression of prairie religious expression is treated in Titley's chapter entitled "Senseless Drumming and Singing," but Victorian perceptions of the religions of the Plains Indians have not been discussed as part of the context for this legislation, and they are important to our understanding of its adoption.

44 Josephy, *Now that the Buffalo's Gone,* 80.

45 "Impressions Regarding Missionary Efforts amongst the Indians . . . " (GA, A.T586A, 3,469, Archdeacon John William Tims Papers, 1872–1953), 7. Tims was an Anglican missionary working for the Church Missionary Society.

46 Georgeen Barrass, *Canon H.W. Gibbon Stocken, among the Blackfoot and Sarcee* (Calgary: Glenbow Alberta Institute, 1976), xi.

47 Robert Nathanial Wilson, "Diary 1881–1888," June 21, 1881 (NAC, MG29, E47).

48 See, in particular, Robert Jefferson, "Notes and Correspondence Re: Customs and Culture of Cree Indians, Battleford, Saskatchewan, 1911–1919" in "Notes on the Western Cree," and his notes on the Sun Dance, 1911 (GA, M585, A.J45), 4.

49 Paget, *People of the Plains,* 29.

50 *Ibid.*

51 Robert Nathaniel Wilson, "Ethnographical Notes on the Blackfoot 'Sun-Dance,'" March 29, 1897 (GA, M4422), 46.

52 Annual Report of Superintendent Steele, Commanding Macleod District, Fort Macleod, November 30, 1889 (Canada, *Sessional Papers,* vol. 12, no. 13, 1890), 65.

53 Jefferson, *Fifty Years,* 91.

54 Goddard, "Sun Dance of the Cree of Alberta," 305.

55 John McDougall, *Pathfinding on Plain and Prairie,* 1898 rpt. (Toronto: Coles Publishing Company, 1970), 70.

56 John Maclean, *The Indians of Canada: Their Manners and Customs,* 1889 rpt. (Toronto: Coles Publishing Company, 1970), 267.

57 Maclean, *Indians of Canada,* 299, 302–03.

58 Ramsay Cook, *The Regenerators: Social Criticism in Late Victorian English Canada* (Toronto: University of Toronto Press, 1985), 4–5, 176–77.

59 Maclean, *Indians of Canada,* 304–05.

60 *Ibid.*, 315.

61 *Ibid.*, 322.

62 Judy Zegas, "North American Indian Exhibit at the Centennial Exposition," *Curator* 19, no. 2 (1976):170. See also Joan Lester, "The American Indian: A Museum's Eye View," *The Indian Historian* 5, no. 2 (1972):30.

63 Monseigneur Pascal, Vicar-Apostolic of Saskatchewan, was cited in the *Ottawa Evening Journal,* December 9, 1896 (NAC, RG10, vol. 3,825, file 60,511-1).

64 Sarah Carter, "The Missionaries' Indian: The Publications of John McDougall, John Maclean and Egerton Ryerson Young," *Prairie Forum* 9, no. 1 (1984):27–44.

65 *The Regina Leader,* July 26, 1883, 1.

66 *Ottawa Evening Journal,* December 9, 1896.

67 *The Regina Leader,* June 14, 1894, 8.

68 A messianic movement based on indigenous northern Paiute and northwest plateau teachings and Christian millennium beliefs, the Ghost Dance religion had spread throughout the Sioux communities in the North and South Dakota areas. According to Omer Stewart, "faithful dancing, clean living, peaceful adjustment with whites, hard work, and following God's chosen leaders would hasten the resurrection of dead relatives and the desired restoration of the 'good old days' of Indian prosperity." During world renewal, Whites would be quietly removed (see Omer Stewart, "The Ghost Dance," in *Anthropology on the Great Plains,* ed. W. Raymond Wood and Margot Liberty [Lincoln: University of Nebraska Press, 1980], 180). While the Ghost Dance movement was not directly responsible for the wars against the Sioux (1890–91), it did provide the American government with a rationale for the military pressure that resulted in the massacre at Wounded Knee.

69 Sergeant Albert Mountain to Officer Commanding, Battleford, March 23, 1894 (NAC, RG10, vol. 3,825, file 60,511-1), 2.

70 Mandelbaum, *Plains Cree,* 218. The dance was introduced by the Sioux who had fled to Canada after the Battle of the Little Big Horn.

71 *Ibid.*

72 Gary Simons, "Agent, Editor, and Native: The Attitudes of the Western Canadian Press to the Department of Indian Affairs, 1880–1891" (Master's thesis, Queen's University, 1984).

73 *Ibid.*, 83.

74 Jefferson, *Fifty Years,* 40.

75 Father J. Hugonnard to Indian Commissioner, Department of Indian Affairs, November 23, 1903 (NAC, RG10, vol. 3,825, file 60,511-1), 2–3.

76 Hayter Reed, cited in Anthony Looy, "The Indian Agent and His Role in the Administration of the North-West Superintendency, 1876–1893" (Ph.D. diss., Queen's University, 1977), 295.

77 Father J. Hugonnard to Indian Commissioner, Department of Indian Affairs, November 23, 1903 (NAC, RG10, vol. 3,825, file 60,511-1), 1.

78 "Chief Piapot and the Sun Dance," 1921 (GA, M4252, Austin G. McKitrick Papers), 5.

79 *Ibid.*

80 Father Lacombe, cited in Looy, "Indian Agent," 295.

81 Lawrence Vankoughnet to Edgar Dewdney, December 4, 1889, cited in Looy, "Indian Agent," 295.

82 Hayter Reed to Reverend J.W. Tims, April 21, 1891 (GA, A.T586A, 3,469, Archdeacon John Williams Tims Papers).

83 Maclean, *Indians of Canada,* 263; 302–03.

84 D.L. Clink to the Indian Commissioner, June 19, 1893 (NAC, RG10, vol. 3,825, file 60,511-1), 1.

85 Department of Indian Affairs to the Indian Commissioner, July 12, 1893 (NAC, RG10, vol. 3,825, file 60,511-1), 1.

86 Richard Altick, *Victorian People and Ideas* (New York: W.W. Norton and Company, Inc., 1973), 134.

CHAPTER 5

1 D.L. Clink to the Indian Commissioner, June 19, 1893 (NAC, RG10, vol. 3,825, file 60,511-1), 1.

2 A.E. Forget, Regina, September 20, 1895, Annual Report to the Department of Indian Affairs for the Year Ended June 30, 1895 (Canada, *Sessional Papers,* no. 10), 199.

3 Annual Report of A. Bowen Perry, Superintendent Commissioner, Depot Division, North-West Mounted Police (Canada, *Sessional Papers,* no. 15, 1896) 64.

4 Marion Boswell, "'Civilizing' the Indian: Government Administration of Indians, 1876–1896" (Ph.D. diss., University of Ottawa, 1978).

5 Looy, "Indian Agent," 91.

6 James Smart to Superintendent General of Indian Affairs, December, 1900 (Canada, *Sessional Papers,* no. 27, 1901), xxxii.

7 F.H. Paget to Agent Markle, June 6, 1896 (NAC, RG10, vol. 3,825, file 60,511-1), 1. The letter confirmed that the Waywayseecapo people had given up their dance "very reluctantly."

8 Agent A. McNeill to Indian Commissioner, May 20, 1896 (NAC, RG10, vol. 3,825, file 60,511-1), 1.

9 *Ibid.,* June 12, 1896 (NAC, RG10, vol. 1,354, file 76, part 3, "RCMP 1896: Sun Dance at File Hills").

10 Jefferson, *Fifty Years,* 82.

11 J.D. McLean to G. Forget, July 2, 1898 (NAC, RG10, vol. 3,825, file 60,511-1), 1.

12 Assistant Indian Commissioner to J. Day, July 4, 1907 (NAC, RG10, vol. 3,825, file 60,511-2), 1.

13 *Ibid.*

14 David Laird to Agent J. Wilson, July 11, 1898 (NAC, RG10, vol. 3,825, file 60,511-1), 1.

15 Hugh Dempsey, *Red Crow, Warrior Chief* (Saskatoon: Western Producer Prairie Books, 1980), 213.

16 Comptroller White to J. Smart, February 3, 1901 (NAC, RG10, vol. 3,825, file 60,511-1), 1.

17 Inspector James Wilson, Annual Report to the Commissioner, North-West Mounted Police, Regina, December 1, 1900 (Canada, *Sessional Papers,* no. 28), 54.

18 Kehoe, "The Ghost Dance Religion in Saskatchewan," 50. Harry Brown's second Sun Dance on the Poundmaker Reserve was attended by an American anthropologist, probably Donald Cadzow.

19 John Jennings, "The Northwest Mounted Police and Canadian Indian Policy, 1873–1896" (Ph.D. diss., University of Toronto 1979), 96–97.

20 Titley, *Narrow Vision,* 166.

21 Barron, "Indian Pass System"; Carter, "Indian Movement." Barron traces the creation of the pass system to Hayter Reed, who was the Assistant Indian Commissioner at the time. For specific reference to the use of the pass system and the Sun Dance, see Canada, *Sessional Papers,* Annual Report of the Department of Indian Affairs for the Year Ending 31 December 1881 (Ottawa: Queen's Printer), 82.

22 Hayter Reed, cited in B. Bennett, "Study of Passes for Indians to Leave their Reserves" (Ottawa: Treaties and Research Centre, Department of Indian and Northern Affairs, 1974), 3.

23 Irvine, cited in Jennings, "Canadian Indian Policy," 289.

24 Wilson, cited in Bennett, "Study of Passes," 6.

25 A. McNeill to Indian Commissioner, June 12, 1896 (NAC, RG10, vol. 1,354, file no. 76, part 3, "RCMP 1896: Sun Dance at File Hills"), 1.

26 Barron, "Indian Pass System"; Bennett, "Study of Passes"; and Carter, "Indian Movement."

27 F.H. Paget to Commissioner, North-West Mounted Police, May 30, 1896 (NAC, RG10, vol. 3,825, file 60,511-1), 7.

28 See Dempsey, *Red Crow,* 203–14.

29 *Ibid.,* 208.

30 R. Burton Deane, Superintendent Commissioner, Lethbridge and Macleod Districts, Annual Report to Commissioner, North-West Mounted Police, November 30, 1898 (Canada, *Sessional Papers,* no. 15, 1899), 27.

31 Dempsey, *Red Crow,* 208.

32 *Ibid.,* 207.

33 *Ibid.,* 213.

34 Hayter Reed to C.C. Chipman, July 9, 1895 (NAC, RG10, vol. 3,825, file 60,511-1), 1; Agent Wright to Deputy Superintendent General of Indian Affairs, September 30, 1895 (NAC, RG10, vol. 3,825. file 60,511-1), 1.

35 E. Yeomans to Secretary, July 11, 1907 (NAC, RG10, vol. 6,809, file 470-2-3, part 5), 1.

36 Goddard, "Sun Dance of the Cree of Alberta," 305.

37 Peter Douglas Elias, *The Dakota of the Canadian Northwest: Lessons for Survival,* Manitoba Studies in Native History 5 (Winnipeg: The University of Manitoba Press, 1988), 119.

38 Mandelbaum, *Plains Cree,* 370.

39 "No Sun Dance," *Manitoba Morning Free* Press, July 1, 1895 (NAC, RG10, vol. 3,825, file 60,511-1); see also Agent Wright to Superintendent General of Indian Affairs, September 21, 1896 (Canada, *Sessional Papers,* no. 14, 1896, 67), 1.

40 A. Bowen Perry, Regina, to the Superintendent Commissioner, Depot Division, Annual Report, 1895 (Canada, *Sessional Papers,* no. 15, 1896), 64.

41 Hayter Reed to A.E. Forget, July 9, 1895 (NAC, RG10, vol. 3,825, file 60,511-1).

42 Commissioner of Indian Affairs to Superintendent General of Indian Affairs, September 21, 1896 (NAC, RG10, vol. 3,825, file 60,511-1), 1.

43 *Ibid.*

44 Sargeant Des Barres, Report of the Proceedings of Court held at Indian Agent's Office, Crooked Lake, Assiniboia, July 17, 1896 (NAC, RG10, vol. 3,825, file 60,511-1), 1.

45 Watetch, *Payepot and His People,* 44–45.

46 *Ibid.,* 45.

47 *Ibid.*

48 W.P Stewart, *My Name is Piapot,* 103–04.

49 David Laird to Superintendent General of Indian Affairs, October 15, 1902 (Canada, *Sessional Papers,* no. 27, 1903), 188; see also David Laird to Secretary, Department of Indian Affairs, July 17, 1908 (NAC, RG10, vol. 3,825, file 60,511-2), 1.

50 J. McLean to Agent W. Sibbald, May 12, 1910 (NAC, RG10, vol. 3,825, file 60,511-2), 1.

51 P.J. Williams to Indian Commissioner, January 15, 1897 (NAC, RG10, vol. 3,825, file 60,511-1), 1. Peyasiw-awasis (or Thunderchild) had been one of the headmen originally allied with Big Bear. Thunderchild and Lucky Man had eventually led some 200 of Big Bear's followers into treaty and had remained loyal to the British government during the Saskatchewan Uprising of 1885.

52 *Ibid.*

53 *Ibid.*

54 J. Cotton, Commanding "C" Division to Commissioner, North-West Mounted Police, January, 1897 (NAC, RG10, vol. 3,825, file 60,511-1), 2.

55 *Ibid.*

56 *Ibid.*; and J. Cotton to Commissioner, North-West Mounted Police, January 25, 1897, Report: Indians, Arrest at Battleford for Participating in Give Away Dance (NAC, RG18, vol. 1,382, file 76).

57 Constable T. Hosken to Officer Commanding, December 14, 1897, Report: Indians, Arrest and Trial of "Yellow Bird" for Encouraging to start a Give Away Dance (NAC, RG18, vol. 1,382, file 76), 2.

58 *Ibid.*

59 Report of Inspector Wilson (Canada, *Sessional Papers,* no. 12, 1902), 91.

60 *Ibid.*

61 David Laird to Secretary, Department of Indian Affairs, February 28, 1903 (NAC, RG10, vol. 3,825, file 60,511-1), 1.

62 *Ibid.*

63 Caldwell and Coleman to Minister of the Interior, May 20, 1903 (NAC, RG10, vol. 3,825, file 60,511-1), 1.

64 Wilson Wallis, *The Canadian Dakota,* Anthropological Papers of the American Museum of Natural History 41, part 1 (New York: The American Museum of Hatural History, 1947), 126.

65 Kennedy, "Qu'Appelle Industrial School," 196.

66 William Trant, J.P., N.W.T. Report: Judicial District of West Assiniboia, Deposition of Witnesses, May 18, 1903 (NAC, RG10, vol. 3,825, file 60,511), 3. Cappo testified that the dance had been conducted between the hours of 6:00 p.m. and midnight, and that beef, bannock, and tea were consumed approximately every half hour. The sponsor of the dance, Etchease, provided the food. Cappo pointed out: "[Etchease] did not ask us to eat; we all went and helped ourselves and paid nothing. We ate it all and then went away." Cappo further testified that some giveaways continued for four nights until about eighteen months later, when they were stopped. In reference to the relationship between the giveaway or the Circle Dance and disruptive behaviour, he commented: "I know what excitement means. Indians do not get excited at either of these dances." Approximately thirty people from three reserves attended the ceremony.

67 *Ibid.,* 2.

68 "Indian Dances Stopped," *Toronto Globe,* May 27, 1903 (NAC, RG10, vol. 3,825, file 60,511).

69 William Trant Report (NAC, RG10, vol. 3,825, file 60,511), 3.

70 Assistant Indian Commissioner to Secretary, Department of Indian Affairs, June 15, 1903 (NAC, RG10, vol. 3,825, file 60,511-1), 1.

71 *Ibid.*

72 Father J. Hugonnard to Honourable David Laird, March 31, 1903 (NAC, RG10, vol. 3,825, file 60,511-1), 1.

73 "Indian Dances Stopped," *Toronto Globe,* May 27, 1903 (NAC, RG10 vol. 3,825, file 60,511-1).

74 William Trant Report (NAC, RG10, vol. 3,825, file 60,511), 7.

75 P.C.H. Primrose, Superintendent Commanding "D" Division, Macleod, Annual Report to Commissioner, North-West Mounted Police, Regina, December 1, 1903 (Canada, *Sessional Papers,* no. 28), 76.

76 *Ibid.*

77 "Injustice to Poor Old Indian," *The Telegram,* February 18, 1904 (NAC, RG10, vol. 3,825, file 60,511-2).

78 Pearson Bell to Commanding Officer, North-West Mounted Police, January, 1904 (NAC, RG10, vol. 3,825, file 60,511-2), 1.

79 Commissioner A.B. Perry, Regina, Annual Report to Sir Wilfrid Laurier, December, 1901 (Canada, *Sessional Papers,* no. 28), 4; Commissioner A.B. Perry, Regina, Annual Report to Sir Wilfred Laurier, December 15, 1902 (Canada, *Sessional Papers,* no. 28), 74; James Wilson, Inspector Commanding Regina District, Annual Report to the Commissioner, North-West Mounted Police, Regina, December, 1902 (Canada, *Sessional Papers,* no. 28), 75; James Wilson, Superintendent Commanding Regina District, Annual Report to the Commissioner, North-West Mounted Police, Regina, December, 1903 (Canada, *Sessional Papers,* no. 28), p. 96; and, Commissioner A.B. Perry, Regina, Annual Report to Sir Wilfred Laurier, January, 1904 (Canada, *Sessional Papers,* no. 28), 4.

80 Hayter Reed to Superintendent General of Indian Affairs, December 2, 1896 (Canada, *Sessional Papers,* no 14., 1897), xxxii.

81 A.E. Forget, Assistant Indian Commissioner, September 20, 1895, Annual Report to the Department of Indian Affairs for the Year Ended June 30, 1895 (Canada, *Sessional Papers,* no. 10), 99.

82 Hayter Reed to Deputy Superintendent General, June 21, 1892 (NAC, RG10, vol. 3,876, file 91,749), 1.

83 Agent D. Clink to Indian Commissioner, June 19, 1893 (NAC, RG10, vol. 3,825, file 60,511-1), 2.

84 Agent C. Paul Schmidt to Department of Indian Affiars, August 1, 1913 (NAC, RG10, vol. 3,826, file 60,511-3), 1.

85 Titley, *Narrow Vision,* 67.

86 *Ibid.,* 177. Duncan Campbell Scott was born in Ottawa in 1862. His father, William, was a Methodist preacher. During his earlier years, Duncan lived in numerous towns and villages in both Quebec and Ontario, and it was at this time that he became familiar with local Indian populations. He received his formal education at the Wesleyan College in Stanstead, Quebec. In 1879, his father, a John A. Macdonald supporter, had exerted his influence among his political connections and obtained employment for his son as a copy clerk with the Department of Indian Affairs. He later became renowned as a poet and writer. Much of his literary work revealed a strong admiration for British imperialism and its humanitarian objectives with regard to indigenous peoples. The "Indian" theme also predominated in his works, and, while he admitted that Indians were capable of being "civilized," especially through missionization, education, and interbreeding with Whites, he nevertheless tended to portray them as irrational, violent "savages." Some of his writings, however, did reveal the philosophical underpinnings of nineteenth-century humanitarianism, and he was equally adept at depicting Indians as the

"doomed race" whose existence was assured only by the benevolent policies of a paternalistic government program. Scott became the Deputy Superintendent General of Indian Affairs in 1913 and occupied the position until 1932 (see Titley, *Narrow Vision*, 23–36).

87 *Ibid.*

88 Duncan Scott, *General Instructions to Indian Agents in Canada* (Ottawa: Department of Indian Affairs, October 25, 1913), 15.

89 *Ibid.*

90 *Ibid.*

91 Titley, *Narrow Vision*, 173.

92 "Programme of Old Time Dances," 1929 (GA, M331, Joseph Francis Dion Papers), 3.

93 Graham was born in the Ottawa Valley area, and his father had travelled to the West with the Wolseley Expedition of 1870. Graham Senior later received a position in the Indian Department as an official in the Manitoba Superintendency. By 1885, his son, William Morris, had followed in his father's footsteps and had also chosen to pursue a career with the Department (see Titley, *Narrow Vision*, 184).

CHAPTER 6

1 Tobias, "Treaty Rights Movement," 247.

2 Citation from petition submitted by Thunderchild and Fineday, in Assistant Indian Commissioner Stewart to J. Day, July 4, 1907 (NAC, RG10, vol. 3,825, file 60,511-2), 1.

3 *Ibid.*

4 Joe Ma-ma-gway-see to Secretary, September 19, 1908 (NAC, RG10, vol. 3,825, file 60,511-2), 1–3.

5 *Ibid.*

6 Chief Thunderchild to Department of Indian Affairs, June 4, 1914 (received) (NAC, RG10, vol. 3,826, file 60,511-4, part 1), 1.

7 *Ibid.*

8 J. Rowland to J.D. McLean, June 10, 1915 (NAC, RG10, vol. 3,826, file 60,511-4, part 1), 1.

9 Memorandum, James Campbell to Secretary, January 22, 1909 (NAC, RG10, vol. 3,825, file 60,511-2), 7.

10 *Ibid.*

11 W. Grant to Secretary, July 2, 1906 (NAC, RG10, vol. 3,825, file 60,511-2), 1.

12 J. Wright to the Indian Commissioner, June 21, 1898 (NAC, RG10, vol. 3,825, file 60,511-10), 1.

13 J.A. Mitchell, Extract from Report of the Muscowpetung Agency, December 1900 (NAC, RG10, vol. 3,825, file 60,511-10), 1.

14 Assistant Indian Commissioner J. McKenna to Secretary, November 4, 1903 (NAC, RG10, vol. 3,825, file 60,511-1), 1.

15 Petition, Assiniboine Reserve to Honourable Frank Oliver, 1906 (NAC, RG10, vol. 3,825, file 60,511-2), 2.

16 *Ibid.*

17 W.S. Grant to Secretary, July 2, 1906 (NAC, RG10, vol. 3,825, file 60,511-2), 1.

18 "Notes of Representations Made by Delegation of Indians from the West," Alex Gaddie, Interpreter, Department of Indian Affairs, January 24, 1911 (NAC, RG10, vol. 4,053, file 379,203-1).

19 *Ibid.*, 31.

20 *Ibid.*

21 *Ibid.*

22 Tobias, "Treaty Rights Movement," 247.

23 "Deputation back from Ottawa," *Manitoba Free Press,* July 3, 1911 (NAC, RG10, vol. 4,053, file 379,203-1).

24 *Ibid.*

25 Alex Gaddie to David Laird, May 1, 1911 (NAC, RG10, vol. 3,826, file 60,511-3), 1.

26 Annual Report of Superintendent J.D. Moodie, Commanding Regina District, to Commissioner Royal North-West Mounted Police, Regina, October 24 (Canada, *Sessional Papers,* no. 28), 128–29.

27 *Ibid.,* 129.

28 W. Millar, Indian Agent, Crooked Lake Agency, Broadview, to Frank Pedley, Deputy Superintendent General of Indian Affairs, May 26, 1912 (Canada, *Sessional Papers,* no. 27, 1913), 142.

29 Reverend Father Hugonnard to Frank Oliver, April 28, 1911 (Canada, *Sessional Papers,* no. 27, 1913), 1.

30 Assistant Indian Commissioner to Secretary, June 15, 1903 (NAC, RG10, vol. 3,825, file 60,511-2), 1.

31 J.D. McLean to Indian Commissioner, January 5, 1903 (NAC, RG10, vol. 3,825, file 60,511-1), 1.

32 Gresko, "White 'Rites' and Native 'Rites,'" 177.

33 L. Thompson to Honourable Frank Oliver, March 19, 1906 (NAC, RG10, vol. 3,825, file 60,511-2), 1.

34 J. Markle to Indian Commissioner, June 13, 1896 (NAC, RG10, vol. 3,825, file 60,511-1), 1.

35 G.H. Wheatley to Indian Commissioner, May 31, 1897 (NAC, RG10, vol. 3,825, file 60,511-1), 1.

36 *Ibid.*

37 A.E. Forget to G.H. Wheatley, June 3, 1897 (NAC, RG10, vol. 3,825, file 60,511), 1.

38 J.A. Mitchell, Extract from Report of the Muscowpetung's Agency, December, 1900 (NAC, RG10, vol. 3,825, file 60,511-1), 1.

39 J.A. Markle, Extract from Report on the Crowfoot Boarding School, February 14, 1916 (NAC, RG10, vol. 3,826, file 60,511-4, part 1), 1.

40 Edmund Morris, *The Diaries of Edmund Montague Morris: Western Journeys 1907–1910,* transcribed by Mary Fitz-Gibbon (Toronto: The Royal Ontario Museum, 1985), 140.

41 L. Thompson to Honourable Frank Oliver, March 19, 1906 (NAC, RG10, vol. 3,825, file 60,511-2), 1.

42 Petitioners, Assiniboine Agency to Honourable Frank Oliver, 1906 (NAC, RG10, vol. 3,825, file 60,511-2), 2.

43 T. Cory to Secretary, March 13, 1909 (NAC, RG10, vol. 3,825, file 60,511-2), 1.

44 Glen Campbell to Department, March 30, 1912 (NAC, RG10, vol. 3,826, file 60,511-3), 1.

45 Joe Ma-ma-gway-see to Secretary, September 19, 1908 (NAC, RG10, vol. 3,825, file 60,511-2), 1.

46 Little Bird and the Wandering Crees to Superintendent General of Indian Affairs, March 10, 1911 (NAC, RG10, vol. 3,826, file 60,511-3), 1. Approximately fifty people wanted to celebrate the Thirst Dance.

47 D. McLean to Superintendent General, March 17, 1911 (NAC, RG10, vol. 3,826, file 60,511-3), 1.

48 Jefferson, *Fifty Years,* 40 and 83.
49 *Ibid.*
50 J. Markle to Indian Commissioner, June 13, 1896 (NAC, RG10, vol. 3,825, file 60,511-1), 1.
51 A. MacDonald to Indian Commissioner, June 15, 1896 (NAC, RG10, vol. 3,825, file 60,511-1), 1.
52 J. Wright to Indian Commissioner, June 21, 1898 (NAC, RG10, vol. 3,825, file 60,511-1), 1.
53 Magnus Begg to Superintendent General of Indian Affairs, August 17, 1895 (Canada, *Sessional Papers,* no. 14, 1896), 137.
54 Wasichunashi, Jimmy Shepherd to Indian Department, February 3, 1909 (received) (NAC, RG10, vol. 3,825, file 60,511-2), 1.
55 Father H. Grandin and eighteen petitioners to Bishop Legal of St. Albert, July 9, 1908 (NAC, RG10, vol. 3,825, file 60,511-2), 1.
56 *Ibid.*
57 Kennedy, "Qu'Appelle Industrial School," 195.
58 J. Wright to Indian Commissioner, June 21, 1898 (NAC, RG10, vol. 3,825, file 60,511-1), 1. She-sheep stated that he had "eight sacrifices given to him which he [would] offer up at a Smoke Dance which only takes part of one night." She-sheep also asked the agent for provisions of meat and tea, and these were supplied.
59 W. Dilworth to Assistant Deputy and Secretary, January 7, 1915 (NAC, RG10, vol. 3,826, file 60,511-3), 1.
60 *Ibid.,* March 10, 1914 (NAC, RG10, vol. 3,826, file 60,511-3), 1.
61 H. Nichol to Secretary, February 16, 1911 (NAC, RG10, vol. 3,825, file 60,511-2), 1.
62 J.D. McLean to H. Nichol, February 21, 1911 (NAC, RG10, vol. 3,825, file 60,511-2), 1.
63 Mandelbaum, *Plains Cree,* 219.
64 Hayter Reed to Reverend J.W. Tims, April 21, 1891 (GA, A.T586A, 3469, Archdeacon John William Tims Papers, 1872–1953).
65 Report of the Indian Commissioner, Regina; A. Forget, to the Honourable Superintendent General, September 22, 1896 (Canada, *Sessional Papers,* no. 14, 1897), 287–302.
66 *Ibid.*
67 J. Wright to Indian Commissioner, June 21, 1898 (NAC, RG10, vol. 3,825, file 60,511-1), 1.
68 Father J. Hugonnard to Secretary, November 20, 1913 (NAC, RG10, vol. 3,826, file 60,511-3), 1–2.
69 David Laird to Secretary, June 23, 1908 (NAC, RG10, vol. 3,825, file 60,511-2), 1–2. McDougall had been organizing Indians to participate in the Calgary exhibition without the express permission of the Indian agent or the Department. See also *Winnipeg Free Press,* October 19, 1908 (NAC, RG10, vol. 3,825, file 60,511-2).
70 Reverend John McDougall cited in *Winnipeg Free Press,* October 19, 1908 (NAC, RG10, vol. 3,825, file 60,511-2).
71 James Campbell to Deputy Superintendent General, May 29, 1906 (NAC, RG10, vol. 3,825, file 60,511-2), 1–2.
72 A. MacDonald to Superintendent General, July 20, 1896 (Canada, *Sessional Papers,* no. 14, 1896), 166.
73 S. Swinford, Annual Report, Assiniboia-Touchwood Hills Agency, July 20, 1899 (Canada, *Sessional Papers,* no. 14, 1900), 183.
74 J.P. Day to Indian Commissioner, July 4, 1908 (NAC, RG10, vol. 3,825, file 60,511-2), 1.
75 *Ibid.*

CHAPTER 7

1 Department of Indian and Northern Affairs, *Historical Development of the Indian Act,* 120–21.

2 *Ibid.,* 121.

3 *Ibid.,* 127; and see Titley, *Narrow Vision,* 48–51, for an examination of the issue.

4 Department of Indian and Northern Affairs, *Historical Development of the Indian Act,* 131–32.

5 J.D. McLean to W. Grant, July 9, 1906 (NAC, RG10, vol. 3,825, file 60,511-2), 1.

6 Duncan Scott to Joseph Laroque, August 17, 1914 (NAC, RG10, vol. 3,826, file 60,511-3), 1.

7 Frank Pedley to T. Cory, March 9, 1909 (NAC, RG10, vol. 3,826, file 60,511-4), 1. Pedley, a Toronto lawyer, was appointed to the Deputy Superintendent position in 1902.

8 Kayasowatam to Commissioner of Indian Affiars, November 25, 1914 (NAC, RG10, vol. 3,826, file 60,511-3).

9 *Ibid.*

10 G. Wheatley to Superintendent General of Indian Affairs, September 9, 1902 (Canada, *Sessional Papers,* no. 27, 1903), 123; Frank Pedley to J. Gordon, April 28, 1908 (NAC, RG10, vol. 3,825, file 60,511-2), 1.

11 David Laird to Deputy Superintendent General of Indian Affairs, November 3, 1909 (NAC, RG10, vol. 3,826, file 60,511-3), 1; see also Keith Regular, "On Public Display," *Alberta History* 34, no. 1 (1986):1–10, and Jon Whyte, *Indians in the Rockies* (Banff: Altitude Publishing Company Limited, 1985) for discussions of Indian involvement in exhibitions.

12 David Laird to Deputy Superintendent General of Indian Affairs, November 3, 1909 (NAC, RG10, vol. 3,826, file 60,511-3), 1.

13· *Ibid.*

14 David Laird to Indian Commissioner, Report, June 30, 1908 (Canada, *Sessional Papers,* no. 15, 1909), 196; R. Logan to Secretary, October 4, 1910 (NAC, RG10, vol. 3,825, file 60,511-2), 2.

15 Father Hugonnard to Secretary, November 2, 1913 (NAC, RG10, vol. 3,826, file 60,511-3), 2.

16 G. Weadick to Honourable Thomas Crowthers, April 24, 1913 (NAC, RG10, vol. 3,826, file 60,511-3), 1.

17 Indian Agent to Secretary, May 3, 1908 (GA, BE.31, .B655, A102, Blood Indian Agency Papers 1899–1944; Blood Indian Agency Correspondence, 1903–1909, file 21), 2.

18 Glen Campbell to Secretary, December 11, 1913 (NAC, RG10, vol. 3,826, file 60,511-3), 1.

19 J. McKenna to Secretary, February 1, 1908 (NAC, RG10, vol. 3,826, file 60,511-2), 2.

20 Brief, Bill No. 114, Amendments to the Indian Act, 1914 (NAC, RG10, vol. 6,809, file 470-2-3, part 6), 18–19.

21 *Ibid.,* 20.

22 Brief, Bill No. 114, Amendments to the Indian Act: "Of Dances on Reserves"; and "The Sun Dance and Other Dances Which Occur in Open Air in Summer" (NAC, RG10, vol. 6,809, file 470-2-3, part 6), 21–22.

23 *Ibid.,* 21.

24 Draft Bill, 1914 (NAC, RG10 B3, vol. 6,809, file 56,402). The amendment was assented to on June 12, 1914. See "An Act to Amend the Indian Act" (S.C. 1914, c. 35, 4–5 George V) in *Indian Acts and Amendments, 1868–1950,* 132.

25 "An Act to Amend the Indian Act" (S.C. 1914, c. 35, 4–5 George V) in *Indian Acts and Amendments, 1868–1950.*

26 Morris Zaslow, *Reading the Rocks: The Story of the Geological Survey of Canada, 1842–1972* (Toronto: The Macmillan Company of Canada Limited, 1975), 279.

27 *Ibid.*

28 R. Brock to Duncan Scott, March 28, 1914 (NAC, RG10, vol. 6,809, file 470-2-3, part 6), 1. Brock was the Director of the Geological Survey of Canada from 1907 to 1914. The Victoria Memorial Museum in Ottawa came under his jurisdiction in 1907.

29 R. Brock to Duncan Scott, April 2, 1914 (NAC, RG10, vol. 6,809, file 470-2-3, part 6), 1.

30 *Ibid.*

31 William Graham to Duncan Scott, May 31, 1915 (NAC, RG10, vol. 3,826, file 60,511-4, part 1), 1.

32 *Ibid.*, June 11, 1915 (NAC, RG10, vol. 3,826, file 60,511-4, part 1), 1.

33 *Ibid.*, July 21, 1915 (NAC, RG10, vol. 3,826, file 60,511-4, part 1), 1.

34 J.D. McLean to William Graham, 21 July, 1915 (NAC, RG10, vol. 3,826, file 60,511-4, part 1), 2.

35 Duncan Scott to all agents, August 19, 1915 (NAC, RG10, vol. 3,826, file 60,511-4, part 1), 1.

36 Titley, *Narrow Vision,* 175.

37 J.R. Hooper to Commissioner, Crime Report, June 3, 1915 (NAC, RG10, vol. 3,826, file 60,511-4, part 1), 1.

38 J.A. Rowland to J.D. McLean, July 20, 1915 (NAC, RG10, vol. 3,826, file 60,511-4, part 1), 1–2. The lawyer was apparently unaware of the parameters of the legislation.

39 The Alexander Reserve in Alberta.

40 Inspector Commanding Southern Saskatchewan District to the Commissioner, June 23, 1919 (NAC, RG10, vol. 3,826, file 60,511-4A), 1.

41 F. Hasse, "Sun Dance," *RCMP Quarterly* 34, no. 4 (1969):54.

42 *Ibid.*

43 Corporal G. Gill to Officer Commanding, August 18, 1921 (NAC, RG10, vol. 3,826, file 60,511-4A), 1.

44 William Graham to Secretary, September 22, 1921 (NAC, RG10, vol. 3,826, file 60,511-4A), 3.

45 *Ibid.*, 3–4.

46 William Graham to Duncan Scott, October 2, 1922 (NAC, RG10, vol. 3,827, file 60,511-4B), 2.

47 Randall Brown, "Hobbema Sun Dance of 1923," *Alberta History* 30, no. 3 (Summer 1982):3. Scott had agreed to allow the ceremony to be held provided that the prohibitions in Section 149 were upheld.

48 Dominion of Canada, "Report of Superintendent G.L. Jennings, September 30, 1927," *Report of the Royal Canadian Mounted Police,* cited in *Annual Report of Cortlander Starnes, Commissioner to the Honourable Minister in Control of the RCMP,* 30.

49 *Ibid.*

50 Saskatchewan Indian Cultural College, "Interview with Pierre Lewis, the Son of the Rain Dance Maker," *Kataayuk,* np.

51 William Graham to Duncan Scott, December 22, 1922 (NAC, RG10, vol. 3,827, file 60,511-4B), 1.

52 G. Gooderham to William Graham, December 18, 1922 (NAC, RG10, vol. 3,827, file 60,511-4B), 1.

53 William Graham to Secretary, September 22, 1921 (NAC, RG10, vol. 3,826, file 60,511-4A), 3.

54 *Ibid.*

55 J. Gooderham to Assistant Deputy and Secretary, February 12, 1915 (NAC, RG10, vol. 3,826, file 60,511-3).

56 "The King versus Big Chief Face," submitted by M.S. McCarthy to the Department, December, 1915 (NAC, RG10, vol. 3,826, file 60,511-4, part 1); Sargeant R. Nicholson, Crime Report – Re: George Tanner . . . Swan Lake Reservation, Man., Illegal Dancing, Indian Act, July 25, 1926 (NAC, RG10, vol. 3,827, file 60,511-4B).

57 Harry Hotani and Marpiyaska to Secretary, 1917 (NAC, RG10, vol. 3,826, file 60,511-4, part 1), 1.

58 *Ibid.*

59 W. Cromling to Duncan Scott, June 6, 1917, "Memorandum of Dances held by Indians of Wahpaton Sioux Reserve, Prince Albert" (NAC, RG10, vol. 3,826, file 60,511-4, part 1).

60 James MacDonald to Assistant Deputy and Secretary, February 14, 1918 (NAC, RG10, vol. 3,826, file 60,511-4A), 1.

61 *Ibid.*

62 J. Molly, Report: Patrol to Hollow Water Reserve, Lake Winnipeg, February 21, 1921 (NAC, RG10, vol. 3,826, file 60,511-4A), 1.

63 Hodgson Detachment, Report: Patrol to Bloodvein and Jackhead Indian Reserves, Lake Winnipeg, March 9, 1921 (NAC, RG10, vol. 3,826, file 60,511-4A), 1.

64 J. Molly, Report, March 8, 1920 (NAC, RG10, vol. 3,826, file 60,511-4A), 1. In Sargeant Mann, "Re: Lizard Point I.R. Rossburn, Man., Assistance to Indian Department, July 11, 1923" (NAC, RG10, vol. 3,826, file 60,511-4B), a report was made regarding the dismantling of a medicine lodge.

65 Superintendent G. Jennings, "Re: Sauteau Indians Dance at Craig Lake, Saskatchewan, Saskatchewan Indian Act," September 8, 1925 (NAC, RG10, vol. 3,827, file 60,511-4B), 1.

66 G. Sheppard to Officer Commanding, Report, December 12, 1925 (NAC, RG10, vol. 3,827, file 60,511-4B).

67 E. Moore, Report: Alleged Pagan Dances – Dinorwic Indian Reserve, Dinorwic, Ontario, July 4, 1938 (NAC, RG10, vol. 8,481, file 1/24-3, part 1), 1. Prosecutions were made under Section 140 of the Indian Act. In his report, Moore detailed the numerous instances of offerings of material goods, which consisted of: (i) gifts presented by the sponsor; (ii) those offered by the initiates to their mentor; (iii) other spiritual offerings of goods; and (iv) a suspected offering of a dog.

68 "An Act to Amend the Indian Act" (S.C. 1914, c. 35, 4–5 George V), in *Indian Acts and Amendments, 1868–1950*, 134.

69 J.D. McLean to George Race, October 4, 1918 (NAC, RG10, vol. 3,826, file 60,511-4A), 1.

70 Cole and Chaikin, *An Iron Hand,* 147. See "Proposed Amendments to the Indian Act," submitted by the Deputy Superintendent General 18/1/36 to the Honourable Superintendent General (NAC, RG10, vol. 6,810, file 470-2-3, part 9), 1.

71 Cole and Chaikin, *An Iron Hand,* 148.

72 "Proposed Amendments to the Indian Act," submitted by Deputy Superintendent General 18/1/36 to the Honourable Superintendent General (NAC, RG10, vol. 6,810, file 470-2-3, part 9), 1–2.

73 J. McLean to Chief Thunderchild, June 8, 1917 (NAC, RG10, vol. 3,826, file 60,511-4, part 1), 1.

74 Chief Walter Ochapowace to J.D. McLean, October, 1917 (NAC, RG10, vol. 3,826, file 60,511-4, part 1), 1.

75 *Ibid.*

76 J.D. McLean to E. Taylor, October 12, 1917 (NAC, RG10, vol. 3,826, file 60,511-4, part 1), 1.
77 S. Macdonald to Wm. Graham, August 14, 1922 (GA, Battleford Indian Agency Reports, 1904–1935, box 1, file 2), 3.
78 H.A. English, Field Matron, Report of Field Matron for Month of November, 1915 on Little Pine['s] Reserve (NAC, RG10, vol. 10,243, file 1/1-16-3, vol. 1), 1.
79 *Ibid.*
80 Bennett McCardle, "Government Control of Indian 'Medicine Men' in Canada," Treaty and Aboriginal Rights Research of the Indian Association of Alberta (Ottawa: The Indian Association of Alberta, 1981), 3–4.
81 Duncan Scott to William Graham, October 4, 1921 (NAC, RG10, vol. 3,826, file 60,511-4A), 1.
82 J. Dilworth to Assistant Deputy and Secretary, February 2, 1917 (NAC, RG10, vol. 3,826, file 60,511-4, part 1), 3. This program had its parallel in the United States.
83 Carter, "Indian Reserve Agriculture," 353.
84 William Graham to Duncan Scott, July 4, 1925 (NAC, RG10, vol. 3,827, file 60,511-4B), 1.
85 William Graham to Secretary, October 29, 1928 (NAC, RG10, vol. 3,827, file 60,511-4B), 1.
86 *Ibid.*
87 Titley, "W.M. Graham," 30.
88 Eleanor Brass, "The File Hills Ex-Pupil Colony," *Saskatchewan History* 6, no. 2 (1953):67.
89 William Graham to Secretary, September 22, 1921 (NAC, RG10, vol. 3,826, file 60,511-4A), 1–2.
90 William Graham to Duncan Scott, December 3, 1921 (NAC, RG10, vol. 3,826, file 60,511-4A), 1–2.
91 *Ibid.*, July 21, 1915 (NAC, RG10, vol. 3,826, file 60,511-4, part 1), 2.
92 Titley, *Narrow Vision,* 178.
93 *Ibid.*
94 See Chapter 8 for discussion of these 1923 Sun Dances.
95 William Graham to Duncan Scott, July 9, 1923 (NAC, RG10, vol. 3,827, file 60,511-4B).
96 *Ibid.*, July 2, 1931 (NAC, RG10, vol. 3,827, file 60,511-4B).
97 Duncan Scott to J.D. Coté, September 12, 1914 (NAC, RG10, vol. 3,826, file 60,511-3), 1; J.D. McLean to the Colonial Photographic Company, January 23, 1914 (NAC, RG10, vol. 3,826, file 60,511-3), 1; A. Rafton-Canning to Department, January 14, 1914 (NAC, RG10, vol. 3,826, file 60,511-3), 1.
98 J.A. Markle, Inspector of Indian Agencies and Reserves for Alberta Inspectorate 1915, Report (Canada, *Sessional Papers,* no. 27, 1916), 83. In a 1911 petition for Indians to join such a travelling show, organizers indicated that participants would not only be issued travel funds, but also be paid a salary of $7 a week and receive board for each man for a period of six months. The only required services included participation in a parade wearing traditional garb once a day. The letterhead on the petition billed the show as "Western Canada. No. 1 Show. Direct from Calgary, Alberta. Pictorial, Athletic and Variety Company. High Class Specialties. Life Motion Pictures. Also Featuring Genuine North American Indians (Blackfoot Tribe)" (see Clarence Dangerfield to R.N. Wilson, March 5, 1911 [GA, BE 31, .B655, A102, Blood Indian Agency Papers, 1899–1944, Blood Indian Agency Correspondence 1910–1912, file 100], 1).
99 W. Dilworth to Assistant Deputy and Secretary, February, 1917 (NAC, RG10, vol. 3,826, file 60,511-4, part 1).
100 Titley, *Narrow Vision,* 180–81.

101 *Ibid.*
102 *Ibid.*, 181.
103 Duncan Scott to Charles Stewart, October 1, 1926 (Dominion of Canada, *Annual Departmental Reports*, 1925–26, vol. 2), 1.
104 Duncan Scott to William Graham, September 24, 1928 (NAC, RG10, vol. 6,810, file 470-2-3, part 8), 1.
105 Duncan Scott to T. Murphy, July 28, 1931 (NAC, RG10, vol. 3,826, file 60,511-4A).
106 *Ibid.*
107 Indian and Northern Affairs Canada, *Indian Acts and Amendments,* 180.
108 *Ibid.*, 142.
109 *Ibid.*, 175.
110 "An Act to Amend the Indian Act" (S.C. 1926–27, c. 32, 17 George V) in *Indian Acts and Amendments, 1868–1950*, 142.
111 J. Murison to Department, July 11, 1932 (NAC, RG10, vol. 3,827, file 60,511-4B), 1.
112 Acting Director to Department of Indian Affairs to the Commissioner, Royal Canadian Mounted Police, July 19, 1941 (NAC, RG10, vol. 10,243, file 1/1-16-2), 1. Peyote was blamed for the death of a family who were members of the Louis Sunchild Cree Band in Alberta. Sunchild was a Peyote priest whose movements were monitored. There was an instance in 1952 in which his car was searched and paraphernalia associated with the Native American Church was discovered. Peyote was confiscated. See: H.J. Wilson to the Department of the Minister of Justice, June 15, 1953 (NAC, RG10, vol. 10,243, file 1/1-16-2); Constable J. Mead to the Department of Indian Affairs, Report, March 17, 1952 (NAC, RG10, vol. 10,243, file 1/1-16-2).
113 "Devil's Brew or Sacred Potion?" *The Winnipeg Tribune*, December 2, 1954 (clippings in files, NAC, RG10, vol. 10,243, file 1/1-16-2).
114 *Ibid.* The Native American Church was incorporated on October 10, 1918, in Oklahoma; it was an attempt by American Indians to counteract the government suppression of the Peyote religion by "legitimizing" it as an organization based on an acceptable White format. Its theology was syncretic in that Indian beliefs were combined with those of Christianity. Its strong ethical code stressed "brotherly" love, honesty, family responsibilities, self-reliance, and the avoidance of the excessive use of alcohol. Peyote was ritually used as a sacrament and for healing (see J.S. Slotkin, *The Peyote Religion: A Study in Indian-White Relations* [New York: Octagon Books, 1975], 58).

CHAPTER 8

1 Sluman and Goodwill, *John Tootoosis*, 117.
2 Brian Titley, "The League of Indians of Canada: An Early Attempt to Create a National Native Organization," *Saskatchewan Indian Federated College Journal* 1, no. 1 (1984):54.
3 *Ibid.*, 53–63.
4 Titley, *Narrow Vision,* 102.
5 Ahenakew, *Voices*, 69 and 72.
6 Sargeant F. Mann to Officer Commanding, July 11, 1925 (NAC, RG10, vol. 3,827, file 60,511-4B), 1. In a report entitled "Re: Alleged Medicine Dance – Lizard Point, I.R.," Mann was obviously perplexed regarding his role in terminating what appeared to be a "legal" dance.
7 A. Messner to Minister of the Interior, June 20, 1925 (NAC, RG10, vol. 3,827, file 60,511-4B), 1.

8 Corporal W. Wilkins, Report Re: Chief Red Dog (Indian) Sec. (115) Indian Act, File Hills Reserve, Saskatchewan, July 8, 1932 (NAC, RG10, vol. 3,827, file 60,511-4B), 1.

9 RCMP Report, Piapot Reserve, June 15, 1931 (NAC, RG10, vol. 3,827, file 60,511-4B), 1.

10 Red Dog Starblanket to Mr. Scott, February 1918 (NAC, RG10, vol. 3,826, file 60,511, part 1), 1.

11 Petition from Indians of White Bear's Band to Department, February 4, 1929 (NAC, RG10, vol. 3,827, file 60,511-4B), 3. This petition was accompanied by a letter from the law office of W. Williams, Barrister, Carlyle, Saskatchewan.

12 Barristers Miller and Wilson to Superintendent General, October 22, 1928 (NAC, RG10, vol. 3,827, file 60,511-4B), 1.

13 J.D. McLean to Barristers Miller and Wilson, December 5, 1928 (NAC, RG10, vol. 3,827, file 60,511-4B), 2.

14 E.S. Stephenson to Secretary, Department of Indian Affairs, February 20, 1929 (NAC, RG10, vol. 3,827, file 60,511-4B), 1; and the Acting Assistant Deputy and Secretary to E.W. Stephenson, March 7, 1929 (NAC, RG10, vol. 3,827, file 60,511-4B).

15 James Dempsey, "The Indians and World War One," *Alberta History* 31, no. 3 (1983):2.

16 Grant, "Indian Affairs," 34.

17 Henry Two Bears to Department, April, 1932 (NAC, RG10, vol. 3,827, file 60,511-4B), 2.

18 W. Murison to Secretary, April 28, 1932 (NAC, RG10, vol. 3,827, file 60,511-4B), 1. Two Bears was a Wahpeton Dakota. See also A.F. Mackenzie to George Will, May 6, 1932 (NAC, RG10, vol. 3,827, file 60,511-4B).

19 N. McLeod to Superintendent, June 17, 1931 (NAC, RG10, vol. 3,827, file 60,511-4B), 1.

20 Blackbird to Deputy Superintendent, July 3, 1933 (NAC, RG10, vol. 3,827, file 60,511-4B), 1.

21 Superintendent Commanding "G" Division to Commissioner, RCMP, November 1, 1920 (NAC, RG10, vol. 3,827, file 60,511-4A), 1–2.

22 G. Neff to Department, July 8, 1933 (NAC, RG10, vol. 3,827, file 60,511-4B), 1.

23 A. Messner to Minister of the Interior, June 20, 1925 (NAC, RG10, vol. 3,827, file 60,511-4B), 1.

24 F. Harker to Minister of Indian Affairs, June 15, 1920 (NAC, RG10, vol. 3,827, file 60,511-4A), 1.

25 Duncan Scott to William Graham, June 25, 1920 (NAC, RG10, vol. 3,827, file 60,511-4A), 1–2.

26 Chief Matoose to Department, April 20, 1932 (NAC, RG10, vol. 3,827, file 60,511-4B), 1.

27 *Ibid.*

28 D.A. Cadzow, Pennsylvania Historical Commission, to General Scott, May 3, 1932 (NAC, RG 10, vol. 3,827, file 60,511-4B), 1.

29 David Mandelbaum, Plains Cree Notebook 2, June 27 to July 1, 1935 (SA), 36.

30 *Ibid.*, 37.

31 *Ibid.*

32 David Mandelbaum, Plains Cree Notebook 1, June 23, 1934 (SA), 29.

33 Watetch, *Payepot and His People*, 46–47.

34 *Ibid.*

35 *Ibid.*

36 Grant, "Indian Affairs," 35.

37 *Ibid.*

38 Kanipitataw, Robert Chief, Peter Thunder, Touissant, Calling Bull, John Quinny to Duncan Scott, March 6, 1919 (NAC, RG10, vol. 3,827, file 60,511-4A), 1.

39 *Ibid.*, W. Sibbald to Secretary, 1919 (NAC, RG10. vol. 3,827, file 60,511-4A), 1.
40 Duncan Scott to G.H. Gooderham, Indian Agent, May 5, 1923 (NAC, RG10, vol. 3,826, file 60,511-4A); Titley, *Narrow Vision,* 178.
41 M. Christianson, Inspector of Indian Agencies, Regina, to W. Graham, June 14, 1923 (NAC, RG10, vol. 3,827, file 60,511-4B), 1.
42 RCMP Inspector W. Lindsay to the Commissioner of the RCMP, May 17, 1923 (NAC, RG10, vol. 3,827, file 60,511-4B). See also Brown, "Hobbema Sun Dance."
43 "Sun Dance of the Crees at Hobbema by Special Permission of Government," *Edmonton Journal,* July 21, 1923 (NAC, RG10, vol. 3,827, file 60511-4B).
44 Watetch, *Payepot and His People,* 46–47.
45 Sergeant, Alberta Provincial Police, Wetaskiwin Department to Commissioner, Report Re: Complaint of Indian Agent W.G. Askey, Contravention of Indian Act, July 26, 1925 (NAC, RG10, vol. 3,827, file 60,511-4B), 1.
46 Inspector W. Murison, Regina, to the Secretary, Department of Indian Affairs, June 15, 1933 (NAC, RG10, vol. 3,827, file 60,511-4B), 1.
47 Corporal V.W. Hope to Officer Commanding, July 17, 1921 (NAC, RG10, vol. 3,827, file 60,511-4A), 1.
48 Telegram to Secretary, July 24, 1924 (NAC, RG10, vol. 3,827, file 60,511-4B), 1.
49 Constable J. Murray, Report: Sun Dance, Big River Indian Reserve, No. 118, Sask., July 1, 1932 (NAC, RG10, vol. 3,827, file 60,511-4B), 1.
50 Report: Chief Red Dog (Indian), Sec. (115) Indian Act, File Hills Reserve, Saskatchewan, July 9, 1932 (NAC, RG10, vol. 3,827, file 60,511-4B), 1.
51 J. Ostrander to Secretary, July 15, 1933 (NAC, RG10, vol. 3,827, file 60,511-4B), 1.
52 David Mandelbaum, Plains Cree Notebook 1, June 22, 1934 (SA), 14–15.
53 *Ibid.*
54 *Ibid.*, "David Mandelbaum Fieldnotes," David Mandelbaum Fieldnotes, June-July 1935 (GA, Randall Brown, M4327, Notes, Article and Clippings Re: Plains Indians and Sun Dance, 1819–1977), 25–42. Mandelbaum had forwarded copies of a portion of his fieldnotes to Randall Brown and these were donated to the Glenbow Archives.
55 *Ibid.*, "Little Pine Sun Dance," David Mandelbaum Fieldnotes, June 2 (GA), 39.
56 *Ibid.*, July 1935, III-3.
57 *Ibid.*, July 3, 1935, III-10.
58 Corporal G. Gill, Crime Report Re: Walter Blackbird, Indian – Engaging in Illegal Indian Sun Dance, June 26, 1921 (NAC, RG10, vol. 3,826, file 60,511-4A), 1. Ruth Landes reported that the ceremony was held publicly in June of 1920 and 1921; after these years, it was held "secretly" (see Ruth Landes, *Ojibwa Sociology,* Columbia University Contributions to Anthropology, vol. 29 [New York: Columbia University Press, 1937], 110).
59 Corporal G. Gill, Report Re: Mayzenahweeshick, Indian – Engaging in Illegal Indian Dance, July 30, 1921 (NAC, RG10, vol. 3,826, file 60,511-4A), 1–2.
60 James Howard, *The Plains-Ojibwa or Bungi: Hunters and Warriors of the Northern Prairies with Special Reference to the Turtle Mountain Band,* Reprints in Anthropology, vol. 7 (Lincoln: J. and L. Reprint Company, 1977), 162.
61 Wallis, *Canadian Dakota,* 351.
62 Watetch, *Payepot and His People,* 45.
63 F. Harker to Minister of Indian Affairs, June 15, 1920 (NAC, RG10, vol. 3,826, file 60,511-4A), 2. Harker reported that an officer had been furnished as a guard for Sun Dances in the Edmonton Agency for the previous few years. See also Chief Ne-Shaw-Shove to

Department, December 29, 1924 (NAC, RG10, vol. 3,827, file 60,511-4B), 1; A. Messner to Minister of the Interior, June 20, 1925 and March 16, 1926 (NAC, RG10, vol. 3,827, file 60,511-4B), 1; and Cecil St. John to Secretary, May 14, 1926 (NAC, RG10, vol. 3,827, file 60,511-4B), 1.

64 Chief Ne-Shaw-Shove to Department, December 29, 1924 (NAC, RG10, vol. 3,827, file 60,511-4B), 1.

65 Clipping from *The Observer,* "Letters to the Editor," n.d. [1920s] (NAC, RG10, vol. 3,826, file 60,511-4, part 1). Dilworth was also accused of holding a "fat" job and doing nothing on the Blood reserve.

66 Sluman and Goodwill, *John Tootoosis*, 142.

67 David Mandelbaum, "General Remarks about Sun Dance," David Mandelbaum Fieldnotes, June 23, 1934 (GA), 17.

68 Watetch, *Payepot and His People*, 45.

69 See the following documents (all NAC, RG10, vol. 3,827, file 60,511-4B): S. Mikisman to Department, June 15, 1929, 1; William Graham to S. Mikisman, June 25, 1929, 1; Fergus Imlach to Deputy Superintendent General, June 27, 1921, 1; J. Ostrander to Secretary, May 18, 1932, 1; Report: Chief Red Dog (Indian), Sec. (115) Indian Act, File Hills Reserve, Saskatchewan, July 9, 1932, 1; J. Ostrander to Secretary, July 15, 1933, 1; G. Neff to Department, July 8, 1933, 1; J. Ostrander to Secretary, July 15, 1933, 1.

70 Imlach Fergus to Deputy Superintendent General, June 27, 1931 (NAC, RG10, vol. 3,827, file 60,511-4B), 1.

71 J. MacMillan to Department, July 7, 1932 (NAC, RG10, vol. 3,827, file 60,511-4B), 1.

72 J. Ostrander to Secretary, July 15, 1933 (NAC, RG10, vol. 3,827, file 60,511-4B), 1–2.

73 Tarasoff, *Persistent Ceremonialism*, 97–98.

74 David Mandelbaum, "General Remarks about Sun Dance," David Mandelbaum Fieldnotes, June 23, 1934 (GA), 28.

75 *Ibid.*, 27.

76 *Ibid.*, Plains Cree Notebook 1, June 23, 1934 (SA), 25.

77 *Ibid.*, "General Remarks about Sun Dance," David Mandelbaum Fieldnotes, June 22, 1934 (GA), 28.

78 *Ibid.*, June 23, 1934, 41.

79 *Ibid.*, "Little Pine Sun Dance," June 2, 1935, 11–40. One form of sacrificial offering was to fast in the Thunderbird Nest constructed in the crux of the sacred pole.

80 *Ibid.*, "General Remarks about Sun Dance," June 23, 1934, 28.

81 *Ibid.*, 38.

82 *Ibid.*

83 *Ibid.*, 32.

84 *Ibid.*, 42.

85 *Ibid.*, "Little Pine Sun Dance," June, 25–42; and June 2, 1935, 39.

86 *Ibid.*, July 3, 1935, III-10.

87 *Ibid.*, III-14.

88 *Ibid.*, III-9 and 10.

89 *Ibid.*, July 2, 1935, III-1.

90 *Ibid.*, *Plains Cree,* 198.

91 *Ibid.*, Plains Cree Notebook 3, July 29, 1934 (SA), 33.

92 Watetch, *Payepot and His People*, 42.

93 Mandelbaum, *Plains Cree,* 183.

94 *Ibid.*

95 *Ibid.*, Plains Cree Notebook 2, July 1, 1935 (SA), 36–37.

96 *Ibid.*, "General Remarks about Sun Dance," June 23, 1934 (GA), 31. At the 1934 Thirst Dance, he was described as wearing "a 'porcupine' (roach) in back of head, a feathered halo-like attachment, dyed red. He wore a beautifully beaded hide shirt that came down to his knees. Wore hide leggings and beaded moccasins. His shirt was the finest example of beadwork that I so far have seen. . . . Had yellow and blue dots all over his face" (31).

97 *Ibid.*, Plains Cree Notebook 7 (Informant: Fine Day), September 19, 1934 (SA), 27.

98 Wallis, *Canadian Dakota.*

99 *Ibid.*, 332.

100 *Ibid.*

101 *Ibid.*, 335.

102 *Ibid.*, 351. Informants reported that piercing had stopped some fifty years previously at Portage la Prairie.

103 Sluman and Goodwill, *John Tootoosis,* 142.

104 David Mandelbaum, Plains Cree Notebook 7, July 25, 1935 (SA), 32.

105 *Ibid.*

106 Corporal G. Gill, Crime Report Re: Illegal Indian Dance – Buffalo Point, July 25, 1921 (NAC, RG10, vol. 3,827, file 60,511-4B), 1. Informants stated that participants had blankets around them so that they couldn't identify who was performing the piercing.

107 Corporal G. Gill, Crime Report Re: Walter Blackbird, Indian – Engaging in Illegal Indian Dance, June 26, 1935 (NAC, RG10, vol. 3,826, file 60,511-4A), 32. Ruth Landes was told that Ne:nekawigi:jigweb attended the Sun Dance at Dominion City (Roseau River) in June 1907 and brought it to Buffalo Point after receiving instruction from Wa:bas (see Landes, *Ojibwa Sociology,* 110).

108 James Donaghy to Mrs. John Gowdy, September 10, 1928 (United Church Archives, Conference of Manitoba and Northwestern Ontario, University of Winnipeg, Reverend James A. Donaghy, "The Swan Lake Reserve and Mission from 1875 to 1927"), 1.

109 James Howard, *The Canadian Sioux* (Lincoln: University of Nebraska Press, 1984), 142.

110 Constable A.J. Stretton, Report Re: Indian Act – Thunderchild Reserve. Re: Alleged Sun Dance and Give-Away Dance, June 2, 1929 (NAC, RG10, vol. 3,827, file 60,511-4B), 1.

111 Wolfe, *Earth Elder Stories,* 60–64.

112 *Ibid.*, 64.

113 *Ibid.*

114 David Mandelbaum, Plains Cree Notebook 4 (Informant: Sweet Grass), July 16, 1935 (SA), 54.

115 James Macdonald to Assistant Deputy and Secretary, July 5, 1917 (NAC, RG10, vol. 3,826, file 60,511-4B, part 1), 1.

116 Henry Two Bears, Prince Albert, Saskatchewan, to the Deputy Minister, Department of Indian Affairs, May 12, 1917 (NAC, RG 10, vol. 3,826, file 60,511-4, part 1), 1.

117 Wabigoon petitioners to Superintendent General, 1938 (NAC, RG10, vol. 8,481, file 1/24/-3, part 1), 1–2.

118 *Ibid.*, 2.

119 Bull Plume and 52 signatures to Department, February 11, 1915 (NAC, RG10, vol. 3,826, file 60,511-3), 2.

120 *Ibid.*

121 Arthur White Elk to Sir R.L. Borden, 1915 (NAC, RG10, vol. 3,826, file 60,511-4, part 1), 1. For response to White Elk's petition, see Memorandum, J.D. McLean to Honourable Dr. Roche, December 15, 1915 (NAC, RG10, vol. 3,826, file 60,511-4, part 1), 1.

122 Daniel Little Axe to Secretary, June 8, 1915 (NAC, RG10, vol. 3,826, file 60,511-3), 1–2.

123 Daniel Little Axe to Department, February 12, 1915 (NAC, RG10, vol. 3,826, file 60,511-3), 1.

124 Mandelbaum, *Plains Cree,* 203.

125 *Ibid.*, 216–17.

126 *Ibid.*, 216.

127 *Ibid.*, 214. Mandelbaum noted the introduction of the Cowboys Society on the Little Pine Reserve in 1925 and the Worthless Society on Poundmaker in the 1930s. Another dance performed at the Pow-wow was the Dakota Dance acquired from the Canadian Dakota. Sham battles were part of the content of this dance (217–18).

128 *Ibid.*, 218. As in the Pow-wow, the choice of partners may have been determined by kinship and status.

129 *Ibid.*, 219.

130 Howard, *Canadian Sioux,* 93–99.

131 Trotter and Company to Superintendent General, May 15, 1924 (NAC, RG10, vol. 3,827, file 60,511-4B), 2–3.

132 *Ibid.*

133 *Ibid.*

134 *Ibid.*, 1–2.

135 *Ibid.*

136 See Omer Stewart, *Peyote Religion,* Civilization of the American Indian Series 181 (Norman: University of Oklahoma Press, 1987), for a comprehensive history of the Peyote religion.

137 Howard, *Canadian Sioux,* 180.

138 A.K. Coates to Secretary, May 9, 1941 (NAC, RG10, vol. 10,243, file 1/-16-2), 1.

139 Acting Inspector, Department of Indian Affairs, to Commissioner, Royal Canadian Mounted Police, July 19, 1941 (NAC, RG10, vol. 10,243, file 1/-16-2), 1.

140 Constable J. Mead, Report to Department, March 17, 1952 (NAC, RG10, vol. 10,243, file 1/-16-2), 1.

141 E.W. Cousineau to R. Bottle, 1954 (NAC, RG10, vol. 10,243, file 1/-16-2), 1.

142 W. Cockburn to E.S. Jones, December, 1954 (NAC, RG10, vol. 10,243, file 1/-16-2), 1.

143 Verne Dusenberry, *The Montana Cree: A Study in Religious Persistence*, Stockholm Studies in Comparative Religion, no. 3 (Stockholm: Almqvist and Wiksell, 1962), 178.

144 Titley, "W.M. Graham," 59.

CHAPTER 9

1 Ahenakew, *Voices,* 123.

2 Taylor, *Canadian Indian Policy,* 199; Bartlett, *Indian Act of Canada*, 6.

3 Harold Hawthorn, ed., *A Survey of the Contemporary Indians of Canada: A Report on Economic, Political, Educational Needs and Policies*, vol. 1 (Ottawa: Queen's Printer, 1966 and 1967), 369–70.

4 *Ibid.*

5 Scott, cited in Hawthorn, *Survey of Contemporary Indians of Canada,* 367–68.

6 T.R.L. MacInnes, "The History and Policies of Indian Administration in Canada," 1946 (NAC, RG10, vol. 6,812, file 480-2-1), 8.

7 Barbeau, *Potlach among the B.C. Indians*. Marius Barbeau had been hired to work in the Victoria Memorial Museum in 1911. He conducted many field trips among Canadian Northwest Coast cultures and was responsible for acquiring extensive artifact collections for the major eastern Canadian and American museums.

8 *Ibid.*, 91.

9 *Ibid.*, 92.

10 Reverend John Antle, cited in LaViolette, *Struggle for Survival*, 92. The M.S. Columbia was a ship piloted by Reverend John Antle, who visited villages along the coast.

11 *Ibid.*, 91.

12 See, for example, the article entitled, "The Potlach: A Plea for the Modification of the Law Prohibiting Potlaches," written by Rene Duncan for the *Log*, cited in LaViolette, *Struggle for Survival*, 92 and 93.

13 LaViolette, *Struggle for Survival*, 94.

14 *Ibid.*

15 Cole and Chaikin, *An Iron Hand*.

16 Frank Speck, "An Ethnologist Speaks for the Pagan Indians," *The Crozer Quarterly* 18, no. 3 (July 1941):213–18 (NAC, RG10, vol. 6,811, file 470-3-6, part 1).

17 *Ibid.*, 214.

18 *Ibid.*, 216.

19 Ronald Haycock, *The Image of the Indian: The Canadian Indian as a Subject and a Concept in a Sampling of the Popular National Magazines Read in Canada, 1900–1970* (Waterloo: Waterloo Lutheran University, 1971), 29.

20 *Ibid.*, 29.

21 *Ibid.*, 30.

22 *Ibid.*, 36.

23 *Ibid.*, 33.

24 *Ibid.*, 41–42. Weekes's article, "Poundmaker the Peacemaker," was published in *Canadian Magazine* 81 (April 9, 1934):10, 29–30.

25 Haycock, *Image of the Indian*, 41–42. Cooper's article, "The Brave They Fought with Cannons," was published in *Maclean's Magazine* 64 (July 1, 1951):16–17, 34–36.

26 Haycock, *Image of the Indian*, 43.

27 *Ibid.*, 51.

28 "Final Act of the First Inter-American Conference on Indian Life," held at Patzcuaro, State of Michoacan, Mexico, April 14–24, 1940 (NAC, RG10, vol. 6,823, file 494-17-2).

29 See the following: "Liaison – New Zealand," 1940–1952 (NAC, RG10, vol. 8,587, file 1/1-10-2); "Liaison – Union of South Africa," 1949–1962 (NAC, RG10, vol. 8,588, file 1/1-10-3); "Liaison – International Labour Office," 1949–1962 (NAC, RG10, vol. 8,588, file 1/1-10-4); "Liaison – United States," 1937–1958 (NAC, RG10, vol. 8,589, file 1/1-10-6- 1); "Liaison – Royal Canadian Humane Society," 1939–1951 (NAC, RG10, vol. 8,589, file 1/1-10-8); "Liaison – United Nations Educational, Scientific and Cultural Organization," 1947–1951 (NAC, RG10, vol. 8,590, file 1/1-10-11-1).

30 Hawthorn, *Survey of the Contemporary Indians of Canada*, 362.

31 *Ibid.*, 360–61.

32 *Ibid.*, 360. At this time provincial governments were responsible for only fur and game management.

33 *Ibid.*, 360–61; see also T.C. Loram, cited in Hawthorn, *Survey of the Contemporary Indians of Canada,* 360, who was contrasting the Canadian and American level of public debate on Indian policy.

34 See Hugh Dempsey's biographical essay on Mountain Horse in Mike Mountain Horse, *My People the Bloods,* ed. Hugh Dempsey (Calgary: Glenbow-Alberta Institute and the Blood Tribal Council, 1979), v–xi.

35 *Ibid.*, 109–10.

36 *Ibid.*, 72.

37 *Ibid.*, preface.

38 Dempsey, cited in Mountain Horse, *My People the Bloods,* x.

39 Ruth Matheson Buck has collated Ahenakew's manuscripts on Thunderchild and "Old Keyam" and published them in a volume entitled *Voices of the Plains Cree.* Buck provides important biographical information on Ahenakew in her introductory remarks to the volume. See also Edward Ahenakew, R-1 (SA, Reverend Edward Ahenakew Papers, files 1–12).

40 *Ibid.*, 13.

41 *Ibid.*

42 *Ibid.*, 140. See Appendix, this volume, for a poem written by the minister on the suppression of Plains Cree religion.

43 *Ibid.*, 139–40.

44 *Ibid.*, 18–19.

45 SA, Ruth Buck Papers, R20 113. See newspaper article in file entitled "Kindly, Yet Severe Criticism of Treatment of Indians is Voiced by Native Clergyman," *Saskatchewan Daily Star,* June 1, 1918.

46 Dion, *My Tribe.*

47 Joseph Dion, "Programme of Old Time Dances," 1929 (GA, M331, Joseph Francis Dion Papers), 1.

48 *Ibid.*, "Index, Dances and Societies," 1929 (GA, M331, Joseph Francis Dion Papers), 12.

49 *Ibid.*, 33.

50 *Ibid.*, 28.

51 *Ibid.*, 33.

52 *Ibid.*, 10–11.

53 Sluman and Goodwill, *John Tootoosis,* 148. The Allied Bands later became the Protective Associaton for the Indians and their Treaties. Sluman and Goodwill noted that the first leaders were Ben Pasqua and Andrew Gordon (Pasqua Reserve), Harry Ball and Abel Watetch (Piapot Reserve), and Pat Cappo and Charles Pratt (Muscowpetung Reserve).

54 *Ibid.*, 148.

55 *Ibid.*, 160.

56 Cuthand, "Native Peoples," 34.

57 Noel Dyck, "Native People: Political Organizations and Activism," in *The Canadian Encyclopedia,* ed. E. Hurtig (Edmonton: Hurtig Publishers, 1985), 1,221.

58 Ian Johnson, *Helping Indians to Help Themselves: A Committee to Investigate Itself, The 1951 Indian Act Consultation Process,* Treaties and Historical Research Centre (Ottawa: Indian and Northern Affairs Canada, 1984), 15.

59 *Ibid.*, 16.

60 *Ibid.*; Bartlett, *Indian Act of Canada,* 6.

61 Johnson, *Helping Indians,* 17.

62 *Ibid.*, 22.

63 "Brief of the Protective Association for Indians and their Treaties to the Honourable The Minister of Indian Affairs for Canada," September, 1945 (NAC, RG10, vol. 6,811, file 470-3-6, part 1).

64 *Ibid.*, 2.

65 *Ibid.*, 2–3.

66 *Ibid.*, 18.

67 *Ibid.*

68 *Ibid.*, 17.

69 *Ibid.*, 23.

70 Department of Indian and Northern Affairs, *Historical Development of the Indian Act,* 143.

71 Canada, Parliament. Special Joint Committee of the Senate and the House of Commons Appointed to Examine and Consider the Indian Act, *Minutes of Proceedings and Evidence*, no. 12, Monday, April 21, 1947 (Ottawa: 1946–1948), 552.

72 *Ibid.*, no. 12, Tuesday, April 22, 1947, 671.

73 *Ibid.*, no. 19, Thursday, May 8, 1947, Appendix ES, "Submission of the Union of Saskatchewan Indians," 956 and 983; and no. 18, Monday, May 5, 1947, Item 11, "The North American Brotherhood of Canada," 854.

74 *Ibid.*, no. 21, Tuesday, August 13, 1946, "Brief from United Farmers' Organization of the Stablo Tribe, Sardis, British Columbia," 850.

75 "Brief of the Protective Association for Indians and their Treaties to the Honourable the Minister of Indian Affairs of Canada," September, 1945 (NAC, RG10, vol. 6,811, file 470-3-6, part 1), 22.

76 *Ibid.*, 29.

77 *Ibid.*, 30.

78 Canada, Special Joint Committee of the Senate and the House of Commons, no. 19, Thursday, May 8, 1947, Witness: Chief Joseph Dreaver, former President of the Saskatchewan Indian Association, 960.

79 *Ibid.*, no. 19, Thursday, May 8, 1947, Witness: John Tootoosis, President of the Union of Saskatchewan Indians, 560–61.

80 Diamond Jenness, cited in Johnson, *Helping Indians*, 24.

81 *Ibid.*, 25.

82 Canada, Special Joint Committee of the Senate and the House of Commons, no. 29, Tuesday, June 3, 1947, Witness: T.F. McIlwraith, 1,533.

83 *Ibid.*, 1,532.

84 *Ibid.*

85 *Ibid.*

86 Department of Indian and Northern Affairs, *Historical Development of the Indian Act*, 156.

87 "Brief of the Protective Association for Indians and their Treaties to the Honourable The Minister of Indian Affairs for Canada," September, 1945 (NAC, RG10, vol. 6,811, file 470-3-6, part 1), 22.

88 Cole and Chaikin, *An Iron Hand*, 68.

89 "Regulations with Respect to Teaching, Education, Inspection, and Discipline for Indian Day Schools, Made and Established by the Superintendent General of Indian Affairs Pursuant to Paragraph (a) of Section 114 of the Indian Act," in "Regulations Governing Indian Schools," Final Draft Section 8 (a–d), November 14, 1952, section (c) (NAC, RG26, vol. 70, file 39), 2.

90 Department of Indian and Northern Affairs, *Historical Development of the Indian Act*, 170.

91 Canada, Special Joint Committee of the Senate and the House of Commons, no. 21, Tuesday, August 13, 1946, Petition: Albert Many Fingers, Percy Creighton, Chief Shot on Both Sides, John Cotton, Morris Many Fingers, A.C.E. Wolf, Charlie David, Jim White Bull, Jack Hind Bull, Blood Agency, Cardston, Alberta, to Mr. Norman Lickers, Liaison Officer, Joint Committee on Indian Affairs, July 24, 1946, 876.
92 Hawthorn, *Survey of the Contemporary Indians of Canada,* vol. 1, 362.
93 *Ibid.*

SUMMARY AND CONCLUSIONS

1 Secretary of State, Langevin (Commons Debates, June 7, 1869) cited in Department of Indian and Northern Affairs, *Historical Development of the Indian Act,* 48.
2 J.E. Hodgetts, *Pioneer Public Service: An Administrative History of the United Canadas* (Toronto: University of Toronto Press, 1955), 207.
3 D.C. Scott, Evidence to Commons Committee to consider Bill 14, 1920 (NAC, RG10, B3, vol. 6,810, L-3), cited in Department of Indian and Northern Affairs, *Historical Development of the Indian Act,* 123.
4 Brooke Larson, "Shifting Views of Colonialism and Resistance," *Radical History Review* 27 (1983):14.
5 See: Erich Kolig, *The Silent Revolution: The Effects of Modernization on Australian Aboriginal Religion* (Philadelphia: Institute for the Study of Human Issues, 1981); and Brian Bullivant, *Pluralism: Cultural Maintenance and Evolution* (Clevedon: Multilingual Matters Limited, 1984). On the Maori, see Ward and David Ausubel, "The Maori: A Study in Resistive Acculturation," *Social Forces* 39 (1960):218–27.
6 Francis Prucha, *The Great Father: The United States Government and the American Indians,* vol. 2 (Lincoln: University of Nebraska Press, 1984), 646.
7 United States Department of the Interior, Federal Agencies Task Force, *American Indian Religious Freedom Act Report,* P.L. 95-3341, August, 1979, 6.
8 Prucha, *Great Father,* 713.
9 Curtis Jackson and Marcia Galli, *A History of the Bureau of Indian Affairs and Its Activities among Indians* (Palo Alto: R and E Research Associates, Inc., 1977), 6. The "short-hair order" was meant to destroy all physical manifestations of indigenous behaviour such as the wearing of long hair (which had sacred meaning) by males and the use of sacred paint by both sexes. In addition, "Indian costume and blanket" were to be replaced with "citizen's clothing."
10 Prucha, *Great Father,* 802.
11 Vine Deloria Jr. and Clifford Lytle, *American Indians, American Justice* (Austin: University of Texas Press, 1983), 54.
12 For an excellent discussion on modernization and ceremonial time and space, see Edward Hall, *The Dance of Life: The Other Dimension of Time* (New York: Anchor Press, 1984).
13 Sam Gill, *Beyond "The Primitive": The Religions of Nonliterate Peoples* (Englewood Cliffs: Prentice-Hall, Inc., 1982), 87.
14 See: Cole and Chaikin, *An Iron Hand*; Philip Drucker and Robert Heizer, *To Make My Name Good* (Berkeley: University of California Press, 1967); Gresko, "White 'Rites' and Indian 'Rites'"; Kennedy, "Qu'Appelle Industrial School"; and Titley, *Narrow Vision.*
15 Duncan Scott to William Graham, October 4, 1921 (NAC, RG10, vol. 3,826, file 60,511-4A), 1.

16 Tarasoff, *Persistent Ceremonialism,* 25.
17 Interview with Elizabeth Ogle (born 1896) in Saskatchewan Indian Cultural College, *Enewuk.*
18 Watetch, *Payepot and His People,* 45.
19 O'Brodovich, "Little Pine Cree," 23.
20 Tarasoff, *Persistent Ceremonialism,* 217.
21 J. Wright to Indian Commissioner, June 21, 1898 (NAC, RG10, vol. 3,825, file 60,511-1), 1.
22 A. Trotter and Company to Superintendent General, May 15, 1924 (NAC, RG10, vol. 3,827, file 60,511-4B), 2–3.
23 Howard, *Canadian Sioux,* 142.
24 *Ibid.,* 142. Also see Elias, *Dakota of the Canadian Northwest,* 213, with reference to the use of the threat of expelling the Dakota back to the United States.
25 Hugh Dempsey, personal communication, November 10, 1983, 1.
26 *Ibid.* Also see Hanks and Hanks, *Tribe under Trust,* who support this conclusion.
27 Liberty, "Suppression and Survival," 122–25.
28 *Ibid.,* 133.
29 Kehoe, "Ghost Dance Religion," 49.
30 Donald Cadzow, "Bark Records of the Bungi Midewin Society," *Indian Notes,* Museum of the American Indian, 3, no. 2 (1926):124. Cadzow noted: "These sacred barks were given to the writer on condition that they be kept in the museum forever, and that duplicates of the more important ones be made on durable paper and sent to the society; for the two old *kichimitos,* or past-masters, feared that the originals would become lost, as the Canadian Government has forbidden the performance of the Midewin ceremony, and the fraternity is slowly becoming extinct."
31 Kehoe, "Ghost Dance Religion"; and Tarasoff, *Persistent Ceremonialism.*
32 Anonymous, personal communication, 1988.
33 Anonymous, Roseau River, personal communication, 1988.
34 Hanks and Hanks, *Tribe under Trust.*
35 *Ibid.*
36 Cuthand, "Native Peoples," 38–39.
37 Reverend James A. Donaghy, "The Swan Lake Reserve and Mission from 1875 to 1927" (United Church Archives, Conference of Manitoba and Northwestern Ontario, University of Winnipeg), 19.
38 See O'Brodovich, "Little Pine Cree," and Tarasoff, *Persistent Ceremonialism.*
39 Watetch, *Payepot and His People,* 47–48.
40 Hanks and Hanks, *Tribe under Trust,* 167–68.
41 *Ibid.,* 170.
42 Shimpo and Williamson, *Socio-cultural Disintegration,* 217 and 223.
43 Joseph Jorgensen, "Religious Solutions and Native American Struggles: Ghost Dance, Sun Dance and Beyond," in *Religion, Rebellion, Revolution: An Interdisciplinary and Cross-cultural Collection of Essays,* ed. Bruce Lincoln (New York: St. Martin's Press, 1985), 114.
44 *Ibid.,* 117–19.
45 Braroe, *Indian and White;* Hanks and Hanks, *Tribe under Trust;* Kehoe, *Persistent Ceremonialism;* O'Brodovich, "Little Pine Cree"; and Shimpo and Williamson, *Socio-cultural Disintegration.*
46 Hawthorn, *Survey of the Contemporary Indians of Canada,* 69.
47 *Ibid.,* 159.
48 *Ibid.,* 122.

49 Jorgensen, *Sun Dance Religion,* 232.
50 Noel Dyck, "Indian, Métis, Native: Some Implications of Special Status," *Canadian Ethnic Studies* 12, no. 1 (1990):39.
51 Hanks and Hanks, *Tribe under Trust,* 109.
52 Cuthand, "Native Peoples," 39.

Bibliography

PRIMARY SOURCES

Archival Sources

Archives Section, Ethnology Division, Canadian Museum of Civilization, Ottawa, Ontario (CMC)

Barbeau, Marius. "The Potlach among the B.C. Indians and Section 149 of the Indian Act," n.d.

Archives, Glenbow-Alberta Institute, Calgary, Alberta (GA)

Battleford Indian Agency Reports. Letterbooks, Volumes 1 and 2, 1904–1935.
Blood Indian Agency Papers, 1899–1914.
Brown, Randall. Notes, Articles and Clippings Re: Plains Indians and Sun Dance, 1819–1977.
Dion, Joseph Francis. Joseph Francis Dion Papers.
Fraser, William. "Plains Cree, Assiniboine and Saulteaux (Plains) Bands, 1874–84," 1963.
Jefferson, Robert. Notes and Correspondence Re: Customs and Culture of Cree Indians, Battleford, Saskatchewan, 1911–1919.
Mandelbaum, David. David Mandelbaum Fieldnotes. In Randall Brown, Notes, Articles and Clippings Re: Plains Indians and Sun Dance, 1819–1977.
McKitrick, Austin. Chief Piapot and the Sun Dance (circa 1921). Recollections and Biography as Methodist Missionary, 1861–1943.
Tims, Archdeacon John William. Archdeacon John William Tims Papers, 1872–1953. Impressions Regarding Missionary Efforts amongst the Indians.
Wilson, Robert Nathaniel. Articles and Ethnographic Notes Re: Blackfoot Legends and Customs, Blood Reserve, 1897.

National Archives of Canada, Ottawa, Ontario (NAC)

Department of Citizenship and Immigration Records. Record Group 26. Volume 70, File 39. Regulations Governing Indian Schools.

External Affairs Records. Record Group 25, A1, A5.

Indian Affairs. Record Group 10, Black Series. Volume 3,825, File 60,511-1. Manitoba and North-West Territories – Correspondence Regarding Indian Dances More Particularly the Sun Dance, 1889–1903.

————. Volume 3,825, File 60,511-2. Manitoba and Northwest Territories – Correspondence Regarding Indian Dances More Particularly the Sun Dance, 1904–1911.

————. Volume 3,826, File 60,511-3. Manitoba and Northwest Territories – Correspondence Regarding Indian Dances More Particularly the Sun Dance, 1909–1915.

————. Volume 3,826, File 60,511-4. Manitoba and Northwest Territories – Correspondence Regarding Indian Dances More Particularly the Sun Dance, 1915–1918.

————. Volume 3,826, File 60,511-4A. Manitoba and Northwest Territories – Correspondence Regarding Indian Dances More Particularly the Sun Dance, 1918–1922.

————. Volume 3,827, File 60,511-4B. Manitoba and Northwest Territories – Correspondence Regarding Indian Dances More Particularly the Sun Dance, 1922–1933.

————. Volume 3,827, File 60,511-5. Correspondence Regarding Stampedes and other Celebrations, 1915–1935.

————. Volume 3,876, File 91,749. Sun Dance, Piapot Band, 1892–1895.

————. Volume 4,053, File 379,203-1. Notes on representations made by delegation of Indians from the West. A. Gaddie, Interpreter, Department of Indian Affairs, January 24, 1911.

————. Volume 6,808, File 470-2-3, Part 1. Indian Act – Amendments, 1880–1887.

————. Volume 6,808, File 470-2-3, Part 4. Indian Act – Amendments, 1893–1894.

————. Volume 6,809, File 470-2-3, Part 5. Indian Act – Amendments, 1904–1916.

————. Volume 6,809, File 470-2-3, Part 6. Indian Act – Amendments, 1906–1920.

————. Volume 6,810, File 470-2-3, Part 8. Indian Act – Amendments, 1920–1928.

————. Volume 6,810, File 470-2-3, Part 9. Indian Act – Amendments, 1930–1938.

————. Volume 6,811, File 470-3-6, Part 1. Joint Committee of the Senate and the House of Commons on Indian Affairs. Proposals of Interested Organizations, Agencies, 1946–1947.

————. Volume 6,812, File 480-2-1. Correspondence and Statistics Regarding the History of Indian Administration, 1919–1914.

————. Volume 6,823, File 494-17-2. Correspondence and Reports Re: U.S. Indian Legislation, 1913–1936.

————. Volume 8,481, File 1/24-3, Part 1. Potlach and Sun Dance.

————. Volume 8,587, File 1/1-10-2. Liaison – New Zealand, 1940–1952.

————. Volume 8,588, File 1/1-10-3. Liaison – Union of South Africa, 1949–1962.

————. Volume 8,588, File 1/1-10-4. Liaison – International Labour Office, 1949–1962.

————. Volume 8,589, File 1/1-10-6-1. Liaison – United States, 1937–1958.

————. Volume 8,589, File 1/1-10-8. Liaison – Royal Canadian Humane Society, 1939–1951.

————. Volume 8,590, File 1/1-10-11-1. Liaison – United Nations Educational, Scientific and Cultural Organizations, 1947–1951.

————. Volume 10,243, File 1/1-16-2, Volume 1, 1926–1955. Miscellaneous Federal and Provincial Legislations. Food and Drug Act, Opium and Narcotics Act.

————. Volume 10,243, File 1/1-16-3, Volume 1, 1895–1956. Federal Legislation: 1. Food and Drug Act; 2. The Medical Act; 3. Indian Medicine Man.

Indian Affairs. Record Group 10B3, Black Series. Volume 6,809, File 56,402. Indian Act – Amendments.

Northwest Mounted Police/Royal Canadian Mounted Police Records. Record Group 18. Volume 1,354, File 76, Part 3, 1896.

_____. Volume 1,382, File 76, 1897.
Privy Council Records. Record Group 2, Series 18.
Secretary of State and Ministry of Indian Affairs Records. Record Group 6, Series A1, C1.
Wilson, Robert Nathanial. Diary 1881–1888.

Saskatchewan Archives Board, Regina, Saskatchewan (SA)

Ahenakew, Edward. Reverend Edward Ahenakew Papers.
Buck, Ruth. Ruth Buck Papers.
Mandelbaum, David. Plains Cree Notebooks 1 to 8, June to September, 1934. Crooked Lakes
    Agency, File Hills Agency, Carlton Agency, Battleford Agency.
_____. Plains Cree Notebooks 1 to 12, June to September, 1935. Sweet Grass Reserve, Fineday
    Interviews.
Manuscript Collection. Mr. Z. Hamilton, Saskatchewan Historical Society.
Piapot. Manuscript Collection.

*United Church Archives. Conference of Manitoba and Northwestern Ontario,
University of Winnipeg, Winnipeg, Manitoba.*

Donaghy, Reverend James A. The Swan Lake Reserve and Mission from 1875 to 1927. Journal
    and Letters.

Published Primary Sources

Ahenakew, Edward. *Voices of the Plains Cree*. Ed. Ruth Buck. Toronto: McClelland and Stewart
    Limited, 1973.
Bloomfield, Leonard. *Sacred Stories of the Sweet Grass Cree*. Anthropological Series No. 11,
    National Museum of Canada, Bulletin No. 60. Ottawa: Department of Mines, 1930.
Brass, Eleanor. *I Walk in Two Worlds*. Calgary: Glenbow Museum, 1987.
Canada. *Sessional Papers. Annual Report of the Department of Indian Affairs, 1885–1951*. Ottawa:
    Queen's Printer, 1886–1952.
Canada, Parliament. Special Joint Committee of the Senate and the House of Commons Appointed
    to Examine and Consider the Indian Act. *Minutes of Proceedings and Evidence, 1946–1947*,
    Ottawa, Ontario.
Dion, Joseph. *My Tribe The Crees*. Calgary: Glenbow-Alberta Institute, 1979.
Erasmus, Peter. *Buffalo Days and Nights*. Ed. Irene Spry. Calgary: Glenbow-Alberta Institute,
    1976.
Graham, William. *Treaty Days: Reflections of an Indian Commissioner*. Introduction by James
    Dempsey. Calgary: Glenbow Museum, 1991.
Halliday, William. *Potlach and Totem and the Recollections of an Indian Agent*. London: J.M. Dent
    and Son Limited, 1935.
Hind, Henry Youle. *Narrative of the Canadian Red River Exploring Expedition of 1857 and of the
    Assiniboine and Saskatchewan Exploring Expedition of 1858*, Volume 2, rpt. Edmonton: M.G.
    Hurtig Limited, 1971.
Jefferson, Robert. *Fifty Years on the Saskatchewan*. Canadian Northwest Historical Society
    Publications, 1, No. 5, Battleford, Saskatchewan, 1929.

Maclean, John. *The Indians of Canada: Their Manners and Customs.* 1889, rpt. Toronto: Coles Publishing Company, 1970.

McDougall, John. *Pathfinding on Plain and Prairie.* 1898, rpt. Toronto: Coles Publishing Company, 1971.

Merivale, Herman. *Lectures on Colonization and Colonies.* London: Oxford University Press, 1928.

Morris, Alexander. *The Treaties of Canada with the Indians of Manitoba and the North-West Territories.* 1880, rpt. Toronto: Coles Publishing Company, 1971.

Morris, Edmund. *The Diaries of Edmund Montague Morris: Western Journeys 1907–1910.* Transcribed by Mary Fitz-Gibbon. Toronto: The Royal Ontario Museum, 1985.

Mountain Horse, Mike. *My People the Bloods.* Ed. Hugh Dempsey. Calgary: Glenbow-Alberta Institute and the Blood Tribal Council, 1979.

Paget, Amelia. *The People of the Plains.* Toronto: Ryerson Press, 1909.

Scott, Duncan. *General Instructions to Indian Agents in Canada.* Issued by Duncan C. Scott, Deputy Superintendent General of Indian Affairs, Department of Indian Affairs, Ottawa, October 25, 1913.

The Assembly of First Nations and the Canadian Museums Association. *Turning the Page: Forging New Partnerships between Museums and First Peoples.* A Report Jointly Prepared by the Assembly of First Nations and the Canadian Museums Association, Ottawa, 1992.

Newspapers

Manitoba Free Press
Ottawa Evening Journal
The Regina Leader
The Standard
The Winnipeg Tribune

Photographic Collections Consulted

Glenbow-Alberta Institute, Calgary, Alberta.
National Archives of Canada, Ottawa, Ontario.
Provincial Archives of Manitoba, Winnipeg, Manitoba.
Saskatchewan Archives, Regina, Saskatchewan.
United Church Archives (Victoria University), Toronto, Ontario.
United Church Archives, Conference of Manitoba and Northwestern Ontario, University of Winnipeg, Winnipeg, Manitoba.
Western Canada Pictorial Index, University of Winnipeg, Winnipeg, Manitoba.

Ethnographic Collections Consulted

Canadian Museum of Civilization, Ottawa, Ontario.
Glenbow Museum, Glenbow-Alberta Institute, Calgary, Alberta.
Manitoba Museum of Man and Nature, Winnipeg, Manitoba.
Royal Ontario Museum, Toronto, Ontario.
Royal Saskatchewan Museum, Regina, Saskatchewan.

Personal Correspondence

Dempsey, Hugh. Letter to Author. November 10, 1983.

Kehoe, Alice. Letter to Author. November 5, 1981, and September 20, 1982.

Mandelbaum, David. Letter to Author. May 5, 1981, October 5, 1982, April 12, 1984, and August 11, 1986.

SECONDARY SOURCES

Books

Abbott, Frederick. *The Administration of Indian Affairs in Canada*. Washington, D.C.: Department of the Interior, 1915.

Aberle, David. *The Peyote Religion among the Navaho*. Chicago: Aldine Publishing Company, 1966.

Altick, Richard. *Victorian People and Ideas*. New York: W.W. Norton and Company, Inc., 1973.

Anderson, Alan, and James Frideres. *Ethnicity in Canada: Theoretical Perspectives*. Toronto: Butterworth and Company Limited, 1981.

Atimoyoo, Pat. *Nehiyaw Ma tow we na: Games of the Plains Cree*. Saskatoon: Saskatchewan Indian Cultural College, 1980.

Axtell, James. *The European and the Indian: Essays in the Ethnohistory of Colonial North America*. Oxford: Oxford University Press, 1981.

Barman, Jean, Yvonne Hébert, and Don McCaskill, eds. *Indian Education in Canada: The Legacy*. Vol. 1. Vancouver: University of British Columbia Press, 1986.

Barrass, Georgeen. *Canon H.W. Gibbon Stocken, among the Blackfoot and Sarcee*. Calgary: Glenbow-Alberta Institute, 1976.

Barron, F. Laurie, and James Waldram, eds. *1885 and After: Native Society in Transition*. Regina: Canadian Plains Research Centre, 1986.

Bartlett, Richard. *The Indian Act of Canada*. Regina: Native Law Centre, University of Saskatchewan, 1988.

Beals, Alan. *Culture in Process*. New York: Holt, Rinehart and Winston Inc., 1967.

Berkhofer, Robert. *The White Man's Indian: Images of the American Indian from Columbus to the Present*. New York: Vintage Books, 1979.

Berndt, Ronald, and Catherine Berndt, eds. *Aborigines of the West: Their Past and Their Present*. Nedlands: University of Western Australia Press, 1979.

Bodley, John. *Victims of Progress*. Menlo Park: The Benjamin Cummings Publishing Company, Inc., 1982.

Bolt, Christine. *Victorian Attitudes towards Race*. London: Routledge and Kegan Paul, 1971.

Braroe, Neils Winther. *Indian and White: Self-Image and Interaction in a Canadian Plains Community*. Stanford: Stanford University Press, 1975.

Brown, George, and Ron Maguire. *Indian Treaties in Historical Perspective*. Ottawa: Department of Indian and Northern Affairs, 1979.

Brown, Joseph Epes. *The Spiritual Legacy of the American Indian*. New York: Crossroad Publishing Company, 1982.

Bullivant, Brian. *Pluralism: Cultural Maintenance and Evolution*. Clevedon: Multilingual Matters Limited, 1984.

Burridge, Kenelm. *A New Heaven New Earth: A Study of Millenarian Activities.* New York: Schocken Books, 1967.

Carter, Sarah. *Lost Harvests: Prairie Indian Reserve Farmers and Government Policy.* Montreal and Kingston: McGill-Queen's University Press, 1990.

Cole, Douglas. *Captured Heritage: The Scramble for Northwest Coast Artifacts.* Vancouver: Douglas and McIntyre Limited, 1985.

Cole, Douglas, and Ira Chaikin. *An Iron Hand upon the People: The Law against the Potlatch on the Northwest Coast.* Vancouver: Douglas and McIntyre Limited, 1990.

Cook, Ramsay. *The Regenerators: Social Criticism in Late Victorian English Canada.* Toronto: University of Toronto Press, 1985.

Cowie, Isaac. *The Company of Adventurers: A Narrative of Seven Years in the Service of the Hudson's Bay Company during 1867–74 on the Great Buffalo Plains.* Toronto: William Briggs, 1913.

Crysdale, Stewart, and Les Wheatcroft, eds. *Religion in Canadian Society.* Toronto: Macmillan of Canada, 1976.

Cumming, Peter and Neil Mickenberg, eds. *Native Rights in Canada.* Toronto: Indian-Eskimo Association of Canada, 1972.

Curtin, Phillip. *The Image of Africa: British Ideas and Action, 1780–1850.* Madison: University of Wisconsin Press, 1964.

Daugherty, Wayne, and Dennis Madill. *Indian Government under Indian Act Legislation 1868–1951,* Parts One and Two. Ottawa: Department of Indian and Northern Affairs Canada, 1980.

Deiter McArthur, Pat. *Dances of the Northern Plains.* Saskatoon: Saskatchewan Indian Cultural Centre, 1987.

Deloria, Vine Jr. *God is Red.* New York: Dell Publishing Company, Inc., 1973.

Deloria, Vine Jr., and Clifford Lytle. *American Indians, American Justice.* Austin: University of Texas Press, 1983.

Dempsey, Hugh. *Red Crow, Warrior Chief.* Saskatoon: Western Producer Prairie Books, 1980.

_____. *Big Bear: The End of Freedom.* Vancouver: Douglas and McIntyre Limited, 1984.

Department of Indian and Northern Affairs. *The Historical Development of the Indian Act.* Ottawa: Department of Indian and Northern Affairs, 1975.

_____. *Contemporary Indian Legislation, 1951–1978.* Treaties and Historical Research Centre. Ottawa: Department of Indian and Northern Affairs, 1981.

_____. *Indian Acts and Amendments, 1868–1950.* Ottawa: Department of Indian and Northern Affairs Canada, 1981.

Dippie, Brian. *The Vanishing American: White Attitudes and the U.S. Indian Policy.* Middletown: Wesleyan University Press, 1982.

Drucker, Philip. *Cultures of the North Pacific Coast.* New York: Harper and Row Publishers, 1965.

Drucker, Philip, and Robert Heizer. *To Make My Name Good.* Berkeley: University of California Press, 1967.

Dugan, Kathleen. *The Vision Quest of the Plains Indians: Its Spiritual Significance.* Studies in American Religion, Volume 13. New York: The Edwin Mellen Press, 1985.

Dusenberry, Verne. *The Montana Cree: A Study in Religious Persistence. Stockholm Studies in Comparative Religion,* No. 3. Stockholm: Almqvist and Wiksell, 1962.

Elias, Peter Douglas. *The Dakota of the Canadian Northwest: Lessons for Survival.* Manitoba Studies in Native History 5. Winnipeg: The University of Manitoba Press, 1988.

Ewers, John. *The Horse in Blackfoot Indian Culture.* Bureau of American Ethnology, Bulletin 159. Washington: Smithsonian Institution, 1955.

Ferguson, F.G. *Studies in Tuberculosis.* Toronto: University of Toronto Press, 1955.

Fey, Harold, and D'Arcy McNickle. *Indians and Other Americans.* New York: Harper and Row Publishers, 1959.

Firth, Raymond. *Elements of Social Organization.* Boston: Beacon Press, 1951.

Fisher, Robin. *Contact and Conflict: Indian-European Relations in British Columbia, 1774–1890.* Vancouver: University of British Columbia Press, 1977.

Frazer, Sir James. *The Golden Bough: A Study in Magic and Religion.* London: Macmillan and Company Limited, 1960.

Fried, Morton. *The Evolution of Political Society: An Essay in Political Anthropology.* New York: Random House, 1967.

Friesen, Gerald. *The Canadian Prairies: A History.* Toronto: University of Toronto Press, 1984.

Gascoigne, Bamber. *The Christians.* London: Jonathan Cape Limited, 1977.

Getty, Ian, and Donald Smith, eds. *One Century Later: Western Canadian Reserve Indians Since Treaty 7.* Vancouver: University of British Columbia Press, 1978.

Getty, Ian, and Antoine Lussier, eds. *As Long as the Sun Shines and Water Flows: A Reader in Canadian Native Studies.* Nakoda Institute Occasional Paper No. 1. Vancouver: University of British Columbia Press, 1983.

Gill, Sam. *Beyond "The Primitive": The Religions of Nonliterate Peoples.* Englewood Cliffs: Prentice-Hall, Inc., 1982.

_____. *Native American Religions: An Introduction.* Belmont: Wadsworth Publishing Company, 1982.

Grant, John Webster. *Moon of Wintertime: Missionaries and the Indians of Canada in Encounter Since 1534.* Toronto: University of Toronto Press, 1984.

Grobsmith, Elizabeth. *Lakota of the Rosebud: A Contemporary Ethnography.* New York: Holt, Rinehart and Winston, 1981.

Hall, D.J. *Clifford Sifton: A Lonely Eminence 1901–1929,* Volume 2. Vancouver: University of British Columbia Press, 1985.

Hall, Edward. *The Dance of Life: The Other Dimension of Time.* New York: Anchor Press, 1984.

Hanks, Lucien, and Jane Hanks. *Tribe under Trust: A Study of the Blackfoot Reserve of Alberta.* Toronto: University of Toronto Press, 1950.

Harris, Marvin. *The Rise of Anthropological Theory.* New York: Thomas Y. Crowell Company, 1968.

Hawthorn, Harold, ed. *A Survey of the Contemporary Indians of Canada: A Report on Economic, Political, Educational Needs and Policies,* Volumes 1 and 2. Ottawa: Queen's Printer, 1966 and 1967.

Haycock, Ronald. *The Image of the Indian: The Canadian Indian as a Subject and a Concept in a Sampling of the Popular National Magazines Read in Canada 1900–1970.* Waterloo: Waterloo Lutheran University, 1971.

Helm, June, ed. *Symposium on New Approaches to the Study of Religion.* Seattle: Washington Press, 1964.

Hodgetts, J.E. *Pioneer Public Service: An Administrative History of the United Canadas.* Toronto: University of Toronto Press, 1955.

Howard, James. *The Canadian Sioux.* Lincoln: University of Nebraska Press, 1984.

_____. *The Plains-Ojibwa or Bungi: Hunters and Warriors of the Northern Prairies with Special Reference to the Turtle Mountain Band.* Reprints in Anthropology, Volume 7. Lincoln: J and L Reprint Company, 1977.

Hoxie, Frederick. *A Final Promise: The Campaign to Assimilate the Indians, 1880–1920.* Lincoln: University of Nebraska Press, 1984.

Jackson, Curtis, and Marcia Galli. *A History of the Bureau of Indian Affairs and Its Activities among Indians.* Palo Alto: R. and E. Research Associates, Inc., 1977.

Johnson, Ian. *Helping Indians to Help Themselves – A Committee to Investigate Itself. The 1951 Indian Act Consultation Process.* Treaties and Historical Research Centre. Ottawa: Department of Indian and Northern Affairs Canada, 1984.

Jorgensen, Joseph. *The Sun Dance Religion: Power for the Powerless.* Chicago: University of Chicago Press, 1972.

Josephy, Alvin. *Now That the Buffalo's Gone: A Study of Today's American Indians.* Norman: University of Oklahoma Press, 1984.

Kehoe, Alice. *North American Indians: A Comprehensive Account.* New Jersey: Prentice-Hall Inc., 1981.

Kelly, Lawrence. *The Assault on Assimilation: John Collier and the Origins of Indian Policy Reform.* Albuquerque: University of New Mexico, 1983.

Kolig, Erich. *The Silent Revolution: The Effects of Modernization on Australian Aboriginal Religion.* Philadelphia: Institute for the Study of Human Issues, 1981.

LaBarre, Weston. *The Peyote Cult.* 4th ed. New York: Schocken Books, 1975.

Landes, Ruth. *Ojibwa Sociology.* Columbia University Contributions to Anthropology, Volume 29. New York: Columbia University Press, 1937.

Lanternari, Vittorio. *The Religions of the Oppressed.* New York: Alfred A. Knopf, 1963.

LaViolette, Forrest. *The Struggle for Survival: Indian Cultures and the Protestant Ethnic in British Columbia.* Toronto: University of Toronto Press, 1973.

Leacock, Eleanor, and Richard Lee, eds. *Politics and History in Band Societies.* Cambridge: Cambridge University Press, 1982.

Lee, R., and M.S. Marty, eds. *Religion and Social Conflict.* New York: Oxford University Press, 1964.

Lehmann, Arthur, and James Myers, eds. *Magic, Witchcraft, and Religion: An Anthropological Study of the Supernatural.* London: Mayfield Publishing Company, 1985.

Lessa, William, and Evon Vogt, eds. *Reader in Comparative Religion: An Anthropological Approach.* New York: Harper and Row, Publishers, 1979.

Lewellen, Ted. *Political Anthropology: An Introduction.* South Hadley: Bergin and Garvey Publishers, Inc., 1983.

Lincoln, Bruce, ed. *Religion, Rebellion, Revolution: An Inter-disciplinary and Cross-cultural Collection of Essays.* New York: St. Martin's Press, 1985.

Lorimer, Douglas. *Colour, Class and the Victorians: A Study of English Attitudes Towards the Negro in the Mid-Nineteenth Century.* New York: Holmes and Meier, 1978.

Mails, Thomas. *Sundancing at Rosebud and Pine Ridge.* Sioux Falls: The Center for Western Studies, 1978.

Mandelbaum, David. *The Plains Cree: An Ethnographic, Historical, and Comparative Study.* Regina: Canadian Plains Research Center, 1979.

Mason, Philip. *Patterns of Dominance.* London: Oxford University Press, 1970.

Olson, James, and Raymond Wilson. *Native Americans in the Twentieth Century.* Provo: Brigham Young University Press, 1984.

O'Toole, Roger. *Religion: Classic Sociological Approaches.* Toronto: McGraw-Hill Ryerson Limited, 1984.

Pandian, Jacob. *Culture, Religion and the Sacred Self: A Critical Introduction to the Anthropological Study of Religion.* Englewood Cliffs: Prentice-Hall, Inc., 1991.

Patterson, E. Palmer. *The Canadian Indian: A History Since 1500.* Don Mills: Collier-Macmillan Canada, 1972.

Philip, Kenneth. *John Collier's Crusade for Indian Reform, 1920–1954.* Tucson: University of Arizona Press, 1977.

Ponting, J. Rick, and Roger Gibbins. *Out of Irrelevance: A Socio-Political Introduction to Indian Affairs in Canada.* Scarborough: Butterworth and Company Limited, 1980.

Porter, Bernard. *The Lion's Share: A Short History of British Imperialism, 1850–1970.* New York: Longman Group Limited, 1975.

Powell, Joy, Vicki Jensen, Vera Cranmer, and Agnes Cranmer. *Yaxwattan's.* Alert Bay: U'mista Cultural Society, n.d.

Nabokov, Peter, and Robert Easton. *Native American Architecture.* New York: Oxford University Press, 1989.

Price, Richard, ed. *The Spirit of Alberta Indian Treaties.* Montreal: Institute for Research on Public Policy and Indian Association of Alberta, 1979.

Prucha, Francis, ed. *The Indian in American History.* New York: Holt, Rinehart and Winston, 1971.

_____. *Indian Policy in the United States: Historical Essays.* Lincoln: University of Nebraska Press, 1981.

_____. *The Great Father: The United States Government and the American Indians.* Volumes 1 and 2. Lincoln: University of Nebraska Press, 1984.

Rasporich, A.W., ed. *Western Canada Past and Present.* Calgary: McClelland and Stewart West, 1974.

Ray, Arthur. *Indians in the Fur Trade: Their Role as Hunters, Trappers and Middlemen in the Lands Southwest of Hudson Bay.* Toronto: University of Toronto Press, 1974.

Robinson, Ronald, and John Gallagher. *Africa and the Victorians: The Official Mind of Imperialism.* London: The Macmillan Press, Limited, 1978.

Rowley, C.D. *The Destruction of Aboriginal Society: Aboriginal Policy and Practice,* Volume 1. Canberra: Australian National University Press, 1970.

Russell, Dale. *Eighteenth-Century Western Cree and Their Neighbours.* Archaeological Survey of Canada, Mercury Series Paper 143. Ottawa: Canadian Museum of Civilization, 1991.

Sahlins, Marshall. *Tribesmen.* Englewood Cliffs: Prentice-Hall, Inc., 1968.

_____. *Stone Age Economics.* Chicago: Aldine Publishing Company, 1972.

Saskatchewan Indian Cultural College. *Kataayuk: Saskatchewan Indian Elders.* Saskatoon: Saskatchewan Indian Cultural College, 1976.

_____. *Enewuk.* Saskatoon: Saskatchewan Indian Cultural College, 1979.

Scott, Duncan Campbell. *The Administration of Indian Affairs in Canada.* Toronto: Canadian Institute of International Affairs, 1931.

Shimony, Annemarie. *Conservatism among the Iroquois at the Six Nations Reserve.* Yale University Publications in Anthropology 65. New Haven: Yale University, 1961.

Shimpo, Mitsuru, and Robert Williamson. *Socio-cultural Disintegration among the Fringe Saulteaux.* Saskatoon: University of Saskatchewan, 1965.

Sinclair, Keith. *A History of New Zealand.* London: Oxford University Press, 1961.

Slotkin, J.S. *The Peyote Religion: A Study in Indian-White Relations.* New York: Octagon Books, 1975.

Sluman, Norma, and Jean Goodwill. *John Tootoosis: A Biography of a Cree Leader.* Ottawa: The Golden Dog Press, 1982.

Snow, John. *These Mountains are Our Sacred Places*. Toronto: Samuel Stevens, 1977.

Spicer, Edward, ed. *Perspectives in American Indian Culture Change*. Chicago: The University of Chicago Press, 1961.

_____. *Cycles of Conquest: The Impact of Spain, Mexico, and the United States on the Indians of the Southwest, 1533–1960*. Tucson: University of Arizona Press, 1972.

Spier, Leslie. *The Prophet Dance of the Northwest and its Derivatives: The Source of the Ghost Dance*. General Series in Anthropology 1. Menasha: George Banta, 1935.

Stearns, Mary Lee. *Haida Culture in Custody: The Masset Band*. Seattle: University of Washington Press, 1981.

Stevens, F.S., ed. *Racism – The Australian Experience: A Study of Race Prejudice in Australia*, Volume 2. New York: Taplinger Publishing Company, 1972.

Stewart, Omer. *Peyote Religion*. Civilization of the Americas Indian Series, Volume 181. Norman: University of Oklahoma Press, 1987.

Stewart, W.P. *My Name is Piapot*. Maple Creek: Butterfly Books Limited, 1981.

Stocking, George W. Jr. *Race, Culture, and Evolution*. New York: The Free Press, 1968.

_____. *Victorian Anthropology*. New York: The Free Press, 1987.

Surtees, Robert. *Canadian Indian Policy: A Critical Bibliography*. Bloomington: Indiana University Press, 1982.

Tanner, Adrian. *Bringing Home Animals: Religious Ideology and Mode of Production of the Mistassini Cree Hunters*. St. John's: Institute of Social and Economic Research, Memorial University of Newfoundland, 1979.

Tasaroff, Koozma. *Persistent Ceremonialism: The Plains Cree and Saulteaux*. Canadian Ethnology Service Paper Number 69, Mercury Series. Ottawa: National Museums of Canada, 1980.

Taylor, John. *Canadian Indian Policy During the Inter-War Years, 1931–1939*. Ottawa: Indian and Northern Affairs Canada, 1984.

_____. *Treaty Research Report: Treaty Four (1874)*. Ottawa: Treaties and Historical Research Centre, Indian and Northern Affairs Canada, 1985.

_____. *Treaty Research Report: Treaty Six (1876)*. Ottawa: Treaties and Historical Research Centre, Indian and Northern Affairs Canada, 1985.

Thrupp, S.L., ed. *Millennial Dreams in Action*. The Hague: Mouton and Company, 1962.

Titley, E. Brian. *A Narrow Vision: Duncan Campbell Scott and the Administration of Indian Affairs in Canada*. Vancouver: University of British Columbia Press, 1986.

Turnbull, Colin, *The Human Cycle*. New York: Simon and Schuster, 1983.

Tylor, Edward. *Primitive Culture: Researches into the Development of Mythology, Philosophy, Religion, Language, Art and Custom*. London: J. Murray, 1871.

United States Department of the Interior. Federal Agencies Task Force. *American Indian Religious Freedom Act Report, P.L. 95-341, August, 1979*.

Vanstone, James. *The Simms Collection of Plains Cree Material Culture from Southeastern Saskatchewan*. Fieldiana Anthropology, New Series Number 6 (1983).

Vecsey, Christopher, ed. *Handbook of American Indian Religious Freedom*. New York: The Crossroad Publishing Company, 1991.

Voget, Fred. *The Shoshoni-Crow Sun Dance*. Norman: University of Oklahoma Press, 1974.

Wallace, Anthony. *The Ghost Dance Religion and the Sioux Outbreak of 1890*. Chicago: University of Chicago Press, 1965.

Wallis, Wilson. *The Canadian Dakota*. Anthropological Papers of the American Museum of Natural History 41, Part 1. New York: American Museum of Natural History, 1947.

Ward, Allan. *A Show of Justice: Racial "Amalgamation" in Nineteenth Century New Zealand.* Canberra: Auckland University Press, 1974.

Watetch, Abel. *Payepot and His People.* Saskatoon: Modern Press, 1959.

Whyte, Jon. *Indians in the Rockies.* Banff: Altitude Publishing Company Limited, 1985.

Wilson, Bryan. *Magic and the Millennium.* New York: Harper and Row, 1973.

Winks, Robin. *British Imperialism: Gold, God, Glory.* New York: Holt, Rinehart and Winston, 1963.

Wolf, Eric. *Europe and the People without History.* Berkeley: University of California Press, 1982.

Wolfe, Alexander. *Earth Elder Stories.* Saskatoon: Fifth House, 1988.

Wood, W. Raymond, and Margot Liberty, eds. *Anthropology on the Great Plains.* Lincoln: University of Nebraska Press, 1980.

Zaslow, Morris. *The Opening of the Canadian North, 1870–1914.* Toronto: McClelland and Stewart Limited, 1971.

_____. *Reading the Rocks: The Story of the Geological Survey of Canada, 1842–1972.* Toronto: The Macmillan Company of Canada Limited, 1975.

Articles and Reports

Aberle, David. "A Note on Relative Deprivation Theory as Applied to Millennarian and other Cult Movements." In *Millennial Dreams in Action,* edited by S.L. Thrupp, 209–14. The Hague: Mouton and Company, 1962.

Albers, Pat, and Seymour Parker. "The Plains Vision Experience: A Study of Power and Privilege." *Southwestern Journal of Anthropology* 27, no. 3 (1971): 203–22.

Amiotte, Arthur. "The Lakota Sun Dance: Historical and Contemporary Perspectives." In *Sioux Religion,* edited by Raymond DeMallie and Douglas Parks, 75–89. Norman: University of Oklahoma Press, 1988.

Ausubel, David. "The Maori: A Study in Resistive Acculturation." *Social Forces* 39 (1960): 218–27.

Barman, Jean, Yvonne Hébert, and Don McCaskill. "The Legacy of the Past: An Overview." In *Indian Education in Canada: The Legacy.* Volume 1, edited by Jean Barman, Yvonne Hébert, and Don McCaskill. Vancouver: University of British Columbia Press, 1986.

Barron, Laurie. "The Indian Pass System in the Canadian West, 1882–1935." *Prairie Forum* 13, no.1 (1988): 25–42.

Bennett, B. "Study of Passes for Indians to Leave their Reserves." Report. Ottawa: Treaties and Research Centre, Department of Indian and Northern Affairs, 1974.

Bienvenue, Rita. "Comparative Colonial Systems: The Case of Canadian Indians and Australian Aborigines." *Australian-Canadian Studies: An Interdisciplinary Social Science Review* 1 (1983): 30–43.

Brass, Eleanor. "The File Hills Ex-Pupil Colony." *Saskatchewan History* 6, no. 2 (1953): 66–69.

Brown, Randall. "Hobbema Sun Dance of 1923." *Alberta History* 30, no. 3 (Summer 1982):1–8.

Cadzow, Donald. "Mr. Cadzow's Field Trip of 1925." *Indian Notes.* Museum of the American Indian 3, no. 1 (1926): 48–50.

_____. "Bark Records of the Bungi Midewin Society." *Indian Notes.* Museum of the American Indian 3, no. 2 (1926): 123–24.

_____. "Peace Pipe of the Prairie Cree." *Indian Notes.* Museum of the American Indian 3, no. 2 (1926): 82–94.

_____. "Expedition to the Canadian Northwest." *Indian Notes.* Museum of the American Indian 4, no. 1 (1926): 61–63.

_____. "Smoking Tipi of Buffalo Bull the Cree." *Indian Notes.* Museum of the American Indian 4, no. 2 (1926): 271–80.

Carter, Sarah. "Agriculture and Agitation on the Oak River Reserve, 1875–1895." *Manitoba History* no. 6 (1983): 2–9.

_____. "The Missionaries' Indian: The Publications of John McDougall, John MacLean and Egerton Ryerson Young." *Prairie Forum* 9, no. 1 (1984): 27–44.

_____. "Controlling Indian Movement: The Pass System." *NeWest Review* (May 1985): 8–9.

Collier, John. "The Indian New Deal." In *The Indian in American History*, edited by Francis Prucha, 93–98. New York: Holt, Rinehart and Winston, 1971.

Cuthand, Stanley. "The Native Peoples of the Prairie Provinces in the 1920s and 1930s." In *One Century Later: Western Canadian Reserve Indians Since Treaty 7,* edited by Ian Getty and Donald Smith, 31–42. Vancouver: University of British Columbia Press, 1978.

Dempsey, James. "The Indians and World War One." *Alberta History* 31, no. 3 (1983): 1–8.

Dyck, Noel. "Indian, Métis, Native: Some Implications of Special Status." *Canadian Ethnic Studies* 12, no. 1 (1980): 34–46.

_____. "Native People: Political Organizations and Activism." In *The Canadian Encyclopedia,* edited by E. Hurtig, 1,221–22. Edmonton: Hurtig Publishers, 1985.

_____. "An Opportunity Lost: The Initiative of the Reserve Agricultural Programme in the Prairie West." In *1885 and After: Native Society in Transition,* edited by Laurie Barron and James B. Waldram. Regina: Canadian Plains Research Center, 1986.

Elkin, A. "Aboriginal-European Relations in Western Australia: An Historical and Personal Record." In *Aborigines of the West: Their Past and Their Present,* edited by Ronald Berndt and Catherine Berndt, 285–320. Canberra: University of Western Australia Press, 1979.

Fisher, Robin. "Historical Writing on Native People in Canada." *The History and Social Science Teacher* 17, no. 2 (1982): 65–72.

Galbraith, John. "The Humanitarian Impulse to Imperialism." In *British Imperialism: Gold, God, Glory,* edited by Robin Winks, 71–75. New York: Holt, Rinehart and Winston, 1963.

Gartrell, Beverley. "Colonialism and the Fourth World: Notes on Variations in Colonial Situations." *Culture* 6, no. 1 (1986): 3–17.

Glock, Charles. "The Role of Deprivation in the Origin and Evolution of Religious Groups." In *Religion and Social Conflict,* edited by R. Lee and M.S. Marty, 27–29. New York: Oxford University Press, 1964.

Goddard, Pliny Earle. "Notes on the Sun Dance of the Sarsi." *Anthropological Papers of the American Museum of Natural History* 16 (1919a): 271–82.

_____. "Notes on the Sun Dance of the Cree in Alberta." *Anthropological Papers of the American Museum of Natural History* 16 (1919b): 295–310.

Grant, S.D. "Indian Affairs Under Duncan Campbell Scott: The Plains Cree of Saskatchewan, 1913–1931." *Journal of Canadian Studies* 18, no. 3 (1983): 21–39.

Gresko, Jacqueline. "White 'Rites' and Indian 'Rites': Indian Education and Native Responses in the West, 1870–1910." In *Western Canada Past and Present,* edited by A.W. Rasporich, 163–81. Calgary: McClelland and Stewart West, 1974.

Grobsmith, Elizabeth. "The Lakhota Giveaway: A System of Social Reciprocity." *Plains Anthropologist* 24, no. 84, part 1 (1979): 123–31.

Harper, Allan. "Canada's Indian Administration: Basic Concepts and Objectives." *American Indigena* 6, no. 4 (1946): 297–314.

Hasse, F. "Sun Dance." *RCMP Quarterly* 34, no. 4 (1969): 54–55.

Hultkrantz, Ake. "Prairie and Plains Indians." In *Iconography of Religions, Section X, North America,* edited by Th.P. Van Baaren, L. Leertouwer, and H. Buning. Leiden: E.J. Brill, 1973.

Jacobs, Wilbur. "The Fatal Confrontation: Early Native-White Relations on the Frontiers of Australia, New Guinea, and America: A Comparative Study." *Pacific Historical Review,* no. 40 (1971): 283–309.

Jorgenson, Joseph. "Religious Solutions and Native American Struggles: Ghost Dance, Sun Dance and Beyond." In *Religion, Rebellion, Revolution: An Interdisciplinary and Cross-cultural Collection of Essays,* edited by Bruce Lincoln, 97–128. New York: St. Martin's Press, 1985.

Kaplan, Martha. "*Luve Ni Wai* as the British Saw It: Constructions of Custom and Disorder in Colonial Fiji." *Ethnohistory* 36, no. 4 (1989): 349–71.

Klein, Alan. "Plains Economic Analysis: The Marxist Complement." In *Anthropology on the Great Plains,* edited by W. Raymond Wood and Margot Liberty, 129–40. Lincoln: University of Nebraska Press, 1980.

————. "The Political-Economy of Gender: A 19th Century Plains Indian Case Study." In *The Hidden Half: Studies of Plains Indian Women,* edited by Patricia Albers and Beatrice Medicine, 143–73. Lanham: University Press of America, Inc., 1983.

Kopytoff, Igor. "Classification of Religious Movements: Analytical and Synthetic." In *Symposium of New Approaches to the Study of Religion,* edited by June Helm, 77–90. Seattle: Washington Press, 1964.

Larmour, Igor. "Edgar Dewdney, Indian Commissioner in the Transition Period of Indian Settlement, 1879–1884." *Saskatchewan History* 33, no. 1 (1980): 13–24.

Larson, Brooke. "Shifting Views of Colonialism and Resistance." *Radical History Review,* no. 27 (1983):3–20.

LaViolette, Forrest. "Missionaries and the Potlach." *Queen's Quarterly* 58 (1951): 237–51.

Leacock, Eleanor, and Richard Lee. "Introduction." In *Politics and History in Band Societies,* edited by Eleanor Leacock and Richard Lee, 1–20. Cambridge: Cambridge University Press, 1982.

Lee, David. "Piapot: Man and Myth." *Prairie Forum* 17, no. 2 (1992): 251–62.

————. "Foremost Man, and His Band." *Saskatchewan History* 36, no. 3 (1983): 94–101.

Leighton, Douglas. "A Victorian Civil Servant at Work: Lawrence Vankoughnet and the Canadian Indian Department, 1874–1893." In *As Long as the Sun Shines and Water Flows: A Reader in Canadian Native Studies,* edited by Ian Getty and Antoine Lussier, 104–19. Vancouver: University of British Columbia Press, 1983.

Lester, Joan. "The American Indian: A Museum's Eye View." *The Indian Historian* 5, no. 2 (1972): 25–31.

Liberty, Margot. "Suppression and Survival of the Northern Cheyenne Sun Dance." *Minnesota Archaeologist* 27, no. 4 (1965): 120–43.

————. "The Sun Dance." In *Anthropology on the Great Plains,* edited by W. Raymond Wood and Margot Liberty, 164–78. Lincoln: University of Nebraska Press, 1980.

Linton, Ralph. "Nativistic Movements." *American Anthropologist,* n.s., no. 45 (1943): 230–40.

Little, J. "Legal Status of Aboriginal People: Slaves or Citizens." In *Racism – The Australian Experience: A Study of Race Prejudice in Australia,* Volume 2, edited by F.S. Stevens, 77–94. New York: Taplinger Publishing Company, 1972.

Long, T. "The Development of Government Aboriginal Policy: The Effect of Administrative Changes, 1829–1977." In *Aborigines of the West: Their Past and Their Present,* edited by

Ronald Berndt and Catherine Berndt, 357–66. Nedlands: University of Western Australia Press, 1979.

MacInnes, T.R. "History of Indian Administration in Canada." *Canadian Journal of Economics and Political Science* 12, no. 3 (1946): 387–94.

Maduro, Otto. "New Marxist Approaches to the Relative Autonomy of Religion." *Sociological Analysis*, no. 38 (1977): 359–67.

Mandelbaum, David. "The Plains Cree." *Anthropological Papers of the American Museum of Natural History* 37 (1940): 163–316.

_____. "The Plains Cree Remembered." In *Proceedings of the Plains Cree Conference, Fort Qu'Appelle, October 24–26, 1975*, pp. 74–78. Regina: Canadian Plains Research Center, 1979.

McCardle, Bennett. "Government Control of Indian 'Medicine Men' in Canada." Treaty and Aboriginal Rights Research of the Indian Association of Alberta, 6 pp. Ottawa: The Indian Association of Alberta, 1981.

McCaskill, Don. "Native People and the Justice System." In *As Long as the Sun Shines and Water Flows: A Reader in Canadian Native Studies*, edited by Ian Getty and Antoine Lussier, 288–98. Vancouver: University of British Columbia Press, 1983.

McNab, David. "The Colonial Office and the Prairies in the Mid-Nineteenth Century." *Prairie Forum* 3, no. 1 (1978): 21–38.

_____. "Herman Merivale and Colonial Office Indian Policy in the Mid-Nineteenth Century." In *As Long as the Sun Shines and Water Flows: A Reader in Canadian Native Studies*, edited by Ian Getty and Antoine Lussier, 85–103. Vancouver: University of British Columbia Press, 1983.

McQuillan, D. Aidan. "Creation of Indian Reserves on the Canadian Prairies, 1870–1885." *Geographical Review* 70, no. 4 (1980): 379–96.

Miller, J.R. "Owen Glendower, Hotspur, and Canadian Indian Policy." *Ethnohistory* 37, no. 4 (1990): 386–415.

Milloy, John. "The Early Indian Acts: Developmental Strategy and Constitutional Change." In *As Long as the Sun Shines and Water Flows: A Reader in Canadian Native Studies*, edited by Ian Getty and Antoine Lussier, 56–64. Vancouver: University of British Columbia Press, 1983.

Moone, Janet. "Persistence with Change: A Property of Sociocultural Dynamics." In *Persistent Peoples*, edited by George Castille and Gilbert Cushner, 228–42. Tucson: University of Arizona Press, 1981.

Mooney, James. "The Ghost-Dance Religion and the Sioux Outbreak of 1890." *Bureau of American Ethnology, Annual Report*, no. 14 (1896), 645–1,136.

O'Brodovich, Lloyd. "Plains Cree Acculturation in the Nineteenth Century: A Study of Injustice." *Na'pao* 2, no. 1 (1969a): 2–23.

_____. "Plains Cree Sun Dance: 1968." *The Western Canadian Journal of Anthropology* 1, no. 1 (1969b): 71–87.

Ray, Arthur. "The Northern Great Plains: Pantry of the Northwestern Fur Trade, 1774–1885." *Prairie Forum* 9, no. 2 (1984): 263–80.

Regular, Keith. "On Public Display." *Alberta History* 34, no. 1 (1986): 1–10.

Saliba, John. "Religion and the Anthropologists 1960–1976," part 1, *Anthropologica*, n.s. 18, no. 2 (1976): 179–213.

Schlesier, Karl. "Rethinking the Midewiwin and the Plains Ceremonial Called the Sun Dance." *Plains Anthropologist* 35, no. 127 (1990): 1–27.

Scott, Duncan Campbell. "Indian Affairs, 1867–1912." In *Canada and its Provinces,* Volume 7, Section 4, *The Dominion,* edited by A. Shortt and A.G. Doughty, 593–626. Toronto: Glasgow, Brook and Company, 1914.

Sharp, Paul. "Three Frontiers: Some Comparative Studies of Canadian, American, and Australian Settlement." *Pacific Historical Review,* no. 24 (1955): 369–77.

Sharrock, Susan. "Crees, Cree-Assiniboines, and Assiniboines: Interethnic Social Organization on the Far Northern Plains." *Ethnohistory* 21, no. 2 (1974): 95–122.

Simmons, William. "Culture Theory in Contemporary Ethnohistory." *Ethnohistory* 35, no. 1 (1988): 1–14.

Skinner, Alanson. "Political and Ceremonial Organization of the Plains-Ojibway." *Anthropological Papers of the American Museum of Natural History,* no. 11 (1914a), 475–512.

_____. "Political Organization, Cults and Ceremonies of the Plains Cree." *Anthropological Papers of the American Museum of Natural History,* no. 11 (1914b), 513–42.

_____. "The Sun Dance of the Plains-Cree." *Anthropological Papers of the American Museum of Natural History,* no. 16 (1919a), 283–94.

_____. "The Sun Dance of the Plains-Ojibway." *Anthropological Papers of the American Museum of Natural History,* no. 16 (1919b), 311–15.

Spier, Leslie. "The Sun Dance of the Plains Indians: Its Development and Diffusion." *Anthropological Papers of the American Museum of Natural History* 17, part 6 (1921), 451–527.

Spry, Irene. "The Tragedy of the Loss of the Commons in Western Canada." In *As Long as the Sun Shines and Water Flows: A Reader in Canadian Native Studies,* edited by Ian Getty and Antoine Lussier, 203–28. Vancouver: University of British Columbia Press, 1983.

Stanley, George. "Introductory Essay." In *As Long as the Sun Shines and Water Flows: A Reader in Canadian Native Studies,* edited by Ian Getty and Antoine Lussier, 1–26. Vancouver: University of British Columbia Press, 1983.

Stewart, Omer. "Origin of the Peyote Religion in the United States." *Plains Anthropologist* 19, no. 65 (1974): 211–33.

_____. "The Ghost Dance." In *Anthropology on the Great Plains,* edited by W. Raymond Wood and Margot Liberty, 179–87. Lincoln: University of Nebraska Press, 1980.

_____. "The Native American Church." In *Anthropology on the Great Plains,* edited by W. Raymond Wood and Margot Liberty, 188–96. Lincoln: University of Nebraska Press, 1980.

Stonechild, Blair. "The Uprising of 1885: Its Impacts on Federal Indian Relations in Western Canada." *Saskatchewan Indian Federated College Journal* 2, no. 2 (1986): 81–96.

Taylor, John. "Canada's North-West Indian Policy in the 1870s. Traditional Premises and Necessary Innovations." In *Approaches to Native History in Canada.* Papers of a Conference held at the National Museum of Man, October 1975, edited by D.E. Muise, 104–10. Ottawa: National Museum of Canada, 1977.

Titley, E. Brian. "W.M. Graham: Indian Agent Extraordinaire." *Prairie Forum* 8, no. 1 (1983): 25–41.

_____. "The League of Indians of Canada: An Early Attempt to Create a National Native Organization." *Saskatchewan Indian Federated College Journal* 1, no. 1 (1984): 53–63.

Tobias, John. "Protection, Civilization, Assimilation: An Outline History of Canadian Indian Policy." *The Western Canadian Journal of Anthropology* 4, no. 2 (1976): 13–30.

_____. "Indian Reserves in Western Canada: Indian Homelands or Devices for Assimilation." In *Approaches to Native History in Canada.* Papers on a Conference held at the National Museum of Man, October 1975, edited by D.A. Muise, 89–103. Ottawa: National Museum of Canada, 1977.

_____. "Canada's Subjugation of the Plains Cree, 1879–1885." *Canadian Historical Review* 64, no. 4 (1983): 519–48.

_____. "The Origins of the Treaty Rights Movement in Saskatchewan." In *1885 and After: Native Society in Transition,* edited by F. Laurie Barron and James Waldram, 241–52. Regina: Canadian Plains Research Centre, 1986.

Tooker, Elizabeth. "The League of the Iroquois: Its History, Politics, and Ritual." In *Northeast, Handbook of North American Indians*, Volume 15, edited by Bruce Trigger, 418–41. Washington: Smithsonian Institution, 1978.

_____. "Iroquois Since 1820." In *Northeast, Handbook of North American Indians,* Volume 15, edited by Bruce Trigger, 449–65. Washington: Smithsonian Institution, 1978.

Tootoosis, John. "Modern Indian Societies." In *Proceedings of the Plains Cree Conference, Fort Qu'Appelle, October 24–26, 1975,* 74–78. Regina: Canadian Plains Research Center, 1979.

Townsend, Joan. "Ranked Societies of the Alaskan Pacific Rim." Rpt. from *Alaska Native Culture and History,* edited by Yoshinobu Kotani and William Workman, 123–56. Oska: National Museum of Ethnology, 1980.

_____. "The Autonomous Village and the Development of Chiefdoms: A Model and Aleut Case Study." In *Development and Decline: The Evolution of Political Organization,* edited by H. Claessen, M. Smith, and P. VandeVelde, 1–57. South Hadley: Bergin and Garvey, 1985.

Trigger, Bruce. "Ethnohistory: The Unfinished Edifice." *Ethnohistory* 33, no. 3 (1986): 253–67.

Turner Strong, Pauline. "Fathoming the Primitive: Australian Aborigines in Four Explorers' Journals, 1697–1845." *Ethnohistory* 33, no. 2 (1986): 173–94.

Turvey, Guy. "The New Zealand Maori and the Process of Acculturation: An Historical Perspective." *Na'pao* 12 (1982): 26–34.

Upton, Leslie. "The Origins of Canadian Indian Policy." *Journal of Canadian Studies* 8, no. 4 (1973): 51–61.

Wallace, Anthony. "Revitalization Movements." *American Anthropologist* 58, no. 2 (1956): 264–81.

_____. "Origins of the Longhouse Religion." In *Northeast, Handbook of North American Indians,* vol. 15, edited by Bruce Trigger, 442–48. Washington: Smithsonian Institution, 1978.

Wallis, Wilson. "The Sun Dance of the Canadian Dakota." *Anthropological Papers of the American Museum of Natural History,* no. 16 (1919): 319–85.

_____. "The Canadian Dakota." *Anthropological Papers of the American Museum of Natural History* 41, part 1 (1947): 1–226.

Warburton, T. Rennie. "Religion and the Control of Native Peoples." In *Religion in Canadian Society,* edited by Stewart Crysdale and Les Wheatcroft, 412–22. Toronto: Macmillan of Canada, 1976.

Weist, Katherine. "Giving Away: The Ceremonial Distribution of Goods among the Northern Cheyenne of Southeastern Montana." *Plains Anthropologist* 18, no. 60 (1973): 97–103.

Zegas, Judy. "North American Indian Exhibit at the Centennial Exposition." *Curator* 19, no. 2 (1976): 162–73.

Theses and Dissertations

Andrews, Isabel. "The Crooked Lakes Reserves: A Study of Indian Policy in Practice from the Qu'Appelle Treaty to 1900." Master's thesis, University of Saskatchewan, 1972.

Boswell, Marion. "'Civilizing' the Indian: Government Administration of Indians, 1876–1896." Ph.D. diss., University of Ottawa, 1978.

Carter, Sarah. "The Genesis and Anatomy of Government Policy and Indian Reserve Agriculture on Four Agencies in Treaty Four, 1874–1897." Ph.D. diss., University of Manitoba, 1987.

Jennings, John. "The Northwest Mounted Police and Canadian Indian Policy, 1873–1896." Ph.D. diss., University of Toronto, 1979.

Kehoe, Alice. "The Ghost Dance Religion in Saskatchewan: A Functional Analysis." Ph.D. diss., Harvard University, 1964.

Kennedy, Jacqueline. "Qu'Appelle Industrial School: White 'Rites' for the Indians of the Old North West." Master's thesis, Carleton University, 1970.

Leighton, J. Douglas. "The Development of Federal Indian Policy in Canada, 1840–1890." Ph.D. diss., University of Western Ontario, 1975.

Looy, Anthony. "The Indian Agent and His Role in the Administration of the North-West Superintendency, 1876–1893." Ph.D. diss., Queen's University, 1977.

Mandelbaum, David. "Changes in Aboriginal Culture following a Change in Environment, as Exemplified by the Plains Cree." Ph.D. diss., Yale University, 1936.

Milloy, John. "The Plains Cree: A Preliminary Trade and Military Chronology, 1670–1870." Master's thesis, Carleton University, 1972.

O'Brodovich, Lloyd. "The Plains Cree of Little Pine: Change and Persistence in Culture Contact." Master's thesis, University of Saskatchewan, 1969.

Pettipas, Katherine. "Severing the Ties that Bind: The Canadian Indian Act and the Repression of Indigenous Religious Systems in the Prairie Region, 1896–1951." Ph.D. diss., University of Manitoba, 1988.

Regular, Keith. "'Red Backs and White Burdens': A Study of White Attitudes towards Indians in Southern Alberta, 1896–1911." Master's thesis, University of Calgary, 1985.

Schwarz, D. Douglas. "Plains Indian Theology as Expressed in Myth and Ritual, and in the Ethics of Culture." Ph.D. diss., Fordham University, 1981.

Simons, Gary. "Agent, Editor, and Native: The Attitudes of Western Canadian Press to the Department of Indian Affairs, 1880–1891." Master's thesis, Queen's University, 1984.

Taylor, John. "The Development of an Indian Policy for the Canadian North-West, 1869–79." Ph.D. diss., Queen's University, 1975.

Usher, Jean. "William Duncan of Metlakatla: A Victorian Missionary in British Columbia." Ph.D. diss., University of British Columbia, 1968.

Weaver, Sally. "Health, Culture and Dilemma: A Study of the Non-Conservative Iroquois, Six Nations Reserve, Ontario." Ph.D. diss., University of Waterloo, 1967.

Index

Aborigines Protection Act of 1886 (Australia) 31
Aborigines Protection Board of Western Australia 31
Aborigines Protection Society (Britain) 21, 38
Act for the Gradual Civilization of the Indian Tribes, 1857 (Canada) 39
Ahenakew, Edward 193, 200–01
Allied Bands 84, 203
American Indian Peyote movement 191
American Religious Freedom Act (US) 7
Antle, John A. 195
Astakasic 136
Australia
– British/Aborigines relations in 29–31
– views of J. Frazer on religions of 24–25

Ball, Harry 15, 169
Baptiste 118
Barbeau, Marius
– on 1914 Indian Act amendment 194–95
Battle River Sun Dance (1893) 107
Bear Dance 53–54
Beardy, Chief 70
Begbie, Matthew 94
Belaney, George Stanfield (Grey Owl) 197
Belcher, Jonathan 35
Bell, C. Pearson 121
Bell, Robert 67
Big Bear 11, 13, 71
– protests Treaty Six 68–69
Big Chief Face 155

Big Child 69
Big Rib 113
Big Road 134
Bill 14 145–46
bison hunt 47–49
Black, Joseph 156
Blackbird 170
Blake, Edward 93
Blanshard, Richard 89
Bond Head, Francis 38
Bran (Cree man) 117–18
Bridgman, Maude 196
British East India Company
– relations of with indigenous peoples 28
British Native Imperial policy 18–19, 22, 28–40, 66, 213–14
– Aboriginal sovereignty recognized in 32, 36
– assimilative strategies in 30
– intellectual foundations of 19–26
– land rights recognized in 30, 35–36
– in Africa 27–28
– in Australia 29–31
– in British Columbia 88, 89–90
– in British North America 34–40
– in India 27–28
– in New Zealand 32–33
– in Oceania 34
British North America Act, 1867 36–37, 39
Brock, Reginald 151
Buffalo Bull 176
Bull Shield 110

Cadzow, Donald
– argues for Aboriginal religious freedom 172
Caldwell and Coleman (legal firm) 119
Calf Shirt 110
Calgary Stampede 163–64
callers, Cree 50
Campbell, James 129–30
Capitulation of Montreal, 1760 35
Carlisle Indian School 38
Cheepoostatin 109
Christianity
– assimilative role of 79–80
– imposed by schools 80
– incorporation of in Cree religion 183
Christie, William 66
Christmas Tree Dance 188
churches
– education controlled by 79–80
– support of for Indian policy 132
Circle Dance 169
Colborne, John 37
Collier, John 197
Coming Day 82, 184
Commodore 121
Cooper, Al 197
Cotasse 176
Cree council, Qu'Appelle, 1857 64
criers, camp 50
Criminal Code, Section 208 124
cultural property, protection of 165
Curry, John 174
Cutknife Hill, Battle of 71

dances and dancing, secular
– contrary to government policy 146–47,
     150–52, 169
– creation of new 188–89, 190
Darling, Major General 37
Davin, Nicholas 79
Day Walker 179–80
Deane, R.B. 113
Dempsey, Hugh
– editing of Mountain Horse's work 200
Dewdney, Edgar 13, 70, 79
Dion, Joseph 201–03
Douglas, James 40
– land policy of 89–90
Dreaver, Joseph
– on denominationalism 207

Duck Lake Council of 1884 70
Duncan, William 89

Eagle Ribs 110
education, Aboriginal 79–82, 145, 215
– denominationalism in 79–80, 206–07, 209
– poor quality of 81–82
– resistance to 80–81
elders
– powers of diminished 73
– role of in cultural continuity 60–61
Elk Dance 53–54
Ermineskin 171, 174
Etchease 119–21

factionalism 83, 84, 207, 226–27
farms and farming, Aboriginal
– government policy on 74–77, 124
– Plains Cree success at 82–83
Fauch, Harry 181
Federation of Saskatchewan Indians 204
Fiddle Dance 176
File Hills colony 82
Fineday, Charles 83, 110, 183–84
– arrests of 152, 153
– invokes treaty rights 128–29
Finnie, Richard 197
First Inter-American Conference on Indian Life
     198
Forget, Amedee E. 107, 117, 134, 140
Four Clouds 180
Fraser, Blair 197
Frazer, James
– on religious evolution 24–25

Gaddie, Alex 131, 132
generations
– separation of 83, 226–27
Geological Survey of Canada
– anthropological work of 150–51
Gilbert, George 157
Gipps, Governor of South Australia 30
giveaway ceremony 54–56
Give Away Dance 53–54, 186–87
giveaways 3, 98–99, 182–83, 186–88
– modifications to 138, 187–88
– persistence of 155–57
– purposes of 54–55, 183, 188–89
Glenelg, Lord 32, 38

Godsell, Philip 197
Gradual Enfranchisement of Indians and the
    Better Management of Indian Affairs Act,
    1869 65
Graham, William 82, 123, 124–25, 146, 160–63
– policies of 131, 151–52, 160–63, 194
– relations with Piapot 14
– views on ceremonials 154
Grant, W. 130–31
Greater Production Program 78
Grey, George, Governor of South Australia 30,
    32

Haka (Maori war dance) 34
Hamasak 94
Hamat'sa rituals 96
Hau Hau (Maori religion) 33, 214
Hawthorn, Harold 198
Hawthorn/Tremblay Report 229
Hay (Grass) Dance 119, 188
headmen, Cree 50
healers, traditional 122
Heavy Shield's wife 113
Hopson, Peregrine 35
Horse Dance 53–54
Hotain 156
House of Commons (Britain), Select Committee
    on Aborigines (Australia) 29
House of Commons (Britain), Select Committee
    on the Hudson's Bay Company 89
Hudson's Bay Company
– Select Committee recommendations on 89
– support for Aboriginal people 114, 171–72
Hugonnard, Joseph 102, 103, 120, 132
humanitarian lobby 19–21
humanitarianism
– in British Native Imperial policy 18–19, 32

images of Aboriginal peoples
– creation of 100–02, 196–97
Indian Act, 1869 (Canada) 39
Indian Act, 1876 (Canada) 17, 37, 73–74,
    87–89, 211–14
– Joint Senate and House of Commons
    Committee on, 1945–48 204–10
– purpose of 17–18
– 1885 amendment to ban potlatch 3
– 1895 amendment, Section 114 95–97; acts
    prohibited by 110; arrests under 115–22,

133; inconsistent with customary law
    128–29; to suppress religion 96–97, 113–14
– 1911 amendment to expropriate lands 77
– 1914 amendment, Section 149 149–51,
    152–54, 175–76; Aboriginal interpretation of
    151; arrests under 155–57, 177; criticism of
    194–95; White opposition to 150
– 1918 amendment 157
– 1919 amendment to expropriate lands 78–79
– 1927 amendment, Section 106, to protect
    cultural property 165
– 1930 amendment, Section 185, to prohibit
    freedom of assembly 165
– 1933 amendment to prohibit public
    appearances 164
Indian Act, 1951 (Canada) 210
– assimilative goals of 212
Indian Advancement Act of 1885 72
Indian Affairs, Department of 3, 37, 108–09,
    145, 194
Indian Affairs Branch (Canada) 36–37, 69
Indian Affairs (US) 197–98
Indian agents 108, 109–10, 157, 162
– Aboriginal views of 129, 130, 151
Indian Association of Alberta 203, 206
Indian commissioners 69, 107–08
Indian policy (Canada) 39, 40–41
– Aboriginal responses to 127, 128; apathy
    76–77; compliance 134, 174, 186;
    compromise 128, 130, 133–34, 133–39,
    136–37, 138–40, 174–75, 177, 178–79, 222;
    millenarianism 71; resistance – *see* resistance
    strategies, Aboriginal; support 92, 146–47
– assimilative strategies in: Christianization
    142; education 79–81, 142, 145–46, 206–07,
    209; political incorporation 39, 145–46;
    restriction of freedom of movement 111–13;
    settlement on farms 74–77, 124; suppression
    of religious practices 96–97, 107, 113–14,
    123–24
– goals of 3–4, 99–100, 104–05, 194, 204,
    209–10, 214–15
– inconsistent implementation of 142–43,
    175–76
– White opposition to 99, 112, 121–22, 130,
    149, 158, 169, 172, 174–75, 194–95, 195–97
Indian policy (US) 197–98
– ban on ceremonials 214
Indian Reorganization Act of 1934 (US) 197–98

Irvine, A.G.
– condemns pass system 112

Jefferson, Robert 99, 109, 136
Jenness, Diamond
– on Indian legal status 208
Johnson, William 36

Kacucumau, Jim 183
Kah-pee-cha-pees 115
Kanipitataw 174
Kenemotayo, Joseph 152–53
Kenemotayo, Seeahpwassum 152
Kennedy, Arthur 89
Kennedy, Blind 182
Kennedy, Daniel 133
Kenny, Harvey 181
King, Harvey 181
King Movement (New Zealand) 33
kinship 45–46, 47, 208
– family breakdown 83
– relations of Indians and government 129
– rules of 189
Kubinase, Jim 177
Ky-ass-i-kan 118

Lacombe, Albert 104
Laird, David 110, 117
lands, Aboriginal 212
– Cree protest loss of rights to 66–68
– expropriation of 77–79
– Indian rights to denied (B.C.) 89–90
– rights recognized by Canada 65
law, customary 46, 72–73, 128–29
– in New Zealand 33
leaders, Aboriginal
– loss of political power of 72, 84, 115
– selection of controlled by government 65
leaders, camp 50
leaders, Plains Cree 49–51
League of Indians of Canada 203
League of Indians of Western Canada 84, 203
Little Axe, Daniel 188
Little Blanket 13
Little Pine 11, 13
– protests Treaty Six 69
Lomas, William 91–92
Lorne, Marquis of 69–70
Loud Voice 131

Lubbock, John
– on religious evolution 23
Lucky Man 13, 69

Macdonald, John A. 92–93
McDougall, John 99, 101
– argues for religious freedom 141–42
McIlwraith, T.F.
– supports Indian policy 208–09
McKenna, J. 148
McLean, J. 117
Maclean, John 101, 104
– on indigenous religions 99–100
Macleod, James 111
McNeill, A. 109
Maitland, Peregrine 37
Ma-ma-gway-see, Joe 128, 129–30
Mandelbaum, David
– argues for religious freedom 172
Many Shot 134
Maori (New Zealand) 32, 33
– religious practice of 34
– resistance strategies of 33
– socio-economic organization of 31–33
– see also New Zealand
Markle, J.A. 108, 163
Marx, Karl
– on cultural differences 25
Masked Dance 53–54
Matoose 115, 172
Mayzenahweeshick 177
Medicine tipi ceremony 182
Meighen, Arthur 77
Merivale, Herman 18, 26–27, 88
Metlakatla 89
Micmac 35
Middleton, S. 199
Midewiwin 53–54, 157, 187
millenarianism 71
Miller and Wilson (legal firm) 169
missionaries
– views on Aboriginal religion: in Africa 27; in Canada 101, 115, 137–38; in India 27–28
Morgan, Lewis Henry 23
– on social evolution 25–26
Morris, Alexander 68, 69
Motokix Society 113
Mountain Horse, Mike 199–200

movement of Indians, freedom of. *see* pass
  system
Moving Slowly Dance (Omaha Grass Dance)
  188
mutilation, ritual 15, 58, 97, 98, 136, 137

names and naming
– to create kinship 47, 129
Native American Church 165–66, 191
Native Circuit Courts Act of 1858 (New
  Zealand) 33
Neill, A.W. 158
– opposes seizure amendment of 1918 158,
  195–96
Neotamaqueb 123–24
New Zealand
– Maori-British relations in 32–33
non-interference, principle of
– in imperial policy 29–30, 34
North American Indian Brotherhood 203–04
North-West Mounted Police
– creation of 87
– refusals to arrest 154
– support for ceremonies 110–11, 112, 113
North-West Territories Act 64–65
Nutlam Society 96

O-kan-ee (Cree man) 117–18
Oberly, John 214
Oceania
– British policy in 34
Ochapowace
– deposed as leader 158–59
Oldman River, Battle of 64
Oliver, Frank 131
Order-in-Council of June 23, 1870 65
Osowwahshtim (Brown Horse) 186

Paget, Amelia 98
Paget, Frederick 108
pan-Indian movement 167–68
Panapekesis
– legal appeal of 130
Panipekeesick, Felix 180
Pas-ke-min 118
pass system 111–13, 155, 164
Patty (Cree man) 117–18
Paull, Andrew 203, 204

Pedley, Frank
– views on dancing 146–47
Perry, Charles
– proposes seizure amendment 158
peyote 165–66, 191
Peyote Road (religion) 191
Piapot 9–16, 12–13, 15
– charged with resisting arrest 118–19
– deposed as leader 137
– illegal conviction of 116
– protests Treaty Four 11–12, 13
– protests Treaty Six 68–69
Pidcock, R.H. 94
Pipestem Bundle Dance 53–54
Pitchenesse
– arrests of 157
Plains Cree
– bands 44–45
– economic activities of 46–49, 63–65, 82–83
– justice systems of 46
– kinship systems of 45–46, 47
– loss of political autonomy 71–72
– military organization of 51
– numbers of 44
– political systems of 46, 49–51, 83
– religious systems of 51–61, 103
– seasonal movements of 47–48
– social structures of 44–46, 83; and
  detribalization policy 72, 74, 76
– territorial shifts of 43–44, 64
potlatch 3, 88, 90–91
– economic functions of 90–91
– White views on 90–92
Potlatch Law 92–95, 209
– criticism of 94, 194–95
– enforcement of 93–94, 96, 104
– public debate on 94–95
– *see also* Indian Act, 1876
Poundmaker 13, 68, 71, 75
– protests Treaty Six 68–69
poundmakers
– work and spiritual power of 49
Pow-wow 170, 188–89
Powell, Israel 90, 91, 92
power, spiritual 52–53
Prairie-Chicken Dance 53–54
Pratt, Richard 38
Proclamation of 1763 (for British North
  America) 36

Proclamation of 1858 (for India) 28
Prophet movements 88–89
Protective Association for Indians and their
    Treaties 204, 205, 207, 209
The Protectors (Australia) 30–31
Provencher, J.A.N.
– recommends assimilation 65–66
Pyakwutch (Clean Earth, Harry Brown) 111,
    224

Queen Victoria Protective Association 204
Queensland Act of 1897 (Australia) 31

race theory 21
Rain Dance 179–80
Red Crow 113
Red Dog 169, 176
Red Pheasant
– protests Treaty Six 68–69
Reed, Hayter 72, 76
– detribalization policy of 74
– insistence on pass system 112
– views on ceremonies 103, 104
– views on shamans and healers 122
religious ceremonials, Aboriginal 53–61
– commercialization of 119, 128, 140–41,
    147–48
– creation of new 188–89, 190
– and cultural continuity 3, 103, 137, 176–77,
    216–17, 225
– economic functions of 54–55
– legislation against 3, 88, 93, 95–97, 110,
    113–14, 149–51, 152–54
– modification of 135–37, 177, 178, 180–81,
    187–88, 188
– persistence of 142, 160, 161, 163, 166, 178
– secularization of 122–23, 139–40, 159–60,
    163–64, 169
– White support for 110–14, 130, 139–42, 169,
    171–72, 180
– White views on 96–99, 102–03, 104, 148–49
– see also dances and dancing
religious evolution theory 23–25
religious systems
– missionary views on: in Africa 27; in
    Canada 101, 115, 137–38; in India 27–28
– revitalization of 228–29, 231
– and social organization 25
– syncretism in 181, 190–92

reserves (Australia) 30
reserves (Canada) 71–72
– Cree role in selection of 68
Resident Magistrate Court (New Zealand) 33
resistance strategies, Aboriginal 67–68, 67–71,
    114, 219–21
– confrontation 118–19, 172–73, 175–76
– defiance 80–81, 176
– delegations 131–32
– legal appeal 120–21, 130–31, 133, 171
– persistence 142, 173–74, 175, 178, 222–23
– petition 16, 127–31, 133–36, 168–71, 170–71
– political organization 84–85, 167–68, 198,
    203–04, 210
– treaty-rights movements 84, 128–29, 131
– White support for 110–14, 130, 134–35, 147,
    174–75
revival meeting 190
Ringatu (Maori religion) 33
Round Dance 53–54
Rowland, J. 129
Running Rabbit 134
Running Wolf 113

sacred pipestem bundle 53
Sake-pa-kow 118
Sapir, Edward 150
Saskatchewan Indian Association 84, 203
Saskatchewan Uprising of 1885
– role of Cree in 71
schools. see education, Aboriginal
Schurz, Carl 79
Scott, Duncan Campbell 151
– policies of 164–65, 194, 212
– views on religious ceremonies 123–24
Scow, Johnnie 195
settlement of the West
– effect of on Indian land title 87
Seymour, Frederick 89
Shaboqua, Mark
– arrests of 157
shamans and healers 52, 159
sharing and reciprocity 49, 55–56, 59
Shave Tail 121
She-sheep 136–38
Shouter 59, 182, 189
Singing Before 113
Smith, Joe 121

Smith, W. Robertson
- on religion and social organization 25
Smoke Dance 138
Smoking Tipi Ceremony 53–54
social evolution theory 20, 21–23, 100–01
social theory
- of race 21
- of religious evolution 23–25
- of societal evolution 20, 21–23, 100–01
Soldiers Settlement Act 77–78, 167, 203
sovereignty, Aboriginal
- recognized by government 68
Speck, Frank
- opposes Indian policy 196
Spencer, Herbert
- on religion and social organization 25
Sproat, Gilbert 90
Standing Through the Earth 186
Star Blanket 69, 81, 134
Starblanket, Adelard 176
Starblanket, Allen 176
status, Indian, legal 87, 146, 208
- *see also* wardship
status, social 49–50
- ideology of 52–53, 83
Steele, S.B. 99
Stephen, James 32
Stephenson, E.W.
- opposes suppression of ceremonies 169
Stocken, H.W. Gibbon 97
Stony, Albert 175
Sun (Thirst) Dance 3, 53–54, 56–61, 97–98
- economic aspects of 58, 59
- ideology of 57, 59–60
- modification of 135–37, 179, 184, 186
- political meanings of 61
- purposes of 183–85
- social meanings of 60
Sunchild, Louis 191
Sweetgrass (Cree headman) 68
Swimmer, Sam 83

Tamanawas (medicine ceremonies) 93
Tangi (Maori funeral ceremony) 34, 214
Taytapasahsung 121–22
Te Kooti Rikirangi (Maori religious leader) 33
Te Ua Hamene (Maori religious leader) 33
Tea Dance 139, 169, 190
Thanksgiving Promenades 139

The Queen vs. Etchease of the Muscowpetung
    Reserve 119–21
Thoma, Joseph 68
Thompson, Levi 133
Three Persons, Tom 163
Thunderbird bundle 54
Thunderchild 69, 110, 117–18
- invokes treaty rights 128–29
- statement on religious freedom 168
- threatened with deposition 159
Tims, William 104
- on Blackfoot Sun Dance 97
Tootoosis, John 204
- on denominationalism 207
Tott, Charles 152–53
Travers, Chief Councillor 156
treaties 66–70
- Aboriginal protests against violations of
    70–71, 128–29, 131
- resistance to 68–70, 84
- Robinson, 1851 66
- Treaty One 66
- Treaty Two 66
- Treaty Four 67, 79, 207; terms of, 67
- Treaty Six 68–69, 79–80; resistance to
    68–70; terms of 68
- Treaty Seven 79
Treaty Days celebration 170
Treaty of Waitangi (New Zealand) 32
treaty-rights movements 84, 128–29, 131
Trutch, Joseph 89
Two Bears, Henry 170
Tylor, Edward
- on cultural differences 23–24

Union of Saskatchewan Indians 84, 204, 206
United Farmers' Organization of the Stablo
    Tribe 206

vagrancy law
- used to ban gatherings 124
Vankoughnet, Lawrence 92, 104
vision quest 52–53
Vowell, Arthur 95

Wa-pa-ha (Cree man) 117
Wanduta 119, 133
war bundle 53

wardship 72, 87, 197, 212
– in British Native Imperial policy 31
warfare 64
Warrior Societies 51
– loss of functions of 73
Watetch, Abel 16
wealth
– ideology of 55–56, 83, 215–16
– redistribution of 3, 49, 54–56, 59, 90–91,
   98–99, 183
Weekes, Mary 197
White, Fred 110–11
White Elk, Arthur 188

White Man's Wife 113
White Pup 134
Wilson, James 110
Wilson, Robert 98
Winnipeg Stampede 147, 148
Wiremu Kingi (Maori chief) 33
Witchcraft Suppression Act of 1899 (Africa) 27
World War One
– Aboriginal participation in 167, 170, 172–73

Yellow Bird 118
Yellowfly 206